THE COMPLETE **IDIOT'S** GUIDE® TO

Understanding Islam

Second Edition

by Yahiya Emerick

ALPHA

A member of Penguin Group (USA) Inc.

Dedicated to my son for the joy of faith he brings to my heart.

ALPHA BOOKS

Published by the Penguin Group

Penguin Group (USA) Inc., 375 Hudson Street, New York, New York 10014, USA

Penguin Group (Canada), 90 Eglinton Avenue East, Suite 700, Toronto, Ontario M4P 2Y3, Canada (a division of Pearson Penguin Canada Inc.)

Penguin Books Ltd., 80 Strand, London WC2R 0RL, England

Penguin Ireland, 25 St. Stephen's Green, Dublin 2, Ireland (a division of Penguin Books Ltd.)

Penguin Group (Australia), 250 Camberwell Road, Camberwell, Victoria 3124, Australia (a division of Pearson Australia Group Pty. Ltd.)

Penguin Books India Pvt. Ltd., 11 Community Centre, Panchsheel Park, New Delhi—110 017, India

Penguin Group (NZ), 67 Apollo Drive, Rosedale, North Shore, Auckland 1311, New Zealand (a division of Pearson New Zealand Ltd.)

Penguin Books (South Africa) (Pty.) Ltd., 24 Sturdee Avenue, Rosebank, Johannesburg 2196, South Africa

Penguin Books Ltd., Registered Offices: 80 Strand, London WC2R 0RL, England

Copyright © 2004 by Yahiya (J. A.) Emerick

Interpretation of the printii   number of the first series of numbers is the year of the book's printing; the rightmost number of the second series of numbers is the number of the book's printing. For example, a printing code of 04-1 shows that the first printing occurred in 2004.

Printed in the United States of America

Note: This publication contains the opinions and ideas of its author. It is intended to provide helpful and informative material on the subject matter covered. It is sold with the understanding that the author and publisher are not engaged in rendering professional services in the book. If the reader requires personal assistance or advice, a competent professional should be consulted.

The author and publisher specifically disclaim any responsibility for any liability, loss, or risk, personal or otherwise, which is incurred as a consequence, directly or indirectly, of the use and application of any of the contents of this book.

Most Alpha books are available at special quantity discounts for bulk purchases for sales promotions, premiums, fund-raising, or educational use. Special books, or book excerpts, can also be created to fit specific needs.

For details, write: Special Markets, Alpha Books, 375 Hudson Street, New York, NY 10014.

Publisher: *Marie Butler-Knight*
Product Manager: *Phil Kitchel*
Senior Managing Editor: *Jennifer Chisholm*
Senior Acquisitions Editor: *Randy Ladenheim-Gil*
Development Editor: *Jennifer Moore*
Production Editor: *Janette Lynn*

Copy Editor: *Ross Patty*
Illustrator: *Jody Schaeffer*
Cover/Book Designer: *Trina Wurst*
Indexer: *Angie Bess*
Layout: *Angela Calvert*
Proofreading: *Donna Martin*

Contents at a Glance

Contents

Appendixes

Foreword

Islam is one of the fastest growing religions in the world. At present, the United States is home to somewhere over five million Muslims. Islam has attracted and transformed the lives of activists, rappers, politicians, artists, athletes, academics, and even scores of students in the Midwest. However, even with the number of Americans converting to Islam increasing exponentially each year, Islam still remains shrouded in mystery. With all of the misunderstanding that revolves around this belief, why are so many people accepting its way of life? What answers does Islam hold for the many cultures and ethnicities that kneel for prayer five times a day saying: "God is Great; God is One"? The answer may lie in its ability to bring about balance.

When I first met Yahiya Emerick I saw a man in balance: a true son of the hearty American Midwest—canoe, corndogs, and all—who could recite prayers in flawless Arabic. Inspired by the writings of Emerson and Thoreau, he could also cite the chapter and verse of various laws and edicts of the Qur'an. Yahiya could give heart-thumping Friday sermons at the mosque and then easily pull a pack of teens together to go camping in the "sticks." I witnessed a man juggling his American identity and his Islamic soul and gracefully striking a balance. Since converting to Islam in his freshman year at Michigan State University more than 14 years ago, Yahiya Emerick has been writing, researching, and publishing texts about Islam. Specifically, his goal is to examine what is truly advocated within the essence of Islam, rather than what is done (incorrectly) in the name of Islam. In this book, he clarifies the incongruent actions of some Muslims and holds them up against the light of the Holy Qur'an to illustrate what Islam advocates and prohibits.

Yahiya Emerick presents a bird's-eye view of the Islamic tapestry in a logical and easy-to-understand format. The thread: knowledge that spans three continents. The pattern: events of the past and the present. The finished product: a garment to be worn by you as a reminder of the journey you have taken. He places each design, each point in history, at close range so as to elucidate the true impact of Islam's place in history. Be it medicine or mathematics, the role of Islam is presented as more than just a month of fasting and women wearing dark veils.

Yahiya Emerick has definitely paid his dues. Whether it's working as an assistant principal and teacher in a Muslim school or leading the Friday prayer, he manages to present an image of tangibility. His example is seen as a reminder for the youth he teaches: Islam is not an unapproachable belief. It is a system that balances economics, politics, morality, and social structure as a simple way of life—from God we came; to Him shall we return.

This book has its own balance. It pulls no punches on any of its topics. It examines Islam on a level plane—no smoke and mirrors—just a clear investigation of a spirituality, a way of life, that has been unfairly vilified by the American media and warped into contradictory tokenism by those who appear to be Muslim in name only. In this text, Islam is presented as a way of life that does not thrive in stasis. Islam emerges as a living spirituality whose core beliefs and social systems, established more than 1,400 years ago, still meet the challenging and complex human needs of the new millennium.

Islam is a spirituality that continues to attract Americans regardless of their race, culture, class, and gender. I am confident that this book will open a multitude of new eyes to a spirituality that is not as exotic as it is made to seem. Enjoy the journey into Islam!

—Qasim Najar

Founding member of the Islamic Foundation of North America

Introduction

Imagine learning that there are over a billion people in the world, one sixth of humanity, who follow a religion that you never really studied in school. This little-known religion is called *Islam*. Perhaps you've heard the name before or developed some opinions about it based on what you've seen in the news. However, if you're like most people, you might not know a great deal about Islam. Well, you've taken the first step toward understanding more about this mysterious way of life, and you may find yourself pleasantly surprised to learn what it really teaches.

Islam shares many of the characteristics that are familiar to followers of Judaism and Christianity. In fact, Islam considers itself a related ideology that fits into a tight chronology with these two other religions. As the population of Muslims rises in many Western countries, and as the West continues its interaction with the traditional Muslim world, for good or ill, the challenges and need for tolerance and an accurate understanding of each other's faith and values has given rise to a curiously refreshing debate on both sides about the nature and place of the other in our increasingly inter-connected world. In this spirit of dialogue and discovery (and even highly spirited debate), it is no wonder that some people have begun to speak of a Judeo-Christian-Islamic heritage for the West.

Islam is the fastest-growing religion in the West. If current trends continue, in a few years there will be more Muslims in America, for example, than Jews or Protestants! Mosques now dot the skyline views of many American cities, and the changing face of America's schools has its share of children wearing head scarves and round caps called Kufis. All of this serves to highlight the need for people to understand their Muslim neighbors and their religious and cultural traditions.

Islam is a way of life and a philosophy of living that millions of people consult in their daily affairs. It has its own answers to such questions as why are we here, who is God, what kind of life should a person lead, and what happens to us after we die? It also has its own program for improving one's heart, mind, and spiritual strength. Through a daily regimen of prayer, supplication, good works, and a strong commitment to faith, Muslims, or followers of Islam, try their best to live in harmony with their fellow men and women and even with their environment.

Napoléon Bonaparte once wrote that if people followed the way of Islam, there would be true harmony and brotherhood in the world at long last. Bernard Shaw also echoed the same sentiment in his writings, though he went a step further stating, *"One day the West will accept Islam."* On the flip side there are those who view Islam as a potential rival for Western dominance and present Muslims in a negative light.

Samuel P. Huntington, Daniel Pipes, and Steven Emerson are three prominent writers who have published books or articles that paint a picture of Muslims that is highly critical and even dangerous. How should you here in the West view Muslims, then?

This book will help you understand who Muslims are, what they believe, what rituals they perform, what civilization they built, as well as what challenges they face. Although the history of interaction between the Muslim and Christian worlds has often been fraught with conflict, there have been many periods of peace and understanding that have enriched both societies. One of the greatest periods of peace and intellectual development for European Jewry was during the era of Muslim rule in Spain. This has often been called a golden age for the Jewish people. Indeed, Christian-Muslim-Jewish relations were not always as strained as they seem to be today, and through mutual respect and tolerance the followers of each of these three monotheistic religions can reacquaint themselves with that spirit of tolerance that reigned in so many places before.

The stamp of Islam and its civilization can be found in many aspects of our society today. Economic terms such as *bank* and *check*, as well as scientific words like *horizon* and *alcohol* come from the world of Islam. Did you ever study algebra or chemistry? Have you ever enjoyed lemonade or sugar? Do you dream of going on safari, or have you ever read an almanac? Do you enjoy the works of Plato (which Muslims transmitted to the West), or have you read the poems of Rumi? These and many other words, discoveries, and intellectual achievements are gifts from Muslim society to the West.

Islam has a very appealing belief system that has been embraced by converts for decades now, and its rituals give meaning to people from all walks of life. Many prison systems across the United States now actively encourage their inmates to learn about Islam, recognizing the discipline and civilizing effect it has on the prison population. In some urban areas, Muslims have been credited with ridding neighborhoods of drugs and prostitution and working with local officials to revitalize depressed areas. Islam can and will continue to make positive contributions in every society in which its followers settle.

I hope you will enjoy learning about Islam and discovering that Muslims are not as different as you thought. In the future you will be seeing a greater Muslim presence in the West. And as Muslims take their place in the melting pot, I hope we can all see that the flavors they will add will enrich our lives for the better.

Here's What You'll Find Inside

This book is divided into seven parts.

Part 1, "Introducing Islam," opens for you the world of Islam from an insider's point of view. In this part, you will learn about some of the reasons for the unfortunate relations the Christian and Muslim worlds have had for centuries. You will also discover the reason why knowledge of Islam has often been lacking in modern school curriculums.

Part 2, "The Spiritual World in Islam," introduces the Muslim concept of the four stages of life, the three levels of the soul's journey to truth, and the Day of Judgment. The Islamic view of Heaven and Hell and their purpose will also be laid out before you. The story of creation all the way up to the Last Day will present a thrilling journey into an alternate conception of the universe and our place in it.

Part 3, "The Five Pillars of Islam," explores the famous five pillars of Islam in great detail and shows how each pillar influences the life of a Muslim. This discussion includes a full account of the Islamic concept of social justice and action. *Jihad*, which is often mistakenly labeled as *holy war*, and the Islamic duty of activism will also be highlighted.

Part 4, "Islam and Other Religions," gives a full account of the relations between Christians, Jews, and Muslims from the beginning of Muhammad's mission until our own time. The Qur'an contains quite a lot of discussion on Muslim relations with the followers of other religions and goes into great detail about the merits and drawbacks of both Judaism and Christianity. In this part, I'll also touch upon the rise of interfaith dialogue.

Part 5, "Regulating Life Within the Laws of Islam," introduces you to the sources for Islamic teachings, how they are interpreted, and how a code of life can be derived from them. You'll learn about issues related to Islamic Law, such as dietary restrictions, male/female relations, community life, ceremonies, and celebrations. You'll also explore the purpose of a mosque.

Part 6, "The History of Islam," takes you on a panoramic overview of the breadth and depth of the world of Islam from the Prophet Muhammad to the present day. I also cover the influence of Islam on Europe, the Golden Age of Muslim Spain, the glorious Mughals and Ottomans, and the Christian/Muslim wars over Palestine and Eastern Europe. This will help you understand better how Islam and the Western world have interacted over the centuries.

Part 7, "The Legacy of Islam," highlights the contributions of Muslims to the growth of civilization, globalization, and modern technology. Great Muslim thinkers and explorers will be introduced, and the era of Colonialism will be fully explored. Moving to today's world, we will tackle the thorny issues that seem to divide the followers of Islam, Christianity, and Judaism, and how world affairs today are influenced by events in the Muslim world. The meaning behind September 11 and the false use of religion to justify it will also be brought to light.

Extras ...

To make your learning experience even more enjoyable and insightful, you'll find sidebars sprinkled liberally throughout the text that include interesting tidbits of information.

Just the Facts

This sidebar confronts myths about Islam with authentic information. These can be quotes, points, or comparisons. This is one of the most important types of information you will find, given that stereotypes and misunderstandings about Islam are rampant today.

Ask the Imam

In this sidebar, you will find issues about religious application to daily life. Tough questions need equally strong answers, and Islam doesn't back down when solutions are needed. By the way, an Imam is the title for a religious leader in the Muslim community.

Translate This

This sidebar includes definitions of words common in Islam that you may have never heard before.

It Is Written

This sidebar includes actual quotes from the Qur'an, the sayings of Muhammad, and the writings of prominent Islamic scholars and others through the centuries. What better way to learn than to let the sources speak for themselves!

Acknowledgments

I really want to thank the people who made this book possible. This is my first book in the *Complete Idiot's Guide* series, and the support I received has been overwhelming. To Jacky Sach, my literary agent, I extend my gratitude for encouragement and helpful feedback. A special thank you for Randy Ladenheim-Gil, my initial editor, for all the kind assistance she extended in the completion of this manuscript. The staff at Alpha Books has also been exceptional. Michael Koch deserves kudos for the hard task of making sense of my endless files in the first edition. Finally, and most importantly, I would like to thank my wife for shouldering more than her fair share of family responsibilities during my time working on this book.

Special Thanks to the Technical Reviewer

The Complete Idiot's Guide to Understanding Islam was reviewed by an expert who double-checked the accuracy of what you'll learn here, in order to ensure that this book gives you everything you need to know about Islam. Special thanks are extended to Reshma Baig.

Trademarks

All terms mentioned in this book that are known to be or are suspected of being trademarks or service marks have been appropriately capitalized. Alpha Books and Penguin Group (USA) Inc. cannot attest to the accuracy of this information. Use of a term in this book should not be regarded as affecting the validity of any trademark or service mark.

Part 1

Introducing Islam

What is the religion of Islam really about? Although you might have already heard a lot about this religion, you might not feel like you've learned what its actual teachings are. Is Islam being given a fair hearing? Beyond all the hype and stereotypes, Islam is, in fact, a genuine spiritual tradition that more than a billion people worldwide are associated with. That's quite a lot of public support! Why, then, is Islam so often presented in such a disparaging manner? Have there been unfortunate circumstances in relations between the Muslim world and the West that would cause long-standing myths and prejudices to take root? Have essentially political events around the globe been used to unfairly taint an entire people and their beliefs?

In reality, Islam is a peaceful religion with teachings that cover every area of life. The philosophy of Islam begins with God and ends with the inevitable journey of all people back to their Creator. Concepts that are already familiar to people in the West, such as righteousness, Heaven, Hell, and angels, make Islam seem less mysterious and more comprehensible than most people would think. In this part, I will be exploring the Islamic conception of God and why there is so much misunderstanding about this great faith in the world today.

Why Has Islam Become So Important?

In This Chapter

- ◆ Learn why understanding Islam is now more important than ever
- ◆ Consider how stereotypes have affected the Western view of Islam
- ◆ Take a brief look at where Muslims live and how they got there
- ◆ Understand how the Muslim world affects your life here in the West

It may be surprising to learn that Islam is the fastest-growing religion in the world today, outpacing Christianity, Buddhism, and all other belief systems through a mixture of conversion and natural increase. However, even more eye-opening is the fact that Islam is also the fastest-growing religion in North America. With nearly 2,000 mosques spread throughout the continent, and populations approaching one million in some urban areas, learning about this often misunderstood and mysterious faith has become more important than ever.

There are many reasons why our knowledge of Islam is so deficient. Centuries of on-again, off-again conflict between the Muslim and Christian worlds have built up long-standing prejudices that have led each side to dismiss the other's relevance in world affairs. Although this hostility has often set the tone for relations between the world's two largest faiths, the damage done to tolerance and mutual respect is not irreparable. My purpose, then, is to reveal the world of Islam to you from the inside so you can gain a greater appreciation of who Muslims are, what Islam teaches, and how Muslims view what's happening in the world today.

The Muslims Are Coming!

Signs of the growth of Islam in the United States, Canada, and recently in Mexico are evident everywhere. Mosques are being built in neighborhoods where once only churches and synagogues stood. Women who wear scarves covering their hair are now a common sight in many towns and cities. Moreover, Muslim holidays are gaining official recognition in such places as Los Angeles, Toronto, and New York; and the U.S. Postal Service has even issued stamp designs commemorating Muslims and Islamic themes (Malcolm X and Ramadan stamps, for example). In addition, an increasing number of employers are accommodating the religious needs of their Muslim workers in the same way they respond to the needs of their Jewish workers.

The Malcolm X stamp honors a well-known Muslim American leader.

On a personal level, many people are finding that some of their neighbors or fellow college students practice the Islamic way of life or that some of their children's classmates are Muslims. Others may be just curious about a religion they hear more and more about and never really learned much about. Clearly Islam is beginning to enter the mainstream of community experience, and the more you learn about your Muslim neighbors the better you will be able to understand each other and work together for the common good.

Given the dramatic rise in the number of Muslims, especially in the West, why do Westerners apparently know so little about the faith that claims over one billion followers all over the world? This gap in knowledge has had a profound effect on our society and its willingness to integrate the next wave of newcomers to our shores, namely people with Muslim heritage. To illustrate the danger we face today from our own lack of knowledge, consider that after the September 11, 2001, terrorist attacks in the United States, otherwise educated and tolerant people suddenly found themselves blaming an entire religion and all of its followers for the actions of fewer than two dozen individuals. Why did the president of the United States, George W. Bush, have to declare publicly that "Islam is a peaceful religion"? It is because most Americans don't know enough about Islam, and a lot of what they've been told isn't true, or is true of only a minority of the Muslim population.

Translate This

Islam is the proper name to use when referring to the religion practiced by Muslims. It is an Arabic word that means two things: to surrender your will to God and to acquire peace in your soul. The legitimacy of using this word comes from the Muslim Holy Book, the Qur'an; and it is the only name Muslims use to refer to their religion. A **Muslim** is a follower of Islam.

Why Didn't I Learn More About Islam in School?

So you made it through high school and maybe college and managed to learn a little bit of everything along the way. Then one night you sit down to watch the evening news and find yourself listening to a report about *Islamic terrorists*, followed by another one highlighting the holy month of *Ramadan* as it is celebrated in a major American city. The next morning you read an article in the newspaper about an *Islamic state* that has passed a law prohibiting women from driving. On the way to work you turn on your car radio and listen to an in-depth National Public Radio story about a Muslim immigrant father "stealing" his child away from his estranged American wife and her heart-wrenching struggle to rescue her baby.

You may reflect for a moment on what a diverse world we live in. However, you may become

Just the Facts

When someone commits a crime, the religion of the individual is rarely mentioned. But when a person who happens to have a Muslim name does some act of violence, whether for religious or personal reasons, their religious affiliation is nearly always mentioned. This kind of surreptitious innuendo and guilt-by-association seems patently unfair to Muslims.

influenced by the slant of the reporting to view Islam as some monstrous religion with demonic values incomprehensible to civilized people. If you are a thinking individual, however, who likes to form opinions for yourself after looking at all the evidence, perhaps, in times of quiet contemplation, the realization hits you: I really don't know much about Islam. What does it teach? Is it as bad and dangerous as it is portrayed in the media? Why do so many people seem to be following it? What should I know about Islamic customs given that my new co-worker may be a Muslim and I saw a girl with a scarf on her head at my child's school? Heck, who is this *Allah* they always talk about? Is He the same God as ours?

Raising these questions enables you to confront the power of stereotypes and how they can damage relationships between people of diverse backgrounds. You also may realize, when you reconsider what you know about Islam, that your education has a gaping hole in it. In the same way that 30 years ago you were learning about the merits and drawbacks of Communism, today's schools and universities are scrambling to fill the knowledge void regarding the relevance of Islam and the Muslim world. In previous decades, the religion of Islam and Muslim culture were hardly given more than a cursory treatment in history classes, even though the Muslim impact on world civilization was at least as great as that of European or Chinese culture.

Ask the Imam

Never use the term *Mohammedanism* to refer to Islam. It is considered offensive to Muslims because it implies that Muslims worship Muhammad. Western academics, who coined this term, were merely following a familiar pattern: Christ worshipper = Christian, Buddha worshipper = Buddhist. But Islam does not teach the worship of Muhammad. Islam views him as a man who was given a mission to teach people about God.

European and American educators have literally voided a large chunk of human history and thrown it into a kind of vague limbo. To follow the flow of history, as presented in typical high school textbooks, both modern and yesteryear's, is to go from the ancient world to the Greeks, Romans, and finally into the Enlightenment, the Reformation, and the world since Colonialism, with few detours at all. This omission of the world of Islam can best be explained by a cultural bias driven by fear and tinged with a little arrogance. Why should Islam matter? After all, the West conquered the Muslim world and broke it up into many tiny states, each powerless and dependent. With the Muslim world no longer a threat to the dominance of the West, the West could focus on other more important things. And it is a well-known fact that the victor often writes the history books according to his own version of events.

The attitude that the study of Islam has evoked in the Western world seems to have been little more than: "Oh, Mohammed made it all up, and a bunch of his fanatics chased people around with swords for a while until the enlightened West took control of the Muslim world and civilized it." Western writers, often called *Orientalists*, have expressed this simplistic and narrow view in their studies throughout most of the last four hundred years. Only recently have modern scholars taken a fresh look at Islam and Muslim civilization and gained a new appreciation for its values, legitimacy, and contributions to the rise of the modern world.

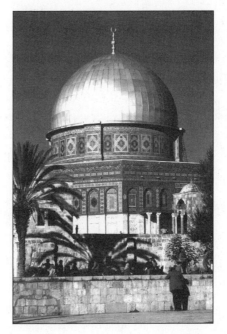

Muslim civilization has produced many beautiful monuments, such as the Dome of the Rock in Jerusalem.

(Photo by Luke Powell)

It is due to this disparaging frame of mind that knowledge of Islam has been largely absent from the curriculum of schools across Europe and the Americas, save for chapters that mention how the "heroic" West captured Palestine during the Crusades. Although the situation is now improving dramatically, some of the old attitudes still remain, and the information about Islam that is being brought to the general public is often incomprehensible to Muslims, who see their faith being maligned or routinely misrepresented almost with impunity.

The Backlash Against Islam and Muslims

The outrageous events of September 11, in particular, have unleashed an equally outrageous Pandora's Box of bigotry and prejudice against this world religion and its followers. The Council of American Islamic Relations (CAIR) released a report in May of 2004 outlining a 70% increase in anti-Muslim bias and violence in the United States, and that was just covering the prior year of hate-crime statistics. In addition, an attitude of blanket condemnation and guilt-by-association has made Muslims feel vulnerable, harassed, and humiliated, especially in places where they are more visible in the community. Consider some of what has been publicly said by leading politicians and opinion makers in the United States that has given fuel to this intolerable and un-American bigotry:

◆ "The nation has been invaded by a fanatical, murderous cult ... We should invade their countries, kill their leaders, and convert them to Christianity."

—Syndicated columnist Ann Coulter, *National Review Online*, September 2001

◆ "We're not attacking Islam, but Islam has attacked us. The God of Islam is not the same God. He's not the son of God of the Christian or Judeo-Christian faith. It's a different God, and I believe it is a very evil and wicked religion."

—Franklin Graham, *NBC Nightly News*, November 2001

◆ "Islam is, quite simply, a religion of war, and [Muslims] should be encouraged to leave. They are a fifth column in this country."

—Lloyd Lind, Free Congress Foundation, in his recently published booklet: "Why Islam is a Threat to America and the West."

◆ "I think Mohammed was a terrorist."

—Jerry Falwell, on CBS's *60 Minutes*, October 2002

◆ "I believe that Muslims in this country are a fifth column ... The vast majority of Muslims in this country are very obviously loyal, not to the United States, but to their religion ... the reason they are here is to take over our culture and eventually take over our country ... You think we should befriend them; I think we should kill them."

—Jay Severin, host of a popular Boston area morning talk show on WTKK-FM, April 2004

◆ "[Muslims attacked us] because we're a Christian nation, because our foundation and roots are Judeo-Christian and the enemy is a guy named Satan ... We in the army of God, in the house of God, in the kingdom of God have been raised for such a time as this."

—Lt. General William G. Boykin, October 2003

These ignorant, prejudicial, and inflammatory statements are, unfortunately, all too common today, though for the most part it is Muslims who notice their frequency and their effect on our freedoms. This rhetoric of hate has now filtered down into the lives of ordinary Muslim Americans, who have become frequent victims of discrimination in public and private places as well as targets of harassment, verbal assault, and hate crimes.

The irrational fear of Islam (called Islamophobia) often influences even official United States government policy, with strong echoes of the unjust treatment of Japanese Americans in World War II. The infamous immigration registry program enacted just after September 11, in which tens of thousands of Muslim immigrants were forced to undergo a special re-registration (and the subsequent detention and expulsion of thousands of law-abiding Muslim immigrants) sent shock waves through Muslim America. This sad state of affairs has done much to damage many Muslims' faith in American freedom and fairness.

The unfortunate wars in Afghanistan and Iraq and the accompanying nationalist bravado have made Muslims, no matter where they came from or what they believe in, the new worldwide boogeyman that Red Communism used to be during the Cold War. The situation has deteriorated so rapidly that Kofi Annan, the Secretary-General of the United Nations, remarked in January of 2004, "One of the most disturbing manifestations of bigotry today is Islamophobia … Since the September 11 terrorist attacks on the United States, which were condemned throughout the Muslim world, many Muslims, particularly in the West, have found themselves the objects of suspicion, harassment, and discrimination." Please see Chapter 28 where I discuss September 11 and its impact on the Muslim and non-Muslim world in more detail.

Clearly the time for a more thorough and accurate exploration of Islam and Muslims has come. Who better to ask what their religion is about than Muslims?

Muslims, Muslims Everywhere!

In the rivalry between the old Soviet Union and the West, the rest of the world played the role of either allies or enemies (or even "dominoes"). South America, Asia, and Africa were the battlefields on which the war for superpower dominance was fought by proxy. Indeed, a large segment of the world was treated literally as a fill-in-the-flag spot on the map. These would be the dozens of Muslim countries ranging from Morocco to Indonesia and all the Muslim territories that had been incorporated into non-Muslim nations over the past two centuries. In the world of James Bond, the Muslim world provided only interesting locations for so-called first-world struggles and intrigues.

With the passing of the Cold War, the deck has been reshuffled. Now nations vying for dominance must treat each region and country individually in their quest for allies and business partners or in their desire to rein-in potential "rogue states." Enter the Muslim world. Where once you had a patchwork of weak dictatorships, monarchies, and sham democracies that were manipulated by the Soviets and the West quite shamelessly, now you have legitimate countries, with their own visions and aspirations. There are even many new nations, created out of the ruins of the Soviet Union, with Muslim majorities, whose future direction and orientation are watched closely by the West. Within Europe itself, many restless ethnic groups are struggling for states they can call their own, Muslim minorities included, and the U.S. Army now patrols many former battle zones in the Muslim-populated Balkans.

Just the Facts

Did you know that during the Cold War, 37 Muslim countries were allied to the West, or were at least Western-leaning, while only 6 were leaning toward the Soviets?

It can seem confusing at times: news about Muslims coming in from Africa, Europe, Asia, the Middle East, and North America. Just where is the Muslim heartland, anyway? How can a religion we know so little about have followers almost everywhere on the globe from Suriname in South America to Estonia in Eastern Europe? The answer to this question lies not in geography but in history. Islam began in Arabia with the Prophet Muhammad in 610 C.E. and spread rapidly to the east, west, and north, mainly because of the zeal of Arab armies and the disloyalty of the peasantry who, under Persian and Byzantine rule, often looked upon the Muslims as liberators.

Within a hundred years, converts from North Africa, Syria, Iraq, and Iran continued to expand the borders of the Islamic Empire until the classic heartland of Islam consisted of a broad swath of territory, encompassing all the land between Spain and western China. The Turkish Ottomans later spread their rule over much of southeastern Europe, resulting in the mass conversion of the Albanians and Bosnians, whose brand of Christianity had been under persecution from the Orthodox and Catholic churches. A further combination of immigration, trade, missionary activity, and displacement resulted in Muslims being in the far-flung places we find them today.

Translate This

C.E., or Common Era, is used to refer to dates in this book rather than the more familiar A.D. or B.C. on account of their overtly religious tone.

An old mosque in Bulgaria is a testament to the Muslim presence in Eastern Europe.

(Photo courtesy of Aramco)

Does Islam Encourage War?

Does Islam command its followers to wage war against unbelievers or kill them without provocation? This is a popular misconception among Westerners, and the statements of a few radicals in the Muslim world don't help to end this false idea in peoples' minds. Christianity has also had its run-ins with radicals who have tried to distort its noble teachings for dubious and violent ends. Just think of abortion clinic bombers, the Inquisition, or the many wars of religion among Christian Europeans in past centuries. Islam, like Christianity, forbids the taking of any human life except for a just cause under the law, such as capital punishment for convicted murderers or traitors, deaths that naturally occur in wartime, or for self-defense. (See Chapter 14 for a more thorough look at Islam's concept of the Just War.) The *Qur'an* has this to say about taking a life:

> Don't take a life which Allah has made sacred except by way of justice and law: thus does He command you that you may learn wisdom. (Qur'an 6:151)

Just the Facts _____

The **Qur'an**, which is often spelled *Koran* in English, is believed by Muslims to be the literal speech of God as revealed to the Prophet Muhammad. The word *Qur'an* means *The Reading*.

The Qur'an never says to fight and kill people who are not believers for the sake of them not being believers, although one of its verses, which is often quoted out of context, does say "to fight the unbelievers wherever you find them." However, this command was revealed when a state of war existed between the first Muslim community and their stronger opponents, the idol worshippers of Mecca. The command was directing the Muslims not to run away from a fight with oppressors, but instead to go headlong into battle with the people who had been attacking them without mercy for so long. Here are the Qur'anic verses that command Muslims to fight:

> Fight in the way of Allah against those who fight you, but don't be the aggressors, because Allah doesn't approve of aggression. Fight them wherever they are found, and drive them out from where they drove you out, because being oppressed is worse than being slaughtered …. But if they cease being hostile, remember that Allah is the Forgiving, the Source of All Mercy. But if they continue to oppress [people], then battle them until oppression is no more and justice and faith in Allah prevails. If they seek peace, then you seek it as well, but continue to pursue the evil-doers. (Qur'an 2:191–194)

Muslim Missionary Efforts

The spread of Islam was accomplished not only through the conquest of land but also through the willing conversion of many of the inhabitants. Even as Christianity spread throughout Europe and the Americas by means of a mixture of missionary work and war, so too did Islam have its more prominent missionary side. A large tract of land stretching from central China down through Cambodia, Vietnam, Thailand, Malaysia, and the Philippines and into Indonesia saw the rapid conversion of huge populations, a result due almost exclusively to the efforts of individuals who were interested in teaching their beliefs to others. Most of these missionaries were either primarily businessmen or wandering mystics. No Muslim armies ever entered that part of the world. Ironically, Indonesia and the surrounding countries now boast the largest Muslim populations found on the globe.

It Is Written

There is no forcing anyone into this way of life. The truth stands clear from falsehood. Anyone who rejects wrongdoing and believes in Allah, has grasped a firm handhold that never breaks, because Allah hears and knows everything. (Qur'an 2:256)

The Qur'an forbids forcing someone to convert to the faith. Despite popular stereotypes of fanatic Muslims with the Qur'an in one hand and a sword in the other, Islam does not teach this type of conversion method; modern Western writers who have taken a fresh look at history now almost unanimously declare that forced conversion was not a method used during the rapid Muslim expansion.

Today in America, Canada, Mexico, and Europe, the number of converts to Islam is rising each year. There are no organized soul-saving crusades, no TV shows in prime time, no magnetic personalities filling stadiums each month in a different city, and certainly no central planning unit to bring Islam to the Western public. Instead religious and cultural trends among certain groups have continued to evolve. For example, the conversion rate of African Americans to Islam has remained steady since the days of Malcolm X and the Nation of Islam. As the number of converts rises, so does the general acceptance of Islam as a viable life choice in the African-American community.

America now sports more than a million African American converts to Islam alone. Caucasian women who marry Muslim immigrants often convert to the faith, either before or after marriage, and it is estimated that there are more than 200,000 such converts in North America today. A surprising movement of Hispanic Americans, especially Puerto Ricans, into the Islamic religion has also continued to grow and expand in recent years. Thus, you can see how the conversion factor contributes to the growth of Islam in unexpected places.

How Did Muslims Get There? Thank the British!

In addition to land conquests and missionary efforts, another factor is responsible for the spread of Islam: the efforts of the British, who were looking for a cheap labor supply for their *colonial* plantations. In the eighteenth and early nineteenth centuries, the British imported tens of thousands of Muslims from India to South America, South Africa, the Caribbean, and elsewhere. Their descendants have continued to practice Islam. Suriname, for example, a small nation just north of Brazil, has a population that is over 30 percent Muslim, the rest being Hindu and Christian.

Translate This _____

Colonialism refers to the era beginning in the sixteenth century when European countries invaded and eventually took control of most of the rest of the world. Nearly every region on Earth from South America and Africa to Asia and the Middle East came under the direct military occupation of Britain, France, Portugal, the Netherlands, Russia, or Belgium. The latest Muslim region to regain its independence was in Central Asia after the fall of the Soviet Union. A few Muslim territories still remain under occupation.

Recently, immigration from Lebanon has resulted in a sizable Muslim population in Argentina, and the Muslim immigrants of Britain and France are well known. In short, Muslims inhabit every corner of the globe, and their growth has been due to a wide variety of factors. The Muslim heartland, then, stretches from Morocco to Indonesia and Bosnia down to Tanzania, with important fringe populations all over the world.

If it seems that news from the Muslim world is suddenly more prominent and noticeable these days, it's not because in the past Muslims were sleeping or because they previously didn't exist. It's because now each and every Muslim country has suddenly become more valuable to the West. Given the Western dependence on fossil fuels, especially oil and gas, and the need to ensure easy access to foreign markets for Western companies, the trends in every Muslim country are watched closely.

The Muslim world now stretches from South America to China. The shaded areas have the heaviest concentrations of Muslims.

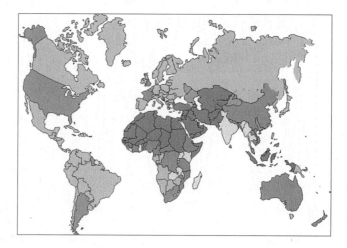

The Arab oil embargo and the rise of OPEC in the seventies made people take notice that numerous people have a history and values that the West does not fully understand. Other events, such as the Arab/Israeli conflict, the Gulf Wars, and the shifting balance of power in the Middle East, have confirmed the view that Americans need to know more about what forces drive people who live in those places. Stay tuned: As the years pass, the volume of news about or originating from the Muslim world will only increase.

Is There Really a Clash of Civilizations?

When Westerners think about Islam, well-worn stereotypes of veiled women, bearded men, exotic food, and an incomprehensible language tend to come to mind. Islam is considered by many to be an alien culture that can't possibly have any relationship or commonality with normal Western values. This belief has an unfortunately long history and dates back 1,400 years, to the era of the Byzantine Roman Empire when the Muslim world and Europe most often met on the field of battle. The Muslim world was still young then, and the vitality of youth caused it to expand its frontiers, much like the European nations did hundreds of years later, when they achieved near total world dominance.

From the year 622 C.E. when Muhammad, the Prophet of Islam, gained control of the Arabian city of Medina, until the close of the sixteenth century, the Muslim world was continually expanding in one direction or another. Although there were many setbacks, such as the loss of Spain in 1492 or the Mongol invasions in the thirteenth century, the Muslim world overcame most of these challenges and continued its outward march. During this time, the Christian world lost all of North Africa, the Middle East, and much of Eastern Europe to Islam.

As a counterstrike, the Crusades (the Christian invasion of Palestine in the eleventh and twelfth centuries) showed Europe that it could wrest land away from "the Saracens," as Muslims were called at the time. Vilification of Islam and Muslims reached a crescendo throughout Europe during this period, and European kings and Catholic priests portrayed Muslims as children of the Devil who must be exterminated. Although the Crusades ultimately failed, the Europeans, who never shook off their image of Muslims as being nearly subhuman, came back with a vengeance in the eighteenth century and by the close of World War I came to dominate over 95 percent of the Muslim world.

Just the Facts

The growth of Islam during the early centuries of its existence was a difficult phenomenon for Western Christianity to comprehend, and misunderstanding, prejudice, fear, and, in some cases, hatred have characterized much of the history of encounters between the two faiths.

—Jane I. Smith, author of *Islam in America*

Sadly, in all of this fighting back and forth, little effort was made to understand the values of the other side, and the greatest legacy both Westerners and Muslims are struggling with today is the fear with which each civilization regards the other. These stereotypes have led many Americans and Europeans to conclude that Islam is incompatible with "modern" values centered on democracy, personal rights, equality before the law, and tolerance for the views of others. You may be surprised, however, to learn that the values of Judaism, Christianity, and Islam are not as different as you might think. It is imperative, then, that the truth be told and that the actual beliefs of Islam be examined closely. Western Christian civilization and Islamic civilization have looked each other in the eye for centuries and done nothing more than give each other bruises. The necessities of the modern world have made a re-examination of that mode of exchange a priority.

Bridging the Next Gap

Muslims are quite puzzled these days when it comes to sorting out their relationship with the rest of the world. On the one hand, many Muslim countries have allied themselves to Western interests, opened their markets to international trade, and have become valued trading partners. On the other hand, when someone like Saddam Hussein comes along, they suddenly find themselves made out to be monsters and killers. Indeed, the number of anti-Muslim incidents during the first Gulf War in 1991 rose all across America as mosques were defaced and vandalized and ordinary Muslims were jeered at and taunted in the streets. These people, mind you, were American citizens who had nothing to do with the Iraqi regime and what it did during its invasion of Kuwait. Moreover, Muslims in America were almost completely unanimous in their condemnation of Iraq's unprovoked attack of Kuwait. At the most, they wanted the war to end quickly because innocent civilians in Iraq were being harmed by the intense bombing raids that seemed to hit nonmilitary targets with ever greater frequency.

The coalition of nations that then-President George H. Bush assembled to oust the Iraqis included more than a dozen Muslim nations who contributed men and material to the war effort. Only one Muslim nation, Jordan, failed to express its disapproval, and it abstained out of fear of Iraqi retaliation. (Iraq is Jordan's neighbor.) Yet throughout this conflict, even though the Muslim world joined in to fight on the American side, the Western media failed to adequately identify Muslims as allies of the West. Instead, Muslims as a group were sometimes presented as *supporters* of Saddam Hussein simply on account of a few well-televised, anti-American protests in Palestine and Jordan, and the American public may have been given the wrong impression that the Gulf War was a war between the West and the Arabs (read: Islam). It only became worse in 2001 after the September 11 attacks, with Islam itself being blamed for anything and everything that a small cadre of zealots operating under the name of Al Qaeda carried out.

Translate This

The name Muslims use when referring to a mosque is *masjid.* This translates as *the place of bowing down.*

Indeed, even though the vast majority of Muslims had no allegiance to or sympathy for either Saddam Hussein or Osama bin Laden, the leader of Al Qaeda, still Muslims have been made to feel like a suspected fifth column, ready to betray America in a second. This fear has been borne out at the local level through the vandalism of some of our religious centers and the daily harassment we face in the streets, our schools, and places of work. So Muslims have often asked the question: What does it mean when Muslims, many of whom are American citizens, are made to look like the enemy on account of the actions of a few in far away places? This feeling is not unlike how

Japanese Americans felt during World War II when they were rounded up and detained for "security" reasons. Hypocrisy and racism was obvious then, and Muslims feel as if they are the current "foreign" group suffering from misinformation, hysteria, stereotypes, and collective judgments.

Hollywood hasn't helped to dispel these erroneous ideas either. Movies such as *Not Without My Daughter, True Lies, Black Hawk Down, Under Siege,* and *Delta Force* have served to paint Muslims as wife-beaters, bomb-throwers, and swarthy immigrants whose loyalty cannot be trusted. Caricatures of Islam and Muslims are staples of American television, and the types of insults and barbs being slung against them would raise howls of protest and marches in the streets if they were directed toward African Americans, Jews, or Hispanics today, as they were in the past. But Muslims have not yet organized an effective, nationwide antidiscrimination movement to correct such stereotyping and maligning. Several organizations such as the Council on American-Islamic Relations (CAIR) and the Arab-American Anti-Defamation League have been established in recent years and have made some strides in influencing the way many news organizations report on Islam and the Muslim community in America. But there is a long way to go before Islam and Muslims achieve the same level of sensitivity from the popular media that other religious and racial groups have.

Grace Halsell, the former speechwriter for U.S. President Lyndon Baines Johnson wrote in 1994 that …

> Phrases such as *Muslim militant* and *Islamic terrorist* appear so often in the U.S. media it is as if word processors were programmed to produce only such pairs. Muslims, now numbering about one billion, are aware of the stereotype. Do these Muslims tend to see duplicity in U.S. Middle East policy? Do they perceive that the U.S. and Europe make the same stereotypical judgment for all Muslims, all over the world? If they are not seeing Muslims as authentic human beings, will they deem them expendable? Is this why, they ask, the Americans and the West can so easily turn a blind eye to a genocide of Muslims in Europe?

It Is Written _____

I hope that in the next century we will come to terms with our abysmal ignorance of the Muslim world. Muslims aren't a bunch of wackos and nuts. They are decent, brilliant, talented people with a great civilization and traditions of their own, including legal traditions. Americans know nothing about them. There are people in that part of the world with whom we are simply out of touch. That's a great challenge for the next century.

—U.S. Supreme Court Justice Anthony Kennedy, December 1999

It would be nearly impossible for me to express in words, however, the frustration that Muslim Americans have felt in their efforts to undo the many forms of stereotypes directed against their religion and communities. But suffice it to say that many Muslims feel that they have been treated unfairly by the media, entertainment industry, and political establishments. As Muslims gain a greater sense of participation in the modern melting pot of ideas and as more people become increasingly comfortable with their Muslim neighbors, realizing they are not as different as they thought, then real progress toward breaking down barriers can be made. Until then Muslims are watching anxiously as each wave of misinformation washes over the television screens and newspaper pages of this otherwise tolerant nation.

Muslims have been migrating to the West in great numbers over the last five decades for the same reasons that other people immigrate: a chance at a more prosperous economic life for themselves and their families. This movement of Muslims into the neighborhoods of North America has given Westerners the chance to come into contact with Muslims and learn directly from them about their values and beliefs. This opportunity is one of the many benefits of our current time. When your children meet Muslim children, they discover that Muslims are not very different from themselves. As mosques start to take their place alongside churches and synagogues in the landscape of the West, the opportunity to bridge one of the last great remaining cultural gaps becomes a possibility.

The Least You Need to Know

- The study of Islam in Europe and North America has been colored by false stereotypes that have hindered good relations and been the cause of much misunderstanding and hostility.

- Muslims are found in every corner of the world and have a history and culture that is as rich as any other.

- The population of Muslims is rising in North America and Europe due to immigration and also to conversion.

- Muslims in general feel they have been stereotyped and are being treated unfairly by the media and entertainment industries.

- Nearly all Muslim countries in the world are either allies of the West or are friendly to the West.

- It is unfair to point to a few villains in the Muslim world and then blame all Muslims for the actions of a very few.

2

Food for the Soul

In This Chapter

- ◆ Understand how Muslims conceptualize their purpose in this life
- ◆ Discover the God of Islam
- ◆ Learn why Muslims say the physical universe is surrendered to God
- ◆ Discover the spirit world according to Islam
- ◆ Find out what Muslims believe about natural human morality

In Chapter 1, I discussed the reasons for the general lack of information about Islam among people in the West. I also explored some of the reasons for the cultural prejudice and bias that many Muslims feel as they attempt to make their homes and communities in lands that have been traditionally Judeo-Christian in their orientation. Now I will turn to the religion of Islam itself. What does this mysterious religion teach about God and our place in the universe? Does it have a well-defined cosmology as Judaism and Christianity do, with a definite purpose in the world? What are the codes of belief that Muslims live by? What happens to Muslims after they die? The answers to many of these questions may be surprising in that the ideas and concepts you are about to learn are not as alien or foreign as you might expect.

The Muslim lifestyle is based on faith in God, leading a morally upright life, following a set of daily rituals to remind oneself of his or her allegiance to God, and doing good works to improve the lives of all living things. The reward for such a lifestyle is eternity in Heaven. The penalty for utter self-indulgence may be a stint in Hell.

The Core Beliefs of Islam

Islam has seven fundamental beliefs that every Muslim must accept as a part of his or her religion. Over the course of the next several chapters, I will be taking a closer look at each of these beliefs. In Arabic the title of this group of teachings is the *Emanul Mufassil,* or *Faith Listed in Detail.* Every Muslim learns this formula as a part of his or her religious training.

The seven core beliefs are ...

- ◆ Belief in God
- ◆ Belief in the angels
- ◆ Belief in the revealed Books of God
- ◆ Belief in God's many prophets
- ◆ Accepting that there will be a Last Day
- ◆ Belief in the divine measurement of human affairs
- ◆ Belief in a life after death

Just the Facts

Muslims must learn a minimal amount of the Arabic language in order to perform their prayers and participate in certain rituals.

We All Have the Same God

The foundation of Islamic teachings begins with God, whom Muslims call *Allah.* The name Allah comes from the Arabic language and means literally *the one and only God,* as opposed to any old god with a small "g." The Qur'an itself declares that Allah is the same God that spoke to the Jews and Christians. Therefore, when Muslims speak about God, they have in mind that it is the God of Abraham, Moses, Jesus, *and* Muhammad. Even Arab Christians, who speak the Arabic language, say "Allah" when they talk about God. (The Spanish word for God is *Dios,* yet nobody makes the claim that it is a different God!)

The Qur'an states it this way:

> Tell [the Jews and Christians], 'We believe in the Revelation which has come down to us [the Qur'an] and in that which came down to you [the Torah and Gospel]; Our God and your God is one; and it's to Him we surrender.' (Qur'an 29:46)

Muslims prefer to use the name *Allah* no matter what language is being spoken. This is because this proper name for the supreme deity cannot be made plural or altered in any way grammatically in Arabic. I will use the terms *Allah* and *God* interchangeably throughout this book.

The name Allah as it is written in Arabic script.

One of the most memorized passages of the Qur'an, the famous *Ayatul Kursi*, or Verse of the Throne, gives a good introduction to the way in which Muslims view God. It goes like this:

> Allah! There is no god but He, the Living, Who needs no other but Whom all others need. He is never drowsy nor does He rest. Space and the Earth belong to Him; who can intercede without His consent? He knows everything people have done and will do, and no one can grasp the least of His knowledge, without His review. His throne extends over the heavens and the Earth and He doesn't tire in their safekeeping. He alone is the Most High, the Lord Sovereign Supreme. (Qur'an 2:255)

The Islamic concept of our place in the universe hinges on the notion that Allah, or God, is the only true reality. There is nothing that is permanent other than God. Everything exists because of His will and everything depends on Him whether we recognize it or not. Allah is eternal and uncreated. Everything else in the universe is created. Created things will pass away and return to Allah for His review. Not even the stars will last forever.

According to the method of reasoning used in the Qur'an, the proof for God's existence is found in four areas:

1. The natural world with all its complexity and beauty. This is a sign of an intelligence in the universe because only a designing mind could have constructed it.

2. Our human abilities and capacities for thought, belief, invention, creativity, and moral choices. No animal or plant can do what we do. We are like the other creatures of Earth but so very different and unique.

3. The revelation of God's guidance and the existence of religion. They show that there is a right way and a wrong way to live life. Prophets, Holy Books, flashes of insight—all these serve as proof that guidance is real and purposefully directed.

4. Finally, our inner feelings. These propel us to seek the meaning in things and show us that we have a soul or spirit that seeks harmony with nature, the universe, and a higher power. The human will is, by definition, inclined to seek the answer to questions that concern more than mere physical existence.

The Universe Is Muslim!

In the realm of creation, Islam makes a clear distinction: There is God *and everything besides Him*. With created things (the *everything besides Him*), there are two basic categories: whatever is *surrendered* to God's will and whatever is *resisting* His will. You are either following God's way or the wrong way. All inanimate matter, such as rocks, comets, water, and even atoms, follows well-defined natural laws regarding their motion, atomic structure, properties, and qualities. Islam holds that God established *all* natural laws, and thus every physical material in the universe is surrendered to His will—that is, everything does what it was created to do. In that vein of thought, then, the entire nonliving universe is considered to be *surrendered* to God. The whole universe follows Islam!

It Is Written

Do [some people] seek a way of life other than the way of Allah? Is this what they do even though everything within space and the Earth surrenders willingly or unwillingly to Him? Certainly they will return to Allah. (Qur'an 3:85)

Thus, the Qur'an states that the entire physical universe is Muslim. How can this strange statement be explained? If the word *Islam* means to surrender to Allah and to acquire peace, then someone or something that does this is called a *Muslim*, or surrendered one. That is how the label *Muslim* can be applied to things other than people. Note the similarity between the words *Islam* and *Muslim*. Both have the letters *S, L,* and *M.* The way Arabic works is simple. You take a base of consonants that have a plain meaning (a root word) and then you add or subtract prefixes and suffixes and alter the vowel patterns to form new, related words. Think about the English word *cover.* You can have *covered, recover, unrecoverable, covering, uncovered, undercover,* and so on. Arabic works in a similar fashion. So the name of the religion is *Islam* and a person or thing that follows Islam is called a *Muslim,* or surrendered one, and because the term is generic it can be applied to nonliving things as well—whatever follows God's will (Islam) is a Muslim.

Animals and plants are also considered to be Muslim in that they follow their innate instincts, which are sort of like their programming. God states in the Qur'an that He taught animals how to do what they do, such as birds flying, bees making honey, plants growing in response to rain, and so on. He even goes so far as to declare that all living plants or animals praise Him in their own way, this praise being an expression of their submissiveness to their Creator. Have you ever wondered why birds sing, frogs croak, or cats meow all night? Not all of it is for mating and establishing territory! Some of it may be for the pure wonder of being alive. The great Sufi poet, Jalaluddin Rumi, said it best when he wrote the line: "I am joyful in the world because the world is joyful in Him."

> ### Ask the Imam
>
> All Islamic teachings come from only two sources: the Qur'an and the Hadith, or sayings of the Prophet Muhammad. Think of the Qur'an like God's Word and the Prophet's sayings as the living application of the Book.

Aladdin Rubbed the Wrong Lamp

Now let's move on and look at the other category of created things. These are the living creatures that are not *automatically* Muslim, or surrendered to God's will and laws. Primarily, I will be talking about human beings and another type of creature called the *jinn.* *Jinns* are similar to the genies so often portrayed in Western literature as wild and crazy spirits. Despite popular folklore, however, Islam does not teach that there are *jinns,* or genies, in lamps or magic rings. Sorry, Aladdin. On the contrary, Islam proposes that these unique life-forms exist for their own sake and that we have no control over them in daily life.

> ### Translate This
>
> The term *jinn* means hidden. Although the word can be applied to anything you don't see, such as bacteria or people hiding behind a mountain, its main use is to signify a type of invisible creature that is made by God and that exists in another realm or dimension.

Jinns are the real cause of supernatural phenomena and paranormal events, not ghosts. *Jinns* inhabit another dimension in which you cannot see them, and they have no substance you can detect. They can be good or evil in their disposition. The evil *jinns* prey upon human beings by goading us into doing wrong. Good jinns ignore us. They do not have as much free will as we humans do precisely because they already know without any doubt that Allah exists. The Qur'an declares that *jinns* are made out of the residue of scorched fire. Muslim scholars have long speculated that *jinns* may exist in the realm of thermal energy or in the x-ray or energy wave spectrums. They can contact us only through our thoughts, in which they can "whisper" suggestions and other types of information in our brains, possibly altering our brain waves. Islam rejects the idea that the spirits of the dead walk the earth as ghosts. Instead, Muslims believe that it is *jinns* who haunt houses, possess people, spook animals, give predictions to psychics, and cause many other inexplicable phenomena. While Christianity relies on the concept of fallen angels to explain the forces of evil, Islam teaches that all angels are good and cannot be corrupted. The angels are all *Muslims* and have no choice in the matter.

Touched by an Angel

Islam accepts the existence of angels, which are called *mala'ikah*. They are made of light energy and can materialize into any form they need to in the physical world. They have no inherent gender. They also have no free will and exist only to serve Allah. Although they're intelligent, they have no serious emotional shortcomings or foibles. Think of them as something like God's robots. They do as they are told, though God is not dependent on them. The following list presents the top four angels and their functions:

- **Jibra'il**   (Gabriel) This angel brings revelations to the prophets.

- **Azra'il**   This angel is the *Malikul Mawt*, or Angel of Death.

- **Mika'il**   (Michael) This angel controls the weather.

- **Israfil**   This angel will blow the horn signaling the end of the universe.

Translate This

Mala'ikah is the term for angels in Arabic. It literally means *ones with power*. Islam does not accept the idea that angels are manifestations of people who have died.

Islam assigns angels to many other types of tasks. One of these is to watch over people and note what they do. Another job of the angels is to look for people who are praising God and to join them. You will be learning more about the different types of angels and their functions as I cover other aspects of Islamic teachings in later chapters.

Accepting the Burden

The Qur'an says that long before God made people He offered the gift of self-awareness and responsibility for one's actions to every living and nonliving thing in the universe. The mountains, the animals, the angels, the planets, the stars, any of these could have accepted and become beings with a power unlike anything in the virtually programmed universe. Anyone or anything that accepted those gifts, called "the trust" in the Qur'an, would transcend nature and be able to conceive of itself and make decisions using an intellect and the power of reason.

Of course with such a gift would come a large measure of culpability for one's actions and spiritual orientation. There is no wrong if a squirrel steals a nut from another squirrel; it's just what squirrels do. Likewise, it is not sacrilege if a bird builds a nest on a place of worship. But when you can *choose* whether or not to do wrong, or to accept or deny God, then you ascend to a whole new level. Now you have *right and wrong, good and evil.* The Qur'an declares that every object in the universe declined this "gift" out of fear of the consequences of not being able to measure up to the task.

Was God Right to Make Us?

Why would God want to give such a gift when He already had complete control over everything in the universe, much like the control a model train enthusiast has over the tracks, cars, and placement of the small figures in a train layout? Why create beings that could choose to love (or hate) on their own? No one can really answer the question of why, for the Qur'an simply states that God created humans and *jinns* for the sole purpose of serving Him and surrendering to His will. That may sound cold or mechanistic, but it really isn't when you look at what people are—physical creatures who

---

Ask the Imam

During the height of Islamic civilization some 800 years ago, Muslim psychologists diagnosed stress this way: The further away you are from God, the more stressed you will be. They then counseled their patients on how to increase their relationship with God through prayer, fasting, aromatherapy, reading, reflection, and self-denial.

It Is Written

What Allah said to the rose and caused it to bloom in hearty laughter, He said to my heart and made it a hundred times more beautiful.

—Jalaluddin Rumi, the Mathnawi

have a built-in need for meaning, love, and purpose. People who don't get these things suffer from depression.

Islam merely says that our most basic needs are fulfilled on the ultimate level when we achieve union with God's goodwill. He is the source for love and all other noble qualities, so the more we love Him and focus on Him the greater peace we feel inside our hearts. Stated plainly, the closer we get to our Creator the more content we become. Recent studies by reputable scientists have found proof that religious people live longer because they are calmer and freer from stress. Hey, I'm sure such people won't argue with that!

There is one possible explanation for why Allah wanted to create beings who could choose to love and follow Him. Although it hasn't been confirmed as fully authentic by our scholars, there is an often circulated saying of the Prophet Muhammad in which he says that God Himself said, "I was a treasure that no one knew. I wished to be known." A more authentic quote from God related to us through the Prophet says that "I created the world for man and man for Me." When you think of the deep love that abides within the meaning of these lines, you begin to realize that life, and the ability to make choices, might not be so bad after all. If love and fellowship with God is the ultimate reward for our right choice, then following God's will is actually the best thing that any one of us could ever do.

God knew what He was doing when He made us this way. Look at it from this angle: When we have children, there is the potential every day for them to be mad at us or hate us, but when they express love for us it is the best thing in the universe. If we didn't take the chance of having them, we wouldn't experience that special love. One moment of genuine love is worth more than weeks of anger. If all we wanted was obedience and nothing more, then we would choose gerbils or dogs for companions in our homes. Allah wants us to love Him as much as He loves us. However, unlike us, He is not dependent on our loving Him, but isn't love a nice thing to receive for its own sake?

Soul Soup

Getting back to the time before there were human beings, when all things and animals declined the offer of self-awareness, we find that God finally made the offer to us. Humans weren't around in physical bodies on Earth. Instead we existed only as a murky prototype and we were with Allah in a sort of primordial soup of spirit matter. Think of all our unformed soul-materiel packed in one large ball, none being individual or unique. It is from this mass of spirit material that each individual human would later get its spirit or soul. (The word for spirit in Arabic is *ruh*.)

Allah offered the gift of self-awareness to that spirit-collective, and it accepted the challenge (though that was foolish, the Qur'an notes). Humans, when they appeared as physical creatures on Earth, would have the freedom to accept or deny God, self-awareness, intelligence, reason, and a moral compass called a *fitrah*, or natural inclination, to help guide them through life. Incidentally, this is how Islam explains our superiority over animal intelligence and abilities. Recent studies into the workings of the brain have even uncovered evidence that we are already "wired" for spirituality. That is, our brains respond to religious stimuli and cause us to feel euphoric.

Translate This _____

Fitrah means your inner nature or moral compass. It steers you to seek out religious experiences and ultimately directs you to accept the existence of God.

Our Compass Points Inward

Why were we implanted with a moral compass? Isn't rational intelligence enough to guide our free choices? That is the claim that humanists and some scientists have put forward in recent years. This theory, however, has failed in many respects. The mere application of reason alone as a means of solving the world's problems may appear a valid procedure on paper, but as Islam points out, all of us have an inherent weakness. We all desire personal pleasure and the fulfillment of our animal urges. These are the instinctual motivations that cause us to hoard food, gather wealth, and procreate. A secular rationalist, thinking himself or herself free of religious obligations, could still act from selfishness, desire, emotion, or anger. As an example, global warming could be solved tomorrow; all the science is there. But people, many scientists and humanists included, want their stereos, their big cars, their air-conditioned homes, and their lighted walkways. Reason would dictate we all need to sacrifice for the common good, but the desire for self-fulfillment and comfort overrides what would otherwise be good, common sense.

Reason alone cannot guide us to right actions given that our animal urges plague us. We need a nudge from inside to counterbalance the animal in all of us. That nudge is our *fitrah*, or inner nature and inclination to seek God. Think of the *fitrah* as that little voice in your head that takes you to task when you do something wrong or that makes you look longingly upon someone performing a selfless act of religious devotion or sacrificing for the greater good. The Prophet Muhammad once said that every child is born with the natural inclination to surrender to Allah, that is, to be a Muslim, but the child's parents make it a Jew, a Christian, or a Zoroastrian. This is a way of saying that our environment can shape and mold us into life patterns that are far from our real nature.

When a child is born, the child enters a world in which the signs of God's creative power found in nature and the child's own *fitrah* seek to influence him or her to believe in God. Other forces, as we shall see, will attempt to take the child's focus away from God. At birth we are also equipped with a kind of free will. What does that mean in practical terms? It means that we humans have the choice of surrendering ourselves to Allah or of rejecting Him, preferring to focus only on creature comforts and temporary worldly interests. Thus we are given the power to choose whether to become Muslim; that is, whether to surrender to God's universal way.

Can You Stand on One Leg?

Interestingly enough, Islam teaches that our physical bodies are already *Muslim* in that our blood flows, our organs work, and our cells reproduce, just as they were made to do. It is within the heart and mind where we have control over our choices and beliefs. It's as if we're half Muslim and half not. The very purpose of our existence, then, is to use our eyes, ears, brains, emotions, and *fitrah* to come to the realization that God is real and that we must surrender our will to His will. By doing so we can join the rest of the universe and exist in harmony with the only true reality that is. There is a faint echo here of the Buddhist and Taoist ideal of being at one with the universe.

By deciding not to fight against Allah's good way, we live a stress-free life in harmony with all things around us. When we say, "I will not fight against you anymore, God," we float peacefully in the great river that is life until we ultimately reach our final destination and return to God as sincere as we can make ourselves.

The Least You Need to Know

- ◆ The word *Islam* means peace and surrender to God.
- ◆ Humans have a kind of free will that God is testing.
- ◆ Islam believes in a spirit world populated by angels and by creatures called *jinns*.
- ◆ People have a moral compass called *fitrah*, which directs them to look for God.

3

Looking at Life the Islamic Way

In This Chapter

- ◆ Find out about the three stages of the soul according to Islam
- ◆ Learn about *Shaytan*, the Islamic word for Satan, and how he came to be
- ◆ Beware of the major sins and how forgiveness from God is obtained
- ◆ Understand the meaning of accountability
- ◆ Learn about the Islamic concept of reward and punishment from God

Philosophers throughout the ages have attempted to tackle the issue of good and evil. What makes a good person go bad, and how can a bad person reform himself or herself? Every religion has its own answer to these questions, and Islam is no different. But whereas other spiritual traditions may emphasize external forces as the primary cause for our sinful behavior, Islam first looks inward. It does so, not with a broad brush by claiming we are evil by nature, such as Christianity asserts, but by delving into the soul and its secrets.

Islam holds that we are all born basically good but have a natural weakness attributable to our physical nature. Social scientists call this our desire for pleasure and aversion to pain. Through these creature instincts we have the capacity to fall into sin. Islam also has the concept of an evil enemy, a Devil that preys upon our hearts and minds. However, this being has only limited power over us and God has given us the tools to combat him. The result is that we can elevate ourselves to a higher level of spirituality or descend to a deplorable moral state. God will judge our faith (*Iman*) and conduct ('Amal) in this great struggle after our physical death and resurrection on the Day of Judgment, and we will be punished or rewarded as a consequence.

Translate This

Iman (sometimes spelled *Emaan* or *Eman*) is the Arabic word for faith or belief. It comes from the root word *amuna*, which means to believe, to trust, and to feel safe.

The Three-Fold Journey

All human beings have three levels of self-development through which they must pass during their lives:

- ◆ **The Animal Self**   Basic instincts and desires

- ◆ **The Accusing Self**   Higher-order questioning of our purpose

- ◆ **The Restful Self**   Transcending worldliness as a focus

These are the stages we pass through as we struggle to come to the final realization that God is, in fact, real and that we ought to move closer to Him. Islam teaches that we are all born sinless and free of sin. This is the condition of our soul upon birth. But being creatures of the flesh, we can be drawn into the pleasures of the flesh as embodied in the world around us. This is best demonstrated in the spoiled child syndrome. No child is born evil, but if a child's every urging and craving is fulfilled, if the child never learns any self-control, then the child becomes unruly and impatient. The soul's journey, Islam would say, got off to a bad start.

The aim of our *fitrah*, or inner nature, is to countermand this trend and elevate our minds to seek God. The journey out of the first stage, our binding tie to seek ever greater resources unto ourselves, is perhaps the hardest of all. The reward for reaching the end of this struggle, however, is eternal reward, though not everyone will reach his or her full potential. As the Qur'an says, "By the soul and the proportion and order given to it; And its innate knowledge of wrong and right; Whoever purifies it will succeed. And whoever corrupts it will fail!" (Qur'an 91:7–10)

The Animal in All of Us

The first stage of our soul is activated from birth and is called the *Animal Self*. During this stage our basic desires for food, sex, creature comforts, and wealth guide our life choices. People who remain stuck in this stage as they grow older wind up living only for themselves and their own pleasure. Think of all those people in the world who do nothing but indulge their whims. No matter how rich or poor, educated or ignorant, famous or unknown, all of us are susceptible to the temptations of our earthly desire for self-satisfaction. Christians call such people hedonists. The Qur'an often refers contemptuously to "the life of this world," describing it as nothing more than "play and amusement, mutual rivalry, hoarding wealth and boasting." "How can you turn down God?" the Qur'an asks, "when He gave you life when you had none. Then He will take back your life and you will return back to Him."

The struggle out of our Animal Self stage is made even harder by the efforts of an evil *jinn* named *Shaytan*. *Shaytan* and all those *jinns* who follow him seek to corrupt and ruin us so that we will eventually forget our Creator. They do this by playing upon our fears, desires, and emotions, ultimately causing us to make bad choices if we succumb to their intimations. As you might have noticed, the spelling of the name *Shaytan* is close to that of *Satan*. But although some of the concepts are similar, there are some important differences between the Islamic view of the Devil and what is believed in the Christian and Jewish religions. You will find more about *Shaytan* and where he came from in Chapter 6.

Translate This

The name *Shaytan*, which is the Islamic term for Satan, means to pull away from. Thus *Shaytan* seeks to pull us away from God. He does this by goading us into seeking ever greater physical pleasure and ignoring our *fitrah*, or inner inclination to seek our Creator.

It Is Written

Shun those studies in which the work that results dies with the worker.

—*Leonardo da Vinci*

Stepping Up to the Plate

When we discard the life-is-a-big-party attitude and begin to pay attention to our *fitrah*, we receive a flash of insight, a deep thought. Here is the chance to enter into the second level of our soul's development, the *Accusing Self*. Now the big questions come flooding in: Why am I here? What's it all for? Is what I'm doing right? What happens to me when I die? Is there a next life?

A person may reflect on the meaning of life for weeks, months, or years until finally becoming motivated to seek spiritual guidance. The person has become ready to look for God. Generally, a person will move toward what is familiar, and thus you can see people becoming fervent practitioners of Christianity, Judaism, Buddhism, and so on. This is all very natural and from the Islamic perspective the practice of any noble spiritual path is better than none at all. Some people fail to have their hunger satisfied by their traditional religion, however, and may begin to explore or experiment with other religions. The Qur'an expects this and postulates that with enough study and research a spiritual wanderer will eventually move beyond those previously revealed (and compromised) religions and into the Islamic way of life that God revealed as His last religious "installment" to the world.

Regardless of the initial path to *enlightenment*, after this second stage has been entered and we realize through our heart and mind that we need God and wholesome values, we can now try to mold our life according to His universal way. We become less attached to the life of this world, more introspective and less irritable and stressed. If we were lucky enough to find the Islamic path, then even greater progress can be made. Through a daily regimen of prayer, reflection, fasting, and study, and a con-sciousness of morality, our heart becomes more and more at ease.

The Supreme Achievement

One day, through devoted effort, we may achieve complete peace and tranquility in our heart. Now we have entered the third and final stage of our soul's development. Nothing in the world has a hold on us any longer. We lead lives of quiet contempla-tion and are not overly discomfited by any tragedy or bounty that may come our way.

We realize we will die and return to God and that this whole life is a test for us. It's not that we become unfeeling, but that we put things in *perspective*, the ultimate perspective.

> **Ask the Imam**
>
> Islam teaches that God sent prophets to every nation and that every racial and ethnic group received some form of divine guidance. Most of the major Jewish prophets and, of course, Jesus are accepted by the Qur'an as true guides from God. The original Torah, Psalms, and Gospel are considered revela-tions from God that came before the Qur'an.

This third stage occurs when a soul becomes a *Restful Self*, awaiting the meeting with the Creator. The individual still has a job, family, and vacations: Islam has no place for monasteries or asceticism. While still maintaining a normal life, the person is no longer living only to satisfy himself or herself, but realizes the higher purpose of life. Thoughts of charity, self-sacrifice, truth, and the simple beauty of life blend together to create a noticeable aura of peace and wis-dom around people whose souls are truly *at rest*.

Sin and Redemption

I've talked a lot about following God's way in your life, so what does it mean to *surrender* to God? For a Muslim, surrendering to God means to believe in Him, to follow a lifestyle that promotes harmony on Earth and among people, and to follow a personal code of morality that can lead to an ever higher understanding of God's nature. God's revelations have guided people throughout history in how to do this. The original Torah, Gospel, scrolls of Abraham, Psalms of David, and countless other religiously inspired texts detail how to achieve such a goal. Islam accepts the validity of them all, though the Qur'an points out that no previous revelation from God has survived without alteration or editing by human hands. The Qur'an, which is considered the last installment of divine guidance to the world, declares itself the culmination of all of God's previous revelations to us and thus is the source for how to live a Godly lifestyle. The Qur'an, incidentally, says it is the one book that God won't allow people to change.

Islam makes a clear distinction between good and evil. Islamic Law, which is derived from the rules contained in the Qur'an and the oral traditions of the Prophet Muhammad, is a detailed code concerned with do's and don'ts, good and evil, and relations among people. A Jewish or Christian person might be very surprised to learn that nearly every virtue one can think of in the Western religious tradition has its counterpart in Islam. Charity, honesty, thrift, compassion, self-control, and integrity are the goals of a Muslim, while dishonesty, violent behavior, greed, jealousy, gossip, and sexual promiscuity are considered sins that deserve to be condemned. Although Islam has no single listing of a "Ten Commandments" or a "Seven Deadly Sins," there are ample Qur'anic verses and prophetic teachings to put together a list of over a hundred virtues and vices for a Muslim to be aware of. Some of these are listed next.

The major sins in Islam are …

- Committing idolatry.
- Stealing from an orphan.
- Committing adultery or fornication.
- Disobeying parents.
- Collecting interest on investments.
- Accusing a chaste woman falsely.
- Giving false testimony.
- Committing murder or suicide.

♦ Committing infanticide.

♦ Enslaving a free person.

♦ Engaging in slander and gossip.

The virtuous deeds in Islam are ...

♦ Speaking the truth.

♦ Being kind to family.

♦ Honoring parents.

♦ Giving in charity.

♦ Feeding the poor.

♦ Fighting against injustice.

♦ Freeing slaves.

♦ Returning borrowed property.

♦ Studying and learning.

♦ Being kind to animals.

Translate This

Tawba means repentance in Islam. The Prophet Muhammad advised us to ask Allah's forgiveness for our sins throughout the day.

Ask the Imam

There is no concept of confession to a priest in Islam or of burnt offerings to atone for sins. Likewise there is no virtue in airing a person's own bad deeds in public. Sin is a private matter between the sinner and God. Only when a person breaks civil laws should the public know about it.

How Does God Forgive?

Islam teaches that when you commit a bad deed, or a sin, it will be held against you on Judgment Day. The only way to remove the stain of that sin is to follow a four-step process of repentance called making *tawba*. To receive God's forgiveness, you must ...

♦ Feel remorseful about the sin.

♦ Repent of your action to God by saying, "My Lord forgive me."

♦ Make restitution for the sin if possible.

♦ Resolve sincerely never to do the sin again. God has promised to forgive our sins if we seek His forgiveness sincerely. If we, despite our best efforts, repeat the same sin later, we can repeat this process again.

Law and Order

In addition, for some sins in which other people's rights or safety were harmed, there are prescribed penalties that must be paid in this life. These are a kind of deterrent to show people that theft, murder, arson, and other social crimes have consequences. Unfortunately, the way the Western media presents it, you would think that in Islam chopping off a hand or a nose or a toe was the norm for punishing people. In fact, there are only a few crimes that incur physical punishment and even then Islamic Law allows the judge to forgo those if mitigating circumstances allow. (The only physical punishments are cutting off the hand for repeated theft, flogging for certain crimes like fornication, and capital punishment for murder, treachery, and the like.) Personal moral sins require only the four-step process of repentance previously outlined, which is done by an individual in private. As you may have noticed, Islamic Law mixes personal morality and civil and criminal law into one overall code in keeping with the religious view that there is no difference between the secular and spiritual realms, though only criminal activity is prosecuted in front of a judge.

 It Is Written _____

Muhammad said, "Allah has recorded both good and bad deeds. Whoever intended to do a good deed and did not do it, Allah writes it down with Himself as a full good deed. But if he intended to do it and did it, Allah writes it down with Himself as worth from ten to seven hundred good deeds, or many times over. But if he intended to do a bad deed and did not do it, Allah writes it down with Himself as a full good deed, but if he intended it and did it, Allah writes it down as one bad deed."

Everything Counts When It Counts

Islam does not accept the Catholic Christian idea that you need to ask a priest to forgive you or pray to a Son of God for deliverance. Even more incomprehensible to Muslims is the Protestant Christian belief of being "saved" in which a person who asks Jesus into his or her heart automatically goes to heaven no matter what the person does later in life, good or bad. Islam teaches that you can save or damn yourself every day through your belief, or lack of it, your actions, good or bad, and your overall record. God's mercy will play a major part on Judgment Day because no human can ever hope to be perfect enough to earn heaven. God, in His mercy, will forgive much and overlook much, but this doesn't absolve us of our responsibility to try to be as virtuous as possible. The Muslim is taught that there is an open line from each of us to God, and when we pray for forgiveness we must each ask God ourselves, every day, until the day we leave this earth.

Our sins, if we don't repent of them, will be held against us. Likewise, good deeds are considered the hallmark of our true faith. Every time we do a good or bad deed it is recorded with God and will be a part of our record come Judgment Day. Islam, however, does not teach that you *earn* your way to heaven, as some Christian theologians have charged. Salvation in Islam is founded on believing in and surrendering your will to God and nothing more. Avoiding sin and leading a righteous life are merely proofs of your faith. A Muslim would respond to the false accusation that Muslims get to heaven by deeds by quoting the Apostle Paul who said, *"Faith without works is dead."* So the emphasis on good deeds in Islam is for another, more noble purpose: to give us a way to measure the strength and veracity of our convictions.

> **It Is Written**
>
> Once a man came to the Prophet Muhammad and asked, "What is faith?" He replied, "When doing good makes you feel good and when doing bad makes you feel bad, then you are a believer." The man asked again, "What is a sin?" The Prophet answered, "When something bothers your conscience, give it up."

The Last Payday

God will reward good even as He will punish evil. This being the case, the more good you do, the more rewards you will get from God. A Muslim, then, is basically given more incentive to do good in the world than to do evil. Think of why Communism failed all over the world. Weren't its precepts noble? No one owns anything; everyone is paid the same, regardless. In practice, however, what happened was that few people worked hard because so many took the attitude that diligent work didn't matter. A hard worker would get no special recognition. Capitalism, on the other hand, succeeds on a certain level because the promise of greater returns for greater effort propels people onward and forward in a mad rush. The Qur'an says, "Every soul has a goal to work towards. Make your goal doing good and race with others for this purpose." (Qur'an 2:148)

Allah rewards us according to the amount of our good deeds. It's a kind of religious capitalism with results that can only make life better for everyone. If more people were eager to help the poor, visit the sick, adopt orphans, and assist the elderly, there would be no need for government welfare, nursing homes, and the like. In addition, the Prophet Muhammad emphasized the inherent value of doing good for others by saying it would make our own faith stronger and increase our satisfaction in life.

Our Report Card

All of our good and bad deeds are recorded in our own individual record. On the Day of Judgment, which will occur sometime in the future, we will be confronted with our book of deeds. Using the yardstick of our faith, deeds, and motivations, we will then be sent to either Heaven or Hell, barring Allah's extra mercy upon souls who would otherwise deserve punishment. Quite simply, the Day of Judgment is when we get our grade for our test in life. Were we greedy and immoral or kind and hopeful in God? An interesting caveat is that on Judgment Day, when our record is read, anyone we ever wronged will be brought in front of us and they will be told to help themselves to our stash of good deeds in order to compensate them for what we did to them in our earthly life. This gives new meaning to the phrase, "Get your affairs in order before you come to regret it!"

It Is Written

The Prophet Muhammad once said, "When a believer sins, there is a dark spot put on his heart, and if he repents and asks for pardon, his heart is polished. But if he keeps on sinning, the dark spots increase until darkness gains ascendancy over his heart."

Christianity teaches that people are already doomed to Hell unless they believe that God's son died for their sins going back to the sin of Adam and Eve. Islam, however, does not teach that people are born sinful. Rather, Islam teaches that we are all born spotless and that throughout our lives we can do either good or bad based on the interplay of our *fitrah*, intelligence, and God's revealed guidance versus *Shaytan* and our lowly animal desires. Salvation in Islam comes from making the choice while alive to accept God and mold your life according to the way of life He has established. That life is based on morality, daily and annual rituals, and repentance for your weakness or misdeeds.

There'll Be Hell to Pay

Why is there the punishment of Hell if we fail God's test? The consequence of rejecting God and staying in the Animal Self stage is that our soul becomes corrupted, or warped. We took our gifts of free will and intelligence and wasted them, burying our *fitrah* in a life filled with meaningless pleasure. In that case, our soul must be repaired before it can enter again into God's presence in the *akhirah*, or next life. Thus, we may find ourselves in Hell where our soul is cleansed by fire of all the dirt we heaped upon it through our immorality and misdeeds in the world. The Qur'an explains the two fates this way:

Just the Facts

Some Western writers have accused Islam of being licentious because of the large number of detailed descriptions of Paradise found in the Qur'an. Islam answers this charge by countering that nearly all of the pleasures of Earth are regulated or even forbidden for a Muslim, so their reward for obeying God in this life is guilt-free indulgence in the next.

Shaytan makes them promises and creates in them false desires, but Shaytan's promises are nothing but deception. [His followers] will have their dwelling in Hell, and they won't find any way to escape it. But those who believe and do what is right will soon be admitted by Us into gardens beneath which rivers flow to live there forever. Allah's promise is the truth and whose word can be truer than Allah's? Anyone who does what is right, whether they are male or female, and has faith, they will enter Paradise and not the least bit of injustice will be done to them. (Qur'an 2:120–123)

When the deserved punishment is finished, the newly cleansed soul may again rejoin God's presence and receive its reward in Heaven for any true belief he or she had and any good done. Some souls, however, are so warped by their owners that they will never get out of Hell and will remain there forever. Think of Hitler or Charles Manson—can anyone ever imagine their redemption? Although, as we are taught to say in Islam, God knows best. In other words, He knows the secrets of our hearts better than we know them ourselves. You will find more about Heaven and Hell in Chapter 6.

The Least You Need to Know

♦ Muslims believe that people are in this life to be tested on whether or not they will surrender to God's will and lead a moral lifestyle.

♦ There are three levels of personal spiritual development: the Animal Self, the Accusing Self, and the Restful Self.

♦ Islam does not teach that humans are inherently sinful. In Islam, sin is not a consequence of birth but rather the result of a choice that the individual has made to commit a bad deed.

♦ God can forgive any person who asks for forgiveness and is sincere. God is more likely to forgive than to punish.

♦ Muslims believe people will be held accountable on a Day of Judgment and will be rewarded by God with eternity in Heaven or punishment in Hell.

Chapter 4

All About Allah

In This Chapter

- ◆ Learn in detail about the Muslim concept of God
- ◆ Revisit the main religious beliefs prevalent in Arabia during Muhammad's time
- ◆ Discover the Ninety-Nine Names of Allah
- ◆ Learn what God means to the ordinary Muslim

Islam has a very well-defined concept of what God is and what He is not. Perhaps no other religion has spent as much time defining God and trying to understand how much we *cannot* understand about Him. Given that Islam categorically forbids making any representations of God, Muslim ideas of God are not affected by changes in social values or mores. For example, until recently in the Western world, God has traditionally been referred to in the masculine gender, and representations show God as a man. Now, as a result of the women's rights movement, some people are using the feminine gender when making references to God. Muslims take a different approach and are content with a concept of God that has far-reaching implications in our modern world.

For the Muslim, God is not personified into forms or shapes created by the imagination of men and women. (How can you paint or carve what you never saw?) The corpus of literature and the arts produced in Islamic civilization are also strangely absent of divine imagery. Although many other religions have prohibitions against making pictures and statues depicting God, only Islam has succeeded so well that the concept is unknown. As you will see, what we lack in artwork about God we make up for in a compelling intellectual and spiritual ideology.

God and Hollywood

The Islamic concept of God has often been called the most uncompromising *monotheism*, next to Judaism, in the world. Islam has a very definite concept of God and how to understand Him, and it has no time for concepts that bring God down to the level of human imagination. With the establishment of Islam as a third major influence in the religious life of North America, Muslims must face a new set of challenges and opportunities. Chief among these is battling the distortions about God and His nature that appear in the mind of the general public and in popular culture.

In addition to promoting disbelief in God, a trend that Islam abhors, today's movies have transformed God into a fun-loving old man, such as in the *Oh, God* movies (starring George Burns) or have typecast Him as a stern, yet fickle being as portrayed by Dustin Hoffman in *Joan of Arc*, or even as a kind of glutton for punishment as in Mel Gibson's *The Passion of the Christ*. Given that Christians worship Jesus as God, the portrayal of a confused blue-eyed flower child in white robes running around Galilee doesn't help the image of God either (think of the musical *Jesus Christ Superstar*). In Hollywood, God seems to be whatever the director wants Him to be. Hey, and you don't even have to pay Him!

> **Ask the Imam**
>
> **Monotheism,** or a belief in a singular, unitary God, is so important to Muslims that they say, "There is no god but *thee* God" over 17 times a day in their daily prayers.

> **Ask the Imam**
>
> Islam forbids all realistic representations of people or animals. Muhammad said that on the Day of Judgment God will command people to put life in what they fashioned. Exceptions are made for children's toys and art for kids.

During the Christian-organized protests of the movie *The Last Temptation of Christ*, Muslim organizations asked their followers not to attend the movie theaters that were showing this controversial film. But whereas Christians were defending the honor of their God, Muslims were more interested in upholding the honor of a man who is considered to be one of the greatest prophets. The same holds true with *The Passion of the Christ*, a movie in which Jesus is beaten up for over an hour. Strangely enough, Christians embraced this movie, though Muslims still counseled each other not to view it. By the way, Muslims shun all movies and cartoons about prophets. Disney's kid-oriented portrayals of such figures as Moses and Joseph and the never-ending stream of made-for-TV movies about David and Jesus are considered in poor taste by Muslims, who see any attempt to represent the physical features of a prophet as wrong.

By showing the face of a prophet, these movies and cartoons give people a false idea about what the prophet looked like and thus they begin to judge that prophet by the actor's looks and performance. People become less interested in the prophet's *teachings* and more so in his *charisma*. When was the last time you saw an unattractive man playing the part of a prophet? How many such movies made you desire to transform your life? These kinds of cinematic portrayals offer a good story, not a God-inspired way of living, which is, incidentally, what the prophets really stood for.

It Is Written

These [false gods] are nothing but names that you have devised, you and your ancestors for which God has sent down no authority (whatever). They follow nothing but conjecture and what their own souls desire! Even though there has already come to them Guidance from their Lord! (Qur'an 53:23)

There Is Only One God

Muslims look aghast these days at the efforts of Western popular culture to promote the idea that we are all gods inside our hearts or that God lives in us, and we can tap into His power like some sort of personal energy reservoir. It seems people are creating God in their own image and justifying any action they engage in by claiming that "God is Love" and so will condone all types of behavior.

It seems sometimes that authentic knowledge of God and a seriousness about what He represents have descended to the level of a joke. Muslims stand, along with sincere people of every monotheistic religion, like lighthouses in the storm, calling people to resist the false suggestions of *Shaytan*, or Satan. Muslims have been among the staunchest defenders in the world of their ideology about God. The Qur'an warned us long ago that the desire of *Shaytan* is to separate us from God, and what better way for him to succeed than to get all of us to call ourselves gods and goddesses or to make up gods of our own!

Does God Show Himself to Us?

Has anyone ever seen God? If you were to believe the claims of televangelists, God comes and visits people in their living rooms all the time. Islam records only one incident in which a person came close to seeing God. The Qur'an records that the Prophet Moses, who is considered to be one of the greatest prophets in Islam, asked Allah if he could see Him. Moses was all alone on Mount Sinai and thought now would be his chance to look upon the Being he loved more than any other. Allah asked him, "Don't you believe in Me?" Moses affirmed that he did but that he wanted to see Allah to satisfy his own longing. Allah said that if Moses could keep his eye on the next mountain then he would see Him. Allah began to materialize His power on the mountain, which shook and rumbled in a great cataclysm. Moses couldn't withstand the sight, however, and passed out without seeing what he wanted to see. His faith was given quite a boost, though! So no one has ever seen God in this life.

Islam on God

As explained in Chapter 2, Islam teaches that its God is the same God as the God of the Jews and Christians. So how does Islam see God in its own terms? How is its view alike yet different from the Judeo-Christian tradition? The first cardinal belief in Islam about God, or Allah, is that He is only one Being, without division, children, or partners. This doctrine is called *tauhid*, or oneness. God is strong enough and capable enough not to need anyone's help or to divide Himself into parts to do different jobs. The Islamic phrase that is most often repeated by Muslims on a daily basis (during prayer) and that reflects these teachings is *La ilaha ill Allah*, which translates as "There is no god other than God." In addition, Muslims are taught that He is not the God of a chosen people nor can any racial or ethnic community lay claim to His exclusive attention. Even Muslims cannot claim exclusive rights to Him as He is, as the Qur'an explains, the *Lord of All Creation*.

Translate This

Tauhid is the Islamic term for oneness. It is derived from the Arabic *Ahad*, which means one. Tauhid implies that God is alone in His divinity with no divisions, partners, or children.

Understandably, the Qur'an completely rejects the Christian Trinity theory. It answers the idea of a three-in-one God with these words: "They are blasphemers, those who say that God is the third of three in a Trinity. There is no god except the One God." (Qur'an 5:73) In the same spirit, Islam would also respectfully disagree with the Jewish belief that God has an all-time covenant with them and a special relationship that divides the entire world by race into Jews and Gentiles. The idea that God makes any kind of racial preferences is reprehensible in Islam. The Qur'an says in this regard, "The Jews and the Christians declare, 'We are the sons of God and He loves us.' Ask them, 'So why does He punish you for your sins (like everyone else)? But no, you are only some people from among the (many) nations He has created.'" (Qur'an 5:17)

The kalimah, or defining statement of Islam is: There is no god other than God. La ilaha ill Allah.

Needless to say, the practice of idolatry in which there are many gods, each with its own sphere of influence, is considered ludicrous by the Qur'an, which says, "God has birthed no son nor is there any god along with Him. If there were many gods, behold each god would have taken away what it had created and some would have lorded it over others!" (Qur'an 23:91)

Pagan Arab Beliefs Before the Coming of Islam

The Prophet Muhammad was born in Arabia in 570 C.E. He grew up in the south-western city of Mecca, which at that time was a major trading town. Although a hand-ful of Christians lived in or around the city, the vast majority of people were Arabs who worshipped idols. Prior to Muhammad's birth the Meccan leaders even banned

Christianity outright in the city limits, seeing that it would threaten their age-old way of life. (Little did they realize what new mes-sage was about to come!) The Meccans, to be fair, did believe in the concept of an overall Creator, (in a fuzzy sort of way) but they felt that the main deity was too remote to be concerned with human affairs. Thus, they ven-erated idols, thinking they were "convenient gods" who would bring luck, safety, good busi-ness deals, and other bounties on a daily basis.

Just the Facts

The pagan Arabs accepted a supreme God over all the demigods they wor-shipped, but they consid-ered Allah to be too powerful and remote to make any difference in their lives.

It is in this context that Muhammad grew up. Interestingly enough, from his earliest age he disliked idol worship, equating it with superstition, and he never engaged in its practice. This is partly why Muslims believe God chose him to be His last prophet to the world. In this he was not entirely alone. An informal tradition of quasi-agnosticism was practiced by a few in the peninsula. These people, who were nicknamed *hanifs*, believed in God but shunned all idolatry and even well-developed religions like Christianity.

Beginning with Muhammad's first exhortations in 610 C.E., we find the earliest revelations of the Qur'an concerned mainly with the evils of worshipping anything else besides the unseen God (a sin called *shirk*) and of the dangers of living an immoral or unjust lifestyle. The Qur'an declared that God is not remote and is not contained in a wood or stone carving. He hears our prayers. He knows our thoughts and actions, and He needs no partners or lesser gods to do His will in the universe.

Translate This _____

Shirk means to hold something else as equal to God. It is considered the greatest sin in Islam because it goes against the fundamental truth about God, namely that He is One. Showing off and boasting are considered signs of *little shirk* because we are competing for greatness with God. We are, after all, made of dust and will die. What right do we have to claim power or status before God?

Mecca is located in south-western Arabia at the junction of several ancient trading routes.

The Middle East

The Qur'an Speaks

One of the most memorized portions of the Qur'an is the short chapter titled "Sincerity," which states:

Tell people that He is One God; Allah, the Eternal Absolute. He neither gives birth nor was He ever begotten, and there is nothing equal to Him. (Qur'an 112:1–4)

For the pagan Arab this message was completely new. In their world, magic, spirits, shamans, luck, totems, and idols were the defining characteristics of religion. Islam challenged the very core of their belief system. Thus it was inevitable that they would oppose Islam when it was first offered to them by the Prophet Muhammad as an alternative belief system.

> **It Is Written**
>
> Every soul draws the results of its actions on none but itself: no bearer of burdens can bear the burden of another. (Qur'an 6:164)

Man and God

Contrary to the beliefs that the pre-Islamic Arabs held, Islam teaches that every person has to face God alone. No one can look to another god or person to save himself or herself in this life or in the next. The Qur'an goes so far as to declare that on the Day of Judgment the false idols in which people placed their hope will be brought forward and made to speak. The idols will reject the people who used to worship them and will taunt them, saying that they were fools for believing in gods of their own making. In desperation the idol-worshippers will even start to blame *Shaytan*, but he will shrug off the blame, saying he only suggested it. He didn't make them call on false gods. The Qur'an is very clear about blame being laid squarely upon our own shoulders. Listen to how cold *Shaytan's* response will be when we try to blame him for our misdeeds.

> And Shaytan will say [on Judgment Day], "It was Allah Who gave you a true promise. I made a promise to you also but I failed in my promise. I had no authority over you except to suggest things to you, but you listened to me. So don't blame me, only blame your own souls. I can't listen to your cries nor can you listen to mine. I reject your former act in associating me with Allah. For wrongdoers (like you) there must be a terrible Penalty." (Qur'an 14:22)

Do Muslims Believe in Original Sin?

If Islam teaches that we all have to bear our own burdens on Judgment Day, how does this idea stack up to Christianity's view that Jesus takes on all our sins? Is there a doctrine of original sin and atonement in Islam? To answer this question, we need to realize that the entire edifice of Christianity hangs on the assumption that because Adam and Eve sinned all human beings have the taint of that original sin on their hearts. According to this theory, everyone is automatically doomed to Hell because of it. God had to divide Himself into parts and send His own begotten child to earth to be killed by people to atone for this first sin. Believing in Jesus' death and rebirth, Christians say, is what saves us from a curse God can't lift otherwise.

Before going further, we need to mention that the Christian concept of God having a son is directly addressed in the Qur'an. Islam considers Jesus to be a prophet of God, born of the Virgin Mary as a special miracle from God. Muslims accept the Virgin birth but consider the lack of a father in Jesus' creation as being on the same level as the lack of parents in Adam's creation. Muslims do not take Jesus' birth as a sign of godhood or as a sign that Jesus was the son of a god. The Qur'an states, "The likeness of Jesus in the sight of God is that of Adam. He created him from dust and said, 'Be' and he was."

Just the Facts

Sometimes God refers to Himself as "We" or "Us" in the Qur'an. A few Christian scholars have suggested that this shows that there is room for the Trinity theory in Islam, but this plural usage of pronouns is merely a common technique called the "Royal We," which is used in many languages. In other words, a powerful king might say, "We decree that ..." even though he is one man. What he is emphasizing by saying *We* is "I *and* My power are decreeing that ...."

The Qur'an even denies that Jesus was killed on a cross. It says that he was not killed or crucified but that it was made to appear so. What happened to Jesus, then? Did he run off to India and study Buddhism like some New Age proponents argue? The Qur'an states only that God saved Jesus and "took him to Himself." Muslims interpret this to mean that God took Jesus to paradise and is keeping him there until he must return to Earth to defeat the anti-Christ. For more details, see Chapter 9.

Islam flatly rejects any notion of original sin and says we are all born pure. Yes, Adam and Eve sinned, the Qur'an says, but God forgave them when they asked for His mercy. No sin was passed on to their descendants. Thus, it is our cumulative faith and actions that determine our salvation. The Qur'an declares that Allah can forgive any sin He wants to, whenever He wants to, and that He has no children nor any need for them to act as sacrifices. Certainly God would never allow Himself to be tortured and killed by His creatures before He would forgive them! The Qur'an explains that it is beneath the majesty of God to do such things. It is no sign of love for a Muslim that God would die for him or her. So the doctrines of original sin and the Trinity have no room in the Islamic concept of God because Islam asserts that God's power is great enough for Him to forgive anything without requiring His death first.

The opening verses of Chapter 2 of the Qur'an are rendered in artistic Arabic calligraphy, eighteenth-century Mauresque style.

(From the private collection of Said Salah, reprinted from the 1840 Paris printing)

How Close Is Close?

But does God's absolute power make Him remote and unconcerned? Islam says no. We can build a personal relationship with Allah because He can hear all our thoughts and because he knows our feelings. He is not far away and cold. "He's as close as our jugular vein" says the popular Qur'anic verse. In the Qur'an Allah says, "Call upon Me. I listen to the call of every person when they invoke Me." Although we don't phrase our creed in quite the same way as Christians might—"Accept Allah into your hearts and be saved"—we do have a similar phrase: *Ataqullah*, which means, "Be aware of God in your heart." The word *taqwa* means consciousness or awareness of God in your life. It also implies self-control, knowing that God is watching you. The more *taqwa* you have in your heart, the closer you are to God. Islam teaches that prayer, fasting, reflection on life and its brevity, and selfless action can cause your *taqwa* to grow.

Allah Has Many Names

The Qur'an provides a very clear picture of God, but not in the style of the Bible. The Bible begins by saying that God made man in *His image*, that is, God looks like a human; whereas the Qur'an declares emphatically that God has no form we can comprehend and that He resembles nothing at all in creation. Like Judaism, Islam completely forbids making representations of God, such as paintings or statues. The Qur'an says, "He is not like anything you can imagine." God is not a human, an animal, or a fuzzy spirit. The rule in Islam is that if you make a mental picture of what God looks like, then God does not look like that at all!

So if God has no form, how can we understand Him? Are we doomed to endless reprimands of "It's a mystery"? In Hinduism or Christianity, there are statues and paintings of God, but Islam says these are all false imagery. How does a Muslim imagine God then? Islam has a unique answer to this human need to rely on appearances. Instead of focusing on God's physical form, we look to His *qualities*. What does God *do?* What is His *nature?* What is He *like?* These are called Allah's Names and Attributes. We use adjectives to describe the nature of God, and through studying them and emulating them we come to a closer understanding of who God really is. The Muslim approach is not to passively look at pictures but to actively participate in knowing the Divine.

It Is Written

Tell them, "Call on 'God' or call on 'the Compassionate' by whatever name you call upon Him (it is well), for to Him belongs the Most Beautiful Names. (Qur'an 17:109)

There is a famous listing called the Ninety-Nine Names of Allah. The list includes such descriptions as the Merciful, the Strong, the Mighty, the Loving, the Everlasting, the Beginning, the Last, the Acceptor of Repentance, the Caring, the Bringer of Peace, the Avenger of Evil, the Living, the Faithful, and so on. Through these Names of Allah we get a feel for the essence of Allah, and thus we no longer have to worry about what He physically looks like. We can know Him by His qualities and actions. The Prophet Muhammad once said that whoever knows and lives by the Ninety-Nine Names of Allah will go to Heaven. This is a way of saying that God's qualities are the best ones to inculcate in yourself, for by doing so, you bring your life closer to His way.

Islam also teaches that God is neither male nor female. After all, if He has no form that we can understand, how can He have a gender? So why, you may ask, do we use the pronoun "He" when referring to God? In Arabic, as in Spanish or French, all nouns are either male or female in gender. A house is considered feminine but a chair is masculine. It's just the way these languages work.

In Arabic there is no word for "it," so the pronoun "He" is used to refer to God, with the full understanding that Allah is not a male. Interestingly enough, the base word *Elah*, which means *a god*, is a feminine word (the *ah* ending signifies femininity in Arabic); yet when you take the proper name *Allah* (*the* God) and use the masculine pronoun *Hoowa* (He is), you are canceling out both male and female genders. The phrase *Hoowa Allah* combines both genders and thus each negates the other. This is the closest thing to "it" that you can get in Arabic and applies to no other words in that language.

Translate This _____

Asma' ul Husna means the "Most Beautiful Names (of Allah)." Muslim homes and mosques will often have artwork consisting of Arabic calligraphy that incorporates Allah's Names, either listing them all or focusing on one.

To summarize, God is a single entity with no divisions, partners, wives, or children. He has no beginning or end. He does not reveal Himself to people, and no human eye is strong enough to behold His power. He can do all that He wishes with no need of a helper. He is not male or female. He has no form we can comprehend. We can know what He is like only through the names He used to describe Himself in the Qur'an. He did not burden us with original sin nor does He ever need to die for any purpose. Idolatry is false. Allah is not a remote God; rather He is active in human affairs and is testing us in this life and giving us the chance to choose to surrender to Him.

The Least You Need to Know

- Islam is a monotheistic religion with no concept of the Trinity.

- Muslims believe that God is all-powerful and that He knows all, sees all, and can do whatever He wishes.

- Original sin has no place in Islamic teachings. Every person has the potential to be good or bad, and there is no need for any atonement or redemption.

- Muslims have no physical description or representation of God. They have an abstract concept that consists of God's qualities, which are embodied in the Names of God.

- In Islam, God is not male or female, nor was He ever born on Earth. He never begets any children and He does not show Himself to people.

Part 2

The Spiritual World in Islam

What is the meaning of our lives here on Earth? What is the soul, where did it come from, and what happens to it after we die? Islam provides its followers with answers to these and many other questions related to both this earthly sojourn and the life to come. Muslims believe that we all have four stages to go through on our great journey called life and that each station has its own unique challenges and rewards.

Islam also has an explanation for the creation of the earth and the appearance of living beings upon it. It differs significantly from the biblical version and has been called more scientifically accurate. The Muslim Holy Book, the Qur'an, goes even further and tells us that life arose for a purpose. All life-forms on this planet, and beyond, have a special duty to live in quiet praise and obedience to the Lord of the Universe.

Although Islam says all nonhuman creatures accomplish this automatically, our kind is the one exception. We have the free choice to accept God or not. The path of Islam gives us a way to surrender ourselves to God if we so choose. Free will is our great burden, and there will be rewards and consequences on account of it.

Chapter 5

The Four Stages of Life in Islam

In This Chapter

◆ Learn what Islam says about the significance of conception, life, death, and beyond

◆ Discover what Islam says about abortion and when it is allowed

◆ Know about the scientific marvels found in the Qur'an

◆ Discover the main duty of the angels who watch over us

◆ Find out what happens to a person's soul after death

There has been a lot of controversy in recent times about the meaning of life and death. When does life begin? When does it end? Does our quality of life determine how long we should live? Islam would say that all of these issues are wrapped up in a larger one—our purpose for being alive. Given that the Qur'an teaches that people exist solely for the sake of learning to surrender to God, it stands to reason that Islam's answers on many of these tough issues would be framed in that context.

Islam puts forward the proposition that human life begins at conception, that the unborn attain personhood at a definite time, and that life after birth is no less than a crucial testing ground where either contentment or frustration will be our lot. However, Islam goes even further by asserting that there exists an undying soul within each one of us that will live on after our physical body has ceased to function. We will still be around after death while we're waiting for Judgment Day, but unlike the fun-loving ghosts in such movies as *Casper* and *Beetlejuice* or the vengeful spirits of *Poltergeist*, Islam tells us that our souls will be put into a kind of storage bin, so to speak, and will get a foretaste of our eventual fate. This is called the Life of the Grave. As you'll see, Islam has quite a lot to say about what will happen there.

Four Lives for Each Life

According to Islam, we all have four well-defined segments of life that we will pass through from our conception in the womb until our death and beyond. These are the stages from the time a soul is joined with the flesh in the womb until we are ultimately in either Heaven or Hell. Each of our four life stages has its own unique challenges and features, and each is considered separate from the other, like a series of doors we must pass through on our journey back to our Creator.

Indeed, the whole concept of life in Islam is that our soul is on loan to us from God. Remember that primordial spirit lump from which all of our souls came and that accepted free will eons ago? Well, that's Allah's property, and when we die He takes back our souls. Of course, now that we have become fully realized individuals we won't be stripped of our uniqueness. He has a different purpose for us then.

The four stages of life are …

- ♦ Life in the womb.
- ♦ Life in the world.
- ♦ Life in the grave.
- ♦ The next life (Heaven or Hell).

I will be discussing the first three stages in this chapter, and the expansive topic of the next life in Chapter 6. As you learn about each stage, notice how the Islamic emphasis on our utter dependability on God is interwoven with the events and features therein.

Life in the Womb

Physical life begins at conception, according to Islam. This is the beginning of the first stage of life for us. In the womb we are in our most vulnerable state. Our bodies are growing and developing, and our soul becomes one with our physical self. It is understandable, then, that Islam has teachings concerning the welfare of the fetus.

Islamic Law recognizes the right of the mother to have a protected pregnancy and the right of the fetus to be brought to term. If anyone assaults a pregnant woman and the fetus dies, the perpetrator must pay penalties and compensation, though the act is not classified as full murder in the same sense of killing an already born person. But the very fact that there are penalties for harming a person in the womb shows that Islam considers this stage of life important and worth protecting.

 It Is Written

[Tell people:] "Come, I will tell you what Allah has prohibited you from doing: don't take any other as His equal; be good to your parents; do not kill your children on a plea of want. We provide supplies for you and for them." (Qur'an 6:151)

Abortion and Islam

The *Shari'ah* (Islamic Law) states that the fetus has rights. No one has the right to kill a baby in the womb, especially when it has no defense. Abortion is quite forbidden. Islam considers it to be taking away the right of Allah to allow—or not to allow—a pregnancy to come to full term. Despite popular ideas today about personal choice and freedom to birth or abort, Islam does not change with the times and stands squarely against *Roe v. Wade*. There is no trend or tradition, however, of opposing abortionists through individual acts of violence, so in that regard Muslims have been hesitant to fully embrace all of the tenets of the Right-to-Life movement, which is known to have a radical fringe element.

 Translate This

Shari'ah is the term used for Islamic Law. This body of legal literature uses the Qur'an and the **Sunnah,** or Prophet's example, along with the opinions of his immediate followers, to provide a ruling on any issue that may confront the Muslim community. There is a mechanism for dealing with new or unusual issues as well called **Ijtehad** in which a scholar can make new legal rulings that follow the spirit of Islamic principles.

As a rebuttal to the main reason given by people for aborting their babies, the Qur'an has formulated this reply: A lack of resources is no excuse to harm a fetus. The Qur'an commands people not to kill their offspring because they are afraid of being poor or because they feel they won't be able to take care of them. God will provide for the newborn *somehow*, the Qur'an states, so let the baby live.

Equally forbidden, as an excuse for abortion, is the desire to have a male child over a female one. Throughout the world, many people misuse sonograms to learn the gender of the baby in the womb, aborting the baby if it will be a girl. This problem is especially prevalent in India and China, and Muslim scholars, basing their decision on clear and direct Qur'anic principles, have denounced the practice as sexist. A pregnancy is considered a gift and a trust from Allah not to be terminated by our choice. The Prophet Muhammad said, "Be kind to daughters and treat them well, for I am also the father of daughters." More importantly the Qur'an addresses the issue of female infanticide point blank and condemns it poetically as a sign of judgment day in the following passage:

> When the sun is covered in darkness, when the stars fall, when the mountains pass away, when the livestock heavy with young are abandoned, when the wild beasts are herded together, when the seas rise, when the souls are sorted, when the baby girl buried alive is asked, for what crime she was killed, when the books are opened, when the skies are laid bare, and when Hell is set ablaze and Paradise is brought near, then, every soul will know what it has prepared. (Qur'an 81:1–14)

Are there any exceptions to the rule that abortion is forbidden in Islam? Yes, but only one. A principle of Islamic Law is that if there are only two bad choices, then take the lesser of the two evils. While the Law does not accept abortion, the law does make an allowance when it is necessary to save the life of the mother. The principle behind this exception is that it is better to keep the life of a wife and mother than to prefer someone who has no social relations yet. So in very clear terms, Islam is extremely pro-life. Only God can decide whether the developing fetus should proceed to term, not us. Even rape or incest is not grounds for an abortion, because the unborn child can't be killed simply on account of the horrible way he or she was conceived. Why should the baby have to pay for the crime?

Islam and Contraception

Contraceptives are generally allowed in Islam as long as they only *prevent* the fertilization of the egg. Destruction of an already fertilized egg crosses the line, according to most recent legal rulings on the subject. Therefore, abortion pills and such have been declared forbidden by the majority of modern Islamic scholars. The entire process after fertilization is considered sacrosanct, as the following passage from the Qur'an illustrates:

O People! If you have any doubts about the Resurrection, [consider] that We created you out of dust, then out of sperm, then out of a clinging thing, then out of a morsel of flesh—partly formed and partly unformed—in order that We may make clear [Our Power] to you. We cause whom We will to rest in the womb for an appointed term then We bring you out as babies then [foster you] so you can reach your age of full strength. Some of you are called to die early and some are sent back to the feeblest old age so that you know nothing after having known much. (Qur'an 22:5)

> **Just the Facts**
>
> The Qur'an uses stunning detail to describe the development of the fetus, calling it a sign of God's power. From correctly identifying the role of sperm in conception to an amazingly accurate depiction of each stage of fetal growth, the Qur'an has been very thorough on this subject. "These facts about human development could not have been known to Muhammad in the seventh century because most of them were not discovered until the twentieth century."
>
> —Keith L. Moore, The Qur'an and Modern Science: Correlation Studies, 1990

When Is a Fetus a Person?

When is a fetus considered a full-fledged person in Islam? This is determined by when it gets a soul. The Prophet Muhammad explained that after 120 days an angel comes to the baby in the womb and breathes the soul into it. Then the angel begins to write in a *book*, which will become that person's book of deeds. The four things that this angel writes are: Will he or she be rich or poor, will the person be happy or sad, how long will the person live, and what will be his or her preferred type of deeds? The answers to these questions are not predetermining the person's fate, however, but merely taking a notation of the future, which God sees as well as He sees the present and the past. I will be discussing the Islamic view of destiny in Chapter 8.

Although it may seem strange to count our time in the womb as a stage of life, it really isn't all that far-fetched. Islam counts the unborn as a

> **Ask the Imam**
>
> Islam defines childhood as any age below puberty. According to the Prophet Muhammad, God does not hold children accountable for their bad deeds. *Shhhh.* Don't tell the kids that! Childhood is the time when children must be taught the skills of living a virtuous life so that when their deeds do count, after the age of 12 or 13 or so, they will have no difficulty.

person-in-process, and as the fetus develops it gains all the necessary physical and mental potential to thrive upon entering the world. Isn't the baby alive in the womb, after all? The Qur'an points out that some babies do not survive their time in the womb because of God's will and that this is a test for the parents. According to Islam, all children who die prematurely will go to Heaven. The Prophet even stated that if a person loses two children and bears their loss with patience, the person will be saved from Hellfire on the Day of Judgment.

The pre-Islamic Arabs had many superstitions about how pregnancy was caused, just as many other civilizations have also had ideas that were outlandish and incorrect. The Qur'an explains the process of fertilization, development, and the birth of the fetus in

Translate This

A chapter of the Qur'an is called a *Surah*. The word *Surah* means two things: a fence or a step up in progression.

great detail. However, you will not find a single passage or group of passages that lay out the stages all in one listing. The Qur'anic method of teaching is often based on presenting a religious idea, then giving a proof from nature that no person could have known at the time, and finally reiterating the principle introduced. This following section about the sun from *Surah*, or Chapter, 91 of the Qur'an provides a good example:

> By the sun and its radiance, and the moon as it reflects, by the day as it reveals, and the night as it covers up. By the cosmos and He Who built it, and the Earth and He Who spread it, and by the soul and He Who perfected it, and gave to it innate knowledge of right and wrong. By the same token know that whoever purifies his soul shall prosper, while whoever corrupts it shall fail. (Qur'an 91:1–9)

By first calling on signs in nature such as the sun as a light-giver and the moon as a reflector, we are introduced to the idea that in a world full of opposites our soul can also be good or bad. Statements that refer to fetal development in the Qur'an, then, are there to give proof to religious concepts. The very first chapter that was revealed to the Prophet Muhammad, while he was meditating in a mountain cave in the year 610 C.E., said, "Read in the Name of your Lord Who created humans from a clinging [zygote]." (Qur'an 96:1–2)

Life in the World

In the teachings of Islam, the moment we are born we enter the proverbial *life of the world*. This is the second stage of life. In this new reality we will need to learn how to lead a moral and upright lifestyle that is pleasing to God. If we are denied the opportunity to learn a godly lifestyle and orientation as children, either because of neglect or abandonment by our parents, then our *fitrah* will help to guide us in seeking such knowledge. When we enter puberty, the standard for adulthood in Islam, God will hold us accountable for our beliefs and actions.

Shaytan and his minions will continually attempt to corrupt us by whispering evil suggestions into our minds. All the pleasures of the world will present themselves on a platter, tempting our lower animal desires. Our primal motivations will rule over us until such time as we begin to use our reason and inner spiritual motivations to train our hearts and minds to seek God. The Qur'an describes this world as an illusory place of deception and play, rivalry and amusement, boasting and hoarding. If we enter adulthood and aren't careful, we just might fall into the trap of becoming an unabashed *hedonist*.

Translate This

Life of the world, or *Hayat ad-Dunya,* is the term used to describe this life and all its challenges and benefits.

It Is Written

The Prophet Muhammad said, "A Muslim, male or female, remains subject to trials [in this world] in respect of self, children and property till he or she faces God, the Exalted, [on the Day of Judgment] in a state in which all his or her sins have been forgiven [on account of their struggles]."

The span of our life, which was recorded in our book of deeds, will not last a minute longer than it is supposed to. While we are alive, however, we will be confronted with a series of challenges and tests in life: The car breaks down; whom should I marry; I got a big raise; someone stole my credit card; my mother passed away, and so on. All of these daily life circumstances happen in order to give us the opportunity to improve ourselves and to draw closer to God. According to Islam, these tests and challenges in life serve a purpose. They can bring out the best in us and cause us to dig deep within ourselves where bravery, courage, perseverance, and fortitude reside. Without being tested, how would we know that we have the guts to carry through in times of crisis? The Qur'an asks, "Do people think they can just say, 'We believe' and they wouldn't be tested in what they claimed? You can be sure We tested those before them and Allah will show those who are true and those who are false." (Qur'an 29:2–3)

Many people take the opposite approach, though, and choose not to rise to the occasion. They fail their tests and forget about God. They resort to lying, cheating, backbiting, corruption, violence, or worse when faced with life's difficult choices. The Qur'an describes them as people who are sitting on the edge of a fence: When times are good, they are satisfied; but when the going gets tough, they engage in evil deeds with no regard for the rights of anyone else.

Does God Try to Fool Us?

Some people have charged that God turns us into unbelievers or believers. There are several verses in the Qur'an that say such things as, "God will mislead them" or "Nobody believes unless it is God's will." When taken out of context, these verses can give a false impression. The Qur'an is very clear about this principle: God *wants* us to believe in Him. He's not going to *keep* us from surrendering to Him. The problem occurs when we reject God *first*. He warned that if we do that, He will let us wander off in error as much as we want. As an added punishment He will cover our hearts with a *veil* and allow the *Shaytan* to tempt us without check so we understand even less about the truth. The more we reject God, the more we lose our way. If we move closer to God, however, He opens our hearts more and more to the reality of all things. The Qur'an puts it this way:

> No soul can believe except by the Will of Allah and He will place doubt in the hearts of those who refuse to understand. You can say to people, 'Hey, look at all the signs of Allah in space and on Earth …' but neither signs nor Warners profit those who won't believe. So do they expect anything besides what happened in the days of the people who passed away before them? Tell them, 'Wait then, for I, too, will wait with you.' In the end We deliver Our messengers and those who believe. Thus is it fitting on Our part that We should deliver those who believe! (Qur'an 10:100–103)

Careful! You're Being Watched

The Qur'an says that we all have two angels who follow us around throughout our lives. They are called the *Kiraman Katibeen*, or the Noble Writers. One figuratively sits on our right shoulder while the other sits on our left shoulder. Their only job is to write in our book of deeds every action, thought, or feeling we have each day. The right-side angel records our good deeds and the left-side angel notes our bad deeds. (Imagine if someone followed you around all day with a camcorder!) Muslim parents often joke with their children that one of their two angels is very busy writing: Which one is getting a tired hand?

This metaphorical book in which the angels are writing is our cumulative record, which we will be confronted with on the Day of Judgment after our death. There is a widely circulated story in the Muslim world to bring home the point of God's omnipotence. A religious scholar, or *Shaykh*, wanted to test his young students. He gave each one a piece of candy and told them to go and eat it where no one could see them. All of the students went away and came back some time later. The teacher asked if everyone had eaten their sweets, and they all raised their hands except one boy. When the *Shaykh* questioned the boy about eating the candy, he answered, "I couldn't find a place where Allah couldn't see me."

The Qur'an calls this life a time of trial and testing to show who among us has the most consciousness of God and behaves the best. "O People!" the Qur'an announces, "We created you from a single pair of a male and a female and made you into nations and groups so you can come to know each other. Certainly the noblest among you in the sight of Allah is the one with the most *Taqwa* [awareness of Allah]." (Qur'an 49:13)

The preferred lifestyle Islam envisions is one based on prayer, repentance, contemplation, responsibility, and morality. Islam doesn't demand that we become perfect. It merely states that we have to use this life to be the best we can be in all spheres of life. The Prophet Muhammad said, "Allah loves a person who, when they do something, they try their best." In the end, though, Allah makes allowances for those who were sincere, regardless of their success.

A Persian miniature painting depicting idyllic village life: ordered and honest in its simplicity.

(Photo courtesy of Aramco)

A Muslim who lives a normal life span is expected to work, marry, have a family, participate in social activities, and do his or her part to advance the cause of Godliness.

Waste and extravagance are to be avoided, and thrift and conservation are praiseworthy values to acquire. In every sphere of life, religious guidance must be consulted and followed. You often see the bumper sticker that reads, "God is my co-pilot." Islam says that if you really believe this, then you must *act* like it and not merely feel smug and do whatever you want. Follow the straight path of surrender to God in your life and you will please the One Whom you will have to face regardless of your personal opinions about His existence on a day that you cannot avoid.

> ### " " It Is Written
>
> According to the Prophet Muhammad, Allah said, "O son of Adam, so long as you call upon Me and ask of Me, I shall forgive you for what you have done, and I shall not mind. O son of Adam, were your sins to reach the clouds of the sky and were you then to ask forgiveness of Me, I would forgive you. O son of Adam, were you to come to Me with sins nearly as great as the earth and were you then to face Me, ascribing no partner to Me, I would bring you forgiveness nearly as great as that."

A person may live for 20, 50, or even 100 years, and every day will still be a continuous challenge to remain on the path of surrender to God. There are no easy tickets to Heaven. There is no salvation moment whereby we are guaranteed admittance to Heaven regardless of what we do for the rest of our lives. If we believe in God one day but reject Him a day later and then die, our whole life will be judged by the condition of our belief when we left the physical world. I'm reminded of a tombstone inscription from a graveyard in New York that begs the reader to consider every moment of life and its implications: "Behold and see as you pass by, as you are now so once was I. As I am now so you must be. Prepare for death and follow me."

Life in the Grave

One of the more graphic and compelling teachings of Islam begins with the moment of our death. Islam teaches that when we are dying, our soul rises in our body and collects in our throat. An angel called *Malikul Mawt*, or the Angel of Death, arrives and is given the task of removing the soul. This angel isn't the handsome young Mr. Death like Brad Pitt in *Meet Joe Black*. He's stern and unflinching in his duty and has no crisis of identity.

So how does the angel remove our soul from our body? Our soul, or *ruh*, is an otherworldly substance. The angel merely takes hold of it as it separates from our physical body and *pulls*. If the person believed in God and led a virtuous life, then the Angel of Death and his assistants gently draw out the soul from the body. But if the soul was that of a person who denied God or a person who led an evil life, then the angels will tear out the soul violently, like yanking cotton through a metal grate.

The exact moment when death is inevitable is described in the Qur'an as a moment of complete realization: "When a dying person breathes his last, when, 'Can any doctor save him?' the people ask, then, in the pangs of death he'll know his time is due. His knees will shake as death approaches and then he will return to his Lord." (Qur'an 75:27–30)

> **Ask the Imam**
>
> Euthanasia is equated with murder and suicide in Islamic Law and is thus completely forbidden. If someone is in a vegetative state, however, our scholars say that their feeding tubes can be removed because our record of deeds stops when our mind stops functioning.

When you take your last breath, you finally know your time is up and you may panic or be filled with regret. But repentance is too late then. God accepts no repentance from a person who is that close to death. When the process is moments away from completion, the cutoff point has arrived. The Qur'an records the final minutes of the Pharaoh's life, just before he was drowned in the Red Sea while chasing the fleeing Israelites. The Pharaoh said, "Now I believe." But God answered by saying he was too late.

> **Ask the Imam**
>
> Muslims don't view death as final. It is merely passing on to another stage of life. Pain is naturally felt at the removal of a loved one from this world. However, no believing Muslim feels that the person is gone forever. Appropriate words of sympathy to tell a grieving person who has lost a loved one are: "To Allah we belong and to Him we return." One may add the line, "May Allah forgive them and grant them a high place in Paradise."

Spirit on a Wing

What happens to the soul now? Islam teaches that there is another world, or parallel reality, if you will, in which only spirit material and energy beings like *jinns* and angels can exist. When we die, our soul is released from every cell of our body and is now in that other realm. The angels who took us out will now hold our soul fixed over our corpse. We can see all of the people gathered around our body, but they cannot see us. We try to speak to them, but they can't hear us. We see everything that happens to our body. When it is finally time to take the corpse to the graveyard, our soul floats along with it. A person who has been good will say, "Take me forward," but a person who has been immoral or faithless will say, "Curses, where are you taking me?"

A good soul will be carried gently by the angels and clothed with shrouds from Paradise. The angels will ascend upward into Heaven and will pass through its gates announcing who the soul is. When they reach the highest place in Heaven, Allah gives the command, "Write My servant's name in *Illiyun*." (*Illiyun* is the record of who will get into Heaven after Judgment Day.) Then the angels are told, "Take him back to Earth because I promised them that from it I created them, into it I return them and from it I will resurrect them once again."

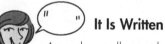

It Is Written

As a day well spent brings happy sleep, so a life well used brings a happy death.
—Leonardo da Vinci

The soul of an evil person is also carried to the gates of Heaven, but when the angels bring the soul there, the gates will not open for the soul to pass through. It is written in the Qur'an that the doors of Paradise will not be opened for someone who rejected Allah. Allah will then command that the person's name should be written in *Sijjin*, which is the register of Hell. Next He will order the angels to return the soul to Earth for the same reason He also returns good souls.

Soul Storage

Even as a person's body is being lowered into the grave and buried, his or her soul is brought down with it by the angels. We will hear the dirt being shoveled in and also the footsteps of the people as they walk away. Then we are alone, but not for long. By the way, it doesn't matter whether our body is destroyed or remains intact. Our soul will stay near the place where our body was last placed. So a person who dies in a fire and whose body is destroyed will find his or her soul sinking into the ground there. Even if the body is cremated and the ashes put in an urn and displayed on a shelf, the soul will sink into the earth somewhere along the way.

Now the life in the grave begins. The term for this life stage is *Barzakh*, or the Partition. It is sometimes referred to as "soul storage." Our soul will wait in this timeless existence until the Day of Judgment. No contact with the living or the souls of the other dead is possible, and we will be aware of nothing except our own selves. Islam does not believe that the spirits of the dead can be contacted by clairvoyants or that departed souls can inhabit the bodies of the living. Muslims believe that evil *jinns* work with psychics and spirit mediums and fool people into believing that they really did talk to their long dead aunt or grandmother. Islam says death is final and there is no coming back.

So what happens to us in the grave? According to the Prophet Muhammad, two angels with black faces and blue eyes are sent to us shortly after burial with an interesting mission. Their names are *Munkar* and *Nakir*. When they arrive, they force our soul to snap to attention. These angels are the Questioners of the Grave, and they ask us three questions: "Who is your Lord?" "What was your way of life?" And finally, "Who was your prophet?"

Islam accepts that there were other prophets sent by God to the world before the Prophet Muhammad. In fact, as mentioned earlier, Islam teaches that all people in the past received some type of divine guidance through an authentic prophet. Muhammad is merely the last of the prophets in a long chain. So the correct answers to those three questions are: "God", "Surrender (or obedience) to God's will," and then the name of the prophet we followed, whether Muhammad, Jesus, Moses, or whoever.

Just the Facts

Near-death experiences are accepted in Islam. The rule is that if it is not your time to go, you will revive. The Qur'an contains several stories in which the main characters wish to return to the world to warn their relatives about the truth of the next life. Jesus, who is considered a prophet in Islam, is said to have revived those who were thought dead.

If we answer all three questions correctly, then something amazing happens. Our good deeds become personified into a being resembling a person who says to us, "I'm here to give you good news. Allah has accepted what you did, and you will receive eternal gardens of delight. This is the day you were promised. I am your good deeds. By Allah I only knew you to be quick in obeying Allah and slow in disobeying Him. May God reward you with good." Then a window is opened to Heaven and another to Hell. We are shown where we would have gone in Hell if we were bad and then we're told to look at the place we will go to in Paradise instead. Then the angels expand the size of our soul storage bin to the size of a large room. A soft warm light fills the space, and we will be told to go to sleep and to dream peacefully until the Day of Judgment. Every day an angel will come and nudge us in our dreams and open a window through which we will see our place in Heaven again.

If we don't answer the questions correctly, and only a true rebel against God will fail the test, then something horrible happens. The angels appear terrifying to us. They strike our spirit body with a heavy mace, and they command our soul storage bin to squeeze in upon us until we feel suffocated. Our bad deeds become personified into a being resembling a grotesque ghoul who says, "I'm here to give you some bad news. I am your evil deeds. By God I only knew you to be slow in obeying God and quick in disobeying Him. May God repay you with evil." Then the angels come to us daily to strike us and force us to look through an open window through which we see our future spot in Hellfire. We stay tormented and screaming until the Day of Judgment.

Islam teaches that animals can hear the screams of those being tormented in the grave. The Prophet Muhammad said that if we could hear their cries, we would faint in terror. He often encouraged us to pray for protection against the *Punishment of the Grave*, as it is called. Time has no meaning there in the real sense, but this experience can be either a pleasant or a terrifying one, and, as Islam says, we will all have to undergo it, whether Muslim or not. Chapter 6 will explore what happens after the life in the grave is over.

It Is Written

Prophet Muhammad told an interesting story about Death. It seems the angel of death was sent to Moses and when he went to him, Moses slapped him severely, spoiling one of his eyes. The angel went back to his Lord, and said, "You sent me to a slave of Yours who does not want to die." Allah restored his eye and said, "Go back and tell Moses to place his hand over the back of an ox, for he will be allowed to live for a number of years equal to the number of hairs coming under his hand." (So the angel came to him and told him the same). Then Moses asked, "O my Lord! What will happen after those years pass?" He said, "Death will happen." Moses said, "Then let me die now."

The Least You Need to Know

♦ Islam counts our time in the womb and our lying in the grave after death as distinct stages of life.

♦ Abortion is all but prohibited in Islam. Saving the life of the mother is the only valid reason for abortion.

♦ Islam says faith can render any situation, good or bad, into a way to please God.

♦ When we die, our soul lives in the grave until Resurrection Day.

♦ Faith and at least an attempt to lead a virtuous life are essential prerequisites for a contented earthly life and a successful afterlife.

6

Islam on Heaven and Hell

In This Chapter

◆ Understand what Islam teaches about the coming Judgment Day and why it is necessary

◆ Understand the process of our soul's final judgment from the Islamic perspective

◆ Learn about the terrifying bridge that spans Hellfire and leads to Heaven

◆ Discover the delights of Heaven

◆ Know what fate awaits those who wind up in Hell

Nearly every religion in the world teaches that there will be some sort of reward or punishment for our actions in this life. Whether it is belief in Heaven, Valhalla, union with the light, or Paradise, a realm of eternal delight for the deserving motivates the followers of any given religion to invest in their ultimate future by straight-jacketing their lives here in order to reap rewards later. In the same way, whether you're talking about Hell, Hades, or the Fire, visions of never-ending suffering are powerful incentives for avoiding immorality and wickedness in this world.

Islam offers a very clear picture of each of these possibilities to its followers. For the Muslim, there is no vague union of our souls in a great nothingness nor a bland pearly gate leading to a street paved with gold. No, for the devoted follower of the Prophet Muhammad, Paradise is presented with such clarity and detail that we can almost taste it. Likewise, Hell is given such a vivid treatment that it can give us nightmares if we're not careful. All of this serves to accentuate the very reason that religion teaches us about an afterlife in the first place: so that we can feel the immediacy of the importance of our beliefs and actions in everything we do and know what is to become of us after death.

Why Have a Judgment Day?

Over one quarter of the Qur'an's verses deal with issues related to the next life or the spiritual world. For the Muslim, this is a naturally appropriate ratio given that Islam teaches that the *real* life is yet to come. This life, the Prophet noted, is like a dream. When we die, we will truly awaken to reality. In Chapter 5, you learned about some of the things that every person will experience after death: the angels drawing out the soul, being placed in the grave, and being visited by angels in *Barzakh*. Now I will turn to what happens afterward. I mean, you can't stay in soul storage forever! Because Islam teaches that the earth will cease to exist one day, all of those stored souls have to go somewhere!

Translate This

Youmul qiyamah means the Day of Standing (Up for Judgment). An alternate name is *youmud deen,* which means the "Day When Ways of Life Will Be Judged." In English we call either one Judgment Day for short.

Life in the grave will last, then, until the Day of Judgment, (known as *Youmul Qiyamah*), when God will gather together every human being and *jinn* who ever lived. No dead soul can rise from its grave and walk the earth in the meantime like a ghost or an apparition. To reiterate, the only time the soul gets out of the grave is after God has caused the world to end in a cataclysmic *Last Day*. Only then is it time to bring all departed souls together for their final reckoning. The fourth and final stage of our life now begins.

To understand the reasoning behind a Judgment Day, we have to remember what the purpose of life is for each one of us. We are here to be tested by God in our ability to master our very *selves*, thereby making us worthy of entering His paradise. The two main proofs of this worthiness lie in our faith and in our actions. Throughout this test, we try to raise our souls to the highest of three levels of development, passing from our animal self, to an accusing or self-reflective self, and hopefully becoming a restful soul at peace. We accomplish this ascension in status through a combination of belief in God, seeking His guidance through His revealed Books and emulating the example of His prophets; and then of a life devoted to good deeds, asking repentance when we stumble. From this philosophy of our purpose, then, the logical conclusion is that there must be an end to this test and that each of us will receive our *grade* eventually. This is what Judgment Day is for.

The Long Arm of the Law

The very idea that criminals and evil people in this world can escape punishment simply by dying is unimaginable. Can Adolph Hitler, with the blood of millions on his hands, escape a more severe retribution than merely expiring in a bunker? Think of all the children who have been abused, animals who have been mistreated, thefts and rapes that have occurred—what kind of universe would say that miscreants can get away with such deeds? The modern mechanistic view of life, which says we are all just intelligent animals who live only once, is the greatest danger to human safety ever conceived. To tell someone that because you live only once go ahead and have fun while you can is a license for any deranged person to harm others with abandon. If it feels good, do it, is not an acceptable mantra for a Muslim.

We must police our own behavior if we are to have safe societies, says the Qur'an. If there is no punishment for crimes, there is no peace. If man-made laws are not enough of a deterrent, then an appeal to higher laws that transcend humans' existence will help for many people. Those who flout both levels of law will get more than a slap on the wrist from God! The Qur'an is very clear about the need for just retribution for those who did wrong and redress for those who were wronged, and it is on Judgment Day that injustice will be paid back. "That will be the Day of ultimate recompense," the Qur'an declares, and Islam is very firm in promoting the full justice that is everyone's right. Even plants and animals whom we have wronged for unjust or cruel reasons will be able to make their claim.

 Just the Facts

People have sometimes criticized the use of harsh punishments for criminals in Islam. However, in societies where Islamic Law is most implemented, crime is nearly nonexistent. By the way, there are not that many harsh punishments to begin with, and the rules for proof are very stringent—almost in the defendant's favor.

When Will It Come?

So when does Judgment Day begin? Is a date given in Islamic sources? Unfortunately, no. The Qur'an records that a group of idolaters went to the Prophet Muhammad and taunted him about this whole concept of a final judgment. They dared him to make it happen right there or to at least tell them when it was supposed to be. A revelation came to him and he recited this argument in rebuttal, "They ask you about the hour, tell them only God knows when it will occur. When it does happen, they will be taken completely by surprise and will wish it never came."

We do know how it will commence and proceed. According to the chronology given in Islamic sources, one day God will initiate a process that will bring about the end of the world. Even as He began it, He will shepherd it to a close. An angel named *Israfil* will sound a note on a massive horn, and the shock wave will permeate the whole of space. In the beginning, Allah had created the universe in a huge explosion (the Big Bang) and was expanding it. Now He will roll it up like a scroll and shut it down. People will still be living on Earth at that time, and they will run in terror as the globe begins to shake and break apart violently. "What is happening with the world?" they'll cry. The Qur'an has many vivid passages describing what will be going on when the Earth is covered in darkness, and here is one of the more famous ones:

> No, but I call your attention to the Day of Resurrection. And no, I call your attention to the accusing voice of every person's own conscience. Do people think that we can't resurrect them or knit their bones together again? Without a doubt we can recreate them down to their very fingertips! Even so, people choose to deny what lies ahead of them, asking, "When will this resurrection day be?" But on that day when fear overshadows their sight and the moon is darkened and joined together with the sun, on that very day people will cry out, "Where can we escape!" But no, there will be no escape. The journey will lead back to your Lord, alone. People will be informed, on that day, of all that they did and left undone. And no, every person will be their own accusing witness, even though they hide themselves in excuses. (Qur'an 75:1–15)

All living beings will die, including the angels and the *jinns*, and all matter in the universe will be destroyed. This is called the Last Day, and it signals that the show is over. Next stop: Judgment. The angels will then be brought back to life, and *Israfil* will sound another note on his horn. All human beings and *jinns* will suddenly appear standing on a huge level plain. The souls of all the dead will be instantly brought out from *Barzakh* and given new bodies that will look like their physical bodies from Earth in every respect, though without the flaws. We will be stunned by what we see and will feel we had lived on Earth for less than a day. Everyone will be naked and without any symbol of status or power. This is called the Resurrection.

Next, all people will be sorted according to what they used to believe in or follow in the physical world. A Muslim, Christian, or Jew will be standing behind Muhammad,

Jesus, or Moses. A Hindu follower of Ganesh will be standing behind a representation of the elephant god. Those who followed Communism will probably be standing behind Karl Marx and so on. This sorting will be absolute, and we can't cut lines or hide in other groups. The angels will be moving us into place, and we have no choice but to cooperate.

The Prophet Muhammad said that the Day of Judgment will last 50,000 years because of the large number of people present. Think of it: Every human being who ever lived will be there. But no one will be concerned with anyone but himself or herself because of the gravity of the situation. The Qur'an says a person will ignore his or her own parents and children because of the worry and suspense on that day. Think back to grade school and how you felt on report card day; then imagine getting a report for your whole life!

People who denied God (called *kafirs*) will be agitated and filled with stress on that day. All the more so because the pit of Hell will be visible in the distance, and all the terrifying moans and booming sounds of massive explosions within it will be heard. The sinners will approach the people who were faithful and virtuous in their lives because these good persons will be bathed in a sheen of light. The sinful will beg for some of that light but will be cordoned off from the righteous.

Allah will be hidden behind a huge veil and will not show Himself, though He will be conducting the judgment proceedings. (He will reveal His true self in Heaven only to those who desired to seek Him alone.) He will run a tight courtroom, and no excuses will be accepted. People will try to bribe the angels or offer to pay a ransom to God for their salvation, but what can they pay with when everything belongs to God? This gives new relevance to the saying, "You can't take it with you."

It Is Written

Muhammad said, "One Day Allah will take the world in His left hand and will roll up the universe in His right. He will say, 'I am the King, where are the kings of the Earth?'"

Translate This

Kafir is the term used in the Qur'an to describe someone who does not believe in God. Although the word is often translated as unbeliever, that is not what it means. In fact, there is no equivalent word for *unbeliever* in Arabic. *Kafir* comes from the word *kaffara*, which means to cover up, conceal, or hide. Thus a person who is a *kafir* hides God's truth and covers his or her heart and mind, refusing to accept the existence of God.

The Judgment Cometh

How will the judgment proceed? The Qur'an and the Hadith give a very detailed picture of the whole affair. There will be no breaks from the assembly. We won't need to eat or drink or sleep. We just wait. When it is our turn to be judged, two angels, one walking in front and the other in back, will escort us before the Judge, Almighty God. The angel in front will announce, "I have his record here with me." Our record will be given to us in our right hand if we were a good person. Those of us who must receive it in our left hand or from behind our back are in big trouble.

Just the Facts

Islam is not against "lefties." The significance of getting your record in your right or left hand on Judgment Day has nothing to do with a person's dexterity in this world.

Next our whole record will be read in our presence. Every thought or deed we ever did will be there, so much so that we will exclaim, "What kind of book is this? It leaves nothing out, great or small!" Our faith in God will be examined in detail and our sincerity measured. We will then be questioned about what we did and why. If we try to lie or be evasive, our body parts will be made to speak and bear witness against us. For example, if we stole something and denied stealing it, we may be surprised to hear our hand talking, saying, "He did it! He did it!"

Other witnesses will be brought forward. Anyone we ever harmed in our earthly life will come and state their claim against us. Our good deeds and evil deeds will be gathered near us in a pile, and people we wronged will be told to help themselves to some of our good deeds. We will be powerless to stop them. We will try to blame *Shaytan*, but he will disown us. People may call to their idols for help, but they will say, "You're on your own!" Then we truly will realize that we are held completely accountable for what we did, and no one can save us.

After the review of our record, our good and bad deeds will be placed on a scale and weighed. We had better hope our good-deed side is heavier! However, our record of prayer will be examined first; if it is found to have shortcomings, then all our good deeds will be thrown out. What good are our deeds if we were deficient in calling on our Lord and praying to Him? Why, you might be wondering, are our deeds weighed if Islam teaches that faith is what brings us salvation? Good deeds are the proof of our faith, as even the Apostle Paul in the Christian Bible noted. So if we did little that was good or right in the world, then what was the value of all our declarations and assertions?

After the review, our victims' payback time, and the weighing of our deeds, we kneel humbly before Allah's presence. He will explain to us the meaning of the evidence, and no injustice will be done or favoritism shown. If we are guilty or innocent, we are made to understand completely and beyond the shadow of a doubt what we deserve. But Allah is a merciful and a loving God. He loves to forgive those who asked for His forgiveness in their worldly life, and thus He will display that great magnanimity that is only His on Judgment Day as well. He may forgive extra sins of ours for no other reason than that He wants to. People who hoped for Allah's forgiveness may find themselves with a spotless record, and the worst criminal may find that due to some small but poignant act of kindness done to a person, plant, or animal, his record may be wiped clean. Other factors that could cause God to forgive unconditionally include taking orphans under our care lovingly, raising and educating three daughters in the best way, being martyred in battle or oppressed by a tyrant, and being dutiful and faithful to our aged parents.

Allah Is Merciful

The Prophet Muhammad once told a story to illustrate this mercy of Allah. A harlot was walking down a road when she saw a deep well. As she climbed down its walls to get a drink, she noticed a thirsty dog pacing back and forth above. She felt pity for it and removed her leather sock, filled it with water, and brought it up for the dog to drink. On account of this act of kindness, God forgave all of her sins.

> **It Is Written**
>
> Muhammad said, "When Allah decreed the Creation He pledged Himself by writing in His book which is laid down with Him, 'Behold, My mercy prevails over My wrath.'"

The Bridge over Hell

Finally our verdict is given: guilty or innocent. We either rejoice or hang our heads in shame as we return to our places in line. Then, when all of the judgments are finished, we must travel on to the next segment of this process. From the Plain of Judgment everyone will move forward to the brink of the pit of Hell. It will be a monstrously huge, gaping hole that you can't even see across. The flames will leap up for miles, and sparks the size of logs will shoot out. The intense heat will be felt by all, and people will be terrified of it. The angels will throw the worst sinners, who were found guilty of the worst crimes, into the flames headfirst without any fanfare or ceremony. The rest of us, whether guilty or innocent, will have to take a harrowing journey over a bridge called the *Sirat*, which spans the chasm of Hell and leads to Paradise on the other side.

The sequence on Judgment Day.

The *Sirat* is as thin as a razor and is studded with jagged edges and spikes. The righteous people and the prophets will zoom right over it and make it to the other side.

Good people who had a few sins that were not forgiven will be cut and bruised as they journey over the bridge to remind them that there are consequences for all bad deeds, but they will make it over as well. Some people will be in tatters when they step off! (We all are healed on the other side.) Sinful people will be able to make it only so far because they will suddenly become snagged by the thorny bridge and will tumble headlong into the pit. Their screams will echo and terrify everyone else. Incidentally, more people will fall in than will make it over.

What if we were not too bad but also not good enough for Heaven and our good deeds weighed exactly the same as our bad? We might find ourselves in an elevated spot between Heaven and Hell called the *Heights*. It is not exactly the same as the Christian conception of purgatory or Abraham's Bosom, but the idea is similar. We will stay there, seeing Hell and fearing it and seeing Heaven and longing for it, until such time as we fully realize that we almost slipped up and went to Hell. Then we will eventually go to Paradise.

The topics of Heaven and Hell are covered quite extensively in the Qur'an and in the Hadith, or the sayings of Muhammad. The details are unerringly stunning. Wherever we end up will be the culmination of our fourth and final stage of life. Our soul, on loan from God, has now been returned to the other realm and is receiving its rewards or torment based on what we did with it in the world. Now I'll explain what Islam says about Heaven and Hell.

Use Your Time Wisely

Islam presents a very vivid picture of the afterlife. According to a saying of the Prophet Muhammad, we should live in this world as if we were merely strangers or drifters. The idea is that we only have a few years to live here on Earth and then we die, so shouldn't we look to the realm of the soul? Isn't the afterlife the most important thing to know about? Shouldn't we spend our life investing in the kind of capital (faith and good deeds) that would make our permanent life worthwhile? But all too often we spend our time running after what is only temporary. Regardless of our awareness of what is to come, however, Heaven or Hell is our final destination.

The Gardens of Paradise

Jannah, or Paradise, is the place where our soul is rewarded for listening to its *fitrah*, or inner nature. Because we had lived a life of faith and good deeds while avoiding bad deeds—which wasn't always easy in a world where *Shaytan* and animal desires compelled people to commit evil actions—we demonstrated that we are the best type of creature God created. Our souls have been purified and are ready for the good life after so much struggle and hardship. The Qur'an tells us: "History

Translate This

Jannah is the word for Heaven in Arabic. It literally means a garden, and thus the English equivalent, *Paradise*, is more often used by Muslims to describe the *good place*.

is a witness! Indeed, humanity is truly lost. Except for those who have faith, do what is right, and who teach each other about truth and perseverance." (Qur'an 103:1–3)

When we step off the *Sirat* (assuming we passed our judgment successfully) and make it to Paradise, we will find a huge wall in front of us with eight gates. Each gate is named after one of the main religious rituals that God established on Earth for us. For example, there will be gates named after Prayer, Charity, Fasting, Struggling Against Evil, and so on. We will enter through the gate that corresponds with the activity we were best at. Some very holy people will be called by the wardens of all the gates simultaneously to enter. In that case they can go through whichever gate they wish! Angels, who will be standing guard in front of each, will greet us as we enter and say, "Peace be upon you! You have done well! Enter here and dwell within."

Just the Facts

The Muslim greeting that is equivalent to "Hello" is *Assalamu alaykum.* This means "Peace be upon you." The reply is the reverse, *Wa alaykum assalam,* which translates as "And upon you be peace."

The total wonderment of Paradise cannot adequately be described in human language, and God says as much: "I have prepared for My servants what no eye has ever seen, nor ear heard, nor any human being ever conceived of" (Hadith). The Qur'an can merely give us mental images drawn from our own life experiences in this world, and thus Heaven is described in very earthly terms, though Muslims understand that many of these descriptions are metaphors to appeal to what we know now. It will seem to us as a land of lively cities, exquisite gardens, rolling meadows, primeval forests, and river valleys. Soulless servants who will resemble us, and who only aim to please, will pamper us at all times. The colors and scents that will greet us at every moment will be so vibrant that we will never grow tired of looking at them.

Whoever was handicapped, lame, infirm, or blind will find that they, along with everyone else, will have perfect bodies. Once an old woman asked the Prophet Muhammad if she were going to go to Heaven. He told her that there will be no old women in Paradise. She bowed her head sadly, but then the Prophet smiled and lifted her head up and said, "There will be no old women in Paradise because you will all be made young again." The woman was overjoyed. We will all be about 30 years of age and in the prime of our physical shape, and we will never feel sick or hurt again. Babies who died will remain as infants, but they will have the run of the place, scurrying around "like pretty green birds all aflutter."

Heaven has seven layers, each more fascinating than the next, and each of us will be taken to our home, which will be located on one of those levels. The level is determined both by the extent of our goodness and by the amount of our prophet's scriptures that we learned by heart while we were alive in the world. Each level is so fantastic, however, that we will not feel any slight or jealousy because of our assigned level. In fact, such sentiments will be unknown in Paradise; no ill talk, gossip, or lying will ever be heard.

We will be able to visit people who live in different levels. Friends and family will meet and lounge in leisure. Husbands and wives will be reunited, if they choose, and socializing will be a major activity. There will be special servants and pleasure mates (called *houris*) in Paradise. They are intelligent yet soulless creatures made only to serve and please us in a world that knows no more vice. Islam is very matter-of-fact about sex and says straightforwardly that guiltless sex is one of the benefits of Heaven.

Wine, another vice that was forbidden in the world, will be allowed there also, and the best food will always be brought to us. We don't need to eat to survive any longer; there we will eat for the joy of it. Paradise contains markets to shop in, fountains to relax near, roads to travel, and endless delights. Boredom will never occur. We will be given silk clothes with jewelry and brocade of the finest quality. The people of Paradise will be quite a sight indeed!

> **Ask the Imam**
>
> Islam does not only teach us to pray to God for admittance into Paradise. Rather, we are taught to ask for the highest place in Paradise. Aim high!

> **It Is Written**
>
> They will live among sylvan forests where there is neither thorn nor bramble, amidst wildly flowering trees that provide cool, expansive shade. There are flowing brooks and fruits of all kinds that never go out of season nor diminish. They will recline in places of honor, with specially created companions who are pure, undefiled, loving and of a similar age. (Qur'an 56:27–38)

Paradise is forever. No one has to leave and we will be at peace with everything in all of creation. Every question we ever had will be answered. Every delight we ever imagined will be ours for the asking and more besides. Even greater than these, however, is the ability to see God, Himself. He can be seen beyond the seventh layer in a fantastic spectacle of indescribable light and sound.

Such is Heaven according to Islam. There are so many vivid descriptions in the Qur'an and Hadith that the immediacy of the next life is brought to the forefront of the Muslims' mind. People of other faiths may have pearly gates and gilded hymnals in mind, but Muslims have a closer look at what's there and long for it that much harder!

No Dancing with the Devil Here!

Hell. The word conjures up images of fire and suffering. Nearly every society has some conception of an ultimate place of punishment for those who committed great evil or seemed to get away with their crimes here on Earth. But the purpose of Hell in Islam is not only to punish, but also to purify. Christianity teaches that Hell is forever for anyone who goes there. Islam, while teaching that some will never get out, also says that some souls will get out after their fixed term of punishment is reached. Then they, too, will go to Heaven. So in Islam, Hell isn't forever for everybody.

Even as the Qur'an describes Heaven in stunning detail, so too does it give a very immediate depiction of Hellfire. To begin with, Hell is not the headquarters of *Shaytan* and his devils, as is the popular idea in Western culture. *Shaytan* has no throne in Hell from which he directs his plans against true believers in God. Hell is a place that God created only for *punishing*. *Shaytan* does not want to go there, and neither does anyone else. Hell is so tremendous that it will never be completely filled. The Qur'an has a verse in which God says that He will ask Hell one day if it is full yet. Hell will respond, "Are there any more to come?"

 It Is Written

> Muhammad said, "Paradise and Hellfire disputed together, and Hellfire said, 'In me are the mighty and the haughty.' Paradise said, 'In me are the weak and the poor.' So Allah judged between them, saying, 'You are Paradise, My mercy; through you I show mercy to those I wish. And you are Hellfire, My punishment; through you I punish those I wish, and it is incumbent upon Me that each of you shall have its fill.'"

Hell has seven layers, just as Heaven does. The lower the level, the worse it gets. Nineteen angels patrol the rim of the chasm and push back anyone who tries to escape. The Prophet Muhammad once remarked that the fire of Hell is 70 times hotter than fire here on Earth. That's worse than an incinerator! Our level in Hell will be determined by how bad we were and how little we believed in God and the afterlife. The inmates of Hell will frequently hear the phrase: "Didn't any Warners come to you? Didn't you listen to what your religious guides were saying?" Angels will administer the many varieties of punishments and will not flinch in executing their duties.

Among the more terrifying punishments of Hell are these:

- Endless columns of fire will enclose the inmates of Hell, and flaming chains will fall upon them. Snakes and scorpions will continuously harass them.

- The inmates of Hell will wear clothing made of burning pitch, drink from fountains of burning oil, eat barbed fruits that look like devil heads, and never have a moment's rest from it. Every time a person's body will be burnt up or destroyed, a fresh body or layer of skin will materialize so that the punishment can be felt anew.

Translate This _____

Jahannum is the name for Hell in Arabic. It is related to the Hebrew word, Gehenna.

- There will be no communicating with anyone else. Isolation will be complete, and nothing but screams and moaning will be heard. No pleas for mercy or cries for a relief will be entertained. Instead, every time the inmates of Hell cry for relief, their punishment will be doubled.

- People will be punished according to their crimes: Faultfinders will scratch their faces with iron nails, liars will rip out their cheeks with iron bars, gossipers will cut off their lips with razors, the greedy will be bitten by snakes, and those who dressed to incite lust in others will be disfigured and made grotesque.

- Fountains of pus and blood and boiling muck will be the only refreshment, and utter hopelessness will be everyone's lot.

Western writers have tried to envision the afterlife for centuries. Dante's *Inferno* is probably the most detailed European concept about the subject. The more dramatic Robin Williams' movie *What Dreams May Come* also attempts to paint a picture of the next life but ultimately falls short of a full representation of how wonderful it will be. Whereas traditional Christianity gives the one-size-fits-all *Lake of Fire*, Islam provides a closer look at what awaits those who denied God and spent their life hurting other people and harming the world in general. The Qur'an quotes God as saying, "You forgot this possibility so this day I will forget you."

Just the Facts _____

Dante's book, *The Inferno*, contains many startling images of the seven layers of Hell. Although he was a Christian, he was influenced by the Muslim concept of the next life. He wrote the book as something of a social and political satire but wound up insulting Islam by making the Prophet Muhammad a character in his story.

Why Does God Punish?

Hell is not the province of a cruel God. It serves a purpose: to purify warped souls. Once a woman and her son were sitting in a gathering listening to the Prophet Muhammad as he gave a sermon. The child wandered away from his mother and tried to put his hand in the fireplace; the mother instinctively snatched her child away to safety. She thought for a moment about what she had done and asked the Prophet how Allah could punish those He loved in Hell when she as a mother wanted only to protect her little one. The Prophet bowed his head and cried softly and then answered her by saying that Allah does not like to punish. He punishes only those who have rejected Him and committed evil actions. Wouldn't the mother also correct her son when he did wrong? Thus, we find the purpose of Hell justified.

If we have been cast into Hell temporarily but have finished our sentence, the angels will locate and remove us, though we will be mere charred skeletons by then. A substance called the Water of Life will be poured over us, and our bodies will regenerate and be restored to us as good as new. Finally, we will be escorted to Paradise and given our full rewards for any good we might have done. Who will stay in Hell forever? Only God knows, and He is never unjust. The lowest level of Hell is for the worst inmates who will have no way out of it ever.

The Least You Need to Know

- Muslims believe in a Day of Judgment where all injustice will be paid back and no one will be treated unfairly.

- Islam teaches that Heaven is eternal, whereas a person's sentence in Hell can range from temporary to forever, depending on his or her crimes.

- Heaven is presented as an ideal adult playground with the best delights in food, comfort, friendship, activities, environment, and physical pleasures of all kinds.

- Hell is described in great detail in Islam. Punishments there often mimic crimes done in this life. Anyone who has any small amount of faith in God will eventually be released and admitted to Heaven.

Chapter 7

In the Beginning ...
An Islamic Perspective

In This Chapter

◆ Learn about the Qur'anic account of the creation of the world

◆ Find out where Islam stands on the evolution and creationism debates

◆ Learn about the role of science in the Qur'an

◆ Compare the Islamic version of the story of Adam and Eve to the biblical account

◆ Discover how Satan became the enemy of humankind

The Qur'an has its own explanation for how the world began and also for how it will end. The Qur'an, however, is not structured in chronological order as the Bible is. Rather, it consists mostly of essays on spiritual topics, and then uses scattered references to history and science to prove the validity of the religious points as they are presented. Most chapters of the Qur'an employ this kind of technique. The history of ancient prophets and nations, the formation of space, the natural world, and the miracle of life are the most common proofs given. When you gather together all of the statements in the Qur'an related to natural phenomenon, for example, and examine them, you'll find an amazingly detailed description of how everything came to be.

In addition to a well-structured explanation of the elements of creation, Islam also has its own account of how people were made and what human activity means throughout history. Such familiar Judeo-Christian concepts as Adam and Eve, the prophets, God's hand in history, and the coming of an anti-Christ have their counterparts in Islam. But as you have already seen with the subjects covered in earlier chapters, Islam has its own version of what each means. Throughout this chapter you will find that the Islamic explanation for how we came here and what it all means is wide in its scope and complexity as well as independent in its own right.

The Creation of the Universe

"Let there be light" is a familiar phrase for Jews and Christians. It signifies the beginning of the universe according to the Bible. In fact, if one were to read the book of Genesis, a very clear and ordered picture of creation would be presented. Does Islam have its own version of creation? You bet. Is it similar to the biblical account in any way? The answer is both yes and no. As you'll see, the Qur'anic presentation of the creation of the universe is both unique and startlingly accurate.

To begin the Islamic narrative of creation, I must go way back to the time when there was *nothing but God.* Muslims believe that God has no beginning and no end and that He exists independently of time or place. His omnipotence is complete, and He is present everywhere, though He is not a part of anything. In a way, you can *almost* compare Him to the concept of the *Force* in the *Star Wars* movies, except that God is very much alive and cannot be used by people for their purposes like some sort of tool. Given that Muslims do not personify God as other religions do, the mental energy involved in understanding His place in the universe has to come from a higher conceptual level. Trying to explain the origin of God is not something Muslims even try to do.

> **Ask the Imam**
>
> Muslims are supposed to look into the natural world for proofs of God's existence. Evidence of His creative genius, says the Qur'an, is found in every aspect of our environment. Science strengthens a Muslim's faith and there has been no conflict between science and religion in Muslim history.

Allah's Notebook

Before God even started the ball rolling, though, He made some rules for Himself to follow. One of these was that He would be kinder and more generous with His soon-to-be-made creatures than He would be stern. He also made laws for the governing of the natural universe that would not change. (God invented physics!) Where did He record all of these rules and laws? Muslims believe that God has a ledger of some sort in which He records whatever He wishes. He does not need this ledger, however, just as He doesn't need the angels to help Him. He just willed it.

In this ledger He also wrote down how long the universe would last and how it would end. Everything in creation, as you learned in Chapter 2, would be *Muslim*, or surrendered to God's will. The only exception to that rule would be those creatures in whom He endowed free will. The Qur'an says, "We did not create space and the Earth and everything in between them except for just ends and for a fixed term." (Qur'an 46:2–3)

Creation in the Qur'an

How did God proceed to make the universe? Did He announce, "Let there be light"? Actually, no. There is no such verse in the Qur'an. What He *did* do will sound very familiar from a scientific point of view. He said the word "Be," and an object like a ball (or something equivalent to it) appeared, and then He split it into pieces. The materials from this initial explosion were the building blocks for all things in the universe. The force of that blast continues to expand and spread this matter in all directions even to this day. The Qur'an is very clear when it says, "Don't the people who hide the truth see that space and the earth were all joined together in one unit of creation and then We split them apart?" (Qur'an 21:30) Does this statement ring a bell? Scientists would call this description amazingly close to the modern concept of the Big Bang.

After this great explosion of matter, the Qur'an mentions that the heavens were filled with a kind of smoke. (For Arabs in the seventh century, this is how interstellar gases would have looked.) The formation of planets and stars soon followed, and the fact that they have regular orbits is stated in the Qur'an, as well: "By the rotation of the stars and the orbit and setting of the planets, by the night as it falls and the morning as it passes, certainly, this is the speech of an honored Messenger." (Qur'an 81:25)

 It Is Written

We built the universe with creative power and We are certainly expanding it. We spread the Earth out wide and how excellent We ordered it! And We created every living thing in pairs so you could get a reminder. (Qur'an 51:47–49)

Interestingly enough, the Qur'an also describes the movement of bodies in space by using the Arabic word for *swim*. Planets and stars are *swimming* in their courses. As we know today, space is not empty and the objects within it move at a measurable pace not unlike a person gliding under water. The Qur'an even correctly identifies the sun as a giver of light (*siraj*) and the moon as a reflector of light (*munir*).

A model of the solar system developed by Muslim astronomers in the sixteenth century.

(Photo courtesy of Aramco)

Six Days and Still No Rest

God finished the creation of the universe in six segments, ostensibly called days, and then mounted the throne of power to govern the universe on the seventh. He did not rest, for as the Qur'an says, He never tires. With that said, Muslims do not believe that the universe is only a few thousand years old, as some religious groups assert. Islam can accept the proposition that the universe is *billions* of years old. How can this be when the Qur'an declares that it took God six days to create everything? The answer lies in the meaning of the Arabic word for day, *youm*. The term *youm* can mean a day as we know it or a segment of time independent of a 24-hour Earth day. The Qur'an further points out that a day to God is not like one of ours. In one verse it says a day to God could be like a thousand years. In another it says that the time it will take the angels to ascend to God for Judgment Day will be a day that is equivalent to 50,000 years of our own time. We simply can't conceive of time in the same way God does. After all, He *made* time. So the length of time in years that it took for creation is negotiable for us.

Out of the six days, or time periods, that God took to create everything, the final two *days* were for creating planets like ours. Our particular planet, and its formation and features, is given more specific treatment in the Qur'an for obvious reasons. Here we find that, as before, we have a large number of inexplicably accurate scientific statements, which the Muslim would say is a sign that the author of the Qur'an could have been none other than God. The Qur'an describes some of Earth's salient features this way:

- Earth is *almost* perfectly round. (The Qur'an actually uses a word that means egglike in shape and in fact, the earth is not a perfect sphere!)

- Earth's surface is described as being spread out like a carpet that can move. (The crust!)

- The mountains have roots like tent pegs to stabilize Earth lest the surface will move and shake us too much. (Plate tectonics!)

- Rain falls from the sky, collects underground, and comes out as springs. (The water cycle!)

- There are different types of clouds, each producing a different type of precipitation. (Rain, hail, sleet!)

- Earth is surrounded by a protective canopy that shields us. (The ozone!)

- The Qur'an uses the word ocean 32 times and the word land 13 times. The ratio is 71.11 to 28.88, the exact figure for the distribution of water and land over the earth.

Muslims are proud to point out that these and many other accurate scientific descriptions were unknown in Muhammad's time. (Is it any wonder verses from the Qur'an are called *ayahs*, or

Translate This

Youm means a day or any period of time in succession. It doesn't necessarily mean a 24-hour Earth day. So when the Qur'an says God took six days to create the universe, it could mean six segments of billions of years each.

Just the Facts

Some people have accused the Qur'an of being disjointed in its organization. This is a misreading of its style and rhythm. The Qur'an uses the following method of argument: It mentions a miracle of nature and then uses that point to accentuate the value of a religious concept. Such semi-independent passages together weave an overall unified message.

Translate This

The Arabic word *ayah* means a sign. Verses from the Qur'an are also called by this term.

signs?) In fact, most of these discoveries were made only within the last 200 years. As Dr. Maurice Bucaille, a French scientist who undertook to study this aspect of the Qur'an, wrote in his book *The Bible, the Qur'an and Science,* "The relationship between the Qur'an and science is ... a surprise, especially when it turns out to be one of harmony and not of discord."

Islam and Evolution

"We didn't come from monkeys!" "Life evolved over millions of years." "God made it all at once!" "How do you explain the dinosaurs?" These are the kinds of arguments and questions that creationists and evolutionists have bandied about for decades. The debate still rages into modern times, and you can even see this war being waged on car bumpers as staunch Christians proudly display their stickers of fish symbols and equally passionate science buffs offer stickers of fish with legs as their response. Where do Muslims stand in this debate? Can Islam contribute anything to help solve this seemingly insurmountable gap?

After already reading about the Qur'an and its reliance on scientific statements to prove its validity, you might get the impression that Islam would lean toward evolution (sometimes referred to as Darwinism, after its founder Charles Darwin). On the other hand, Chapter 2 introduced you to a fantastic world of angels, *jinns,* Judgment Day, and an omnipotent God. Would Islam swing toward creationism as advanced by fundamentalist Christians? Although there has been a lot of debate in recent years among Muslim scholars about this issue, the consensus is that Islam teaches a mixture of both theories. It's a balanced approach derived from the basic Qur'anic assumption that God made everything and that everything follows identifiable physical laws. Let's look at how this synthesis can be accomplished.

> **Ask the Imam**
>
> Do Muslims believe that aliens exist? We certainly can if we choose. The Qur'an contains two verses in which we are told that every creature in the heavens (space) and on the earth praises God. *Phone home, ET!* We'll leave the lights on for you!

First of all, Islam attributes the origin of life only to God. He is the exclusive Author of Existence. In this sense, Islam would say God is the Creator. This makes us creationists after a fashion. The first match-up with an evolutionary idea comes from the Qur'anic statement that God created all living things from water. The animals and plants were here before we humans were, as evidenced by the chronological appearance of Adam and Eve *after* Earth was populated with life-forms. The Qur'an even makes an allowance for the diversity of species and the extreme age of Earth.

The Qur'an states matter-of-factly:

> Don't you see that it is Allah Who sends the rain down from the sky? With it
> We produce plants of various colors. And in the mountains are colored layers of
> rock, some white and red of various tones and some black in hue. And so, too,
> among humans and crawling creatures and cattle will you find a great diversity
> of colors. Those among Allah's servants who have knowledge truly fear Him,
> for Allah is Mighty and Forgiving. (Qur'an 35:27–31)

Armed with these teachings, Muslim scholars have unanimously agreed that the
universe developed over a long period of time and that life arose on Earth through
natural processes. One of God's names, from the Ninety-Nine Names of Allah is,
strangely enough, *Al Bari*, or the *Evolver.* The caveat that Muslims add is that it was
God who provided the spark to those two lonely proteins in the ancient nutrient-rich
sea. He is the one who guided the development of all the diverse life forms on our
planet, and He is the one who authored animal instincts. "Glorify the Name of your
Lord, the Most High, Who creates and completes all things, determines their length,
and directs them to their conclusion." (Qur'an 87:1–3)

Just the Facts

The top two scientific researchers in the Muslim world today, who hold opposing
views on the evolution or instant creation of human beings, are Dr. Maurice
Bucaille and Harun Yahya. Bucaille published his views in the book *What Is the
Origin of Man?* while Yahya wrote his response in the work *Evolution Deceit.*
Both lay out well-reasoned arguments and have contributed a great deal to the
richness of the current debate among Muslims.

This line of argument works well and brooks little dissent among the members of
our community—until we get to the formation of human beings. Here is where the
battle lines are drawn. In general, most Muslims are of the view that God created
humans in a unique way, apart from the evolutionary mechanism. Although a few
theologians argue that humans could have been evolved as well, with Adam and Eve
being the first of our kind in the chain of development, this view is currently in the
extreme minority. So while Islamic theology can generally go along with many aspects
of evolutionary theory with regard to plants and animals, Muslim opinion leans more
strongly toward creationism where human beings are concerned.

This debate in the world of Islam about human development is still underway and
could swing back and forth for a while. Both sides of the argument have their proofs

to offer, and Muslims will be watching to see what happens. What we can say for certain is that Islam takes a position somewhere in between the two extremes of evolution and creationism: accepting the gradual development of life while considering God to be the author of its initiation. Again, the place of human development is the subject of debate, and no consensus has yet been agreed on.

Adam and Eve: A New Perspective

People who are familiar with the biblical account of the first people on Earth will find some similarities with the Qur'anic version. However, there are also important differences that relate directly to the founding doctrines of Christianity and Islam. Before explaining the Muslim thinking about Adam and Eve, I'd like to briefly digress in order to consider the questions of why some stories from the Bible have a counterpart in the Qur'an and whether they give credence to the common Western notion that Muhammad must have learned and copied the Bible. You will be surprised at how Muslims answer this question.

The idea that Islam proposes is that there is one God who has spoken to humanity for as long as we have been here. He has chosen guides called prophets who sometimes leave written messages behind them. When people eventually lose the teachings of their prophet, God raises a new prophet for them who will come with a fresh message that will set the record straight. (This is a promise that God made to Adam and Eve after he forgave them for their transgression in the garden.) Being from the same God, each prophet's message will, of course, share some similar content, even if cultural forms might be a bit different. So how does a message *get lost*? Perhaps people alter or change their revelations or warp the oral traditions out of all proportion over centuries or millennia. Think of the game in which one person whispers a message to another and we then see how the message comes out with the last person. Now multiply this by centuries of transmission and you will see how legends and new rituals can be become part of a faith, though without any authority from the original messenger. The corrupted religious teachings must then be replaced by new, corrected ones. Moreover, if an ancient prophet lived and worked for the guidance of his people, wouldn't a later prophet's revelation make mention of him?

This is a basic tenet of the Qur'an: The prophets that Jews and Christians are familiar with were true, and the Qur'an is merely correcting what has been falsely or erroneously written about them and their teachings. People altered their biographies, edited their revealed messages, and lost many of their precepts. (Many everyday Christians and Jews do not know the history of the Bible and how many times it has been lost, rewritten, and edited, Muslims would point out, though the information is readily available for those who care to seek it out.) So if the Qur'an contains the story of Adam and Eve, or anyone else, it's not because someone copied it, but because Adam and Eve were real people, guided by God, who had real missions. The Qur'an, which is God's last revelation, is merely retelling these stories in a more accurate way.

Besides, at Muhammad's time, there were no Bibles in the Arabic language, nor were books common in Arabia. Even more astounding is the fact that Muhammad never learned to read or write! He was an illiterate in a society where most people could not read. There weren't any Bible colleges, libraries, traveling evangelists, or churches in

Mecca, his hometown. Although there was an odd Christian here or there in central Arabia, none of them were particularly religious, zealous, or knowledgeable. Idol worship and the hard life of the desert were the order of the day, and a person's religion didn't amount to much for most people who were just trying to make it in a harsh land.

> **Ask the Imam**
>
> A Muslim must respect the Holy Books of others and is forbidden to desecrate them or insult them.

Furthermore, when you look into the teachings of Islam and the contents of the Qur'an, you begin to realize that the Qur'an has nothing in common with the Bible as far as structure, tone, voice, grammar, or orientation is concerned. If Muhammad copied the Bible, then the Qur'an would be similar to the Bible, but it is not. There are no genealogies, letters to friends, tribal histories, books of visions, or accounts of doctrinal developments in the Qur'an. What we do have is a book of forceful prose, metered poetry, passionate appeals to reason and faith, and a religious law that is quite distinct. The Qur'an is a uniquely original book.

An Implausible Theory

In recent years some modern Christian evangelists have asserted that there must have been *Christian sages* in Mecca who taught Muhammad theology and religious history. Others go so far as to say that an agent of the pope at that time went to Mecca to fool a local man into founding a new religion. Not only are these theories erroneous, but they are quite a stretch of the imagination. The few Christians who lived in backward Arabia were not knowledgeable scholars, no pope ever wanted to found a new religion in Arabia, and the idol-worshippers of Mecca, who knew Muhammad from boyhood, never charged that priests or evangelists taught him anything. Most Western academic scholars, however, have begun to backtrack from the assertions of previous generations and now accept that Muhammad didn't have any access to the Bible nor to people who knew much about it.

Did Muhammad ever journey outside of Arabia? This is where some people point fingers and say that this is how he must have gotten all his religious knowledge. Yes, he did travel to Syria twice, but in both instances he went as a worker in a caravan and had no time to enroll in a theological seminary or take tutoring in religion from people who spoke Aramaic, Greek, or Persian, languages he didn't understand anyway. His first caravan trip was as a boy of about 10. He accompanied his uncle as a simple caretaker of the animals and never left the caravan. It is reported that a Christian monk saw him during a stopover at a watering hole outside a monastery and predicted to his uncle that he would be chosen by God to bring a divine message, but his uncle dismissed the idea and nothing came of it. The second time Muhammad went to Syria was when he was the captain of a caravan. He was 25 years old and in the employ of a lady who would later ask him to marry her. She sent one of her servants to watch Muhammad closely to see how he conducted his business and all he reported upon the return of the trading expedition was that Muhammad was honest, diligent, and untiring in his discharge of his duties to make money for his employer. If Muhammad had so much free time to study either as a boy or an overseer in a brief caravan trip of three or four weeks, then he would have been the Einstein of his age, and then some!

The Angels Had Us Pegged

Now, getting back to Adam and Eve, the Qur'an begins their story with an announcement. Allah told an assembly of angels that He was going to create a *khalifa*, or caretaker, for the earth. When the angels realized that this new creature, the human being, would have free will, they objected, saying, "Will you create beings there that will cause trouble and shed blood, while we praise Your Holy Name?" From the angels' point of view, to make someone who could choose to be bad was unwise, especially since God already had perfectly obedient creatures like them. Allah told them frankly that He knew what He was doing (and He would later prove it to them). In other words, He had something in mind, and they could never really know the reasons behind His plan.

Translate This

Khalifa means a steward or caretaker. Humans are the stewards of the earth. This is also the title given to the worldwide head of the Muslim political entity. The English spelling is *caliph.*

Then God created the first man and woman from *dust* and placed them in a tropical garden paradise. Their names were Adam and *Hawwa*, or Eve. Where was this garden located? Many Muslims believe that it was in Heaven and that later on the pair were sent down to Earth after having been expelled from it. Others believe the garden was

on Earth in a highland area in East Africa, and
when Adam and Eve were ejected they settled
down in lower country not far from there.
There is a friendly debate over this, as the
Qur'an and sayings of the Prophet Muhammad
are vague about its exact location. This issue,
however, is not essential to Islamic teachings
and is peripheral to our story. I should also
mention that Islam does not sanction the
Judeo-Christian belief that Eve was created
because Adam was lonely. They were both
made for each other's welfare. (The Qur'an
rather romantically describes the relationship
between a man and a woman as if they were
garments for each other, protecting each other.)

> **Ask the Imam**
>
> Was woman created from the rib
> of a man? The Qur'an is silent
> on this, but a saying of the
> Prophet Muhammad relates,
> "Treat women nicely, for a
> woman is created from a rib,
> and the most curved portion of
> the rib is its upper portion. If you
> should try to straighten it, it will
> break, but if you leave it as it is,
> it will remain bent. So treat
> women nicely." (Hadith)

As I explained in Chapter 2 humans were created with a soul, free will, intelligence,
reason, and an inner nature to seek God called a *fitrah*. Adam and Eve also were
endowed with these qualities. Did they have any other special qualities? The Arabic
word used in the Qur'an for human beings, *insan*, can shed more light on our uniqueness. This term is called an "exaggeration noun" in Arabic. It is derived from the
word *onss*, which means easily adjusting or adapting to everything. The express implication is that humans are clever creatures who can adapt to their environment.

The Education of Adam

The Qur'an tells us that God taught Adam all the *names* of everything in his environment. An examination of the root meaning of the Arabic word for name, *ism*, shows
that Adam was made to understand the meaning of nature around him and how to use
it. He could understand his world and could grasp what each plant and animal was
useful for. When the education of Adam was complete, God called the angels to participate in a demonstration of sorts. God wanted to show the angels what He had
meant earlier when He said that He knew what they didn't know about humans and
their value.

God commanded the angels, "Tell Me about all of this (natural phenomena on
Earth)." The angels, who were light-based creatures, had no real understanding of
how the physical world worked, so they expressed their ignorance about such matters.
Then God commanded Adam to tell the angels what he knew about the world. When
he finished fully explaining about the plants and animals and how to understand their

uses, the angels realized that humans were creatures of great worth and had greater insight than they did. Allah declared, "Didn't I tell you before that I know what you don't?"

The First Racist

To signify that they were wrong and deserved to pay their respects to Adam, God commanded the angels to bow to the human beings, much in the same way a defeated opponent in a chess game or martial arts school might bow to the victor. They all bowed together. But that was not the end of this episode. Do you remember the *jinns*, those fire or energy-based creatures that God had also created? They have a habit of following angels around, and some were in the garden, watching the proceedings.

When the angels lost their contest and were commanded to bow, the *jinns* began to bow, too, because when the Creator of the universe says to bow, even if you are not mentioned by name, you bow! But one *jinn* remained stiff and refused to bow. He must have stood out like a sore thumb! His name was *Iblis*. God asked him why he didn't bow along with the angels, and *Iblis* gave a reply that echoes to this day in the prejudices people hold against each other: He said, "I am better than him."

Translate This

Iblis is the original name of *Shaytan*, or Satan, and literally means frustrated.

God had just proven that humans were better than angels, and angels were certainly better than *jinns*, so for *Iblis* to make such an arrogant statement was foolish and uncouth. God ordered him to get out of the garden, saying that he, and his jealousy, were to be rejected. But *Iblis* didn't want to go quietly. He laid down the gauntlet and dared God to another contest of sorts: "If you give me time," he shouted, "I can corrupt [your precious humans] and in the end you will find most of them ungrateful to You."

Now God isn't one to back down from a challenge. Of course, He doesn't need to participate in them, either, because He is God, after all. But the way that the Qur'an tells it, God accepts all of our challenges against Him so that in the end when we lose, we finally understand how wrong we were. God punishes only after someone fully realizes the folly of their ways. For that reason, He lets us stray as far as we want into sin and evil so that when He seizes us, we can't protest the receipt of our just desserts.

So God accepted the challenge and granted *Iblis* time until the Day of Judgment to do his worst to us. *Iblis* boasted, "I will attack them from their front and back and their right and left, and I will create in them false desires and superstitions." (He does this by "whispering" thoughts into our minds.) But in return for allowing *Iblis* virtual eternal life until Judgment Day, God laid down one ground rule of His own that *Iblis* had to obey. He said that *Iblis* could have no power over those who seek protection with Him.

Iblis's name was then changed to *Shaytan.* The word *Shaytan* means to separate, which is an apt description of his goal: to separate us from our Creator. A segment of the *jinn* population decided to follow *Shaytan,* and they are called the *Shayateen,* or Separators. *Shaytan* is evil and frightening and wants to have us sent to Hell, but we have our *fitrah* and God's revealed religious teachings to help us combat him and our animal desires. Note that Islamic thought does not portray him as a red devil with a pitchfork, nor is he a fallen angel as some religions present him. He is a being with the free choice to do good or evil and he chose the latter and will go to hell one day himself because of it.

The Great Test

God warned Adam and Eve about *Shaytan* in a revelation. He told them that *Shaytan* was their declared enemy and was out to corrupt them. These first two people were so innocent that they had no need of clothes, for they felt no shame, nor did they engage in lying or theft because everything was free. Food was within easy reach, and they never experienced hardship of any kind. Sounds like an idyllic life, doesn't it? What could possibly go wrong? How could *Shaytan* hope to corrupt these two virtuous people?

Although Adam and Eve had complete freedom to do as they pleased in the garden, they had to follow one rule: Do not go near or eat the fruit of one particular tree. That was it—one off-limits tree. Was this the *Tree of Knowledge of Good and Evil* spoken about in the Bible? Well, not exactly. You see, in the Bible we read that the forbidden tree had the power to let everyone know about good and evil deeds. Yet in the Qur'anic telling of this story, God is never quoted as saying that this tree was anything special. In addition, the Bible also mentions a *second* tree, called the Tree of Life, which could give anyone enough power to rival God. The Bible says that God was scared lest Adam and Eve eat from that one as well.

It Is Written

According to Muhammad, "Among the first words of revelation given to man were the instructions, 'If you feel no shame then do as you wish.'"

The Islamic version of the story just has the one tree, and nobody tells Adam and Eve it is special—no one except *Shaytan* that is. According to the Qur'an, *Shaytan* came into the garden and tempted both of them to eat from the tree. He told them it would give them eternal life and that their power would never end. This was *Shaytan's* first big lie to humanity. Well, they went ahead and did it. They ate from the tree (and gained no special power). Why, you may ask, would they do what God Himself told them not to? Here we see the strategy of *Shaytan's* sly appeals to our animal self, our desire for more and more. Adam and Eve slipped up because they gave in to their greed for what they weren't supposed to have.

After they ate from the tree, *Shaytan* left them, probably laughing at the fact that it was so easy to corrupt God's "best creation." The Qur'an does not blame Eve for goading her husband into taking a bite, nor does it let Adam off the hook, as the Bible does. In fact, Islam does not specify who ate first at all! The Qur'an lays the blame on them both equally. "They both did wrong," the verse says. Even though other religions assert that women brought sin into the world, Islam makes no such claim and places no stigma on being female. So what happened next? Adam and Eve realized they did wrong and felt ashamed because of it. As their sense of shame grew they wanted to hide and this caused them to question even their nakedness, they began to sew leaves to wear as clothes. The tree they ate from didn't give them any insight into good or evil; rather they felt the shame from within their own conscience. Their innate *fitrah* (orientation) made them feel inadequate and disgraceful.

As a consequence of their disobedience, God ordered Adam and Eve to be expelled from the garden. They were forced out into the wild world to fend for themselves with nowhere to go and nothing to shelter them. God declared that humans would have discord and hatred for each other from now on because of the inherent struggle to survive in the world. Imagine the world hundreds of thousands of years ago: no other people, dangers everywhere, and no safe place to hide. Life was harsh for the first two humans for a while. Even worse was their feeling of separation from God. Their *accusing self* was soon activated, and they sought to find the reasons for their disobedience.

Now whereas Christianity would say that Adam and Eve's failure in the garden put the taint of sin on us all, resulting in an unforgivable *original sin*, Islam states that after a while God had mercy on the repentant and humbled pair and taught them how to ask for His forgiveness. Then, when they implored God for His grace, guess what? He forgave them. End of story. Although they could not return to the garden, the sin was erased and redemption was complete. *Shaytan*, not realizing that people had a way to remove the stain of corruption from their hearts, was furious! Perhaps he realized that his self-imposed mission was going to be harder than he thought.

Later, Adam and Eve had children, and among them were Cain and Abel (*Qabeel* and *Habeel* in Arabic). The Qur'an tells the familiar story of how one murdered the other in a fit of jealousy over an offering. The Qur'an does not, however, assert, as the Bible does, that Cain went somewhere and found a wife and began a new nation. (If Adam and Eve and a few children were all the people in the world, where would Cain find his bride?) He buried his brother, felt remorse for the crime, and nothing more is said of him in the Qur'an.

Just the Facts

Both Jews and Muslims look aghast at the idea of original sin. The Bible even witnesses that "the son shall not bear the iniquity of the father neither shall the father bear the iniquity of the son." (Ezekiel 18:20)

Pass It On

God gave Adam and Eve some important instructions that they were to pass on to their descendants:

> If, and it will happen, there comes to you guidance from Me, whoever follows My guidance will not lose his way, nor fall into despair. But whoever turns away from My message, certainly he will have a life narrowed down and We will raise him up blind on the Day of Judgment. (Qur'an 20:123–124)

Thus God promised to send prophets and guides throughout human history to help combat the ignorance of following our animal desires (and *Shaytan's* prompting). The entire history of the world, from the perspective of the Qur'an, is nothing more than an expression of this eternal battle.

Ask the Imam
Islam does not consider the pain of childbirth that a mother feels as a punishment for Eve fooling Adam into eating from the forbidden tree. The Qur'an doesn't even blame women! In Islam, labor pains are looked upon as a kind of noble suffering on the part of a woman for the sake of her children. Because of the pain she endures during delivery, a woman has some of her sins forgiven!

Do Muslims view Adam in any other way than being the first man? Yes, Islam teaches that he was the first prophet of God on Earth, because he taught his children how to serve God, though in a far simpler way than our modern organized religions. The Prophet Muhammad said that Adam is sometimes allowed to leave the grave and sit in Paradise. He turns his head to the right and sees all of his descendants who follow God and he smiles. When he turns his head to the left and sees how many of his descendants are evil, he cries.

In this account of Adam's life, the major points of difference between the Islamic and Christian versions of the story are …

- God placed people on Earth, not because He was lonely, but because people were to be Earth's stewards.

- *Shaytan*, who thought he was better than we are, challenged God to a contest of sorts saying that he could ruin almost all people morally and spiritually.

- Woman was not created to assuage man's loneliness.

- The forbidden tree was not magical; it was just a test. There was no second tree of eternal life either.

- The woman is not blamed for the pair eating from the tree. Who is to blame is never assigned.

- Adam and Eve were forgiven after repenting and their sin was erased, so there was no *original sin* to pass on to their offspring.

- Frequent prophets were promised to help future generations combat *Shaytan's* jealous desire to ruin all of God's most noble creations, namely, us.

The Least You Need to Know

- The Qur'an has a complete chronology and explanation for how life and the universe began.

- Islam accepts elements of creationism and evolution in explaining the origin of life.

- The Qur'an contains its own version of the story of Adam and Eve. The woman is not blamed for the pair eating from the tree, and there is no original sin.

- God sends prophets to guide people. The messages of the prophets were sometimes lost by later generations.

- The structure of the Qur'an is completely different from the Bible, as is the style and theme.

Chapter 8

The Measurement of Life

In This Chapter

◆ Gain an Islamic perspective on the concept of destiny

◆ Discover how Islam looks at time and its role in our lives

◆ Understand the difference between the principle of Divine Measurement and fate or fatalism

◆ Learn what Islam says about God's knowledge of the future and what we can do about it

Destiny. This word evokes a wide range of responses in people, probably because many of them don't have a clear idea of its meaning, so they unwittingly use the word incorrectly. For example, in popular culture, destiny is often portrayed romantically as a vision of what a person is *supposed* to do. "I go to my *destiny*," intones the motion picture hero as he leaps into the fray, not knowing if he will live or die but trusting to some ultimate purpose in the universe to decide his fate. In real life, too, people call upon destiny, but their use of the word is more therapeutic than romantic. Usually they are trying to justify whatever circumstance befell them that was beyond their power to stop. In such cases, destiny transforms into an undesirable *fait accompli*, of having no say in a matter. The synonymous, yet less desirable term known as *fatalism* then is bandied about. Yet most people would strongly disagree with the idea of an inescapable fatalistic end that must happen despite all our best actions to stop it: So why is destiny often considered benign but fatalism, which is basically similar, considered outrageously negative and self-defeating? Aren't both terms two sides of the same coin?

Muslims have a unique concept about their lives both in the present and the future, but it does not involve either fatalism or destiny in the usual sense. Islam has been accused of teaching fatalism and of promoting an attitude of acceptance that results in inaction and hopelessness. This false notion, which grew out of eighteenth-century European criticism of Islam, is actually a highly inaccurate misinterpretation of Islamic teachings on the subject. Islam has a unique concept called *Divine Measurement*, which gives Muslims hope that they can affect the future with personal effort and which provides a clear explanation for the reasons why things happen the way they do.

Destiny, Fate, or Free Will—Which Is It?

Islam asserts that God is omnipotent. He had no beginning and He will have no end. Because He is outside the realm of time and space, He knows everything that has happened and will happen. He knew that human beings would be valuable creatures when He made them, even though the angels didn't think much of us. He also knew that the first pair of people would sin, and He made a plan for the salvation of their descendants—if any would choose to take it. This would be the test we are all taking in this life.

When Adam and Eve were expelled from the garden, they were sent into a world full of choices. All of us today have just as many challenges to face as they did. We can do right or wrong. We can lead a successful life, or we can blow our chances and miss golden opportunities. But if God is all-powerful and knows the past, present, and future, and has already written for us the span of our life, our economic condition, and so many other things, are we, in fact, locked into an inescapable destiny? Does Islam teach that each of us has an inevitable fate? Are we destined for Heaven or Hell?

This is an important issue. Christianity, especially, has had to wrestle with this topic for centuries, and it took great thinkers such as St. Augustine and Meister Eckhart to provide some answers. Even then, appeals to *Divine Mystery* permeate Christian literature on this and many other subjects. After all, asking why God made the universe when He already knows the future is a pretty powerful question. What does Islam say about this? Free will and the ability to shape our own future must mean something if our test is to be fair.

It's Not Written in the Stars

You might be pleasantly surprised to know that Islam does not teach *fatalism*, or hopeless reliance on what is destined for a person. At the same time, Islam also does not promote the idea of destiny as it is usually understood in the West. *Destiny* implies that there is a future plan designed for each individual that will unfold no matter what happens. On the flip side, Islam rejects the notion that the universe and everything in it is an unplanned exercise in random events. There is order in life, and people can sense it. Some put their faith in a Higher Power and work as they can in life while others seek to discover the ultimate meaning of things and what is to come through their own devices. Many people, in fact, become apprehensive when they think about tomorrow, and they begin to believe that their destiny or future part in the great plan of life can be learned if the right way to discover it can be found. Some claim that destiny is "written in the stars." Such people have devoted followers who throw thousands of dollars their way for a glimpse into tomorrow. Psychics and astrologers are an integral part of Western culture, and their influ-ence is everywhere in newspapers, in society, and even in politics. (Former President Ronald Reagan's own wife is reputed to have contacted psychics while she lived in the White House!)

Just the Facts

Orientalists have charged that Islam teaches abject fatalism, or the belief that personal actions do not matter because we cannot escape what will happen to us. Islam is actually against this kind of a concept. Muhammad said, "Work as you are able because if you don't help yourself, God won't help you either."

Islam, however, says that the position of the stars and planets has no bearing on what will happen to us. For this reason, Muslims are forbidden to engage in astrology. The Arabs had strong superstitions in Muhammad's time, and he worked very hard to dispel them. When his infant son died, an eclipse of the sun happened to occur a few hours later. People started to say that it happened on account of the baby's passing. When Muhammad heard people were saying this, he came before them and said, "The sun and the moon are two signs of God; they are not eclipsed on account of anyone's death or on account of anyone's birth. So when you see an eclipse, glorify and supplicate to God."

On another occasion, Muhammad said that God Himself commented on astrology by saying:

> This morning one of My servants became a believer in Me and one a disbeliever. As for him who said, "We have been given rain by virtue of God and His mercy," that one is a believer in Me, and a disbeliever in the stars. And as for

him who said, "We have been given rain by such-and-such a star," that one is a disbeliever in Me, and a believer in the stars. (Hadith)

Watching Time Go By

So if astrology is out, how can people know what will happen to them in the future? Islam says that we don't *need* to know what will happen tomorrow at all! The reason is that *God* knows; and if we truly trust Him and believe in Him, then we have nothing to worry about. How does this differ from fatalism or destiny? Islam teaches that even though God knows the future, we can still act and make a difference in our ultimate fate. How does Islam balance God's knowledge of the future with our ability to act? The synthesis comes in a grand concept that can almost be described as *managed time*. What do we mean by this?

The Islamic answer begins with God's foreknowledge. God knows the past, present, and future all at the same time. He can do this for one simple reason: He created time and so is not bound by it. Picture a timeline that begins with your birth. As you move to the right you pass through your teen years, college, marriage and family, and ultimately your death. Look at what you just did! You saw it all at once as if you were outside of your own timeline. Islam teaches that God is in this position. Muhammad said that God declared: "People struggle against the passing of time, but I am Time. In My hand is the night and the day."

 It Is Written

Every soul shall taste of death. We are putting all of you to a test by passing you through bad and good conditions, and finally you shall return to Us. (Qur'an 21:35)

So God sees us in any life stage at any time He wants. He won't end our share of time until we reach the amount allotted for us. In the Qur'an, God has laid out the principle that all of us must live, be tested, and then wait for His Judgment. So for Muslims, knowing that God is outside the timeline means that God's foreknowledge is not a worrisome issue for us. That's just the way it is. God's *seeing* what we will do is not Him *making* us do it. Yes, there are times when God is active in the timeline by sending Prophets, allowing catastrophes to befall evil rulers or nations, or answering someone's prayer, but this is balanced by a passiveness in which God allows things to take their own course. "Not a leaf falls but that God knows of it," says the Qur'an in many passages of this type. The only caveat is that God's ultimate objective is that truth and justice prevail in the end. That is why He doesn't plan to have the universe just go on forever, left to its own devices. He will nudge the timeline here and there to keep things more or less on track to a just end (at a time of His choosing) but most of what happens he lets happen because it is what naturally must come in the great interplay of events.

By the way, Islam does not teach that every time there is a disaster that it is God's punishment to man. If an earthquake strikes in a remote, uninhabited region, we may scarcely take note. But if, over many years, people began to settle in the area and another earthquake strikes, then people speak of Divine retribution. But the earthquake would have happened, based on built up pressures in the earth, no matter whether people lived in the area or not. It was just a case of being in the wrong time and place.

What about evil rulers, such as Hitler or Stalin? People have asked how God could allow such abominations to occur under their rule when He is supposed to be a merciful God in charge of everything. The perspective in Islam is that people are given the freedom to act, whether for good or ill, evil or good, and even if it will harm others. The perpetrators of crimes will be punished by God, either by his nudging another people to have the courage to fight back and vanquishing them, or by taking them to task on Judgment Day and then sending them to Hell. Their victims, if they don't get justice in this world from the society of men, will get justice on Judgment Day. The chance to reward people for their courage, especially martyrs who fight to uphold the revealed truths of God's revelations in the face of tyrants, also comes into play. God is only as passive as necessary to let people have a level and fair test of their free will.

Thus, no matter how many times the question pops up: Are we *destined* to do what we do? Does God *force* the criminal to be bad by *decreeing* his future? Islam says no, we are not forced to do anything. To reiterate, God's foreknowledge is not *making* us do what we do. He is merely outside the timeline, looking at us in every stage of our lives. He knows where we will end up tomorrow; however, He is letting time flow, so we can live out our natural lives and experience life for ourselves. Should we still worry then? Is our fate sealed in a way because God knows what will happen? Not at all.

All Things Great and Small

Islam provides a unique mechanism to free ourselves from this kind of worrying about the future. This doctrine is called *Qada* and *Qadr,* loosely translated as Determination and Measurement. *Qada,* which means to determine or to set parameters, covers the span of life for the universe and how it will operate. Gravity causes apples to fall; fire burns combustibles; illnesses can be treated with the right medications; our genes contain a blueprint for how our body will operate, and so on. Using this principle we can live life confidently, knowing that we can make sense of our world and the rules with which it operates.

The second principle to make our lives a little easier is *Qadr*, which means to measure. All things, including people, are dependent on God, and He has measured our life circumstances to provide a varied and challenging test for us to pass. What does this mean in practical terms? Beyond measuring the length of our lives, the interplay of all the different trends around us throws a specific set of challenges our way, so we can make choices and learn to live by faith and virtue—or descend into a life of nihilism and immorality. All along our timelines are stumbling blocks and situations that we must react to. When we consider that God can make sense of everyone's intertwined timelines and how they create a never-ending web of actions and reactions, we can become dizzy trying to conceive of his power of computation!

Translate This

Qadr, or Divine Measurement, is the term Muslims use instead of destiny. It is sometimes translated as *power* in the sense that the ultimate control over the future is with God.

It Is Written

Surely Allah Alone has the knowledge of the Hour [of the Last Day], He is the One Who sends down the rain and He knows what is in the wombs. No one knows what he will earn the next day; and no one knows in what land he will die. Surely, Allah knows all this and is aware of everything. (Qur'an 31:34)

How does this concept of measurement help us to live free from anxiety? Basically, if we say that God has measured the overall circumstances in our life, we can free ourselves from being overly stressed about what happens to us every day. When we are stricken with calamities, our anxiety is reduced and our despair is mitigated because we trust in God's measurement or foreknowledge of our tests. Life, therefore, can really be looked at as a test and not as a series of punishments, and thus a Muslim's belief in the goodness of God and the essential rightness of His overall plan remains intact.

The question remains: Can we change what will happen to us? Does prayer or our active participation in a situation have any effect on the outcome of events? Islam says yes. Muhammad said, "Nothing changes the Divine Measurement except fervent supplications (to God)." As God looks at our timeline, there may be a place where we decide to call on Him for His help. In that case, God may change the course of our future. In so doing, His foreknowledge is not affected because He knows what alterations will occur and when. In His mercy, He may decide at any moment to revise our timeline and respond to our prayers, so Muslims are asked to make supplications to God often.

As you can see, then, Muslims put their trust in God's foreknowledge and accept that what happens to them will be a test. But because we have the power to act and react and even to ask God to change things, Muslims always hold out hope that their active participation can influence the course of their lives. In the end, they trust in God and in His knowledge of their ultimate fate: "Whatever good happens to you is from Allah; but whatever evil happens to you is from your [own] self." (Qur'an 4:79)

What You Can and Can't Do

To gain a greater perspective on how the teaching of Divine Measurement affects the Muslim outlook on life, we can look at what our reactions mean. Islam divides daily life into two spheres: what we have control over and what we do not. We have no control over the circumstances developing around us. The car breaks down; we're get laid off at our job; an earthquake topples the city; we bump into a long-lost friend; we find a bag of money; the dog runs away; and so on. These things just happen. We couldn't prevent them because we didn't know they were coming. Islam says all of these things are a test for us. They were predetermined challenges or merely things that, because of a complex confluence of events, just happened. They were a part of our Divine Measurement.

Now we come to the essence of the Islamic world-view. Even though we often have no control over what happens to us, we do have control over *how we feel and respond*. When a tragedy strikes, do we blame God? When we see a diamond, does covetousness well up within us? When someone does evil to us, do we reciprocate or forgive? When we are alone, do we feel lonely or jubilant? Islam says we have control over our feelings, emotions, and personal actions. *Our test lies in how we respond to what happens around us.* Do we exercise patience (*sabr*) with life's challenges or do we panic and create disorder in our lives and in others? Now if we really think of the complex web of actions and reactions that go on every day in all of our lives, we can begin to appreciate how little our capacity is compared to God's. The Hindu concept of Karma might help here, but Muslims believe in God's *Qadr*, or measurement, not in a passive, impersonal web of actions coming back to us.

Translate This

Sabr is the word in the Qur'an used for patience and perseverance. No matter what tragedy befalls us, if we trust in God and persevere, then we display a proof of our faith.

Living Free of All Worry

God sees the timeline and knows what we will do. He sees what everyone else is doing as well. He knows what challenges will erupt as lives cross, and He knows how natural processes such as tornadoes, rainfall, or sunny days will affect the mix. At the end of each person's timeline, his or her soul is stored in *Barzakh* to await the end of

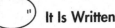

It Is Written

When We give people a taste of Mercy they celebrate and when some hardship afflicts them because of their own failures, behold they're in despair! Don't they see that Allah enlarges provision and restricts it to whoever He pleases? Indeed in this are Signs for those who believe. (Qur'an 30:35–38)

all time when Judgment Day will occur. By then, the universe, which began with the Big Bang, will be "rolled up" (scientists call this the *Big Crunch*) and time will no longer have any meaning.

Muslims live their lives, then, trusting in God and His knowledge of the future. The future is not a threat, nor do we fear what is to come. Whatever challenges meet us in our lives we have to try our best to face them. When we have done our best, we leave it in God's hands. If we are rich or poor, fortunate or sorry, we don't get too worked up about it. Life's tests come from God. We try our best and accept what happens and then try some more. The Qur'an says:

"No disaster can come on the Earth, or on yourselves, that isn't already recorded by Us in a book, and that is indeed easy for Allah. [Remember that] so you don't despair over what you have lost or brag about what you have gained, because Allah doesn't love the arrogant and boastful who are greedy and who urge others to be greedy also." (Qur'an 57:22–23)

Peace from the Pulpit

This next story is a practical example of the peacefulness that belief in *Qadr* can bring. A story is told about a famous Muslim scholar of the past named Abu Hanifa (703–767). He was giving a sermon in a mosque when a man rushed in through a side door, ran up to him, and whispered something in his ear. Abu Hanifa merely answered, "Praise God." The throngs of people gathered there were puzzled as the man ran back out, but they said nothing and the scholar continued his speech. A little while later, just as Abu Hanifa was concluding his talk, the same man came running back in and whispered again into his ear. Abu Hanifa replied once more, "Praise God." When the sermon was finished and the scholar was leaving, a crowd gathered around him and asked him what happened and why he said, "Praise God" twice. Abu Hanifa explained:

The first time the man came to me, he told me all my merchandise was lost at sea in a shipwreck. When I realized that this loss had no effect on my faith in God, I said, "Praise God." The second time he came to me, he told me it was a mistake and that the ship with all my goods on it was now coming into port. When I realized that this also did not cause my heart to become altered I again said, "Praise God."

Islam never teaches that we should sit around and wait for whatever is supposed to happen to us. We must participate, take action, and, when results come in, accept what happened and not be filled with endless "what if's." The Prophet Muhammad advised us to say, "God has planned; He has carried out His plan, and I will be patient." Just because we don't like the results of our life's challenges doesn't mean they weren't good for us. At the same time we have to ask ourselves if we lived up to the challenges and tried our best.

In another famous story about Abu Hanifa, he was leaving a mosque one day when he was accosted by a beggar. The man was not disabled or old so Abu Hanifa asked him why he didn't get a job. The man replied that he was following the teachings of the Prophet Muhammad, who said, "If you would put your trust completely in God, He will provide for you in the same way He provides for the birds: They go out in the morning with their stomachs empty and return in the evening with their stomachs full." Abu Hanifa shook his head and told the man that he had misinterpreted the saying of the Prophet. The man failed to take note of the fact that the birds had to *go out* in the morning and work for their food. The man dropped his bowl and went looking for employment.

Trusting in God and His plan while taking action and then accepting the outcome reflectively is the Muslim way. "Tie your camel and then put your trust in God," the Prophet once told a man who asked which he should do first. On another occasion the Prophet said, "Whoever says our actions don't matter and we must rely on destiny has failed to understand the teachings of Muhammad." God knows the future, and we can rest assured He is the best Planner. People who do not have this kind of faith, however, often resort to fortune-tellers, tarot-card readers, crystal balls, or psychic hotlines because they are afraid of what is to come. Islam says this is a sign of lack of trust in the Creator. It is such a serious crime in Islam that the Prophet Muhammad once said that a person who consults a fortune-teller will not have his or her daily prayers accepted by God for 40 days! The fortune-telling business is considered a sham by Islamic standards. Why is it that psychics sometimes give true predictions? Islam has an answer for that, too.

As I mentioned in Chapter 7, the *jinns* like to follow the angels around. The angels, who are given instructions about whose soul to take or news of what natural disaster will occur, often talk amongst themselves. When the *jinns* overhear something that is going to happen on Earth, they rush to people who claim to be fortune-tellers and pour that knowledge into their minds, mixing in a lot of lies along the way. Thus, when so-called psychics speak, they seem to know certain unknowable things, but they often use this knowledge to give bad advice because they do not guide people to lead God-centered lives. Rather their point of reference is to tell people what they want to hear. That is how they make their money. The Qur'an teaches us that people who delve into this type of business "will have no share in the next life."

A watercolor painting of a Muslim craftsman in the medieval period.

(Courtesy of Aramco)

The Least You Need to Know

- ◆ Islam does not believe in fatalism or in an ultimate destiny that is inescapable.

- ◆ God is the creator of time and is outside of the flow of time, seeing the past, present, and future happening all at once.

- ◆ Muslims are taught to avoid astrology, fortune-telling, and similar activities. Islam teaches they are false professions.

- ◆ Muslims are taught to have perseverance no matter what happens to them, good or bad. This stoic attitude is the hallmark of an individual's level of faith.

- ◆ Muslims believe that God does not test people with more than they can bear. It's up to us to rise to the challenge.

Chapter 9

From Adam to Armageddon

In This Chapter

- ◆ Learn how Islam explains the diversity of religions and cultures in the world
- ◆ Know the function of prophets and Divine Revelation according to Islam
- ◆ Discover the meaning of history in the Qur'an
- ◆ Discover what Islam has to say about Armageddon and the anti-Christ
- ◆ Learn about the role Jesus will play in the end-of-time scenario

The history of the world is filled with a dizzying array of cultures, customs, religions, and beliefs. Islam has its own explanation for the origin of this incredible diversity in our species' spiritual and religious mosaic. All true religion, Muslims believe, began with God. It is merely the fault of people through the centuries that beliefs mutated over time or were lost. Along the way, new values and customs would sometimes emerge, resulting in the great variety of unique local expressions of faith and culture we see today. With regard to our racial and ethnic differences, Islam says that humans are descended from one male and one female and that it is the environment that shaped how we look. So what is the meaning of history for a follower of Islam?

According to the nineteenth-century German philosopher Georg Wilhelm Friedrich Hegel, there are patterns to history, and those who do not know the past are doomed to repeat it. These two maxims describe the entire saga of the human story and, quite lucidly, mirror the message of the Qur'an. The rise and fall of civilizations is a manifestation of our collective desire to establish a permanent presence in this world. We can gain lessons, the Qur'an suggests, into the purpose of our lives by seeing how previous nations either exalted or ignored God and their ultimate fate. In fact, history for a Muslim can be considered no less than the playing out of episodes in a cosmic script culminating with the inevitable journey of all people back to their Lord.

From the first human couple, Adam and Eve, through the innumerable generations of humanity, the struggle between order and chaos and good and evil in our world has ebbed and flowed. But this process of history will not go on forever. Even as humanity had a beginning, so too will it have an end, and Islam provides us with prophecies about how the conclusion to our story will proceed. The prophets that God sent to the various races and nations of the earth all warned of a coming Last Day. Some gave more-detailed narratives than others, but the basic theme remains the same—at the moment when human civilization is at its height, it will come crashing down, and God's promised Day of Judgment will be upon us all.

No Tower of Babel Here

How does Islam explain the variety of human cultures, languages, religions, and historical experiences we have in our world today? The Bible certainly offers a creative explanation. It says that all people in the ancient days were one nation, and in their arrogance they tried to build a high tower to reach God. This was called the Tower of Babel. Then God decided that it would be a good idea to break people up into different groups lest they become too powerful, so He magically made them all speak different languages. People scattered in a hurry and became the various nations of the earth. Is this how the Qur'an explains the linguistic and cultural diversity in our world? No, in fact, there is no Tower of Babel mentioned in the Qur'an.

It Is Written

According to Muhammad, "There is no superiority of a white over a black or of a black over a white. All of you are the children of Adam and Adam was made from dust."

Islam gives a very reasonable and balanced explanation for the spread of people over the earth and their unique experiences. To begin our narrative, the Qur'an states that the earliest human beings did live together in one community or tribe. Then we learn that the group became too large to sustain a cohesive social life. The Qur'an says that "they fell into disputes with one another and scattered" over the earth. Another interesting verse even gives us a beneficial side effect for this dispersal around the world. It states, "O People! We created you from a single pair of a male and a female and made you into nations and tribes so you can come to know each other. The noblest among you in the sight of Allah is the one with the most spiritual awareness." (Qur'an 49:13)

So Islam views the diversity of languages and cultures in our world as a natural process caused by the movement of people here and there. It is a source of richness, wonder, and discovery. Multiculturalism has a treasured place in Islamic ideology; and according to the Qur'an, the only criterion for differentiating among people lies in the strength of their religious sentiment. Muslims are thus taught that race is not a legitimate standard of measurement. Islam has often been praised for its emphasis on the equality of all people regardless of race, creed, or color. Malcolm X, who had been reared in a racist hybrid of Islam, Christianity, and Black Nationalism, otherwise known as the Nation of Islam, came to discover this when he broke with the movement and undertook a Hajj to Mecca. There he found himself living and praying alongside whites, blacks, browns, and all the other races of the earth.

Given this understanding of natural human movement throughout the world, Muslims thus can agree with anthropologists who have proven that all people can be traced back to a single region in east Africa. What about the diversity of our colors and physical features? Islam makes an allowance for that as well. The Prophet Muhammad once commented on the differences of appearance among people in the Arabian peninsula by pointing out that people in the south of Arabia were darker skinned because the sun was harsher and the climate more extreme. People in central and northern Arabia, he explained, were lighter skinned because the climate was fairer. Thus, environmental factors account for how people look from region to region.

> **Just the Facts**
>
> The number of Muslim converts among Native American Indians is growing steadily each year. Recently, construction of a mosque began on the Great Navajo Reservation located in Arizona.

The Rise of the Prophets

The descendants of Adam and Eve spread throughout Africa, the Middle East, Europe, Asia, and finally the Americas. This process took countless generations, and different groups of people developed a variety of cultural expressions. The Qur'an says that God sent prophets to all those nations during this process of dispersal. Prophets were always chosen from among local people because those born into a community know best how to reach it. Islam makes allowances for the varied rituals and customs that each nation followed by saying that every community received religious features tailored to its specific needs: "To every civilization We have appointed rites and ceremonies which they had to follow, so don't let them dispute with you on this matter, but invite [them] to your Lord, for you are assuredly on the Right Way." (Qur'an 22:67)

It Is Written

Nabi means prophet in Arabic, that is, someone who receives instructions from God and prophecies. *Rasul* means messenger. This is a prophet who also is given a book, an organized body of teachings that can be written down and passed on as a message for generations to come. Both functions can be combined in one individual.

If you think about the many peoples and communities that have existed for the last 500,000 years, the sheer number of prophets must be staggering. There is an unconfirmed saying of the Prophet Muhammad in which he said that God sent 124,000 *nabi*, or prophets, to the world and 313 *rasul*, or messengers, who also received an organized body of laws to pass on. Do we know the names of all these prophets? No, the Qur'an's unique style doesn't include countless names and genealogies. Where stories are pertinent to illustrate a spiritual precept or lesson, there you will find mention of ancient prophets.

The Qur'an clearly states:

> We have already told you the story of some Messengers, but of others We haven't. And Allah spoke directly to Moses. The Messengers gave good news as well as warnings so that people after [the life time] of the Messengers would have no plea [of ignorance] against Allah, because Allah is Powerful and Wise. (Qur'an 4:165)

Only 25 prophets and messengers are mentioned by name in the Qur'an; and their stories, following the Qur'anic method of teaching, are given mainly in the context of providing an example for the religious idea being taught.

How Religion Becomes Lost

What happened to those prophets and their teachings? Does Islam teach that a prophet must always be successful, as some Western scholars have asserted? In general, the Qur'an does not require that a prophet complete his mission successfully. The prophet of the day is only required to try his best. In fact, the Qur'an is very critical of the responses that most people have given to religious guidance. Under the pretense of protecting their cultures, most communities and tribes fought against their prophets. In some cases they even killed or tortured the prophets and their followers, who were mostly drawn from the ranks of the poor and downtrodden in society.

Even though God did His part—sending prophets who spoke with inescapable logic, providing signs in nature of His creative energy, possibly bringing about natural disasters to wake up the people, and sometimes performing miracles to aid the prophet's mission—*Shaytan* was able to convince many civilizations to cling to their old ways:

> Before you We sent [Messengers] to many nations and We afflicted them with suffering and adversity that they might learn humility. When the suffering sent by Us reached them, why didn't they learn humility? On the contrary their hearts became hardened and Shaytan made their [sinful] acts seem alluring to them. (Qur'an 6:42–43)

In a few instances, the people accepted the message of their prophet and became faithful believers. Other peoples might have adopted their prophets' teaching after the prophets had long since been dead. In any case, with the passage of time any given community was likely to alter, forget, or add to the precepts that had been passed down from generation to generation. If there were written revelations, they were probably edited, added to, or lost during wars or natural disasters. After many centuries there often was nothing left of a true prophet's doctrines but a name and a few snippets of advice. The rest of the religion might now consist of legends, idolatry, myths, superstition, and elaborate rituals.

When a prophet's message had been almost completely obliterated, God would send a new prophet who would again likely meet with opposition. Thus, the Islamic explanation for the existence of so many religions in the world is to say that all religions began with a true prophet but mutated over the centuries until they had little in common with their roots. The core message every prophet taught was *surrender to God and do what is right*—in other words, the tenets of Islam—but this message was lost successively until the last revelation given to the Prophet Muhammad.

Because Muslims believe that every nation received guidance from God and also that this guidance did not survive the passage of time unaltered, we automatically must respect the beliefs of other people. This is because a true prophet probably founded that person's religion many thousands of years before. The goal of Muslims, then, is to figure out what remains of authentic guidance from God, as determined by the yardstick of the Qur'an, and then to call upon that person, using any beliefs held in common, to take a look at Islam, the last installment of Divine Guidance.

The Cycle of History

Each major civilization during its rise had its corresponding prophetic messages. Abraham and the Mesopotamians, Moses and the Egyptians, David and the Israelites, Jesus and the Romans, and countless others. The Qur'an tells us that the rise and fall of nations was due primarily to their acceptance or rejection of God. When one nation of oppressors would grow too strong, God would allow a stronger nation to conquer them. The Qur'an says that God gives nations their chance to shine in turns and that He uses some nations to check the influence of others lest tyranny should engulf the whole Earth.

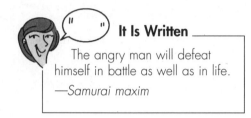

It Is Written

The angry man will defeat himself in battle as well as in life.

—*Samurai maxim*

Beginning with the first human tribe to our present-day world, the forces of good and evil have been locked together in a struggle for the soul of humanity. *Shaytan* incites people to evil while God sends His messages to call them to good. If a people go out of bounds, God sends a disaster upon them or allows them to be taken over by others. Think of the fall of Rome at its most despotic hour or the destruction of the Nazis after they came so close to world domination. The Hand of God moves in the world even as the deceit of *Shaytan* propels people in the worst direction. The only people who have any hope of salvation are those who put their faith in God and lead a life based on virtuous values. This is the ultimate lesson of history, according to Islam. Chapter 103 of the Qur'an expresses it best: "By the passage of time, people are surely in a state of loss. All except those who teach each other about truth and perseverance."

The End Is Near!

Islam asserts that one day the world will end. The march of history from our hunter-gatherer days to our modern space age will not travel onward forever. The earth will be destroyed, and humanity will have to stand for judgment. Before this occurs, however, fantastic events pitting the forces of good against evil will take place. Christians have their Book of Revelation; Jews have their Messianic Prophecies; Hindus have world-ending scenarios of their own. What does Islam say? Will the end come with no warning, or are there signs to watch for? The Qur'an and the words of the Prophet provide a definite scenario for the end of the world and its portents. They also give us a reason why it has to end.

As I've mentioned before, all Islamic teachings are derived from only two sources: the Qur'an and the Hadith, the sayings of the Prophet Muhammad. Muslims consider the Qur'an to be the literal Word of God while the prophetic sayings are Muhammad's explanations of how Islam should be lived, comments about the Qur'an's teachings, and also prophecies of the future. Islam, unlike all other religions, did not develop its doctrines over many centuries through the efforts of many men. Every important aspect of Islamic beliefs and practices came within a span of 23 years, from 610 to 632 C.E. Islam combines both of these sources in its narrative of how the end-of-time scenario will play out.

To begin with, Islam teaches that the life span of the universe is fixed. God began it and will end it one day. The Day of Judgment will follow afterward so that evil can be punished and good rewarded. In Islam, God is considered a righteous Being Who will right wrongs and show appreciation for those who listened to His guidance. The Last Day is necessary, for the ultimate *payback* time will come. Leading up to the Last Day, God will give many signs so that those who are disheartened may gain spiritual strength and those who are rebels against God's teachings may have one last chance to repent and reform. The twin sources of Islam give a complete picture of what these signs will be.

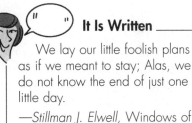

It Is Written

We lay our little foolish plans as if we meant to stay; Alas, we do not know the end of just one little day.

—*Stillman J. Elwell*, Windows of Thought, *1984*

There are two major areas of focus when we look at the end-of-time scenarios. The first concerns human society and the final battle between the forces of *Shaytan* and the forces guided by God. The second concerns physical disasters that will overcome the earth causing its destruction. With regard to the human component, there will basically be tremendous conflicts and battles between nations. Unlike the Book of Revelation in the Bible, however, there is no mention of a climactic melee between angels and demons up in the clouds. All of the battles on Earth will be between people who are either for or against God. The actual destruction of Earth will follow after that. I will begin with the first topic, that of war between nations and people.

Prophecies About the Muslim World

Are Muslims expecting the end of the world soon? Modern conditions, as foretold by the Prophet Muhammad, lead many to believe that the end is indeed near. The greatest of these signs lies in the worldwide condition of the Muslim community. There is no unified Islamic nation encompassing the whole Muslim world, as is called for in the Qur'an. Muslims are not victorious against their foes anywhere in the world, and only recently did the armies of Europe end their military occupation of over 90 percent of the Muslim world. (From the 1800s until the 1960s, most of the Muslim world was ruled by France, the Netherlands, Russia, or Great Britain.)

Just the Facts

The Jewish Old Testament of the Bible warns Jews of God's wrath and the destruction of Zion and its later rebirth by the Messiah. The Christian New Testament warns of a great disaster to befall true believers who will be saved later by a triumphant Jesus. Islam also has a prophetic tradition of predicting the downfall of Muslims until a hero, named the *Mahdi,* comes along who will revive the community.

To make matters worse, in most Muslim countries (save for a few like Malaysia or Pakistan) the free practice of Islam is suppressed. It is so bad that in Turkey, the former seat of the last Islamic Empire, it is illegal for females to wear head scarves in school or for children to be sent to academies to learn about the Qur'an. It would be akin to outlawing yarmulkes in Israel or Bible study groups in America! In Syria, if you speak publicly about corruption in the political system, you may wind up in jail. In Uzbekistan, the prisons are full of people whose only crime was that they wanted to promote basic Islamic moral teachings in their communities. In Algeria, the military canceled democratic elections in 1992 simply because a Muslim political party won the popular vote. From country to country in the so-called *Muslim* world, similar restrictions on the free exercise of Islam exist. How is it possible that the traditional religion of so many countries is suppressed? Most governments in the Muslim world happen to be ultra-secularist dictatorships or corrupt monarchies that consider organized religion a threat to their power. Bet you didn't know that!

Turmoil exists on the economic front as well. Although it may seem that some Muslim nations are generally prosperous, especially when you think of the big oil countries, in fact, the rulers of those nations do not look after the welfare of their people. They spend the nation's resources on building palaces and enriching their relatives in typical despotic fashion. Because of the petty wars being fought in the Muslim world today between tin-pot dictators, Muslims now make up the majority of the world's refugees. The resources of the Muslim world do not benefit their countries of origin, because the oil, timber, gas, diamonds, and other treasures are largely exported to other countries, with the resultant cash being skimmed off by the ruling elite. When the Shah of Iran, Suharto of Indonesia, and Benazir Bhutto of Pakistan were forced from power, did you ever wonder where they got all those *billions of dollars,* stashed in Swiss bank accounts, that were reported by the media?

Multinational corporations make shady deals with the rulers and give tremendous kickbacks and bribes, and the only people who lose are the citizens of the nation whose resources have been sold for too little. Even though the Muslim world was dominant for over a thousand years in world affairs, both economically and politically, today it is a basket case. Prior to World War I, the Ottoman Empire, the last unified multicultural Muslim state, was even referred to as the "Sick Man of Europe" because of both its own failed policies and creeping European Imperialism. The Prophet Muhammad warned that a day would come when the nations of the earth would feed upon the resources of the Muslim world like people eating at a banquet. A man asked the Prophet, "Will we be so few then?" The Prophet answered, "No, you will be numerous."

The Signs of the Hour

Muhammad gave many prophecies about these dire times, and he said that when the signs are evident, we should look for the coming of the anti-Christ, or *Dajjal* as he is known in Arabic. Given these conditions, many Muslims feel that we have entered the beginning of the end-of-time process. In this there is commonality with fundamentalist Christians, who also feel the end of the world is near. Though to be fair, the Muslim world had it far worse during the Mongol invasions, and writers back then thought the end of the world was coming soon as well.

What are these signs of the end-of-time? Islam teaches that after the Muslim world is vanquished and broken up into many competing nations, the practice of Islam will be increasingly difficult for true believers. Muhammad once described this period by saying that holding on to Islam will be like holding onto a hot coal. He also said that Islam came into the world as a stranger and will end up as a stranger again one day. Other signs of the end-of-time include the following:

 Just the Facts

The starting point of the Islamic calendar is the migration of the Prophet Muhammad from the hostile city of Mecca to the friendly city of Yathrib in the year 622 C.E. This event is called the *Hijrah*, or migration. Muslims use the initials *BH* (Before *Hijrah*) and *AH* (After *Hijrah*) in the same way Christians use B.C. and A.D.

1. Abundant riches (oil?) will be discovered under the Euphrates River in Iraq, and people will fight over them, causing much death and destruction.

2. Children will no longer obey or respect their parents.

3. Poor nations will compete with each other to build tall buildings in their cities even as the populace starves.

4. It will be hard to tell men and women apart physically.

5. Women will outnumber men by a huge margin (50:1).

6. Religious knowledge will decrease dramatically and authentic pious scholars will be rare.

7. Wealth will be widespread, and corruption will be rampant.

8. Music, female singers, and alcohol will be prevalent.

9. The worst people will be chosen as leaders.

10. There will be family turmoil in every household.

Looking at this list you might think that the Day of Judgment is coming tomorrow! But things would have to become a whole lot worse, and other similar signs have still to be met. Muslims in the Prophet's own time were often under the impression that the Last Day would soon come upon them. However, the Qur'an teaches that only God knows when it will occur. It could still be a long way away by our timetable. Perhaps it won't come for thousands of years or more. It is this realization that has prevented the formation of doomsday cults or movements in the world of Islam.

The False Prophets

When all the signs do start to fall into place, a series of false prophets will arise in the world. There will be nearly 30 of them, with the last one being the anti-Christ, or *Dajjal*. Before the *Dajjal* appears, though, a great Muslim leader will arise who will unify all faithful Muslims under his banner and will wage many successful campaigns against the enemies of Islam. This leader's title is the *Mahdi*. Muslims look forward to his appearance and expect that many victories from Palestine to India will be achieved. Invading armies from Europe will be vanquished as well. After unifying the Middle East, peace and prosperity will fill the earth, and the economic benefits for all, Muslim and non-Muslim, will be overwhelming. The main base of Muslim authority will then be centered in Palestine when, after an indeterminate amount of time, rumors about the appearance of the *Dajjal* will begin to circulate among the region.

The Prophet Muhammad described the *Dajjal* in great detail. However, whereas the Bible envisions him to be a handsome man who will woo people with his magic and charm, Muhammad said that he will be blind in one eye and will have a mark on his forehead that looks so prominent that you can sense the disbelief in his face. He will have brown, curly hair and will travel throughout the world spreading mischief and trouble wherever he goes with chicanery and deceptive activities. Not surprisingly, the name *Dajjal* translates as liar, or man of deception.

The *Dajjal* will claim that he is a new prophet of God. He will be wealthy and have amazing powers to cure people of their illnesses. *Shaytan* will send some of his evil *jinns* to impersonate the dead so that the *Dajjal* can claim to bring people back to life. Later he will make the claim that he is a god on Earth. The majority of the people in the world, including a few misguided Muslims, will follow him and believe in him. He will therefore amass a lot of military might, which he will use to harass and destroy all vestiges of true religious expression.

The *fitnah*, or turmoil of the *Dajjal* will last for 40 days. During that time, he will gather an army and begin to conquer the Middle East, which had been unified under the *Mahdi*. He will even try to invade the city of Medina in Arabia but will be prevented from entering it by angels who will deter his attacks. The remnants of the Muslim army will gather in Syria and will very quickly find themselves under siege by the *Dajjal's* army. Battles will rage for several days, with the Muslims taking heavy casualties. When all appears lost, the *Mahdi* will call his soldiers together in the evening and receive their pledge to fight to the last man and woman on the following day.

Just the Facts

The *Mahdi* will be a descendant of the Prophet Muhammad and will have the same name. He will be a man whom God will inspire with the mission of uniting the Muslim world.

Translate This

Fitnah means both controversy and turmoil. It is the term used to describe what the *Dajjal* will bring to the world. It is also applied to any period of civil war among Muslims.

While the darkness of night is still upon the Muslim camps in and around central Syria, a rumor of deliverance will spread like wildfire and a voice will be heard saying, "The one who listens to your pleas has come." When the time for the pre-dawn prayer arrives, the Prophet Jesus, who had been saved from dying on the cross thousands of years before and had been kept in Paradise by God, will descend in the midst of Damascus. After joining the Muslims in prayer, he will lead the *Mahdi's* forces against the *Dajjal's* army. The *Dajjal's* soldiers will number 70,000.

On the battlefield, Jesus will command his troops to move aside so that there will be a clear view between him and the *Dajjal*. Upon seeing Jesus, the *Dajjal's* powers will fade and he will make a panicky retreat into Palestine. The Muslims will come down from the mountains and crush the remnants of the enemy army. Jesus will pursue the *Dajjal* to a place named Lydda, which is near an airport south of the present-day city of Tel Aviv in Israel. There Jesus will strike down the *Dajjal* with a lance, and his reign of tyranny will be over.

The Rule of Jesus

What will happen next? Is the game finally over? Is it time for Judgment Day? Not yet. According to the sayings of the Prophet Muhammad, Jesus will speak to the Christians and Jews of the world and convert them to Islam. He will succeed in breaking the worship of the cross and will stop the eating of pork. The army he led will disband and disperse back to their home countries, and only a small contingent will remain with him to serve him. Jesus will be the spiritual head of a transnational government of peace. Everyone in the Middle East will convert willingly to Islam, and there will be no more war for a long time. He will visit Mecca and Medina while on pilgrimage. He won't reign for a thousand years, as Christianity teaches, but will live only 40 more years—the rest of his natural life span. Along the way he will marry and have children. While he is in the world, peace and prosperity will bring countless benefits for all people.

Gog and Magog

The next great challenge for humanity will occur when the nations of the East, the *Yajuj* and *Majuj*, known as Gog and Magog in the Bible, will begin an invasion with forces such as the world has never before seen. They will invade the Middle East and destroy every city and resource in their path. They will completely drain Lake Tiberias in Palestine because of their armies' large requirement for water. Jesus will command the faithful to retreat to Mount Sinai in Egypt because no one will be able to withstand the massive onslaught of the invaders.

When the carnage wrought by the *Yajuj* and *Majuj* becomes so great that all looks lost, Jesus will pray to God for deliverance. His plea will be answered because God will unleash a pathogen or some type of disease upon the enemy that will infect their soldiers and cause their army to crumble from within. The power of the invaders will be broken, and Jesus and his followers will leave the mountain redoubt and return to their homes. Now, many more people around the world will start to convert to Islam, but before this can be fully accomplished Jesus will pass away. He will be buried in Medina next to the grave of the Prophet Muhammad.

The Last Day

We enter the final phase: the end of the world. Three massive sinkholes will open up in the earth. One will be in the east, one in the west, and one in Arabia. A mysterious cloudy haze will envelop the world, making people feel hot with fever, and the sun will rise in the West. Many of the remaining people in the world who do not believe in God will want to convert now, but no conversion will be accepted then. A strange and fantastic beastlike creature will rise from the earth and warn people about the end of the world. A ground fire will ignite in the land of Yemen, driving the people in Arabia to flee to Syria.

A new wave of hypocrisy and heresy will sweep over the world. Vice, crime, and state-sponsored oppression will become rampant. All the remaining faithful Muslims will gather in Syria once more. But by this time, even the few remaining Muslims in the world will have forgotten the Qur'an, and copies of it will not be found anywhere. The earth will start to quake, and the mountains will begin to crumble. As the Qur'an says, "Everything will be in a commotion."

 It Is Written

The Trumpet will [just] be sounded when all beings in the heavens and on earth will pass out except such as it will please Allah [to exempt]. Then will a second one be sounded when behold they will be standing [on the Plain of Judgment] and looking on! (Qur'an 39:68)

The stars will begin to fade; the skies will start to "roll up." The seas will rise, animals will gather in the few remaining patches of land, and terror and fear will grip the people who remain. God will order that all the souls of the dead be raised from their graves and reunited with new bodies on the plain of Judgment. A breeze will pass over the world, taking the souls of any living believers, and they will feel no pain. The earth will be crushed, and the souls of the remaining living people (the sinners) will also be taken. God will then create a new universe with a new Earth, but for humanity the game is over. Everyone will stand before God on a level plain and await his or her judgment.

This is the Islamic view of the end of the world and the establishment of the Day of Judgment. As you can see, there are some similarities with the Christian concept of Armageddon, but the Islamic view has many twists and turns to the story that make it unique in its own right. Again, when will this process start? Only God knows the hour. Muslims today are expecting it to happen sooner rather than later, but thus far people have not been convinced enough to quit their jobs or sell their homes. Undue panic over this issue has no tradition in the Muslim community.

The Least You Need to Know

- The diversity in world religions is caused by the alteration of each prophet's message over many generations.

- Islam does not believe in the superiority of any race over another. The only valid criterion for establishing the value of people is their religiousness and level of faith.

◆ Islam has its own view of Armageddon in which Jesus plays a part, though he will be on the side of Muslims when he returns to Earth.

◆ Muslims believe in an end-of-time scenario that includes the destruction of Earth and the beginning of Judgment Day.

Part 3

The Five Pillars of Islam

How do we live a godly life? Countless sages and seers for millennia have posed this question. Every religion and spiritual tradition seeks to answer this dilemma with its own program of faith, personal improvement, and social activism. Islam also has its own unique system designed to bring about a heightened awareness of God in our lives. Through a constant reaffirmation of faith and the practice of the five pillars of Islam, a Muslim orders his or her life according to the dictates of the Prophet Muhammad.

These religious practices encompass a variety of activities, from fasting and pilgrimage to prayer and active struggle against wrong. It is in this last one, otherwise known as *jihad*, where a large amount of misunderstanding among both Muslims and non-Muslims occurs. In this part, I will take a look at the pillars and practices of Islam and the unique reason behind each one. I will also discuss the role of *jihad* in Islam and why it has become such a misused term.

10

Declaring Faith in Islam

In This Chapter

♦ Learn about the Five Pillars of Islam and their significance

♦ Understand how the rituals and practices of Islam affect Muslims' daily lives at home and in the community

♦ Read up on the Muslim confession of faith

♦ Discover how belief in one God helps Muslims to transcend the material world

♦ Know how Muslims view the place of Muhammad in their religion

Islam has a very detailed philosophy for looking at life and provides a definite statement about our purpose in this world. Beliefs and philosophy, however, must be backed up with a program of life-changing action: daily rituals, meaningful practices, and annual reaffirmations of what it means to be a follower of God. Only when faith is reinforced by action can religious concepts be truly realized. From the perspective of the Qur'an, Muslims can't simply say they believe and then get away with leading any kind of lifestyle they want. What good is faith if it doesn't improve the way you live?

Although every religion asks its followers to engage in rituals to reinforce the precepts of the faith, only Islam requires its followers to keep a daily and yearly regimen of testimony, prayer, fasting, pilgrimage, and charity, commonly known as the *Five Pillars of Islam*. When a person commits to following the Islamic way of living, the commitment is no joke. However, it's not so hard that only a select few can do it. People from every walk of life live Islam every day. The idea is that we gain discipline through the application of Islamic rituals in our lives. The rituals teach us to master ourselves and our motivations so that we can gain control over our physical urges and elevate our minds for a higher purpose.

Introducing the Five Pillars of Islam

Islam has a system of rituals designed to translate our religious beliefs into concrete reality. This serves to keep us constantly aware of our duty to God and helps us avoid the dangers of temptation and complacency. This system is called the *Arkan al Islami*, or Pillars of Islam. In order, they are …

1. **Shahadah**   Testifying our allegiance to God.

2. **Salat**   Daily prayer.

3. **Zakat**   Annual charity.

4. **Saum**   Month-long fasting.

5. **Hajj**   The pilgrimage to Mecca.

Just the Facts

There are four categories of religious action with regard to daily duties in Islamic Law. They range from what you *must* do as a Muslim to what you can choose to do for extra credit on your record or leave off entirely. The categories are as follows:

- ◆ *Fard*   Required duties for all Muslims, such as the five canonical prayers, fasting, etc.

- ◆ *Wajib*   An action that should be done every time the opportunity comes up, such as certain extra prayers or lifestyle practices

- ◆ *Sunnah*   The Prophet's personal example or things he asked people to do without making them a religious duty, such as brushing your teeth after every meal or shaking hands with the right hand

- ◆ *Nafl*   Extra or optional actions that the Prophet did sometimes but not on a consistent basis, such as fasting on certain days, keeping night vigils, etc.

These practices are integrated into the daily routine of every Muslim's life, and they help keep us on the straight path. The Five Pillars remind us of who we are and what we have pledged ourselves to follow. These rituals are so important that they have the legal status of a *fard*, or required duty on the part of a believer. To neglect a required duty is a sin, and the angels will record it in our book of deeds as such. On the Day of Judgment everyone will have to answer for his or her lack of compliance in God's multi-step program for life change and personal transformation. As you learn about each of the pillars, try to put yourself into the Muslim frame of mind and think about how these types of activities could influence your own faith on a daily basis.

The Five Pillars are crucial from the standpoint of Islam, because through their practice we remind ourselves of our real purpose in this world. By praying, fasting, giving in charity, and such we train ourselves to become God-oriented people. Islam has often been praised for its disciplining effect, and the five pillars are the core of that program. Prison wardens throughout the United States, for example, are giving greater freedom to the propagation of Islam among their inmate populations precisely because it makes the prisoners calmer, easier to manage, and more mature.

The Shahadah

Did you know that there is one phrase said at least 17 billion times a day? It is called the *Shahadah*, or *Declaration of Faith*. It is said a minimum of 17 times each day within the daily prayers of each of the 1 billion Muslims on Earth. Anyone who says that people don't praise God enough obviously hasn't met a Muslim!

In Arabic, the most basic *Shahadah* formula is said this way: *Ashahadu an la ilaha ill Allah, wa ashahadu anna Muhammadar Rasulullah.* The English translation is: "I declare that there is no god except God, and I declare that Muhammad is the Messenger of God." This phrase includes the two founding principles of Islam and is sometimes called the Muslim Creed. It is a very strong ideological statement in that it lays out the Muslim frontline position: There is only One God, and Muhammad is His last Prophet.

Translate This

Shahadah literally means to bear witness to or testify to the truth of something. An Islamic martyr is called a *shaheed*, or witnesser, because he or she provided the ultimate proof of their faith, to give their life for God's cause.

What are the benefits of reciting the *Shahadah* so many times each day? Think about it: All Muslims have the chance to remind themselves about the reality of God in their lives. Whereas the hustle and bustle of the daily grind may cause us to forget that we are living through a big test and will have to face God one day, the *Shahadah* and its recitation focuses our hearts and minds on our ultimate purpose. We are here to surrender our wills to God and lead virtuous lives. The Qur'an asks, "Who will take a reminder?" The *Shahadah* is one way to remember.

Uncompromising Monotheism

The *Shahadah* consists of two distinct parts. One is a negation and the second is an affirmation. It is interesting that the first part of the *Shahadah*, the part about believing in God, is phrased in a negating way. It doesn't just come out and say that God is our master; rather it goes a step further and makes the point that there is nothing worthy of our attention or allegiance *other* than God. There is no god but *the* God.

 It Is Written

According to Muhammad, our Lord declared, "I have never endowed My servants with a favor, without a group among them disbelieving in it and saying, 'Stars, it was due to the stars.'" Astrology is forbidden in Islamic Law as a false crutch upon which to interpret the world and events within it.

Ask the Imam

Islam forbids statues, paintings, and drawings of people and animals, equating them with potential idols. Abstract art and drawings, tapestries and fabric, nature scenes, cartoons, and dolls and figurines for children are generally exempted. A minority of very conservative Muslims even consider photographs forbidden, though this issue is hotly disputed among Muslim scholars.

Islam is very expansive in its definition of false gods. Usually idols or statues come to mind when we think about man-made gods, but Muhammad made the point that anything that takes our attention away from our true purpose in life can be a false god. A belief in astrology, slavish adoration of some famous person, or veneration of paintings of people or animals are examples. Furthermore, Islam says that personal arrogance is grounds for having a false god. People who are so full of themselves that they walk the streets puffed up with pride should beware, the Qur'an says, because they've made *themselves* into false gods.

As Muslims, when we affirm the first part of the *Shahadah*, we are saying that we want to dedicate ourselves to living for God alone and that we will not hold anyone or anything as worthy of veneration besides Him. It is a daily pillar of Islam and the first of the five rituals because it establishes the foundation upon which all other Islamic beliefs and practices are built. Billions of times each day people around the world declare that God is the One before Whom there are no others. That's quite a lot of public sentiment!

Are Muslims Idol-Breakers?

In March of 2001, the extremist political group known as the *Taliban*, which ruled Afghanistan until overthrown by the United States later in the same year, became the object of much international criticism for their decision to destroy the ancient Buddha statues in the Bamiyan Valley. Everyone from the United Nations to the Grand Sheikh of Egypt's famed *Al Azhar* religious university appealed for their restraint. The towering statues, which were among the tallest Buddha carvings in the world, was argued to be historic relics worthy of preservation. The Taliban, however, was not persuaded and went forward with their program, completely obliterating the carved stone statues, which had adorned the side of a mountain cliff for almost 2,000 years.

While the Muslim world debated the merits of the Taliban policy, and the non-Muslim world deplored the destruction of this ancient Buddhist art, the Taliban continued with the demolition. The actions of the Taliban bring up an interesting but seemingly contradictory situation. When you look at the situation from the point of view of the *Shahadah*, the Taliban could rightly have claimed that they did nothing wrong, yet to Western minds (and to many Muslim minds as well) their actions were nothing less than those of misguided vandals. In the Taliban's understanding, they were merely destroying idols, or *graven images*, as the Bible would label them. In fact, Taliban representatives expressed their puzzlement at the opposition from the Jews and Christians, whose own religious book, the Bible, also requires the destruction of idols (see Exodus 20:1–5).

Just the Facts _____

The word *Taliban* means "students." This is the name of a movement that began in Afghanistan in the mid-1990s with a handful of religious students who were sickened by the excesses of local warlords. They were never accepted by the majority of Muslims worldwide as good representatives of the faith. Rather, most Muslims understood them to be backcountry rustic types and half-educated bumpkins-with-guns with little understanding of traditional Islamic values.

What many Westerners don't know is that the Taliban was not the first to vandalize the statues. The site had already been severely damaged by the British in the nineteenth century as their armies attempted to conquer Afghanistan several times. An encamped British regiment unconscionably used the Bamiyan Buddhas for target practice and left behind a rubble-strewn mess. In the 1950s, the king of Afghanistan, Zahir Shah, asked for aid from India to restore them as a part of Afghanistan's cultural heritage. Neither the clerics nor people of Afghanistan decried this action as idolatrous. It was only after the country suffered through two decades of first Soviet occupation and then chronic warlordism that some of the grandchildren of the peaceful people of Afghanistan became radicalized and bereft of normal tolerant Islamic values.

The Taliban, which was nothing more than a counter reaction to the chaos prevalent in the civil war–wracked nation, defended their actions by invoking the basic Islamic principle that there must not be any false deities to detract from the worship of God. In their view, they were merely destroying false idols. Mullah Omar, their leader at the time, shrugged off western criticism quite vociferously when he said in 2001, "All we are destroying are stones. I don't care about anything else but Islam." A cultured, religious Muslim schooled in traditional Islamic Law (and having the opportunity of living in a stable society with structure and values passed along through the generations) would never have spoken like that.

Does the understanding of these modern religious zealots mean that Muslims are *supposed* to destroy the idols or relics of other religions? The answer is both yes and no. The destruction of idols, under Muhammad's direct guidance, was implemented in only one era, but it was relaxed later. When Muhammad took over Mecca, the first thing he did was pray to God in thanks. The second thing he did was order the destruction of all the idols that the pagan Arabs had stored in the *Ka'bah*. (The *Ka'bah* is a large cube-shaped building in the center of the city that Muslims believe was originally built by the Prophet Abraham.) That doesn't sound like religious tolerance, does it? But Islam asserts that idol worship was not the purpose for which the *Ka'bah* was built. It was the idolaters who first made the mistake of desecrating a building dedicated to monotheism. The mission of the Prophet Muhammad was to reestablish a place where monotheism would reign and what better place to start than the shrine of Abraham!

Thereafter, Muhammad ordered the destruction only of idols in central and southern Arabia. In the rest of Arabia, the local rulers were rapidly converting to Islam and abolishing their idols on their own. Muhammad said, "There isn't room for two religions in Arabia." So Arabia would be the heartland for the Muslim cause and thus idol worship would not be allowed. However, Muhammad *did* make treaties with Christians and Zoroastrians. This bound the Muslim community to protect the statues of Jesus and the shrines to the god of light. With this principle in force, whenever Muslim armies came into a land and found people worshipping what could be construed as idols, for the most part they left the relics alone. As people in those lands converted through the centuries, they would close, abandon, or alter their shrines to fit into a more Islamic milieu on their own. Although some Muslim conquerors, especially those from only partially Islamized regions, were less than enlightened and destroyed temples or statuary, the vast majority were more or less tolerant of local historical sites. For example, various Muslim dynasties have controlled Egypt for over a millennium and the sphinxes, carvings, and various statues of the Pharaohs are still there!

The Ka'bah, or Cube, is a brick building in Mecca believed to have been originally built by Abraham and his son, Ishmael. It is covered by a large black cloth with verses from the Qur'an embroidered in gold around its circumference. The covering is replaced annually. The old covering is cut into small pieces and distributed variously for gifts and charity.

Just the Facts

The Valley of Baca is the place where, according to tradition, the Prophet Abraham settled his second wife, Hagar, and her son, Ishmael. At that time it was a barren, rocky place. The newly discovered water well that saved the mother and child from perishing attracted wandering nomads, and many centuries later a thriving oasis town named Mecca was established. The Bible mentions this place, its abundant wells, the Ka'bah, and the practice of religious pilgrimage associated with it from the time of Ishmael. "Blessed are they that dwell in thy house … Who passing through the valley of Baca make it a well; the rain also filleth the pools." [Psalms 84:4–6] The Qur'an in verse 3:96 mentions the original name of this valley as Baca, as well.

The principle in Islam is that religion must be a free choice. Therefore, a forced conversion is a worthless one. Muslims ruled Hindu India for nearly a thousand years, yet they did not mandate the forced conversion of all Hindus to the Islamic faith, and to this day Muslims are still in the extreme minority there. Most Hindu conversions to Islam came from free choice, especially from the caste of the Untouchables, who saw Islam as a way out of a bigoted societal structure. Likewise, the Qur'an commands Muslims not to insult the false gods worshipped by other peoples, lest they retaliate and hurl insults against God in their ignorance. Although Muslim governance was not always carried out in an enlightened manner, if Islam had indeed required the destruction of idols in India, there would not be six million gods in their pantheon today (along with the tens of thousands of shrines and temples to go with them). Islamic Law says that we must respect the religious rights of others whether we rule over them or merely live side by side with them.

Because Islam forbids the willful destruction of relics that are being venerated by people in lands outside of Arabia, why did the Taliban destroy the Buddha statues? Quite simply because they were a reactionary movement that operated outside of normal Islamic values. They were a movement shaped by war, social chaos, and intellectual poverty. They disregarded centuries of Islamic thinking on a wide variety of topics and acted as if they were the inheritors of all that is true and right in their religion. This is not a unique phenomenon in world history. All ideologies, whether religious or secular, have suffered from those who would claim to be privy to some secret understanding and then wreak havoc on the lives of all those around them. The Qur'an itself calls for the preservation of religious and cultural sites and even assigns to them a definite purpose to exist. In chapter 40, verse 21, we read, "Don't they travel over the world and see the end of those civilizations that existed before them? They were even superior to (the Meccan idolaters) in strength. (Take a lesson) from the traces and ruins that they left in the land."

And Muhammad Is His Prophet

The second part of the *Shahadah* begins with an affirmation: "I declare that Muhammad is the Messenger of God." This part of the creed lays out the framework within which Islam says a person has to work to be truly obedient to God. The Qur'an, as you will recall, accepts that prophets were sent in the past to various nations. Jesus, Moses, Isaac, David, Abraham—all of them carried the same message from the same God, and they all taught a divinely revealed way of life. Anyone who followed them and their teachings and methods in their historical time would get to Heaven.

Islam also promotes the idea that the messages of these former prophets were lost, altered, or even fabricated by later followers. The Qur'an warns: "Woe to those who write the book with their own hands and then say, 'Here, this is from God,' to traffic with it for a miserable price. Woe to them for what they make and woe to them for what they fake." (Qur'an 2:79) So the mission of Muhammad was to restore the truth of God's authentic message so that people would once again have unimpeded access to God's true way of life.

By stating that Muhammad is God's last Messenger, we are pledging ourselves to practicing what he preached, doing what he did, and looking to him for our role model. Anyone who follows the model of a prophet previous to Muhammad is following a way that has been compromised, thus a common call in the Qur'an is for followers of previous revelation (especially Jews and Christians) to take a look at the last prophet's message to see the truth from their Lord in its unadulterated state. To be a true follower of Moses or Jesus, for example, is to recognize that God spoke to the world one last time and to enter into a way of life that is what their original prophets had taught. There is a special word to refer to a prophet's life example and that is *Sunnah*, or Way of the Prophet. In his last official speech during his last pilgrimage to Mecca, Muhammad said, "I'm leaving two things behind for you. If you hold fast to them you will never go astray. They are the Qur'an and my Sunnah."

Muhammad is not considered divine in Islam. He is not a god. He is not sitting at the right hand of Allah meting out justice, nor is he a savior to whom Muslims can pray. "Muhammad is a man among men," says the Qur'an. Muslims revere him and love him for all of the sacrifices he went through in his struggles with the idol-worshippers of Arabia. He endured unimaginable hardships in order to bring God's last message to the world. He is also considered by Muslims to be the best model of a husband, father, leader, friend, guide, and politician.

He never ordered a palace to be built, even after Islam became triumphant in Arabia, nor did he ever amass any wealth. His total net worth when he died consisted of a reed bed, a jar, and a couple of articles of clothing. He lived an austere, almost Zenlike life all the way to the end. Western scholars and writers have begun to recognize his admirable qualities and comment on them. George Bernard Shaw wrote, "He must be called the Savior of Humanity. I believe that if a man like him were to assume the dictatorship of the modern world, he would succeed in solving its problems in a way that would bring it much needed peace and happiness." (*The Genuine Islam*, vol. 1, no. 8)

Luckily for us, he lived at a time when the world was getting smaller and information could travel faster. His life and sayings have been documented by thousands of individuals who saw him, heard him, lived with him, traveled with him, and watched him from childhood to his assumption of his role as a prophet. Their writings provide a complete picture of who Muhammad was and what he was all about.

> **Ask the Imam**
>
> Muslims learn about their religion from only two basic sources, the Qur'an and the Prophet's *Sunnah*. The **Sunnah**, or Way of the Prophet, is contained in the books of hadiths. These books are the collected sayings and actions of the Prophet, categorized by topic, that were compiled in the first three centuries of the Islamic era.

> **It Is Written**
>
> Once a group of people came to Aishah, the widow of the Prophet, and asked her to describe the Prophet's manners. She said, "His manners were the Qur'an." (Hadith)

Expressions of Respect

Whenever Muslims hear the name of the Prophet Muhammad, they say the following phrase: *Salallahu alayhi wa sallam*, which translates as "the peace and blessings of God be upon him." Both the Qur'an and the Sunnah require us to say this to show our respect; if we don't, it is equated with being stingy. Many Muslim cultures have an entire corpus of music and poetry devoted to praising the Prophet. Muslims believe that whenever we wish peace upon the Prophet, an angel goes to Muhammad's grave and brings this news to his soul, which is resting there. (The souls of the departed remain in their graves in *Barzakh*.) On the Day of Judgment, God will accept the plea of Muhammad to save from Hellfire whomever he asks to be pardoned, up to a certain limit. Only a precious few will be granted the right to intercede on behalf of others on Judgment Day.

The Welcoming Tie

The *Shahadah*, our Declaration of Faith, negates false gods and affirms the way in which we must follow the path to God. The purpose of its frequent recitation is to remind us of those two principles.

The *Shahadah* is the defining statement of Islam. When a person desires to convert to Islam, all he or she need do is believe in what the *Shahadah* teaches and then recite it (or sign it if the converting person is mute) in front of as few as two witnesses. After this utterance, Muslims believe all the former sins of a convert are erased from their book of deeds. There are no lengthy years of study, as there are to convert to Judaism, nor is there a baptism ceremony, as in Christianity. Belief expressed in the heart and tongue is enough to get the spiritual ticket needed to be on the straight path to God.

The Least You Need to Know

- Islam has a unique set of practices called the Five Pillars of Islam, which encompass monotheism, prayer, fasting, charity, and pilgrimage.

- A Muslim must perform the five pillars, or it is counted as a sin.

- The Muslim Creed is called the *Shahadah*, or the Declaration of Faith. It consists of two parts: belief in God and acceptance of Muhammad as a prophet.

- Muhammad is not considered a god, a son of God, or even a savior in the classic Christian sense. He is a man who was chosen by God to deliver a message.

- Muslim conversion rituals consist of merely reciting the *Shahadah* in the presence of at least two witnesses.

Understanding Muslim Prayers

In This Chapter

- ◆ Learn about the Muslim practice of supplication to God
- ◆ Discover the history and meaning of the famous Islamic call to prayer
- ◆ Understand the meaning of the five daily prayers of Islam
- ◆ Unlock the mystery of what Muslims do when they pray
- ◆ Find out about the Muslim rosary and its benefits

Regular prayer, known as *salat* in Arabic, is the second pillar of Islam. It is the ritual having the most direct impact on a Muslim's daily life. Prayer is often a contentious issue in our modern world. As much as people of faith promote its many benefits in public life, those who desire a well-defined separation of church and state often strive to have laws enacted that curtail its practice in public situations. Both sides have reasons for their actions; as Muslims continue to enter mainstream life in the West, they, too, are now increasingly being asked to take sides in this debate. This presents an odd situation in that Islam commands its followers to pray five times each day but then discourages them from participating in the prayers of non-Muslims if they mention topics contrary to Islamic teachings. Is prayer in Islam a public or a private act? The answer is that it is both.

The entire philosophy of prayer in Islam is that it is a way for the individual to elevate his or her mind to seek God. It also has the side benefit of curbing the desire to hearken to immoral inclinations. Images of Muslims lined up solemnly in rows are common staples of newsmagazines, and many in the West have expressed respect for the group discipline that this activity promotes. Public observances thus serve to reinforce within the community the importance of regular prayer and cooperative action. In this chapter, I will be exploring this ritual and its importance. In addition, I will walk with you, step-by-step, through every stage of the Islamic way of prayer so that you can gain an understanding of what it's all about and why this practice won't easily fit into the current debate about prayer in the modern Western world.

Supplication Versus Prayer

"I will extol the Lord at all times; His praise will always be on my lips. My soul will boast in the Lord; let the afflicted hear and rejoice. Glorify the Lord with me; let us exalt His name together." Thus wrote David in Psalm 34 of the Bible. Muslims believe that God revealed the Psalms to this prophet and king for the spiritual fortification of his people. He is further known in Islamic tradition to have been a man much given to piety and fasting. Jews and Christians celebrate his virtues, as well. He was, the Muslim would say, an excellent role model to follow. He was also a man of fervent, passionate prayer, according to the Prophet Muhammad.

Just the Facts

Islam distinguishes between making personal requests to God (du'a, or supplications) and ritual prayer for worship (connectivity, or salat). The former is optional; the latter is a religious duty that must be performed daily by anyone older than nine years old.

Prayer means different things to different people. Some people consider it a magic cure-all for ailments or a quick fix for tough situations—"*If you help me out, God,*" they pray, "*then I'll do such-and-such.*" "*Please God, forgive me.*" "*Help me do well on that test, God.*" These are not prayers, according to Islam, but an attempt by people to have their wants or needs answered. A better word to use for this activity is *supplication*. The Islamic term *du'a*, or Calling on God, is what we label such personal requests. Muslims are encouraged to call upon God for their needs and desires, as long as they are for virtuous goals. God even gets angry if we don't call upon Him regularly because then we are slighting Him by our silence. We need God, the Qur'an intones, He doesn't need us, so when we supplicate often we bring this fact home to our hearts and minds often and thereby reaffirm further our own allegiance to piety.

The Qur'an encourages us to supplicate with the following words:

> Therefore, you should know that there is no god but Allah; implore Him to forgive you your sins and to forgive the believing men and believing women; for Allah knows your activities and your resting places. (Qur'an 47:19)

God has promised to listen to all of our sincere supplications. It doesn't mean He will answer all of them, though, because we may be asking for something that is not in our best interests. For example, we may ask to get rich, thinking all our problems would be solved, but that, in reality, may be a sign of our latent greed or penchant for worldly desires. Muhammad said that God keeps some people poor out of His mercy because they would be arrogant if they were wealthy. He further explained why some of our prayers (supplications) are not answered by saying, "Indeed, your Lord is very modest and generous. He feels shy that His servant should raise up his hands in supplication, and He may let it go unaccepted."

The Qur'an and the hadiths together contain over a hundred ready-made supplications that a person can say to ask God for everything from forgiveness to guidance to recovery from illness. There are even specific ones that Muslims memorize for use during certain times or activities. Supplications can be said in any language, and there are no attendant rituals or requirements other than to raise the hands, palms up, in front of the body as if asking to receive something from somebody. Sincerity is the key to having requests granted. This practice is so important in Islam that Muhammad said that our fervent supplications can even change our future in the timeline that Allah has set for us. Examples of common supplications (*du'as*) include these:

> **Ask the Imam**
>
> When Muslims supplicate, or make personal requests to God, we hold our hands in front of us with both palms up. After asking for whatever we wish, we pass our palms over our faces. We ask for God's blessings with open hands and then wash God's grace over our faces!

- Our Lord, give us the best in this life and the best in the next and protect us from the punishment of the fire.

- O Allah, open for me the doors of your mercy. (Said when entering a mosque.)

- O Allah, You are peace and peace comes from You. You are blessed, O Lord, the Sublime and Generous.

- There is no god but You. Glory to you, indeed I was a sinner.

- O God, in Your name do I die and live. (Said at bedtime.)

- O God, I ask Your guidance due to Your knowledge, and I ask for Your help due to Your ability. For You are able and I am not able, You know and I don't know. Only You know what is unseen. O God, if you know that my request is better for my faith, my livelihood, my situation in life for both the long and short term, then grant my request, make it easy for me and a blessing. If you know my request is bad for me, my livelihood, my situation in life for both the long and short term, then deny it to me and let me forget about it. Then decree for me good in something else and help me to be happy with it. (Said when asking God to guide us in an important decision.)

So you can see that Islam makes a distinction between *supplication* and *prayer*. The Arabic word *salat* is what we would term prayer. *Salat* is the religious ritual that a Muslim must perform five times every day to show obedience and attentiveness to God's call. It consists of a physical routine of bowing and prostrating coupled with a litany of short recited passages and phrases in which we praise God and remind ourselves of our mission here. It is our way of presenting ourselves before God to say, "Here I am, Your obedient servant." As you will see, the Muslim method of performing prayer is one of the more demanding forms of worship but also one of the most rewarding.

Translate This

Salat literally means to connect. A secondary meaning is burning or heat. Thus, when a person makes *salat*, he or she is establishing a hot-link to God.

Why Do We Pray?

The benefits of daily prayers are twofold. The first benefit that daily prayer provides is a constant reminder throughout the day that we are God's servants. The second benefit is that God forgives some of our sins each time we perform *salat*. If we are negligent in our duty and pray only irregularly, then we run a very great risk on Judgment Day. When our good and our bad deeds are about to be examined, Muhammad said that our prayers will be looked at first. If they are found to be full of deficiencies, then God won't even look at the rest of our record. Imagine going to court and having all the evidence that exonerates you declared as inadmissible because of serious procedural mistakes on your part!

Each of the five daily prayers is said within a different fixed time period during the day. There are no exemptions to the religious requirement to perform prayers except for children under puberty, women in their menses, the unconscious, the incapacitated, and the mentally challenged. The official prayer times and their names are as follows:

- ◆ **Fajr** From first light to just before sunrise

- ◆ **Zuhr** Just after noontime

- ◆ **'Asr** Late afternoon

- ◆ **Maghrib** Just after sunset

- ◆ **'Isha** Any time at night

Because the seasons change and the days get longer or shorter throughout the year, the times we pray will move a bit each month. In the summer, our first prayer may start at 4:30 A.M. and our last prayer may be at nearly 10:00 at night! In the winter, our range of prayer may be from 7:30 A.M. to 6:30 P.M. The time for each prayer begins according to the position of the sun and is valid until the next prayer time begins, so there is a lot of leeway and flexibility on the exact moment to make the *salat*. These fixed timings have been laid out in the Qur'an, and no prayer may be said before the official time begins. Any prayer said when the prayer time is over is considered a late prayer and is marked as such by the angels who record our deeds.

The Benefits of Prayer

How does praying at five predetermined points throughout the day help us to be better people? Think about it: Each of the prayers is said at a different strategic time so that no matter what we are doing or how busy we get, we are always aware that we either prayed a few hours ago or will pray again soon. This keeps the mind fresh and aware of our duty to God, and we become much less likely to want to break one of His laws. Who wants to cheat on a business contract when an hour later you are going to stand before God and ask for His favor and guidance? Only a hypocrite would be so brash (and God doesn't count their prayers on account of their duplicity).

I'm often questioned by people about the difficulty in praying so many times each day—"How can you remember when to do it?" "Isn't it hard to pray so much?" These are valid questions because many concerned people get the impression that Islam is hard to follow. It's not as onerous as it sounds. A Muslim becomes used to the routine, and once you're used to something it doesn't become difficult any longer. Observant Jews also pray several times each day, as do Hindus, Buddhists, and others. The idea is that if you truly understand that God is real, you won't hesitate to take every opportunity to pray to Him. The actual prayer ritual takes only 5 to 10 minutes to complete, so in a 24-hour day all God asks is that we set aside time to remember Him for less than 30 minutes of that time.

The Islamic prayer is becoming a much more familiar sight in North America.

The Seven Preconditions

There are seven requirements that must be fulfilled before we begin to pray:

♦ It must be prayer time.

♦ We must wash our hands, face, and feet with water to be ritually pure.

♦ We must wear clean clothes.

♦ A clean place to pray must be available. Prayers can be done in a mosque or anyplace else like a conference room, hallway, or even outside in the grass.

Just the Facts

The time for one of the daily prayers falls just after noon. Muslim students as well as those who have jobs must ask their school or employer for time to complete this religious duty. Many public schools, businesses, and even prisons now cater to the religious obligations of their constituents on this issue.

♦ We must be wearing pants or something equivalent, a shirt, and/or a robe to cover our body. Women add a scarf or veil over their hair to remind them that God does not judge us by our looks or beauty, but by our sincerity.

♦ We must face in the direction of Mecca to signify the unity of all Muslims and show our respect for Abraham's shrine.

♦ We must have the proper intention in our mind about what we're doing.

If these seven conditions are met, then the prayer can proceed.

Just the Facts

The concept of washing before prayer is not a new one. The Bible provides numerous examples of its prophets, priests, and even Jesus washing before praying. Even though this practice has fallen into disuse in modern-day Judaism and Christianity, it is nevertheless an integral part of their ancient religious roots. (See Exodus 30:17–21, for example.)

Cleanliness Is Next to ...

Before Muslims may pray, we must be in a ritually pure condition. This means that we must wash our hands, faces, and feet before we are allowed to make *salat*. The procedure for attaining this cleanliness is called *wudu*, or ablution. Islam teaches that before we present ourselves before God, we must make every effort to look presentable. Would you meet the president with dirt on your face? Would you cook dinner without first washing your hands? Would you go to school in sweats and uncombed hair? Even as we try to make a good impression on others, so, too, does God give us a way to make ourselves fit for His review.

One of the main features of a mosque is the fountain or *wudu* area where Muslims go to make their ablutions. *Wudu* can even be made in a sink; all that's needed is clean water. The entire procedure takes about a minute, and Muslims are encouraged by the Prophet not to waste water while doing so. The state of ritual purity is valid for as long as a person has no bodily waste functions, and doesn't bleed or fall asleep, so a person could make several prayers throughout the day on just one *wudu*. There is a requirement for taking a shower, as well, for those who had intimate relations, or finished their menses. The Prophet Muhammad once said, "The key to heaven is prayer and the key to prayer is being ritually pure."

The Muslim Call to Prayer

When the Muslim community was in its infancy, prayer was a precarious practice. Muhammad lived in Mecca, a city devoted to the business of idol worship. At the age of 40, when God chose him to be a prophet, Muhammad began preaching that there was only one God and that idols were man-made pieces of wood and stone. Understandably, the Meccans, who made their living by catering to the pilgrims who traveled from far and wide to venerate their idols, were furious. They attacked Muhammad through a virulent smear campaign and a bitter propaganda war. When this didn't work, and they saw many people still accepting Islam, the city authorities resorted to violence and even murder.

Muhammad wasn't directly attacked at first, because of his family connections, but other Muslims weren't so lucky. They often had to lie low. When the time for prayers came, there was no public call for people to congregate. Anyone found praying could be attacked, harassed, or ridiculed. No mosques were built in the city, nor would the Meccans have entertained such an enterprise. Islam was under siege. Many Muslims had to hide their identity for fear of persecution, torture, or worse. For 13 long years Muhammad's ever-growing following had to endure immense physical and mental pressure. Most of the converts to Islam in this period, which is called the *Meccan period*, were poor, young, or slaves; thus these early followers had little protection from vengeful families or enraged public officials and their mobs.

Translate This

Masjid an Nabawi is the name for the Mosque of the Prophet in Medina, Saudi Arabia. The former name of this city was Yathrib.

Ask the Imam

Muslims gather for congregational worship service on Friday afternoons. Muhammad explained that God ordained Friday to be the day of gathering to show the precedence of Islam over Judaism and Christianity, whose followers meet on Saturday and Sunday.

Prayer under such circumstances was difficult and unnerving. Muslims could meet only in small, secret rooms, and any Muslim who dared to pray near the *Ka'bah* was immediately set upon and beaten. The followers of Muhammad, who are known as his *sahaba*, or companions, enjoyed no religious freedom of worship in the land of their birth. This situation is akin to the period of Christian persecution by the Romans in the first two centuries of Christianity. There were no church bells in Rome during Nero's time, nor were there any similar devices in Mecca to call Muslims to prayer.

Later on, after Muhammad was invited to migrate with his followers to Yathrib, some 200 miles to the north, the Muslim community was given permission to construct a house of prayer. The first mosque was built in a small town outside of the city called *Quba*, and the great Mosque of the Prophet was soon constructed in the center of the thriving metropolis. The mosque was a simple structure made of mud bricks with a roof of palm leaves, balanced on wooden poles. It was illuminated with torches at night. The appearance of the building wasn't what was important to the early Muslims, however; it was the strength of character of those who entered it.

Islam requires prayer to be performed at five fixed times, and in those days clocks hadn't yet been invented. People told time by the position of the sun. Some way had to be found to let people know that the prayer time had come. Moreover, because Islam taught that prayer in congregation was better in the sight of God than prayer alone, people needed to be informed when the congregation was forming in the mosque. Yet another reason for notifying people is that Muslim men over the age of puberty are required to attend a special service on Friday afternoon in which they hear a sermon. This is called *Salat ul-Jumu'ah* (the Gathering Prayer). Given all of these needs, the Muslim community had to come up with a way to alert people five times each day.

Several ideas were bandied about: bells like those used in churches, horns like those in synagogues, drums, and so on. But Muhammad did not approve of any of them. He prayed for guidance from God on this issue, and the answer came in a unique way. A companion came to the Prophet a few days later and said that in his dreams he saw a man calling out phrases in a loud voice. He was asking people to come to prayer. Muhammad listened to the man's words and declared that this dream came from God. He ordered the man to teach the words to a Muslim convert named Bilal, who had a beautiful voice. (Bilal was an African slave who was freed from his idolatrous master by the Muslims.) Bilal then stood atop a wall of the mosque in Medina (the former city name of Yathrib had been dropped) and called out loudly the following words:

Allahu Akbar, Allahu Akbar.

Allahu Akbar, Allahu Akbar.

Ashahadu an la ilaha ill Allah.

Ashahadu an la ilaha ill Allah.

Ashahadu anna Muhammadar Rasulullah.

Ashahadu anna Muhammadar Rasulullah.

Haya alas Salah. Haya alas Salah.

Haya alal Falah. Haya alal Falah.

Allahu Akbar, Allahu Akbar.

La ilaha ill Allah.

The meaning is as follows:

God is greater, God is greater.

God is greater, God is greater.

I declare there is no god but God.

I declare there is no god but God.

I declare Muhammad is the Messenger of God.

I declare Muhammad is the Messenger of God.

Rush to prayer. Rush to prayer.

Rush to success. Rush to success.

God is greater, God is greater.

There is no god but God.

Just the Facts

Allahu Akbar is actually an incomplete sentence in Arabic. Literally it means, "God is greater than …" The logical question becomes, "Greater than what?" The implication of leaving it as a broken sentence is that no matter how you complete it, God is greater than that, too.

Ask the Imam

Men are always chosen to say the *azan* (sometimes spelled as *adhan*) for two reasons: They have louder voices generally, and the sound of a woman's voice calling through the streets may tempt some men to fantasize about her. Islam believes in protecting the modesty and dignity of women from any unscrupulous men who may be around.

Upon hearing these words, another man rushed to the mosque and told Muhammad that he also had had a dream containing those same words. Thus the Muslim call to prayer, or *azan*, was confirmed. A person who calls the *azan* is termed a *muazzin*. It is not a special office or holy position. Any male can perform it, but Muslims usually appoint the person who has the nicest and loudest voice to do it. No trip to a Muslim country is complete until you've been awakened in the early morning to the sounds of the *azan* floating over the landscape.

Why don't we hear the *azan* being called in the West, even though there are thousands of mosques in Europe and North America? Quite simply, local authorities largely forbid it. Now, Muslims in the West have begun asking for the same rights that Christians have in alerting their followers to their prayers. Whereas the sound of church bells ringing can be heard throughout the day and night in the cities of North America and Europe, Muslims have had only limited success in gaining permission to announce the *azan* outside the mosque with loudspeakers. Perhaps the coming years will see a shift in this restriction.

Humble Pie

The purpose of *salat* is to present ourselves before God as humble servants. *Salat* is performed in a set manner, and the basic rules are the same for Muslims all over the world. The *salat* procedure combines a set of ritualistic movements with memorized passages that are said at specific times. While learning the physical aspects of the prayer is simple, learning by heart the words we must say is a little more challenging. Even more challenging than that is the final goal of *salat*—producing such a meditative state that no distractions are able to take our focus from God.

Why do Islamic prayers combine physical movements with memorized passages and assorted supplications? The answer lies in the makeup of our human selves. In the old days, when a king or noble walked by, the required response was to bow and show one's deference to the power inherent in the office the person represented. We submit physically as a sign of what is in our heart. If we stand stiff-necked and pray merely by saying whatever comes into our mind (and maybe getting emotional along the way), then the heart is humbled to a degree but the body betrays a lack of true deference. The body is left behind. Think about it, if you really believe in the power of God then to bow in submission is no strange or demeaning thing.

Likewise, if our prayer is nothing more than whatever words we feel like saying at the moment, then one prayer would be no better than another. There would be no structure, no dignified way to say to God that we are obedient to Him, rather than a rabble of babbling voices. Islam says that all three of our components (mind, heart, and body) must be unified in prayer for it to be truly meaningful. First, we humble our hearts out of love for God. Then, we recite prayers that God gave us and concentrate on their meanings so we can learn how to remember God throughout our lives. Finally, we bring it all together by bowing down low so we feel with our physical senses what true humbleness means.

Jesus, Moses, Abraham, and many of the previous prophets are recorded in the Bible as bowing down and praying. They didn't stand stiff-necked or kneel on comfortable cushions. No, when they prayed they *fell on their faces* as the Bible often describes it. If we truly believe that God has total power and strength and that we owe our entire existence to Him, then shouldn't we treat Him with more reverence than we do earthly kings and queens, who wear

It Is Written

According to Muhammad, "Your Lord delights at a shepherd who, on the peak of a mountain crag, gives the call to prayer and prays. Then Allah says, 'Look at this servant of Mine. He gives the call to prayer and performs the prayers; he is in awe of Me. I will forgive My servant [all his sins] and admit him to Paradise.'"

Ask the Imam

There are certain times when some of the five daily prayers can be combined and prayed at the same time. Travelers, pregnant women, and nursing women can combine the two afternoon prayers at either one of the times and also the two evening prayers at either time so there is no hardship on such busy people.

only man-made crowns on their heads? Islamic prayers seek to make us really know our proper place before the greatest sovereign of all.

Each of the five daily prayers is performed in a similar way. The only difference between them is the total number of segments in each. The basic procedure to each prayer consists of standing and reciting a chapter from the Qur'an, bowing at the waist and glorifying God, and then prostrating twice on the ground while extolling God's power. This complete segment is called a *Ra'kah*, or unit of prayer. The early morning prayer consists of two units like this, whereas the two afternoon prayers and the night prayer consist of four units. The sunset prayer has three units. The varying number of units serves to give variety to our daily schedule so that we have to keep ourselves aware of what we're doing and also the varying lengths are fitted to the amount of time we may have at different points throughout the day to spend in prayer without it becoming a burden.

The Prayer Described

Let me walk you through a complete prayer procedure modeled on the early morning *Salat ul-Fajr*. Try to put yourself into the mindset of a Muslim, and you will see how this ritual can be very powerful as a source of spiritual rejuvenation and contentment. Let's begin.

After you have met the seven preparatory requirements for prayer, such as ablution and facing Mecca, begin your prayer by raising your hands to the side of your head and saying, in Arabic, *"Allahu Akbar,"* or *"God is greater."* (For the duration of this descriptive narrative I will only give the English meaning of what is said in the prayers.) From that moment onward, you are considered to be cut off from the world. All your attention and focus must be on God. You are presenting yourself to Him and should show proper deference. If you laugh, talk to someone, look around, or do anything similar, then your prayer is broken and you must start again. You must ignore everything that happens around you until you are finished. (Emergencies such as helping an injured person or avoiding imminent danger are valid excuses to interrupt prayer.)

Next, fold your hands over your lower chest with the right hand over the left and recite the first chapter of the Holy Qur'an, which for Muslims is sort of like the *Lord's Prayer*. It is a beautiful summary of the entire message of Islam and reads as follows:

> **Ask the Imam**
>
> Islamic prayers are said in Arabic exclusively so that all Muslims can be unified in their language of worship, in much the same way that Catholicism used to require Latin services. Muhammad even taught non-Arab converts to say the prayers in Arabic. Supplications, however, can be made in any language.

In the Name of God, the Compassionate Source of All Mercy. All Praise be to God, the Lord of all the worlds, the Compassionate Source of All Mercy and Master of the Day of Judgment. You alone do we serve and it is to You alone that we look for help. Guide us on the Straight Path; the path of those who have earned Your favor, not the path of those who have earned Your anger, nor of those who have gone astray. (Qur'an 1:1–7)

These are, in order, the major postures of the Islamic prayer.

Following this you say *"Ameen,"* or *"Let it be so."* Then you must recite one more portion of the Qur'an, of your own choosing. It can be as few as three verses. (Muslims are encouraged to learn at least some of the Qur'an by heart for use in prayer.) Say, *"God is greater"* once again and bow forward at the waist, resting your hands on your knees. Repeat three times, *"Glory to my Lord, the Greatest."*

Then you say, *"God hears those who praise Him,"* and stand back upright with your arms at your sides. After another *"God is greater,"* you get down on your hands and knees and bow your forehead to the ground. Say three times, *"Glory to My Lord, Most High."* Repeat, *"God is greater"* and rise to a sitting position. Declare that God is greater again

Ask the Imam

When a person or group begins to pray, any angels who are nearby come and join in the prayer. The angels then report back to God and tell Him what His servants are doing, though He already knows.

and then bow on your forehead once more, repeating what you said the first time. This ends one unit of prayer. From here you say, *"God is greater"* one last time and then stand up again, fold your hands in front, and begin the whole process over.

The only difference in the second and final unit of movements is that after you recite the opening chapter of the Qur'an, you must choose a different second passage to recite afterward. When you finish with your second and final prostration, you rise to a sitting position and say two short benedictions. The first one extols the beauty of righteousness and faith while the second one is a heartfelt plea for God to bless the noble efforts of both Muhammad and Abraham. Following this you may slip in a supplication of your choice if you wish. Then you end your prayer by turning your face first to the right and then the left, wishing peace upon all those on either side of you by saying, "Peace be upon you and the mercy of God." (Even if there is no one at your side, the angels are there.) This is what Muslims do and say when they pray.

It Is Written

When the Prophet Muhammad uttered the salutation at the end of the prayer, he would say: "O Allah, forgive me my former and latter sins, what I have kept secret and what I have done openly, and what I have done extravagantly; and what You know better than I do. You are the Advancer and the Delayer. There is no god but You."

If a Muslim is praying in a group with other Muslims, then one of them (usually the most knowledgeable) will act as an *Imam*, or prayer leader. The Imam will stand in front of everyone while the rest of the people will form straight rows behind him (or her if the congregation is made up of only women and minors), leaving enough space between each row to bow down. The Imam will recite the passages of the Qur'an out loud while the participants will follow along silently. When it is time for physical movement, the Imam does it first and the rest follow.

Men and women line up in separate rows with all the older men filling the first rows. Then minor-aged children make their own rows in the middle, and finally the oldest women fill up the rearmost rows. If any men are present, a male is always chosen for the Imam. Why don't men and women mix all together in the rows? Given the nature of how we pray with all the bowing and prostrating, many men (and women) might have a hard time concentrating on their prayers if the opposite sex were prostrating just ahead of them. That is why we separate the men and the women in congregational prayer. It has nothing to do with any form of discrimination or symbolic assignment of status. Muhammad, himself, said that there is no decrease in reward for women in the back rows. Although some Muslim cultures take this separation idea to the extreme, such as segregating dinner parties and the like, traditional Islam as it was practiced in its first few centuries was much more progressive on this issue of men and women interacting (in a formal way) in society and community life.

Remembrance of God

After prayer and supplication, there is a third way of reforming our hearts and minds and communicating to God how much we love Him and recognize His love for us. This is called *dhikr*, or Remembrance. It is basically the same as chanting the Rosary in Catholicism, except Islam has a great variety of phrases that we may repeat to bring to mind the reality of God. (There are almost 100 to choose from!)

The whole philosophy of chanting set words or phrases over and over is rooted in psychology: Whatever you fill your mind with, that is what you will tend to believe. This doesn't cause passive complacency, however; rather it conditions and keys the subconscious to surrender to God. Today, even secular motivational speakers such as Anthony Robbins and others stress the power of *positive thinking*. Meditation in any form calms and centers the mind, and for the Muslim, ruminating on God's majesty brings us to this state of deep serenity and calmness. Karl Marx might have said that religion was the opium of the people, but Muslims hold that religion, if properly applied, is the liberator, seeing how it frees us from our inner desires to dominate others and engage in wanton hedonism for no other reason than we want it. As a side note, many Muslims feel that it is excessive music that is the true opiate of society today. People frequently memorize and sing lyrics, and this could be likened to a secular rosary of sorts. What messages do most songs call us to believe in? Think about it. Although music and singing *are* tentatively allowed in Islam (though under more restricted conditions), remembering God is a more productive mental activity, and *dhikr* is considered the best *music* in Islam.

One common *dhikr* phrase is *Alhumdulillah*, which means Praise be to God. By saying this phrase over and over, we make ourselves aware that God *should* be praised. The Sufis, the mystics of Islam, have perfected group *dhikr* and engage

> **Ask the Imam**
>
> Muslims are forbidden to bow to anything on Earth whether it's a king, idol, or an audience for whom we have performed.

> **Just the Facts**
>
> Muslims usually carry beads on a string much like Catholics do. These are called *tasbihs* or *masbahas*, from the Arabic word for glorify. The Prophet Muhammad advised against their use, however, stating that it is better if you use your fingers to count because on Judgment Day your fingers will testify as to how you used them.

in it as part of their daily routine, usually by sitting in a circle with many others. The effect of rhythmic voices, chanting the greatness of God in unison can be quite moving. Are there any rules or methods to *dhikr*? Yes, but they are not complicated. First, *dhikr* should generally be said in Arabic for maximum benefit, though there is no prohibition about using other languages. Any phrase or word may be chosen and chanted. There are longer formulas for remembrance—some are paragraphs long! The Prophet taught us a great many of them, and quite a few carry a reward from God for their performance. Here are some others and their benefits:

♦ There is no power or might save in God. (By saying this *dhikr* often, you will be given a great treasure in Paradise.)

♦ Glory be to God and praise belongs to Him. (If said 100 times, all your lesser sins will be forgiven.)

♦ Glory to God. Praise be to God. God is Greater. (Say each one 33 times before going to bed to center your mind.)

Often after performing the ritual *salat*, you will find Muslims sitting for a few quiet moments "making *dhikr*," to use our phrase for it. When they finish, their minds are relaxed and they have programmed their consciousness to act the part of a virtuous servant of God for the rest of the day.

The Islamic way of performing prayers is both unique and comprehensive. By humbling ourselves before God five times each day, supplicating to God in private moments, and remembering God through the repeated phrases of *dhikr*, we seek to mold our minds and thoughts into a way pleasing to God. *Salat* builds discipline as well and makes a person learn punctuality even as it keeps the mind focused on the true reality of our time here in this world.

The Least You Need to Know

♦ Muslims have to pray five times every day at predetermined times.

♦ The Islamic prayer consists of ritual bowing and the reciting of prayers and glorifications to God.

♦ A clear distinction is made between personal supplication and ritual prayer.

♦ Muslims gather on Friday afternoons for their congregational religious service.

♦ Muslim students and employees need a few minutes every afternoon to perform their obligation of prayer.

Chapter 12

Elevating the Soul

In This Chapter

- Learn about the third pillar of Islam, the practice of *zakat*
- Discover how wealth is regarded in Islam
- Learn about fasting, the fourth pillar of Islam, and the month-long fasting ritual of Ramadan
- Find out what a Muslim learns from charity and fasting

Avarice and gluttony are counted among the Seven Deadly Sins in Catholicism. The effects of these two vices have far-reaching consequences not only for the individual but for society as well. The green-eyed monster, greed, causes envy and hatred by pitting the haves against the have-nots. Those of means become loath to part with their money, while the poor become jealous and spiteful over their woeful condition. The eternal struggle pitting the classes against each other (over the control of resources and wealth) has spawned revolutions and created new ideologies such as socialism and communism. In capitalist nations, the problem of social and economic justice is only partially addressed by scant welfare and social programs whose existence is always begrudged and under constant assault.

Personal gluttony, as expressed in the uncontrolled urge to use and consume for pleasure, engage in sex and other diversions, and take harmful drugs and alcohol, has the disastrous result of causing ill health, addiction, lethargy, family discord, criminal activities, and feelings of hopelessness in its victims. Governments spend billions of dollars each year trying to curb people's excessive appetites and urges. But these programs often don't address the root causes of overindulgence and thus usually return poor results, leaving people more disheartened than before. The term used to describe this backsliding and failure to make long-lasting life changes is *relapse*.

Islam takes these two ailments, greed and gluttony, and considers them in a new light. The problem is not that all our self-help programs are doomed to fail in the face of human intransigence; rather, it is that the root cause of our shortcomings in the first place is often unaddressed: We have forgotten why we are alive. We are not eternally defective as a species or naturally inclined to sin. We are merely forgetful of what life is about, and *Shaytan* uses our desire for pleasure to accentuate this. So to attack this twin-headed beast, Islam prescribes a unique antidote that emphasizes personal reform along with physical action. We can strive for success and even accumulate money—but we are frequently reminded that only faith and good deeds get us into heaven, and we will die one day sooner than we think. Next, we are required as Muslims to pay a portion of our wealth each year like a tax for the benefit of the poor and needy. Islam also says that we can eat and drink and procreate—but a month-long fast from those things will be required of us every year in order to teach us that we have mastery over our desires and not vice versa. We learn to moderate our desires and urges, then, to reach a new level of self-discipline.

The Burden of Wealth

"The rich get richer, and the poor get poorer" is accepted common wisdom. Throughout human history there have always been those who had it a little better than everyone else: finer food, nicer quarters, more profitable businesses, and higher-class lifestyles. These are the stuff of everyone's dreams. But every dream has the potential to become a nightmare and everyone has the potential to fall into misfortune. For every person who lives well, someone else has to make do with much less. Some people even live in desperate, pitiful conditions with no way out and nowhere to turn. There is no worse feeling than seeing one's own children starving or relatives in grave sickness and knowing there is nothing you can do to help them. In such cases, the poor may appeal to the rich for help, and deliverance may come from kind-hearted benefactors. However, another outcome is equally possible: that the wealthy may turn their faces away and choose not to see. It is when the rich fail to remember their blessed position with regard to the fortunes of others that the sins of greed and miserliness come in.

One of the hallmarks of any community is the way in which it treats its weaker members. The Qur'an explains that there are always those who are stronger and wealthier, and that their test in life lies in what they will do with their accentuated capabilities. Likewise, we are taught that the poor and weak are also given their condition as a test and are judged in how they manage their spiritual state and whether they use their God-given talents to at least try to better themselves. The two positions can even be reversed, with a wealthy person suddenly losing it all or a poor soul gaining everything in an instant. (Eddie Murphy and Dan Ackroyd portrayed two such characters in the movie *Trading Places*.) The Qur'an puts it this way: "We alternate these days of varying fortunes among mankind so that Allah may highlight the true believers and take witnesses to the truth from among you." (Qur'an 3:40)

It Is Written

Those who are saved from the greed of their own selves, they are the ones who will prosper. (Qur'an 59:9)

Islam commands its followers to give up a portion of their annual savings for the benefit of the poor. An Islamic government even has the task of imposing this tax on its citizens and using the collected funds for welfare and social programs for the less fortunate. The Qur'an tells Muslims to give this mandated charity with a friendly, jovial spirit, recognizing that all prosperity ultimately comes from God's favor and grace. No matter how much we may boast that we are self-made successes, the Qur'an reminds us, it was really God who created all the conditions that resulted in our triumphs. We pay God back by doing His work in the world. And perhaps the greatest work we can do in His Name is alleviating the suffering of others. That is what the third pillar of Islam, *zakat*, or the Islamic duty of charity, is for.

Translate This

Zakat is usually translated as *poor-due* or *charity*. The word *zakat*, however, literally means to purify. How is charity related to purity? Quite simply, the material world has the potential to distract us from our primary mission: to surrender ourselves to God. Therefore, when we are made to let go of some of our worldly possessions, we learn to force ourselves to let go of some of our greed.

Bah! Humbug!

"Allah has bought from the believers their lives and wealth and in exchange will give them Paradise," states the Qur'an. For Muslims, both our lives and our money are given in pledge to God. When we declare that we believe in Him and seek to follow His will, it follows that we recognize our responsibility to our Lord. Sometimes God requires sacrifice on our part in the great plan He has for the universe. Men and women sometimes have to struggle and die for a just cause. In the same way, there are times when resources are needed to do justice.

That's how Islam looks at wealth: as a proof of faith (or lack of it). What will you do with what you have received, especially when you are asked to give some of it up? Will greed overtake your heart and cause you to sneer at the plight of the less fortunate? How can we learn that wealth has no permanent value in the great test of life that will lead ultimately to the Day of Judgment? Islam requires its followers to give in charity to force them to learn this lesson. Those who hesitate or refuse to pay *zakat* provide evidence from their own actions that they are insincere and focused only on the things of this world. Imam Abu Hamid Al Ghazali, a great Islamic scholar of the eleventh century, explained this concept in his monumental work, *Ihya Uloomuddin*:

It Is Written

In 1889, Andrew Carnegie wrote a small booklet entitled, "The Gospel of Wealth." In it he observed that rich people are "the trustees of their wealth and should administer it for the good of the public."

Worldly goods are an object of love in everybody's eyes, being the means by which they enjoy the benefits of this world; because of them they become attached to life and shy away from death, even though death leads to meeting the Beloved [God]. The truth of our claim to love God is therefore put to the test, and we are asked to give up wealth which is the darling apple of our eye.

The Islamic civilization has produced many beautiful works of functional art such as this vase inlaid with verses from the Qur'an.

(Photo courtesy of Aramco)

If we cling to our wealth with gnarled fingers, such as Ebeneezer Scrooge did in Charles Dickens's *A Christmas Carol*, then we are saying that this life is all we believe in. The Qur'an promises eternal paradise to those who make sacrifices in this life, and one of the sacrifices Islam expects of us is to use our resources for the benefit of the needy and helpless. Because Muslims believe that God is the Creator and True Owner of everything, whatever is placed in our hands throughout our lives is considered to be like a trust. We can't take it with us, and the Qur'an provides a very blunt explanation of the folly of those who look only upon the transitory materials of this world:

> Do any of you wish to have a farm with date-palms, vines and streams and all kinds of fruit, but then to be stricken with old age while your children are still small? [Do you want] your prime lands to be caught in a tornado followed by a fire and have it all burnt up? This is how Allah makes signs clear to you so you may consider. (Qur'an 2:266)

Whatever is in your hand now, Islam reminds us, will be gone very shortly. Financial empires and hard-earned fortunes may outlive our deaths but only for a few days or years. In this regard, Islam is very similar to Taoism and Buddhism with its emphasis on transcending the world. There is an entire corpus of literature, backed up by innumerable Qur'anic verses and hadiths on this subject (and Sufism, an Islamic offshoot, especially emphasizes this part of Islam). Though Islam does not necessarily advocate living the life of a poor hermit, nor does it call wealth a sin, at the same time it challenges people to let go of some of their love of material possessions so that they can become more willing to help those who are less fortunate. When Prophet Muhammad passed away, his personal possessions consisted of only a bed sheet, a bowl, and a shield that he had pawned to a Jewish merchant.

 It Is Written

Whoever spends their wealth in the cause of God, and doesn't follow their gifts with reminders of how generous they were, nor with hurtful humiliation, they shall have their reward with God and they will not be afraid nor will they be sad. (Qur'an 2:262)

Who Must Pay *Zakat?*

Zakat, as a religious duty, is due from anyone who meets the following requirements:

- ◆ The person must have a minimum amount of savings or assets that have been held for at least one year. The value of three ounces of gold is given as the usual figure above which *zakat* is due. In today's terms it would be a minimum of about $1,000. Business assets, cars, farm animals, cash, and even jewelry are also *zakatable*.

Ask the Imam

Can a person intentionally go into debt to avoid paying *zakat*? Islam teaches that a person's actions will be judged by his or her intentions. If someone tries this kind of scheme, God knows about it and will hold that person accountable. Besides, debtors have to wait outside of Paradise until their obligations are forgiven or paid by someone on Earth.

◆ The man or woman must be past the age of puberty and of sane mind. There is no *zakat* due from children or the mentally challenged.

◆ All yearly expenses must be paid, including any debts.

If all conditions are met, then *zakat* in the amount of 2.5 percent of your average annual wealth should be paid to either a government agency designed to collect it or a local mosque or charitable organization for distribution to those who deserve it. This is welfare Islamic style, and because the rate is constant, the wealthy will pay a larger share of money into the fund than the poor will. It is the perfect system for redistributing the wealth!

Who Gets *Zakat* Assistance?

Zakat money is to be given primarily to the poor, the needy, destitute new Muslims, people drowning in debt, needy travelers, refugee relief foundations, widows, orphans, poor relatives, and causes for freeing slaves. As a rule, *zakat* money should be spent in the local area first, where the community lives.

Islam teaches that the disbursing of *zakat* funds should never be done in a way that makes the recipients feel humiliated, for as the Qur'an says, "Kind words are better than charity that hurts." (Qur'an 2:263) A person's economic condition is often beyond his or her control. If we make it seem as if we're doing this person a favor by helping, then we are losing that free spirit of communal assistance, which is the foundation of a society based on brotherhood and sisterhood and which Islam demands of us.

The Sin of Denying Your Brother

Every society has ways to punish tax frauds and cheats. In America you could receive a heavy fine or spend time in jail. In China you might even be shot! In most societies, the implications of refusing to give your fair share are that you don't want to help those in need and that you won't play by the rules of a collective society. Islam feels the same way and counts the nonpayment of *zakat* as a sin that will be addressed on Judgment Day. After all, the amount of *zakat* is only 2.5 percent. Trying to avoid paying it would be a sign of serious greed, and a person who would do so is on the path to Hell.

The fate that awaits people who fail to pay their *zakat* is a frightening one. The mere thought of the dreadful punishment is enough to make one's hair stand on end. The Qur'an is very clear when it says:

> There are people who hide gold and silver to keep it and not to spend it in God's cause. Inform them of a painful punishment. On the day when the fire of Hell will be heated with the wealth they hid, they will be burned on their forehead with a branding iron and on their sides and back. They will be told, "Here is the treasure that you hid for yourselves. Now taste the [worth] of what you hid!" (Qur'an 9:34–35)

Zakat is a reasonable and fair obligation for the benefit of the needy. Islam says the wealthy owe this duty of service because God has given them more wealth than others. Those who try to avoid *zakat*, then, are committing a crime against the poor and are denying them their rights. "In their wealth the needy have a right," intones the Qur'an. Islam does not accept the teachings of communism, with its denial of personal property rights. At the same time the excesses of raw, naked capitalism have the potential to drive large numbers of people into poverty. With the institution of *zakat*, Islam sets a median way between the two extremes so that the poor are given badly needed relief while the rich are saved from the potential sin of greed, which could destroy their souls and send them on the road to eventual ruin. It's a win-win situation for the poor, the rich, and society at large.

The Fast of Ramadan

The fourth pillar of Islam is known as *Saum*, or fasting. During the month of Ramadan, which is the ninth month of the Islamic lunar calendar, Muslims are required to observe a strict fast from dawn until dusk. Since a lunar month has about 30 days in it, what purpose is there in this long and arduous practice? As you will see, the benefits achieved are truly life-changing.

From the very beginning of time, people have been involved with the great struggle to master their bodies and emotions. The urge to eat is one of the most powerful motivations anyone must face. Many people fail and overeat or consume unhealthy foods. Other substances can be abused by our penchant for pleasure: Drugs, alcohol, and cigarettes can pull us down

Just the Facts

Muslim Americans have recently succeeded in convincing the U.S. Postal Service to create a special stamp to commemorate the Muslim fast of Ramadan. It consists of a blue background with calligraphy by a noted American Muslim calligrapher that says "*Eid Mubarak*" or "Blessed Holiday."

just as easily as too many tubs of our favorite ice cream. Sexual addiction is another unique problem that can drive people to commit excesses and cause harm to themselves and others. The rise in AIDS, teen pregnancy, rampant promiscuity, and prostitution has reached the level of national policy issues, and the problem seems to get worse every year.

Reform programs such as diet fads, cold turkey denial, counseling, and alcohol and drug treatment programs are often unsuccessful, leading people to relapse into their self-destructive overindulgence. Merely giving these vices up for a short period won't solve the problem. Is there no way out of personal gluttony? The answer lies not in watching our weight with new pills or eating plans or in wearing a nicotine patch, but in the education of our soul and in curbing its desires from within.

> **Ask the Imam**
>
> Who must fast? Every Muslim over the age of puberty who is sane and healthy enough to do it must observe Ramadan. Those who are exempt are the very young (below puberty), the permanently sick, the elderly who are too weak, and the mentally challenged. Temporary exemptions are given for women in their menses, travelers, and women in labor or after childbirth.

Islam's cure starts with defining the problem as a spiritual identity crisis. When we forget that God exists and is watching us, when we ignore our *fitrah*, or inner nature to seek God, when we fail to live according to God's good laws and forget the advice of the prophets, then we can fall prey to any self-destructive impulse. The solution, then, must begin with strengthening the soul and then bringing the body along in step.

Islam carries with it a fasting component for this reason. We can become better *enlightened* only when we rise above the flesh and recognize the force of our spirit, our very human will. The Qur'an explains the purpose of fasting in this way: "You who believe! Fasting is prescribed for you, as it was prescribed for those before you, so you can gain more spiritual awareness." (Qur'an 2:183) Because the Qur'an has given fasting in Ramadan the status of a religious duty, whose neglect is sinful, the conscientious person resolves to complete the fasting period. It is through this action that the real transformation takes place.

Welcoming Ramadan

When the new moon is sighted, signaling the beginning of the month of Ramadan, Muslims gather and say this prayer: "God is Greater, God is Greater, God is Greater. Praise be to God Who created me and you and Who decreed for you the phases [of the moon] and made you a sign for the universe." Then a short supplication is quietly said in which we dedicate ourselves to fasting in this month.

> **Just the Facts**
>
> There are no special preparations to begin the month of Ramadan. Muslims understand that it is going to be a month of intense religious devotion and a time of self-denial: no food, drink, sex, profanity, fighting, or lying allowed from first light to sundown. The main components of the month will consist of two meals: one before the sun begins to cast its first light and one after sunset. There is also a special prayer service every night in the mosque.

Wake Up! It's Time for Sahoor

Now imagine waking up, long before the first light of the sun has risen over the darkened sky, and taking a small meal, called a *sahoor*, in silence. When the hint of light approaches, the meal has to end and then you pray the morning prayer and read a chapter or two of the Qur'an. During the daylight hours, you must abstain from all food, liquids, inhaled substances, sexual activity, and nutritionally related medicine or any nonessential oral medicine.

In addition, all normally undesirable behaviors are forbidden, with the threat that God won't accept your fasting if you engage in them. No fighting, cursing, arguing, lying, gossiping, or other sins are to be indulged in. Of course, a Muslim must naturally avoid such sins anyway, but sometimes people fall into error if they haven't been reminded of the importance of their actions for a while. Fasting for a month from these vices is the best corrective. If God doesn't accept your fasting, you may not go to heaven no matter what other good deeds you did. There's an incentive for you!

Now you are expected to carry on with your normal day. You have to go to work, take care of the kids, do the lawn work, and anything else that comes up. The difference is that by about 2:00 P.M., time seems to move painfully slow for you. You fight the urge to get that cola, and snacking is out of the question. You also become hyperaware of your behavior and want to avoid committing any sin as much as humanly possible. Doing good deeds is also occupying a prime place in your thinking because in this month your angels record each good deed as doubled or trebled or more.

When the sun finally declines completely past the horizon, the period of fasting is over. You waited the last couple of hours in your home reading the Qur'an alone or with your family and making supplications and *dhikr*. When the last sliver of the sun has fallen past the horizon, the *Muazzin's* call brings a rush of joy to the house. You

Translate This

Iftar means to break your fast with a small meal. The usual *iftar* fare consists of dates, water, or milk.

thank God for His mercy in allowing you to complete the day's fast, and now you're allowed to take a small snack, called an *iftar*, before going to pray the sunset prayer. Families usually join together for *iftar*. When the prayer is finished, you celebrate the end of the day with a joyous dinner at home or in the mosque, where you gratefully partake of food and gain a new appreciation for the value of eating and drinking.

Muslims gather in the mosque for the special late-night prayers held during Ramadan.

After the last regularly scheduled prayer of the day, you might go to the mosque and join in as the congregation prays the special Ramadan prayer known as *Salah al-Tarawih*. Each night the Imam will stand with the other worshippers in prayer and read one thirtieth of the Qur'an aloud until the end of the month when the reading is complete. Then the celebration of the Festival of Fast Breaking, or *Eid ul Fitr*, will engulf the hearts and minds of the community with laughter, joy, and a sense of accomplishment. The holiday begins with the 'Eid Prayer and sermon on the morning after Ramadan ends and lasts two days, with dinner parties, family outings, fairs, carnivals, and great celebrations.

Muslims are expected to give their Islamic center a small donation called *Sadaqat ul Fitr*, or Charity of the Fast Breaking, before the last day of Ramadan. The donations allow the mosque to arrange meals for the poor, allowing everyone to partake in the joys of 'Eid. It is an obligation upon every household, and parents must count their children when figuring out the total to give. It is the equivalent of the cost of one meal per person times the number of people in the house.

One particular night of Ramadan has extra special significance. It is the exact night when the Qur'anic revelation was first revealed to Muhammad in the year 610 C.E. It is known as *Laylat ul Qadr*, or the Night of Power. According to the Prophet Muhammad, it falls on one of the odd-numbered nights in the last 10 days of Ramadan. Many Muslims stay up all night seeking the Lord's forgiveness and guidance.

The Month of Training

What are some of the lessons learned by participating in the Ramadan fast? You would be surprised at the variety. The month of Ramadan provides a sort of spiritual and moral "boot camp." We know that fasting in Ramadan is a duty from God and that any sins may spoil our record of fasting, so we take great pains to be on our best behavior. This intense modification of our habits is designed to help us avoid such sins throughout the rest of the year.

The Blessed Prophet once remarked, "Whoever doesn't give up lying and acting on lies during fasting, then God has no need of him giving up food and drink." On another occasion he warned, "There are many people who get nothing from fasting except hunger and thirst." Clearly, the moral dimension is as important as the physical aspects of fasting.

The lessons learned during Ramadan are many. We learn what it means to be hungry, so we feel more compassion for the poor. We understand how close we are to leaving this world at any moment and how much we depend on food and liquids. We learn to control our animal urges and passions, and we clear our minds and thoughts for serious remembrance of God. We restrain our anger, and we train our habits toward prayer, forgiveness, self-sacrifice, and good behavior. By curtailing sex for the whole day, we force ourselves to train our bodies to obey our will and not to be licentious. There is nothing like the Muslim fast of Ramadan in any other religion for realizing personal reform and self-mastery.

Muslims greet each other on their 'Eid festival with the words, *'Eid Mubarak!* which means, "A Blessed 'Eid to you!" Gift-giving is common, especially for children, and cards are exchanged.

Ask the Imam

There are also occasions to fast throughout the rest of the year. The Prophet Muhammad's personal habit was to fast two days a week (on Mondays and Thursdays).

The reward for a successful Ramadan is no less than the forgiveness of all our sins. Imagine wiping the slate clean with God! So, in addition to all the improvements Ramadan can make in our character and health, we get the slate erased and can start over. (All our good deeds remain; it's only the bad deeds that disappear!) With all these benefits derived from the observance of this blessed month, is it any wonder that Ramadan is the best time of the year for every Muslim?

A surprising number of Christians also observe the Ramadan fast here in North America. They recognize the disciplining effects of the fast and use their time to come closer to God. Every year Islamic centers receive calls from non-Muslims asking how the fast is performed and where they can get a month-long chart showing the start and end times of each day's fast. Employers and schools are also beginning to make accommodations for the needs of their Muslim workers and students.

Because the month of Ramadan falls about a week earlier every year, as the lunar calendar rotates backwards through the solar, Muslims experience differing conditions in their fast. The period of fasting is longer in the summers and shorter in the winters.

As the population of Muslims continues to grow, the awareness of Ramadan will undoubtedly have a positive influence on people of all faiths in the West. Ramadan is all about renewing our commitment to God and undergoing a physical and spiritual training program to increase our intimacy with our faith.

The Least You Need to Know

- Greed and gluttony are considered conditions of the soul and can be cured only with a combination of spiritual advice and a program of action.

- *Zakat*, the third pillar of Islam, is a yearly charity tax on every Muslim that amounts to 2.5 percent of all the person's annually valued assets.

- Ramadan is the name of the month in which Muslims fast from food and drink from first light until sunset.

- Fasting, the fourth pillar of Islam, teaches Muslims to control their desires and urges for worldly satisfaction and to feel empathy for the poor. The reward for successful completion is forgiveness of the individual's sins.

Chapter **13**

Gathering in Mecca

In This Chapter

◆ Learn about the *Hajj*, the annual Muslim pilgrimage to Mecca and the fifth pillar of Islam

◆ Discover what Muslims believe about Abraham and his sons, Isaac and Ishmael

◆ Know all of the rituals of the *Hajj*

◆ Compare Biblical and Qur'anic accounts of Abraham and his family

Throughout the centuries people have held certain places in great esteem. Art lovers adore Paris and flock to its galleries in droves to pay homage to the artists of the past and present. Mountain climbers head for Nepal and its soaring peaks, and aspiring students dream of going to Yale, Harvard, or Oxford. People seeking more spiritually significant experiences usually travel to religious sites. Such holy places, which can be found throughout the world, are often the objectives of pilgrims on very personal quests for enlightenment and moral renewal. Catholics congregate at St. Peter's Basilica in Rome and at sites where the Virgin Mary was reported to be seen. Jews long to visit the Western Wall in Jerusalem, and Protestants consider a trip to Bethlehem as an essential lifetime journey. Buddhists,

Sikhs, and Hindus also have their holy destinations, which draw millions of visitors each year for worship and contemplation.

Of all the religious gatherings in the world, though, there is one that stands out for the sheer magnitude of its size and scope. This is the Islamic pilgrimage, or *Hajj*. It is the largest annual spiritual get-together in the world, with over two million people descending upon a desert oasis city once a year for about a week. The very name of the city itself, *Mecca*, is used to describe a place where multitudes of people may gather. All the major networks from ABC to CNN now offer live *Hajj* coverage every year on prime-time television, and when Hajj season arrives the numbers of people utilizing international travel by car, boat, and plane spikes upwards dramatically. What makes this ritual increasingly noticed by the non-Muslim world, and why has it been veiled in secrecy for so long?

Mecca, the birthplace of Muhammad and home to a shrine with roots going back to the Prophet Abraham, is the center of attention for more than a billion Muslims around the globe. Although every Muslim desires to make this once-in-a-lifetime journey, few non-Muslims know anything about this arduous and self-renewing ritual of Islam. In this chapter, I will help you discover the significance of the *Hajj* and what Muslims hope to achieve by going there. By religious law, no one is allowed in Mecca except followers of the Prophet Muhammad, so prepare to enter a world few outside of Islam have ever seen.

Introducing the *Hajj* Ritual

For over 14 centuries people from all over the globe have undertaken a journey to the Arabian Peninsula for the sake of obeying God. From every nation and every land, using every mode of transportation, Muslim men and women have set their sights on the city of Mecca (sometimes spelled Makkah) in what is today Saudi Arabia. They come to worship God, to renew their faith, to honor God's last prophet, and to look for the meaning of life in a land where most conventional luxuries and worldly distractions are absent. This is the fifth pillar of Islam, known as the *Hajj*.

The *Hajj*, or Pilgrimage, occurs in the twelfth month of the Islamic lunar calendar and lasts from the eighth to the tenth day of that month. It is a journey that all sane, adult Muslims must undertake at least once in their lives if they can afford it and are physically able. It is a ritual with roots that go all the way back to the Prophet Abraham. By choosing an austere desert region for pilgrimage, Muslims believe that God also wanted to show us that the world is really an illusion of sorts and that we are merely travelers here, so we shouldn't get too comfortable.

A view of the city of Mecca with the main religious complex.

The Origin of a Holy Place

The main feature of the city of Mecca is a curious, box-shaped building in the center of town called the *Ka'bah*, or Cube. It is a religious shrine made of bricks and covered by a heavy black cloth embroidered with gold thread. It stands about 50 feet high and measures about 40 feet on each side, with two sides being slightly longer than the other pair. Surrounding it is a large pillared building with tall minarets called the Masjid al Haram. Four thousand years ago, the valley of Mecca, then called *Baca*, was a dry and uninhabited place. That is, until one day when a man traveling in a small caravan brought his wife and young son there and told them that this wasteland was to be their new home.

The man's name was Abraham, and he was instructed by God to bring his second wife, Hagar, and their son, Ishmael, to Arabia from Palestine. This may have been to protect them from any potential conflicts with Abraham's first wife, Sarah, who wanted her child, Isaac, to be the next leader of the tribe after Abraham passed away. Besides being the second wife, Hagar had the unenviable position of having been Sarah's servant before her status was elevated to that of a co-wife. If Abraham had to choose whom to move, guess who had to go!

Muslims believe that God instructed the Prophet Abraham to take Hagar and her son to the wilderness of Arabia and leave them there. He obeyed his Lord and left them with only limited supplies of food and water. Then he made the two-week journey back to Palestine, leaving his little family behind and trusting in God that they would be safe. Hagar and Ishmael pitched a tent and waited. Their supplies quickly ran out, however, and within a few days the mother and son were beginning to suffer the effects of dehydration and hunger. In her desperation, Hagar ran up and down two hills trying to spot any help in the distance, but there was none. Finally, she collapsed next to Ishmael in the center of the valley and prayed to God for deliverance.

Just the Facts

Hagar was a legitimate wife of Abraham, and her son, Ishmael, was his first heir. Although traditional Judeo-Christian thinking favors Isaac, Jewish law makes no distinction regarding the mother of the first-born son. The Bible itself calls Hagar Abraham's *wife* (Genesis 16:3) and thus Muslims would assert that both sons of Abraham were to be blessed through the ages.

The boy struck his foot on the ground, and the action caused a water-spring near the surface to gush forth. The water was cool and sweet. Hagar and Ishmael were saved! With their water supply secure, they were able to trade water with wandering nomads for food and other needs. In time, the Prophet Abraham came back from Palestine to check up on his family in Baca and was amazed to see them the masters of a very profitable well. Ishmael, who was developing a strong sense of wisdom and justice, pleased his father greatly. There is no record in Islam that Ishmael became an archer or was raising his hand against everyone, as the Bible states, perhaps under the influence of a biased unknown author.

Now, as he rested with Hagar and their son, Abraham's great test was about to occur. The aged patriarch saw in a dream that he was sacrificing his son on an altar. When Abraham told his son about this, the boy courageously replied, "Do as you have been commanded." Abraham took the boy into the wilderness and tied him to a stone outcropping. Imagine the stress and anxiety felt by both. Abraham was being asked to take the life of his own beloved son, and the boy was lying there, knowing that his own father was about to kill him. But just as Abraham was about to strike with the knife, an angel came to him and told him to stop, because he had already demonstrated his willingness to give up everything he loved for God's sake. Both father and son rejoiced and found a ram nearby to sacrifice instead.

Just the Facts

The name of the well discovered by Ishmael and Hagar is called the **Well of Zam Zam.** In 4,000 years it has never run dry.

Now, in reading this account you may have noticed that the boy who was going to be sacrificed is not Isaac but Ishmael, which is opposite from the Biblical account of this story. Islam asserts that this story took place in or near the Valley of Baca and that because God spared Ishmael and tested Abraham's faith, a great shrine would be built by the pair in celebration. This would be the forerunner of the present-day *Ka'bah*.

The evidence to support this claim can be derived from the Bible itself, which tells of Abraham being told to sacrifice his *only* son. As you well know, both Ishmael and Isaac were sons of Abraham, with Ishmael being the older, so to call Isaac his *only* son would be incorrect. Jewish law and the customs of the day in Abraham's time do not discriminate between sons born to different wives, so some Muslims have speculated that the name Ishmael was changed to Isaac by people for their own purposes. The chaotic nature of Biblical composition and its many alterations over the centuries certainly can give credence to this view, but whether the story is mentioned in the Jewish scriptures accurately or not is of little importance to Muslims, who believe that the Qur'an is the corrected version of ancient events as revealed by God to the Prophet Muhammad.

The Prophet Abraham then received the revelation from God to build a shrine in the Valley of Baca, dedicated to Him alone. Abraham and his son obeyed without question and constructed a small stone structure that was to be the gathering place for all who wished to strengthen their faith in God. It was meant to be something of a center for monotheism, if you will. The Qur'an recounts part of the story thus:

> Remember when Abraham and Ishmael built the foundations of the House [and prayed], "Our Lord! Accept this from us because You are the Hearing and Knowing. Our Lord! Make us compliant people who bow to You. And of our descendants, make them compliant people, bowing to You also. Show us where to perform our rituals and turn to us because You are the One Who Accepts Repentance and is Merciful." (Qur'an 2:127–128)

As the years passed, Ishmael was blessed with prophethood, and he gave the message of surrendering to God's will to the nomads of the desert. He continued the tradition established by his father of bringing servants of God to the shrine for pilgrimage. Eventually, people began settling in the Valley of Baca, and the name was later changed to "Mecca" (or Makkah). The Qur'an itself notes both the ancient name, Baca, and the modern one, Mecca.

The Hebrew Bible affirms the existence of this great pilgrimage rite at the *Ka'bah* in Mecca (Baca). King David wrote in Psalm 84:

> O Lord Almighty, my King and my God. Blessed are those who dwell in your house; they are ever praising you. Blessed are those whose strength is in you,

who have set their hearts on pilgrimage. As they pass through the Valley of Baca, they make it a place of springs; the autumn rains also cover it with pools. (Psalms 84:4–6)

After many more centuries had passed, Mecca became a vibrant town, mostly because of its reliable water source, but also because of its rising position as a stop on the international caravan route from Yemen and India through to Syria and Europe. But Abraham's religion was not to survive there intact. Gradually, people began to develop false ideas about spirits and a plurality of gods. Finally, after many centuries of accumulated tribal folklore and custom, the shrine of Abraham was turned into a house to store idols and statues, which people worshipped instead of the one, unseen God. It would be many years before the right prophet arose to clean up those false ideas and restore the *Ka'bah* to the worship of the one true God. That prophet, who would be a descendant of the Prophet Abraham through his son Ishmael, was named Muhammad.

Translate This

The main religious shrine in Mecca known as the *Ka'bah*, although it is often referred to as *Baytullah*, meaning the House of God. Muslims don't believe God lives in the *Ka'bah*, however; it is merely the focal point of religious devotion.

Just the Facts

Mecca is located along a corridor of semi-arid land hugging the western coastal region of Arabia and extending for hundreds of miles to the north and south. The region, whose name is *the Hijaz*, receives some annual rainfall but not enough to sustain more than limited agriculture such as date palm or scattered grain production. The summers can be brutally hot, though sporadic rains generally come in the autumn through spring.

Why Do Muslims Go to Mecca?

Every year, thousands of eager Muslims from every country anticipate making the *Hajj*. For many, it is the greatest journey they will ever make and the one goal they've patiently waited for all of their lives. But before performing this important act of service to God, Muslims must have all of their debts paid and all of their worldly affairs put in order. (You never know what will happen to you tomorrow, so it is best to prepare today.) In the past, it was more difficult to get to Mecca, with the journey taking anywhere from months to years, but today it's really quite speedy, and most people spend less than two weeks on their entire trip (although the official Hajj is only three days, there are optional holy rites before and afterward—*and don't forget the shopping and sightseeing when you're done*).

The purpose of the *Hajj* is twofold: to honor the faith and life of the Prophet Abraham and to come together as a community to renew our commitment to God's way of life and to learn the stark reality about the shortness of our lives and our accountability to Him. (Mecca is not considered holy because Prophet Muhammad was born and raised there.) It is not an easy task, though, for Mecca is a hot, dry place for most of the year and the sun is harsh and unforgiving. In addition, some of the rituals performed during the *Hajj* require a fair amount of physical exertion. Add to this the fact that now almost two million people converge on this one small town for about a week each year and you have quite a recipe for hardship and struggle.

Just the Facts

A person who makes *Hajj* is called a *Hajji*. People often add *Al Hajj* (an alumnus of the *Hajj*) as a title to their first name in order to show they have completed it.

But *Hajj* comes with its abundant rewards, making whatever we have to endure well worth it. The first reward is total forgiveness for all our sins. Muhammad said that a perfectly done *Hajj* permits us to enter into Paradise (assuming we maintain our faith for the rest of our lives). We also get the chance to follow in the footsteps of Abraham, whom Muslims revere as the *Friend of God*. By participating in the rituals initiated by Abraham, Muslims feel as though they are with him in spirit. Another benefit is to see the city where the Prophet Muhammad was born. Muslims love him and respect him, and to see the streets he walked on is akin to Christians visiting Jerusalem or Bethlehem and feeling the presence of Jesus. The sense of immediacy is quite satisfying. Finally, the *Hajjis* get the chance to meet Muslims from all over the world; every race and culture is represented, and people's bonds of universal brotherhood are strengthened.

The *Hajj* had such a profound effect on Malcolm X that he renounced racism against whites, even though racism was a cardinal teaching of the patently misnamed Nation of Islam—a skewed organization that mixed a few scant pieces of Islam and Christianity with racial exclusivity. One of the factors in his decision was his experience in Mecca, where he was walking with, sitting with, and living with white Muslims who taught him, through their

Just the Facts

Planning a vacation to Mecca? Don't call the travel agent just yet! The Prophet Muhammad ordered Mecca to be off-limits to anyone who has not yet accepted Islam. You have to convert first, and then you can call the Hilton in Mecca.

example, that the Islamic teaching of equality was better than the Nation of Islam's narrow view of whites as *devils*. When he returned to the United States, Malcolm X changed his name to Al Hajj Malik Shabbaz and left the Nation of Islam.

The Rituals of *Hajj*

Muslims can perform two types of pilgrimages. The smaller pilgrimage, which can be done anytime throughout the year, is called an *'Umrah*. It doesn't count toward the once-in-a-lifetime pilgrimage, however. Rather, it is an act of piety performed to get extra merit. Many Muslim families make the decision to go for *'Umrah* rather than taking a vacation at their favorite resort.

The main pilgrimage, or *Hajj*, must be performed during the second week of the Islamic month called *Dhul Hijjah*. This is the pilgrimage called for in the Qur'an as a duty upon all believers who can afford it. Most people combine an *'Umrah* with the main *Hajj*, doing them back-to-back, and this is the method I will be describing shortly. Regardless of the type of pilgrimage one chooses, however, certain restrictions are placed upon those who undertake this journey for God. These restrictions serve to create uniformity in practice among untold thousands of people and also to emphasize that pilgrimage is no vacation. You're here to worship God, so you have some rules to follow.

All male pilgrims must wear two white garments that are called the *Ihram* (restricting clothes). Stitching is not allowed in the cloth, nor can any straps be used to join the two pieces together. The two garments go on sort of like a toga. Women are allowed to wear whatever clothes they wish. Among the restrictions that every pilgrim must observe are the following:

- No intimate relations

- No shaving or nail cutting

- No colognes or scented oils

- No hunting or killing of any living thing

- No fighting, arguing, or bothering anyone

- Bathing is allowed, but perfumed soaps are frowned upon

On to Mecca!

The *Hajj* begins when a person arrives at a set point outside of Mecca. This point is equivalent to an entry station. Here the pilgrims bathe and change from their normal clothes into their *Ihram* garments and make the intention to do *Hajj*. A bus then takes the pilgrims into Mecca itself, where they will approach the giant complex within which is the *Masjid al Haram*. This is the huge building surrounding the holy places that is ringed with columns and minarets. In the center of the complex, in an open courtyard stands, on holy ground, the *Ka'bah*, covered in a black cloth called the *Kiswah* and embroidered with verses from the Qur'an. All along the *Hajj* journey, the pilgrims chant a special passage over and over until sunset to remind themselves why they are there. The passage should be repeated often with an earnest heart. It is recited as follows: *Labayk! Allahumma labayk. Labayk la sharika laka labayk. Innal hamda wan ni'mata laka wal mulk. La sharika lak.* This translates as: "Here I am at Your service. O God, here I am at Your service. Here I am at Your service, there is no partner with You. Here I am at your service. All praise and all blessings belong to You. All dominion is Yours and You have no partner."

Nothing Like Being There

Now let's join with the pilgrims for a moment and look at the *Hajj* through the eyes of someone performing it. When the awe-inspiring sight of the *Ka'bah* presents itself before us, we join the throngs of pilgrims and walk around it counterclockwise in a great knot of people seven times, pointing toward it and repeating our chanting as we move. This is called the *Tawaf*, or Encircling. Imagine two million people all in the same place doing what we are doing! (The *Hajj* is the largest annual religious gathering in the world.)

The Ka'bah in Mecca.

Muhammad Asad, a Jewish convert to Islam, described his first impression of the *Ka'bah* in these words:

> And there I stood before the Temple of Abraham and gazed at the marvel without thinking (for thoughts and reflections came only much later), and out of some hidden, smiling kernel within me there slowly grew an elation like a song.
>
> Smooth marble slabs, with sunlight reflections dancing upon them, covered the ground in a wide circle around the *Ka'bah*, and over these marble slabs walked many people, men and women, round and round the black-draped House of God. Among them were some who wept, some who loudly called to God in prayer, and many who had no words and no tears but could only walk with lowered heads. (From *The Road to Mecca*)

Many people who have returned from *Hajj* have described their first meeting with the Holy Shrine in similar terms, and any pilgrim, of any faith, can attest to the power of being in a place of holy sanctuary. Continuing onward then, when we have finally completed seven rounds, we make our way to the *Maqami Ibrahim*, or Station of Abraham. Here we offer a prayer by the spot where Abraham was purported to have stood while invoking God's blessings upon the pilgrimage shrine. Next we pay a visit to the fountain that saved Hagar and Ishmael from perishing. The *Well of Zam Zam*, as it is called, has never failed since their time. We drink the water reverently and taste its heavy mineral content. Muhammad said that it is water that can improve one's health dramatically. (Yes, they bottle it and sell it all over the world!)

From there we move to a long covered walkway running between the two hills between which Hagar, in her desperation, ran back and forth. We, too, will walk between those two hills to commemorate her frantic search—but we will walk on a giant tiled path completing seven circuits. The rest of the day we will spend in prayer, study, and reflection. This completes the *'Umrah* portion of our combined *Hajj*, and the next day, which is the eighth day of the month, our compulsory rituals will begin. All during the *Hajj*, pilgrims are expected to ponder the meaning of their lives and what they have done in the world thus far.

> **Ask the Imam**
>
> There is a black stone about the size of a basketball set in a frame in one corner of the *Ka'bah*. It is a meteorite used by Abraham as part of his original shrine. Muslims point to, or kiss, this stone while circling the *Ka'bah* to express their love for Abraham. It is not considered magical or supernatural in nature.

> **Ask the Imam**
>
> Men and women follow the exact same rituals on the *Hajj*. They also pray together in mixed groups, side-by-side, unlike any other time. This is done for the sake of practicality: With millions of people to line up, it is impossible to form separate male and female rows.

The harsh landscape of brown dirt, stunted trees, and black rocks helps to clear a person's thoughts with its absence of flashiness and comfort. (If you've ever been to Arizona or New Mexico, that's what western Arabia looks like.)

The next day, we travel to a barren plain named *Mina* where we spend the day in the open air, praising God and taking stock of our soul. We pass the night in tents and the next morning begin perhaps the hardest part of the journey. (Keep in mind that the temperature during the day is often over a hundred degrees Fahrenheit.) Next, we pilgrims will move to a wide open plain, a few miles outside Mecca, called the *Plain of Arafah*. It is literally a huge, barren wasteland that signifies what it will be like on the Day of Judgment when all people will be lined up and sweltering in the heat. We remain there the whole day until night falls and then travel to another place called *Muzdalifah*.

It Is Written

According to Muhammad, "Whoever performs the pilgrimage for Allah's sake and avoids intimate relations and does not fight with anyone nor abuses anyone, he or she will return home [free from sins] like the day his mother gave birth to him."

While camping there for the night in open tents with the desert wind blowing softly over our campfires, we will join with the other pilgrims in gathering together a set number of small stones that are just the right size for throwing. In the morning we stand together and praise God and then travel back to Mina where we approach a large round roofless enclosure, inside of which are several tall stone pillars. All of us gather around the low wall and throw our stones at the pillars, which represent *Shaytan*, who had tried to dissuade Abraham from sacrificing his son. This exercise is an affirmation that, although *Shaytan* is real, we can fight against him if we are determined, even as Abraham did.

After we have "stoned the Devil," it is time to re-create the test of loyalty that God required of Abraham. God's purpose was not to require Abraham to sacrifice his son but to make Abraham decide whether he loved God more than anything else. Even as an animal was sacrificed instead of Abraham's son, we do the same by offering a sacrifice on a plain about a mile outside the city of Mecca. The sacrificial animals—usually goats, camels, cows, or sheep—are brought for the pilgrims to slaughter. Because there are so many pilgrims, each group of 5 to 10 people will have one animal.

While it may seem bizarre by today's standards to sacrifice animals during religious rituals, we have to look deeper into why it's being done and how. The idea behind the sacrifice is that we are willing to give up what we love for God's sake, just as Abraham was willing to do that. Further still, Islam has very strict rules about how to slaughter an animal. The knife must be sharp, and a swift cut to the jugular vein is all that is allowed. In addition, no one is permitted to slaughter an animal in the presence of another animal. The animal feels no pain, nor is it made to feel scared. This is essentially similar to Jewish kosher regulations.

Unlike the Old Testament of the Bible, which calls for sacrificial animals being burnt on altars, Islam has no such practice. The meat from the slaughtered animals is used to feed the pilgrims, and the majority is distributed to the poor. Nothing is wasted. The meat is processed at a nearby canning factory, and the cans of food are sent to the poor and to refugees all over the world. So looked at from another angle, the rite of sacrifice during the Islamic pilgrimage is another way to help those in need. Where do you think all the meat used in hamburgers and fried chicken comes from? Industry slaughterhouses in the West kill thousands of animals each day in very painful ways *and* in the presence of other animals. Islam is much more humane in its practice and adds a religious dimension once a year besides.

> **Ask the Imam**
>
> Muslims believe that the *Ka'bah* exists on two planes at once, both here on Earth and in Paradise. When Muslims pray anywhere in the world, they face toward the *Ka'bah* as a symbol of their desire to be obedient to God and to go to Heaven. It also provides a sense of unity among Muslims all over the world.

Crew Cut, Anyone?

The official *Hajj* ends on the tenth day of the month, and this is also the day in which Muslims throughout the world celebrate their second main holiday, Eid ul Adha. Muslims are encouraged to make a sacrifice on this day wherever they live and distribute the meat to the poor and needy. As for the *Hajji*, their next step is for men to shave off their hair, signifying their rebirth into true faith. Women don't shave their hair but merely cut a lock. At this point, the pilgrims are released from most of their *Hajj* restrictions, and they can return to Mecca for another *tawaf* around the *Ka'bah*. The next few days of religious ritual are optional and are spent in *stoning* the *Satan-pillars* again, visiting various sites around the city, praying, making supplication, and studying the Qur'an.

On the last day of all rituals, the thirteenth day of the month, we make one final set of farewell passes around the *Ka'bah* and a final supplication imploring God's forgiveness, and then the *Hajj* is complete! Through our journey we have commemorated together the ultimate act of obedience when the Prophet Abraham was commanded to sacrifice his beloved son. Abraham proved he was willing to give up the one thing he truly loved for God's sake. The lesson of the *Hajj*, then, is this: How much are you willing to give up for God?

Continuing the Journey

When the *Hajj* is completed, most pilgrims, following the advice of Muhammad, make a stop in Medina. Medina is the place where the Prophet was able to establish a functioning Islamic society. He predicted that the people of Medina would always be good-natured and religiously minded. While there, we will visit the famed *Masjid an Nabawi*, or Mosque of the Prophet. Today it is a large structure with a dramatic green dome centered over the spot where Muhammad is buried.

The main speaker's pulpit located inside the Prophet's mosque in Medina.

After spending a few days there taking in the historical sights, it is common for Muslim pilgrims to make a final stop in Jerusalem, the city of many of God's great prophets. David, Solomon, Jesus, and others walked its streets, and the Prophet Muhammad even came here once on a kind of mystical journey of the soul accompanied by an angel. The famed *Masjid al Aqsa*, with its spectacular gold dome, marks the spot where Muhammad stood and ascended to heaven for a tour of the next life. More about that in Chapter 21. Although the Israeli authorities have imposed many restrictions on Muslim tourists in recent years, many pilgrims are still able to complete this third leg of what is considered a well-rounded *Hajj* trip.

The *Hajj* is a beautiful way of presenting ourselves before our Lord. This journey is perhaps the hardest thing someone will ever do in his or her life. It is also the yearly gathering whereby Muslims affirm their unity and humility before their Lord. There is no other gathering like this in the whole world. Everyone, regardless of color, race, status, education, economic level, or gender, comes together and is treated as an equal. Everyone stands shoulder to shoulder, together, and no one receives preferential treatment, whether king, president, farmer, or locksmith. Everyone who makes the *Hajj* carries home an experience that changes his or her life forever.

The Least You Need to Know

- Every Muslim who can afford it and who is physically able must make a pilgrimage to Mecca at least once in his or her life.

- Only Muslims are allowed to enter Mecca.

- The *Hajj* ritual consists of a series of activities each designed to teach the pilgrim a different lesson or to commemorate an event from Abraham's life. The main idea behind the *Hajj* is to learn how to let go of what we love in place of God.

- The *Hajj* is the largest religious gathering in the world and is covered by major news networks every year.

- The main religious site in Mecca is the *Ka'bah*. It is a cube-shaped building whose foundation, Muslims believe, was originally constructed by Abraham.

Chapter **14**

Uncovering the Real Story About *Jihad*

In This Chapter

- ◆ Find out why the media often associates Muslims with violence
- ◆ Understand the Islamic view of war and conflict and how it relates to modern times
- ◆ Take a new look at the issue of terrorism
- ◆ Learn about the true nature of *jihad*, which is not what you might have thought
- ◆ Discover the place of social activism in Islam

Perhaps no other term from the world of Islam is as misunderstood in the West as *jihad*. Its very mention conjures up images of swarthy brown terrorists in ragged turbans and robes, Kalashnikov rifles slung over their shoulders, ready to mow down anyone who isn't a believer. It would be easy to believe that these pictures define the term *jihad*. Nightly news reports perhaps unwittingly deliver the wrong kind of message with almost daily stories of one *Islamic* group or another either named *Something-Jihad* or calling for a *jihad* against America, *the Great Satan*. Chanting crowds of flag-burning Third Worlders are often queued to seal the impression that Muslims are a bunch of unruly fanatics.

Just what is a *jihad*, though, and are all the images and events associated with it a valid comparison with actual Islamic teachings? Is there any relationship between events throughout the world and the proper application of religious values? No one would deny that we live in a world filled with injustice. Are Westerners giving a fair hearing to the grievances of the world's poor and downtrodden, who might just be using religion as a veneer over a real political injustice? These are the questions I will attempt to answer in this chapter. Although some of the concepts may be controversial, it must be remembered that there are many sides to any issue, and whenever conflict or injustice is perceived, passions will run very high.

What Is *Jihad?*

The word *jihad* literally means to struggle or strive or to work for something with determination. Although Westerners often assume it means holy war, that is not a correct translation of the Arabic term. The Arabic word for war is actually *harb*, and the word for fighting is *qital*, and neither is construed to be holy or religiously mandated. This is important to know because "making *jihad*" is any action done to further the cause of God no matter how great or small. Providing missionary services in a tough place, going to a far land to study, or even just donating money when it's a hardship can be a type of *jihad*. On the personal level, just trying to curb your undue desires for the forbidden pleasures of this world is considered a type of *jihad*.

However, the word *jihad* is most often associated with the act of physically confronting evil and wrongdoing; hence, it can be applied to the act of fighting as well. But the goal of a physical *jihad* is not to have a big war, gain riches, or kill people; it is to further the cause of Allah and to create justice on Earth. Then, when the evil is removed, or the other side wants peace, Muslims are to make peace as well.

The Qur'an explains for us the reasons why fighting is sometimes a part of *jihad*:

Translate This

Jihad in Arabic means to struggle or strive for something. It does not mean a holy war, as English dictionaries often mislabel it.

It Is Written

Muhammad said the following to some soldiers after they had left the battlefield victorious one day: "You have left the lesser *jihad*, now you are coming to the greater *jihad*. The struggle against yourself."

Let those fight in the Cause of God who sell the life of this world for the next life. To the one who fights in the Cause of God, whether he is killed or achieves victory, We shall soon give him a great reward. And why shouldn't you fight in the Cause of God and of those who, being weak, are mistreated; the men, women and children whose only cry is, "Our Lord! Save us from this land whose people are oppressors and bring to us from You someone who will protect us and bring to us from You someone who will help." Those who believe fight in the Cause of God, and those who reject faith fight in the cause of evil. So fight against the friends of Shaytan. (Qur'an 4:74–76)

Islamic civilization is not a society of vigilantes. It's a religion that teaches the rule of law. It's not up to anyone who feels like it to declare a military *jihad*. Although it seems everyone and their uncle is waving the term around these days, only an Islamic government or a recognized worldwide leader of Islam has the authority to declare a jihad. Neither one exists in the Muslim world right now. Instead, what you have is a large number of small groups, each claiming to uphold the mantle of authenticity. What is interesting to note, however, is that most of these groups arose in response to either a totalitarian regime or a specific attack or invasion from outside their country. Hamas did not exist before Israel was established, Al Qaeda developed from groups that arose during the Soviet invasion of Afghanistan, and the Moro rebels in the Southern Philippines grew as a response to colonialism from the Christian north of their nation. Thus, again we see political grievances being cloaked in the guise of religion. Just as Christians have used their religion as a cover for political agendas, so, too, do some Muslims. The key for the thinking person is not to blame the religion for what some people do. All religions teach good things, but not all who claim to follow their religion (or secular ideas) are good.

Jihad is one of the most misused words in the world today. It means to struggle in God's way. Obviously, planting bombs to harm civilians, flying planes into buildings, murdering captives or kidnapping tourists for ransom is not part of a Godly campaign for truth and justice. Muslims around the world are just as horrified as anyone else when a terrorist crime is perpetrated. We are doubly outraged when people try to attach a religious reason to their dastardly act, no matter which religion is being invoked. If someone does something in a way other than what God ordained, then it is a crime that the individual will have to answer for on the Day of Judgment.

Social Activism in Islam

There are many levels of *jihad*. An important part of our daily life as Muslims is to strive (or "make *jihad*") to improve society. Judaism has its concept of *Tikun Olam*, or perfecting the world, and many other religions have a similar idea. The key phrase guiding Muslims in social improvement campaigns comes from the Qur'an, which says that Muslims must "encourage the good while forbidding evil." Thus, Muslims must be active in the social affairs of any community they live in.

It Is Written

Whoever recommends and helps in a good cause becomes a partner in it. And whoever recommends and helps in an evil cause shares in its burdens and Allah has power over all things. (Qur'an 4:85)

Examples of activities that a Muslim must oppose, or struggle against, are …

♦ The selling of alcohol, pornography, and drugs.

♦ Littering and pollution.

♦ Public disputes that turn chaotic.

♦ Gossip or slander in the media.

♦ Corruption in government.

♦ Pedophilia or spousal abuse.

♦ Cruelty to animals.

These and many other vices are mentioned in Islam as sources of discord and injustice that must be opposed. What are the ways allowed by Islam to change things? An important saying of the Prophet Muhammad with regard to stopping vice is that if you see an evil deed you should try to correct it with your hand or your tongue, or at least feel bad about it in your heart if you think you can do nothing about it.

Islam is a proactive way of life, meaning we are taught to get involved and take action in the defense and promotion of the truth. Why should Muslims try to get involved in the welfare of the society around them? Quite simply because God said, "You are the best community brought out of humanity. You encourage what is right and forbid what is wrong and you believe in Allah." (Qur'an 3:110) That is quite a defining statement!

Muhammad once told an interesting parable to explain the importance of our participation in keeping sin out of our society. He said:

> The example of a person who follows God's orders and limits in comparison to the one who does wrong and violates God's limits and orders is like the example of people drawing lots for seats in a boat. Some of them got seats in the upper deck while the others went to the lower part.

> Those in the lower part of the ship had to pass through the people in the upper decks to get water, and that bothered the people up there. So one of [the people

from below] took an ax and started making a hole in the bottom of the boat. The people in the upper decks came and asked him, "What's the matter with you?"

He answered, "You keep getting bothered by my [passing through your deck] and I really need to get some water." Now if they stop him from doing that, they will save him and themselves. But if they leave him alone, they will destroy him and themselves.

It Is Written

You who Believe, stand up firmly for justice as witnesses before Allah and even [be a fair witness] against yourselves or your parents or your relatives also. And whether it's [against] the rich or poor, too, because Allah can protect both sides the best. Don't follow the lusts [of your hearts] lest you swerve and if you distort [the truth] or decline to do justice, Allah is aware of everything you do. (Qur'an 4:135)

In Arabic, the right or good way is called the *maroof*, and the evil or bad way is called the *munkar*. When we try to make our societies better and oppose evil, we make a safer and more orderly world to live in. Peace and security are the goals of civilization, and Islam gives us the definite prescription for achieving that condition and making it a reality.

What sorts of things should we try to encourage in our societies? Free medical care, aid to the poor and orphans, better schools, accountability in government, clean water and air, humane treatment of animals, and assistance for the elderly and handicapped are good things to start with. All of these have a good track record in classical Islamic civilization, where there was universal health care and free schools for all.

We will never have a perfect world. This life is not the place for perfection. But we can employ our hands, words, and feelings toward making it a better place than how we found it. This is the purpose of encouraging the right and forbidding the wrong in Islam. A person can't feel personally pious yet ignore the decline of morals in his or her own community.

Muhammad once told of an angel who was sent by God to destroy an iniquitous city. The angel was about to cause a natural disaster when he noticed something strange and rushed back to God. "Why haven't you carried out My order?" God asked. The angel reported, "I found one good man there who prays and fasts and praises You, though he keeps to himself and does nothing more." God said, "Then start with that one (destroy him)." Social reform is our duty, and a failure to make things better is tantamount to condoning vice and sin. In the teachings of Islam, *jihad* against the evils of society is just as important as *jihad* on the battlefield.

The Myth of the Holy War

I turned on the evening news to see what was happening in the world. The first report was about a terrorist group named the *Islamic Jihad Brigade*, which was threatening to plant bombs on planes. The second report was about *Muslim extremist* groups declaring a *jihad* against America. The final report was about *Islamic terrorism* against Israel and the new wave of suicide bombers. Any reasonable person might conclude that with the demise of the Soviet Union the next great enemy of freedom-loving people everywhere is Islam. This is an unfortunate conclusion because Islam is not the enemy of the West nor of the Judeo-Christian tradition. On the contrary, Islam is a cousin to the West, and its core values have more in common with modern international norms than most people realize. Why is there such a horrible misperception, then?

Translate This

A *shaheed* is a martyr for the cause of God. The person is guaranteed Paradise as a reward for his or her supreme sacrifice.

A Historical Misunderstanding

As is the case with many ancient prejudices and fears, history and its many twists and turns is the primary culprit for this misunderstanding about Islam. Europe's first encounter with Islam was through the eyes of the Byzantine Empire, which initiated hostilities against Muslims since Muhammad's time. This set the stage for an ongoing condition of hostility, which at times simmered down into a type of cold war. As Byzantine power waned in the eighth and ninth centuries, Muslim armies continued to bite off more and more territory. The Muslim advance stalled for a time, however, due to pressure from the invading Mongols in the thirteenth century, but with the conversion of the Turks to Islam a renewed campaign against the Byzantines was initiated.

So how did Western Europe get dragged into conflict with the Muslim world? Basically, the Catholic Church felt its interests in Jerusalem were being threatened (some Christian pilgrims were reporting interference from the Muslim authorities in the conduct of their rituals) and the Church also felt that a unified western alliance against Islam (under the leadership of the Pope) would reinforce Church influence and hegemony among the rebellious kings of Europe. Thus the era of the Crusades commenced in the year 1098 and introduced the concept among Westerners that the

Muslim world, and thus Islam, was their common foe. The forces of propaganda were quick to follow.

For most of the Middle Ages, Europeans painted an image of Islam that was designed to provoke fear and loathing in the minds of the populace, especially when the rulers were attempting to drum up support for the various Crusades that issued from Europe from time to time until the year 1291. The *Saracens* and the *Turks* (two derogatory European terms for Muslims) were viewed as minions of the Devil whose only desire was to enslave and bring on the worship of Satan. In his book *The Life of Mohammed*, Emile Deir Mongem writes:

> When the war blazed up between Islam and Christianity ... each side misunderstood the other one. It should be admitted, however, that the basic misunderstanding was more on the part of westerners than the easterners ....
> argumentative debaters overloaded Islam with vices, degradation, and abasement without taking the trouble to study it ... (quoted in *The Spirit of Islam* by Afif Tabbarah, page 9, 1978).

Just the Facts _____

Osama bin Laden, along with many of his top henchmen, made it an ongoing habit to issue *fatwas*, or religious verdicts, in which they declared any American could be killed, equating all Americans with being the enemies of Islam. This type of blanket condemnation is so out-of-bounds according to the dictates of traditional Islamic legal theory that even the Taliban issued a public statement in 2000 that bin Laden was not qualified to issue religious verdicts. Obviously, no Muslim government or recognized Islamic organization paid any attention to the ravings of the bin Laden crew.

The nineteenth-century orientalist, Count Henri de Castri goes even further when he comments on the practice of "mercenary poets" and paid storytellers who traveled Europe inciting hatred and misinformation against Islam. "Out of total ignorance of Islam, these songs were charged with hatred against Moslems ... and inculcated such mistaken views in the minds of Christians, even to our present day. Every singer used to consider Moslems as polytheists, disbelievers, and disobedient idolaters." The campaign of anti-Islamic slander was so successful that to this day some textbooks in European and American schools refer to Muhammad as having *epilepsy*, the Qur'an as being copied from the Bible, Muslim armies as forcing conversions on people (by the sword), and Islam as being against science and learning. All of these things are quite untrue, and enlightened Western authors from Arnold Toynbee and Bertrand Russell to Yvonne Haddad and John Esposito have been dispelling these myths in book after book for decades; nevertheless, the message hasn't reached the masses, who still believe numerous false myths concerning Islam.

When Europeans succeeded in occupying virtually the entire Muslim world during the era of Colonialism, they considered their victory over Islam complete. The occupiers closed Islamic schools and colleges all over the Muslim world, arrested and killed religious leaders, disenfranchised the population, and installed as rulers Western-educated natives who were completely dependent on their European masters. But with the end of Colonialism in the mid-1960s, European fears about the return of Islamic power have caused another round of hysteria to grip the Western world.

Virtually all Muslims now feel that the modern Western media have taken on the role of the mercenary poets of the past: presenting an overly negative view of Islam or unfairly connecting violent events with it. They feel that political or regional conflicts are seen only through the eyes of religion, and Islam is blamed for anything that happens. This is unfortunate, because the roots of nearly every conflict in the Muslim world, whether it is the breakup of the former Yugoslavia and its wars, the anti-Muslim riots perpetuated by Hindus in India, the friction between Christians and Jews in Nigeria, the Arab-Israeli conflict, or the existence of rebel groups in places as far flung as the Philippines or Chechnya, are directly related to the meddling of the Europeans in those lands.

As far as Muslim leadership goes, it gets even worse, for sometimes people with Muslim-sounding names will be given an overwhelming amount of exposure when they talk about *jihad,* even when they don't fully adhere to Islamic principles to begin with. For example, after extensively reconstructing the activities and movements of the nineteen hijackers who carried out the September 11th attacks in New York and Washington, it has come to light that some of them had girlfriends or spent time in illicit strip clubs or engaged in otherwise unIslamic behavior. Muslims, among themselves, wondered at the apparent contradictions. On a more international level, Islam forbids dealing in interest money, yet even such supposedly *Islamic* Republics as Iran, Pakistan, and the Sudan routinely engage in this type of activity in their annual budgets and purchases. Clearly many people reference religion only when it suits their interests, so claims to speaking in the name of any religion by anyone must be taken with a grain of salt.

Take the case of Osama bin Laden, who is universally recognized as the mastermind of a network of violent terrorists. After several high-profile terrorist attacks, most notably the attack on the World Trade Center in New York on September 11, 2001, Western media sources aired footage of the one-time Saudi entrepreneur issuing Islamic religious decrees to justify what he had done. Even though Muslims in general were horrified at the brutality of the attack, the false link was made that *terrorism equals Islam.*

Within a day of the attacks Muslim organizations worldwide began issuing condemnations of the heinous and cowardly attack, but these were not aired extensively by the media, so to this day the myth exists that Muslim groups did not speak out against Al Qaeda and its skewed ideology. Oh, by the way, CNN did air footage of people in the Middle East celebrating and cheering the attacks, but it came to light later that that was archived footage that was filmed years before connected to something else. Understandably, Muslims ask the question: What agenda is the media promoting?

A False Alarm

After the United States Federal Building in Oklahoma City, Oklahoma, was bombed in 1995, several mosques were burnt down, Muslim homes were vandalized, and the FBI and the news media were fingering Muslims as the responsible party. They even made all Muslims seem as if they were somehow guilty of some great conspiracy! Then, when the nation found out that it was a white Christian man who did the bombing, did the media apologize to Muslims? Were churches burnt down or pastors deported? Of course not!

All Muslims are asking for is to be treated in a fair manner, as the adherents of other religions are. If a deranged person commits a crime, it doesn't matter what the person's name is, where he or she was born, or what religion the person ascribes to; a crime is a crime and is condemned by all spiritual people, Muslims included. This is an issue that Muslims feel strongly about because it affects them inside as well as outside their community. Indeed, after September 11, average Muslim Americans suddenly found themselves the victims of an alarming number of hate crimes. Children in schools were bullied, people with Muslim-sounding names were attacked, even those who appeared even slightly Middle Eastern such as Sikhs (a small religious group from India in which men are required to wear turbans) were set upon, denied services, arrested, and harassed.

In addition to the alarming crime statistics compiled by the FBI and local law enforcement agencies, Muslims found that political, social, and religious leaders all over the United States began to mount an extremely bigoted and prejudicial campaign against all things Muslim and Islamic. Many people had thought that America, as the leader of the civilized world, would have been beyond group scapegoating and irrational fear mongering, but as Muslims found out, this was not the case. The laws that were enacted immediately after September 11, 2001, also were very discriminatory and downright un-American in nature. Among the more serious indignities that Muslims were told to swallow are the following:

◆ Muslim immigrants specifically were required to register with the Immigration and Naturalization Services (INS) in a special program whose very inception had the underlying message that America didn't trust Muslims from any nation. To make matters worse, many thousands of such voluntary registrants were detained by the INS and eventually deported for minor immigration violations.

◆ Airline flight security has become blatantly laced with racial and religious profiling to the point where Muslims have become apprehensive about using airlines because they fear that anyone with a Muslim name or Muslim attire will be stopped and forced to endure a humiliating search.

◆ A program adopted in late 2002 and implemented in 2003 required all visitors to the United States, mainly from Muslim countries, to be fingerprinted and forced to undergo a much more invasive interview and tracking process than was ever implemented before. It has since been amended to cover a wider range of countries but the initial emphasis on mainly Muslim nations was troubling.

◆ The USA Patriot Act and various other pieces of anti-terrorism legislation enacted in 2002 and 2003 have put at risk the guarantees of constitutional due process and rights to be protected from unreasonable searches and seizures. Muslims feel they have borne the brunt of their far-reaching effects.

Were any of these or similar legal restrictions and biases directed toward the members of any other ethnic or religious group there would have been howls of protest in the halls of Congress. African Americans fought to be freed from discrimination based on their skin color (and the negative connotations that white America had of them) culminating in the Civil Rights movement in the Sixties. Japanese Americans, who suffered great indignities during World War II have only recently gained an official recognition of their suffering from the U.S. government, and Hispanics are still actively fighting against group discrimination, an anti-Catholic bias, and prejudicial treatment in labor laws. Muslim Americans are now only beginning to demand that they be treated as rightful citizens and not to be pigeon-holed and stereotyped based on the actions of a tiny sliver of extremists. Doesn't the promise of America offer better?

Islam on War

What is the position of Islam on war and conflict? Peace on Earth is, of course, the ideal that the world of Islam works toward, and war is abhorred as the last, worst option. However, there are times when there is no alternative but to fight. Every society has its own views about a just war. What do Muslims believe is worth fighting for? According to Islamic Law, an armed struggle can be initiated only for the following three reasons:

♦ To defend your community or nation from aggressors

♦ To liberate people living under oppressive regimes

♦ To remove any government that will not allow the free practice of Islam within its borders

The first two reasons are easy to understand. The third would be necessary if, for example, a country forbade the practice of Islam or its preaching. Obviously from the Qur'an's perspective, such a country is attempting to stop God's religion from being preached. Interestingly enough, Islam does not give people the right to declare a war vigilante style. A group of disgruntled people in country X, for example, doesn't have the sanction to start an armed struggle in the name of Islam, even if they have legitimate grievances. The power to declare war rests only with the properly chosen authorities in an Islamic state (elected by the majority, confirmed and accountable). The leader of the entire Muslim community is the only one who can ask Muslims to enlist in the army and fight in a just war, not someone with a big name or an inflated sense of importance.

> ### Ask the Imam
>
> Muslims who are living in non-Muslim societies are bound by Islamic Law to live peacefully with their neighbors so long as no injustice is being done to anyone. Crime and vice must be opposed regardless.

At the same time, an individual Muslim is not authorized by Islamic Law to tell his followers to go and fight, because the main principle of Islamic governance is mutual consultation, known as *Shura*. Nobody can make a big decision without all of the governmental representatives discussing it first. This is sort of like the Islamic House of Representatives. Given that there is no worldwide Islamic government or forum where political issues can be discussed, rather than declaring *jihad* all over the world, the proper goal of sincere activist Muslims must be the establishment of a political structure acceptable to all Muslims first. In other words, there is no authentic Islamic State right now based on tolerance and justice, so who are these groups looking for enemies in other parts of the world? They should concentrate on their own backyard before peeking into someone else's. Looked at in this light, we can see that most of the Muslim groups in the world engaging in armed struggle have no more legitimacy in Islamic Law than the Crusaders had when they invaded and sacked the city of Constantinople, which was a *Christian* city!

Muslims are actually divided about supporting most of these armed groups for this very reason. They often support the objectives but feel queasy about the methods and the insular ideologies of the participants. The worldwide Muslim community is in somewhat of an awkward position because there is currently no Islamic government functioning today. No, not even Afghanistan or Iran is considered to be adhering to traditional Islamic Law by most of the world's Muslims. So there is no official agency to police the activities of would-be vigilantes or at least provide an authoritative ruling on the legality of their actions.

To get a better sense of what this means, suppose that next year the Catholic Church in Rome is overthrown and the office of Pope is abolished. Then, as the decades progress, you find Catholic populations becoming distinct from each other to the point that they consider other Catholic groups to be heretics. Compound this with nationalistic wars, upheavals, and the rise of totalitarian governments in some Catholic regions. Would some rebel (or freedom) groups arise that used methods of warfare that were against what original Catholicism taught? Undoubtedly, but who would be there to rein them in or at least set the record straight—other competing Catholic factions? This is the situation in the Muslim world right now.

What Makes a Terrorist?

The bitter Arab/Israeli conflict in the Middle East has caused four wars and countless strikes and counterstrikes by both sides. One tactic that has recently become the favored method of resistance by Palestinians fighting to be free of Israeli control (and that gets a lot of media attention) is the use of suicide bombers who often target buses and other public places. Before I address the Islamic position on such actions, I will shed some light on the motivation of the people who do these things. After all, nobody gets out of bed one day and says, "I want to bomb a bus." Keep in mind, Islam does not justify the acts of terrorism committed by people who are driven by passion more than spiritual ideals. I just want to explain what drives some people to violence.

Imagine you are living under the military occupation of a foreign army. Then one day a unit of their soldiers comes and forces your family out of your home at gunpoint and tells you to leave forever because their God gave this land to them. With just the clothes on your back, you and your parents and siblings are thrown out with nowhere to go. You wind up in a makeshift shelter on some barren hills and have to scratch for your sustenance. Your mother is always crying. Your father is frail and looks hopeless, and your siblings are cold and scared, every day. Many other people in similar circumstances join you. Their homes and farms were appropriated, as well. There is no running water, and there are no sewers, no electricity, no schools, and no doctors to help you. Imagine living in such conditions for decades and growing up in squalor.

Then think of how you would feel if you were not allowed to leave your squalid camp without showing an identity card to the soldiers who surround your miserable tin-roof town. The humiliation would be overwhelming.

The only jobs you can find are working in lands that were seized from your parents years before. You labor in the fields and look at the shiny new houses built on the land that had been in your family for generations. The people who live there were born in Europe or elsewhere and have taken your land with no other excuse than, "God gave it to us." You are a second-class citizen with no citizenship rights. Perhaps you join with some of your friends and decide to fight back to regain your land. The soldiers, however, are equipped with tanks and machine guns while all you have are stones or small arms. You lob rocks at the checkpoints in frustration while the soldiers gun down your friends mercilessly. If you get arrested, you're sent to a prison where you are legally tortured and held without trial for years.

> **It Is Written**
>
> A person came to the Prophet Muhammad and asked, "A man fights for treasure, another for fame, and a third for bravery. Whose fighting is for the Cause of God?" The Blessed Prophet answered, "The one who fights so that the Word of God becomes supreme, his fight is for God."

Meanwhile, your baby sister has died because of malnutrition, your uncle's land was recently seized, your cousin's house was bulldozed to the ground, the ramshackle schools are sealed shut, and chances for any kind of future look grim. The soldiers laugh at you, and you see on the side of supply boxes in the prison storeroom the words "Made in America." Your anger at the soldiers and their people is so great that you begin to transfer some of it to those who are supporting them. You don't have an army to fight the invaders; you don't have any hope of organized resistance. Then you think about how to exact retribution, and individual acts of violence such as bombings come to mind. Thus, a terrorist is born. But in his eyes, the real terror was done against him and his people first. He is merely striking back.

From the southern Philippines to Chechnya in Russia, people are taking up arms to right the wrongs that they perceive have been done to them. Given that there are no Islamic governments, it has been left largely up to local people to defend themselves. They find sanction for their choice in the words of the Qur'an: "And those who, when they are oppressed wrongly, help and defend themselves." (Qur'an 42:39) But due to the lack of guidance in the proper conduct of war in Islam, excesses and misguided approaches are often the tools of choice for drawing attention to their cause. Combine this with a sense of abject hopelessness, such as that felt by the Palestinians, and you can see how a few can be duped into becoming suicide bombers with promises of heavenly virgins and the like. With nothing left to live for they come to desire release (and to take as many of their oppressors with them as they can).

Islam and Terrorism

What does Islam say about the kinds of actions such angry young men and women carry out? Try to understand that, first of all, no matter what they say, Islam is often not in the forefront of these people's minds. They feel that they have been wronged and they are looking for revenge. If they shout, "Allah is Great," or give their clandestine groups names that refer to Islamic themes, it is oftentimes more of a veneer than a true orientation. Adolf Hitler and the Nazis sometimes used references to Christianity to justify hostility to the Jews. Slave owners in America repeatedly justified slavery with the excuse that they were Christianizing the blacks, and Hindu fundamentalists in India claim that their attacks on mosques are designed to bring Indian Muslims back to their true religion: Hinduism. People misuse religion quite often, and Islam is misused as much as any other faith.

Just the Facts

Muhammad forbade harming women, children, old people, laborers, people who are not fighting, prisoners, those who surrender, plants (farmlands), and animals. He allowed Muslim soldiers to fight only the soldiers of the other side.

The Rules of War

The rules for the conduct of war in Islam forbid the killing of noncombatants. The Prophet Muhammad never allowed any Muslim soldier to harm women, children, or the innocent. The trouble with bombing a bus or marketplace is that soldiers are not the ones who are killed. Thus, the people who engage in this type of attack are going against the teachings of Islam. According to the Qur'an, "If you kill a life unjustly it is as if you killed all life." (Qur'an 5:32) Suicide bombers are also guilty of ignoring Islamic teachings, because suicide is forbidden in Islam. The Prophet Muhammad said, "Whoever kills himself with a weapon will have that weapon in his hand, and will kill himself forever in the fire of Hell," and yet this is exactly what these people do when they detonate bombs strapped to their bodies. Are there some religious leaders in that part of the world who condone these actions? Yes, there are, but remember that they, too, have been shaped by the same sense of injustice as the rest of the people there. Muslim scholars in other parts of the world condemn these actions as being against the letter and the spirit of the religion.

So we can say that there is no such thing as terrorism allowed in Islam and that people who are attempting to get revenge for injustices done to them are mislabeling their fights as religious in nature. Muslims all over the world affirm this thesis, though it seems sometimes that the only people who are featured in the Western media are those who engage in spectacular acts of savagery and mayhem, such as the insurgents in Iraq who are, as of this writing, engaged in a struggle with American occupation forces. Their struggle is for regaining their independence; it is not about teaching people about religious or moral values.

Harming innocents is forbidden in Islam, so those who engage in activities designed to kill as many people as possible cannot rightly call upon religion to justify their actions. Be that as it may, as I noted above there are some misguided Muslims with legitimate grievances who seem to do everything in the world to make themselves, and Islam, look bad in their pursuit of redress. They say they are *doing jihad;* however, in reality they often break all the rules for carrying out one. Even as Christianity and Judaism have sometimes been wrongfully used to justify the actions of extremists, a small minority of Muslims is doing the same with Islam. The overwhelming majority of Muslims do not support, condone, or engage in such reprehensible acts.

The Least You Need to Know

- Stereotypes of Islam as a violent religion began in the Middle Ages and have persisted into modern times.

- *Jihad* does not mean holy war. It means any exertion in the cause of God.

- *Jihad* is the term usually used to describe a war fought for God's sake; however, even going to school can be a kind of *jihad.*

- Any war for conquest or glory is forbidden in Islam.

- Terrorism is forbidden in Islam, and the actions of people who engage in it and use Islamic slogans are not sanctioned by Islamic teachings.

- Islam has a strong tradition of social activism, and the Qur'an calls on Muslims to oppose vice by working for the welfare of their fellow human beings. Such a struggle is also considered a *jihad.*

Part 4

Islam and Other Religions

In a multireligious world there are bound to be numerous bumps on the road as each religion interacts with another. Islam, as taught by the Prophet Muhammad in the seventh century, existed in a land where idolatry, Christianity, Judaism, Zoroastrianism, and mysticism coexisted. As a result there is a clear track record of relations among all the faiths from Islam's earliest days. This helps Muslims understand multiculturalism and differing religious beliefs and makes us tolerant and accepting of other people's deeply felt convictions.

Although idolatry is generally frowned upon in the Qur'an, Judaism and Christianity have a special status in Islam. Muslims call the followers of each of these two great monotheistic religions "People of the Book." This is a respectful reference to our belief that in the past God revealed His message to prophets whose later followers crafted those two religions. The Prophet Muhammad had both Jewish and Christian acquaintances and always taught Muslims to be respectful and upright toward the sincere adherents of these faiths. In this part, I will explore the relationship between Islam, Christianity, and Judaism in great detail.

15

It's All in the Prophets

In This Chapter

◆ Learn what Islam says about prophets and revelation from God

◆ Find out how Islam describes the major biblical prophets

◆ Discover how Islam views other religions

◆ Understand how Muslims view the Bible

Islam is a faith whose legitimacy lies in the idea that all true religion is part of a historical cycle. Islam asserts that it is nothing less than a continuation of the message given to previous prophets. All prophets taught the same core beliefs, declares the Qur'an, and thus the followers of previously revealed religions must be respected on a certain level. Furthermore, the Qur'an contains the stories of many prophets that are also mentioned in the Bible. These stories, however, are not told in the same manner, and important differences do exist.

Jews and Christians are often mentioned in the Qur'an as people who have received God's guidance in the past. The trials, triumphs, and perceived failures of both of those communities are presented as lessons for Muslims to learn from. Given that Islam teaches that every nation received a prophet from God, a complementary component of this ideology is that all people are equal, regardless of race or color, and are endowed with a standard foundation of human rights that must be respected. As you will see, this intertwining of prophetic history and humanistic values creates a very interesting worldview for the practitioner of Islam.

All Prophets Are Brothers

Any student of world religions soon comes upon a startling discovery: The precepts, beliefs, and practices of all the major religions have an identifiable commonality to them. Judaism teaches its practitioners to pray, as does Hinduism. Islam asks its followers not to harm animals senselessly, as does Buddhism. Christianity orders its adherents to show compassion toward the sick, and so does Zoroastrianism. When a person realizes the incredible similarities in all religions, what should he or she do about it? Would it be prudent then to say that all religions are equal? Islam would answer in the negative, but before I discuss that, let's look at what a few modern researchers have theorized about religion and its origins.

Many thinkers have tried to assert that religion is nothing more than a man-made system for keeping social cohesion. Authorities from diverse disciplines such as Sigmund Freud (psychology), Margaret Mead (anthropology), and Carl Sagan (astronomy) have echoed this view. Under this theory, when emerging human communities needed a way to get people to cooperate, they began calling upon nonexistent gods and spirits that could punish the recalcitrant members of the group if they didn't comply. Other researchers have even postulated that religion was the invention of people who were frightened of the world around them and needed to feel that they had allies in a world full of supernatural phenomena. They cite the proliferation of anthropomorphic gods such as the many river gods, mountain gods, or animal gods found throughout the world.

Although these arguments are interesting and with some merit, at the same time they fail to answer certain fundamental issues that Muslims would assert are evidence for the existence of a higher power. The first issue revolves around the human mind. Recent studies into human psychology have found that people who practice some form of religion are generally more peaceful and freer from worry. They even tend to live longer! If faith increases longevity, well-being, and the general mental condition, then there must be some component in our makeup that either requires it or thrives upon it.

Second, mere mechanical processes cannot explain the existence of a universally accepted standard of right and wrong. Morality and evil are purely human concepts. One doesn't find an emphasis on virtue in the animal kingdom. If the Darwinian survival of the fittest is the way in which life continually develops, then *morality* and *compassion* would actually hold back the strongest from acquiring ever-greater resources and the best mating opportunities. But the very fact that religion has laid a foundation for personal conduct that goes against the basic principles of natural selection is proof that there must be a unique source for our belief in the concept of right and wrong. Muslims would say that God placed a *fitrah*, or natural inclination within us, as part of our innate constitution. In other words, we were born with a conscience.

Just the Facts

The British philosopher Sir Francis Bacon once observed, "A little philosophy brings a man to atheism; diving deep into it brings him back to faith."

The third issue concerns the main features of religion itself. Every religion on Earth has a set of very similar precepts. Whether it is a local tribal religion or a widespread tradition, the core values seem consistent, giving rise to the theory that all religion is, in fact, from a singular source. All religions teach that stealing, adultery, lying, cheating, and murder are wrong. Each also has some form of self-denial rituals to teach enlightenment, prayer methods for communicating with the higher power, and either an oral or a written tradition that is passed on through the generations. The evidence would suggest that the scattered peoples of the world had a single source for most of what they believe.

It Is Written

We raised in every nation a Messenger, saying: "Serve God and keep away from falsehood." After that, God guided some of them while deviation proved true against the others. So travel through the earth and see what was the end of those who denied Our Message. (Qur'an 16:36)

There are other issues that could be explored, but my main focus here is on the multitude of related ideas and the continuity of concepts found in world religions collectively. But there are, to be fair, many major differences among religions as well. This brings me to the question: Why are there so many religions in the world that are similar and different at the same time? What does Islam say about this phenomenon? Islam's answer is straightforward and clear: All revealed religions began with a true prophet from God. People's alterations over time have caused the introduction of varied practices and rituals that may not have any relationship to what their ancient prophet actually taught.

Will the Real Prophet Please Stand Up?

Everything in the material world has a beginning. Likewise, every religion has a main figure who first started to teach it. Islam calls such people prophets and messengers. Whereas some would assert that these people made up their own religious beliefs and promulgated them, Islam would say that all of those founders were really just relaying a message from the same source: God.

The Qur'an puts it this way:

> O Muhammad, We have sent revelations to you just as We sent them to Noah and the Prophets who came after him; We also sent revelations to Abraham, Ishmael, Isaac, Jacob, his descendants, and to Jesus, Job, Jonah, Aaron and Solomon. We revealed the Psalms to David. Revelations were also sent to those Messengers whom We have already mentioned to you and to those whose name We have not mentioned to you, and God spoke to Moses directly. All these Messengers conveyed good news to mankind and admonished them so that, after conveying the message through the Messengers, people would have no excuse to plead against God. Indeed, God is the Mighty, the Wise. (Qur'an 4:163–165)

So Islam accepts all true prophets from God whether He told us their name in the Qur'an or not. Muslims are asked to be tolerant of the religions of other people for this very reason. Upon learning of a different religion, our basic attitude is one of inquiry, not prejudice. Who was its prophet? Was he an authentic prophet from God or a charlatan? What does this other religion have in common with Islam?

Islam recognizes that there is a great diversity of religious expression in the world. To set up every religion as equal with its peers and then to judge them would not be fair. Are there concocted religions? Undoubtedly there are, but at the same time there are other spiritual traditions whose origins are harder to explain. What has sustained Judaism or Buddhism or any of the other major religions for thousands of years? Each religion must be judged on its own merits, not on the sophistication, excesses, or shortcomings of others.

Ask the Imam
Islam does not accept as valid any religion founded between the time of Jesus and Muhammad nor any religion founded since Muhammad.

When Muslims try to identify a potential prophet in a religion they have just encountered, they must first ask several questions. The first question is this: Was the religion founded between the time of Adam and

Muhammad? This is an important question because the Qur'an calls Muhammad the seal and last Prophet to the world. If the religion was founded after the time of Muhammad, then Islam says it is a false religion. To be even more accurate, we find that Prophet Muhammad said, "There were no Prophets sent to the world between Jesus and I." By this stricter definition, any religion, other than Islam, can be preliminarily true only if its founder lived before the removal of Jesus from the world. So the cutoff date for a religion's validity is about 33 C.E., with Islam coming later (in 610 C.E.).

The second question is what did that founding person teach? This is where a little deeper investigation is necessary. Through the use of whatever old records are available, a survey of current practices and their consistency can be conducted. Finally, a thorough comparison with other related religions can help to sweep away centuries of accretions, exposing a more accurate picture of what the ancient ideals were. For example, Buddhism as it is practiced in China is a synthesis of the core principles of Buddhism with folklore, ancestor worship, superstition, and popular myth. When you strip away the baggage, however, you find a religious message not all that dissimilar from Islam. Some Muslim scholars, who have undertaken such a survey, are of the opinion that Buddha might even have been a prophet of God whose teachings became altered through the centuries.

The famed Akbar, who ruled in India during the Mughal period, used to preside over regular interfaith dialogues in which Muslims, Jews, Buddhists, Christians, and Hindus took part.

Other Muslim scholars have attempted to show that Socrates, Lao-Tzu, Hammurabi, and Zoroaster were prophets of God acceptable to Islam. While these theories cannot really be proven with available data, it is interesting to get a peek into how the world of Islam tries to make sense of and integrate the founders of other religions into its own milieu. None of this influences Islamic teachings, however, which are forever enshrined in the Qur'an and in the sayings of Muhammad. This process does serve to accentuate the strain of tolerance inherent in Islamic philosophy, though. If all true religion is from God, then all prophets must be brothers. How can a Muslim discriminate against a follower of another religion?

Introducing the Prophets in Islam

When God banished Adam and Eve from the garden, He said that people would live in hatred and rivalry on the Earth. *Shaytan*, along with our animal desires, would factor greatly in that prophecy. According to Islam, Adam was the first prophet in the world. He has this title because he taught his descendants to love God and loathe the influences of the Devil. As generations marched by, and *Shaytan* attempted to corrupt them, God raised up new prophets to teach people the right way to live again.

In those remote times, the major sins of men and women were not that they disbelieved in God, but that they fell prey to anger and hatred and false ideas. The Qur'an says, "All People were once a single nation; later on they became divided after inventing different lifestyles." (Qur'an 10:19)

> **Ask the Imam**
>
> How does Islam view the mythology prevalent in many societies, such as Greek or Roman mythology? Generally the idea of man gods and fantastic creatures is rejected, being equated with idolatry. With that said, a Muslim must also be reserved in their judgment and ask if perhaps there might be some strands of authentic religious teachings woven into the stories.

The greatest triumph of *Shaytan*, however, was in eventually goading people into worshipping idols instead of God. By working to get people to reject the guidance of God completely, *Shaytan* hoped to counteract the prophecy God gave to Adam and Eve that He would send prophets to guide their descendants. According to Islam, *Shaytan* thought if no one believed in God, no one would listen to His prophets.

How and when did he succeed in doing this? The Prophet Muhammad explained that in the generations prior to the Prophet Noah, there lived five great heroes whose deeds and reputations were known far and wide. When they died, the next generation decided to erect statues of those men to honor them. A few decades later, *Shaytan* implanted the idea into people's thoughts that their fathers actually worshipped these statues and thus veneration of false gods began. This is the Islamic explanation for the origin of idolatry.

From then on, the struggle between God's prophets and the misguided notions of people would be a conflict wrought with violence and great confusion. But God never sent any angels or supernatural creatures to Earth to show people that His power was real. The test would be compromised if God showed His hand too early. Islam teaches that all prophets were plain human beings with no magical qualities or abilities in themselves. The Qur'an explains it this way: "We didn't send any Messengers before you except that they were people whom We inspired. They lived in human communities." (Qur'an 12:109)

> **Ask the Imam**
>
> Christians take the miracles of Jesus as proof that he is the son of God. Muslims believe that God can grant the power to perform miracles to anyone, yet it does not make them into a god.

Sometimes God would grant miracles to these prophets to give the faithless people a chance to reflect. Many of the miracles mentioned as gifts to the prophets in the Bible are also mentioned in the Qur'an. Moses had a staff that turned into a snake. Jesus could heal people. Solomon, according to the Qur'an, could control the *jinns* and understand the languages of animals. But the usual reaction of people to these miracles was often skepticism. People generally didn't believe in what their prophets brought. On one level this attitude is understandable; after all, if a man came to you and said he was a prophet, would you believe him? Probably not.

The Qur'an even comments on people's usual reactions to one of their own claiming prophethood:

> **Ask the Imam**
>
> Muhammad performed several miracles during his ministry. Although they were not as numerous as the miracles granted to Jesus, Muhammad is credited with healing and other such miraculous acts. He always asserted, however, that his greatest miracle was the Qur'an itself.

> Do people find it incredible that We send Our inspiration to a man from among themselves? That he should warn humanity [of the danger of evil] and give good news to the believers that they are held in high esteem in truth before their Lord. The Truth-Hiders just say, "This [revelation he brings] is evidently clear sorcery!" (Qur'an 10:2)

However, prophets were no ordinary men. They had logic and reasoning that could not be explained or denied if given a fair hearing. What would cause people to oppose someone like that? Love for material wealth, sin, or decadence could be definitive factors, for along with bringing a spiritual message, the Qur'an notes that the prophets also brought a message of social reform and personal accountability for one's own behavior. People were asked to change their lives but were prone to resist.

Ask the Imam

Islam teaches that all prophets were sent to their local people only. Muhammad's message, though, was meant not only for the Arabs, but also for the whole world. This idea is affirmed in several passages in the Qur'an.

The basic theme in Qur'anic stories is that people just won't listen, no matter what signs are given them. They have become focused on gods of their own making and don't want to change their lifestyles. They're even willing to resort to violence to protect their unjust ways. The Qur'an charges that "... if you were to dig a tunnel in the earth or raise a ladder into the sky and bring them a sign [they still wouldn't be convinced]." In another place it quotes people as doubting miracles and prophecies by saying, "It's nothing more than magic." For all his many miracles, even Jesus' disciples doubted him sometimes.

Looking at the Characteristics of the Prophets

Many Western scholars have a misconception about the mission of prophets in Islam. They often write that in Islam a prophet is not allowed to fail, so the Qur'an paints a rosy picture of success for God's messengers. This is simply not true. The Qur'an contains several references to prophets who failed to convince their people and even to prophets who were killed by their own communities. It's not that a prophet cannot fail; rather, sometimes people are so obstinate that no amount of convincing will get them to leave their evil ways. The excuse that the Qur'an records as having the least merit but the greatest use is, "We found our parents doing it, so we will do it, too." Then the Qur'an adds, "What! Even though they had no sense or guidance!"

The Qur'an contains many different types of prophetic stories. There are stories of prophets who convinced the poor to follow them but who were attacked by the rich. Other prophets are presented as rulers or kings who worked to guide their nation, whereas others are portrayed as men with struggles in their soul and doubts about what they were doing. It is interesting to note here that the Qur'an often uses these different themes to convince people that Muhammad is also an authentic prophet and is undergoing some of the same trials that previous prophets went through.

Abraham and Muhammad

Are there any qualities that would make God choose a person to be a prophet? You bet there are. In general, people who were given a revelation from God were moral individuals who sought out God with earnest hearts. The Prophet Abraham is portrayed in the Qur'an as searching for God amid an idolatrous society even from childhood. His own father was a maker of idols, so Abraham grew up seeing his dad carving faces in stone and thus understood from an early age that the idols were man-made in the worst sense.

One beautiful passage of the Qur'an has Abraham seeing the stars and praying to them as gods. When they set in the late night, he realizes that they were just heavenly bodies, so he turns to the moon next and finally to the morning sun, thinking each must have been God. When they each set in turn, he realizes that God cannot be found in natural phenomena. A heavenly body is no more a god than a carved idol. Later God revealed his message to the young man, and a prophet was born.

Muhammad also had a unique experience. His father died before he was born, and his mother passed away when he was less than six years old. He was cared for first by his grandfather and then by his uncle. Being an orphan, he was not treated with any special dignity or deference and thus grew up feeling very humble. His mother had sent him to a foster mother in the countryside as a toddler, as was the custom in those days. Here he could learn rural values, which fostered thrift and good character. Because of his time there, Muhammad had better manners than most other children in Mecca. When he was a teenager, he was given the job of tending sheep in the pastures. This gave him a lot of time to think. He developed a reputation for honesty and trustworthiness and never acquired a taste for idol worship. These qualities led him to look for God.

So, if the people selected by God to be His prophets were basically good and introspective before receiving their commission, how did they act after becoming God's elect? Did they ever sin? This is where Islam parts ways with the Jewish and Christian concept of prophethood. Whereas the Bible often makes the

Just the Facts

The Qur'an contains a chapter that starts off by scolding Muhammad for ignoring an old blind man who interrupted him while he was trying to convince a Meccan noble about the merits of Islam. This is an example of an unintentional error in judgment committed by a sinless prophet.

prophets appear sinful and weak, Islam holds that all prophets were *sinless*. What does this mean? Were they demigods? No, they were still men open to human frailties. Sinless doesn't mean *perfect*. It doesn't mean that they didn't make mistakes or errors in judgment on temporal matters. What it signifies is that all persons chosen to be prophets had their records cleared, their hearts purified by God, and thereafter never intentionally did any immoral action again.

Prophethood Is a Men's Club, but Revelation Is Equal

This brings us to the gender issue. In Islam, all prophets and messengers are said to be men. In this, Muslim belief is no different than Judaism. The standard reasons given for this seeming gender discrimination are that …

◆ Men are generally physically stronger, and oftentimes prophets were tortured, starved, or attacked or had to fight in wars.

◆ Men are not burdened with certain functions that make women ritually impure at certain times. Prophets are expected to lead their followers in prayer on a daily basis and receive revelation from the angel Gabriel at a moment's notice. Menstruation (*haidh*) invalidates a ritually pure state (known as *taharah*). Unlike Judaism, however, there is no social stigma for women who are menstruating.

But Islam has a saving grace for the status of women on this issue. Although none of the prophets were females, the Qur'an opens the door to women having received revelation from God. This is akin to the Christian belief that men and women can prophesize. The Qur'an mentions two women in particular who received direct revelation from the Creator. One was the mother of Moses, who received several messages; and the other was Mary, the mother of Jesus, whom an angel visited with direct instructions from God. The Qur'an also mentions the names of several men who received revelations but who were not prophets, such as Khidr and an African sage named *Luqman*. So, taken in that light, the numbers of men and women who received revelations from God, but who were not prophets, could be in the thousands or more.

Prophets on Judgment Day

All prophets will die and be judged on Judgment Day. They don't have to worry about going to Hell, of course, but they will still get a cursory review. Their main job on that momentous day, however, will be as a witness against their followers. People will claim all sorts of false ideas, and even ascribe them to their religion, but their prophet will reject the charges and make it clear what he really stood for.

Islam also teaches that one prophet hasn't died yet. That is the Prophet Jesus. He was saved from being crucified by the Romans and was taken by God to Paradise to live until the end of time. When he is returned to Earth to fight the anti-Christ, otherwise known as the *Dajjal*, he will then marry, have children, live out the rest of his natural life, and die. The Qur'an says, "Every soul shall taste of death." The Qur'an makes no mention of any prophet being carried to Heaven on a flaming chariot, as the Old Testament of the Bible does with Elisha. To travel the highway to the next life and remain, everyone will have to die first.

The Books of God

Islam accepts that written revelations given by God existed before the time of the Qur'an. As you learned in Chapter 9, there are two types of prophets: regular prophets who received prophecies, and messengers who received codified "books" that were meant to be passed down. Tradition states that there were 313 messengers. If we use that figure, it means that there were as many revealed religious texts. These would be the holy books found throughout the world from the ancient Chinese and Greeks to the Toltecs of Mexico or ancient Jews of Palestine. Not every "book," or *kitabullah*, necessarily needs to be written down, according to Islam, because oral transmission would suffice in most cases.

So, where do all these revelations come from? The Qur'an says that God keeps a special book with Him called the "Mother of the Book." This is the source from which all revelations are derived. When a messenger is supposed to receive a message from God, the Angel Gabriel, who is nicknamed the *Spirit of Holiness* in the Qur'an, takes the revelation from the "Mother of the Book" and brings it to the messenger entitled to get it. Because there were so many revelations, Gabriel must have been very busy! Of these many "Books of God," the Qur'an mentions five by name:

- The Scrolls (or leaves) of Abraham (*Suhuf*)
- The Law of Moses (*Taurah*)
- The Psalms of David (*Zabur*)
- The Gospel of Jesus (*Injeel*)
- The Reading of Muhammad (*Qur'an*)

What happened to all the rest of the many revealed books? This problem is best left to literary historians to unravel. Religious texts

Translate This

Kitabullah means the Book of God. The Qur'an is often referred to by this name.

abound throughout the world's ancient civilizations. Some have survived; some have been heavily edited; others were lost or destroyed in the great movement of conquerors and conquered; yet others may survive buried in the recesses of a civilization's historical literature or popular myths. The Qur'an declares, "All [Believers] believe in God, His angels, His Books and His Messengers. They say, 'We do not discriminate against any of His Messengers.'" (Qur'an 2:285)

Thus Islam accepts all previous scriptures and prophets that were truly sent by God. (Fakes and imposters excluded, of course.) The caveat is that all other religious books have had their integrity compromised, and therefore the job of the Qur'an is to correct the mistakes of previous scriptures. "These are the verses of the Book that make things clear." (Qur'an 12:1) Islam does not accept the Bible that was created in the fourth century as being authentic revelation. The Qur'an accuses Christians and Jews of inventing their own scriptures and mixing them with the authentic words of the prophets.

It Is Written

This Qur'an could not be produced by anyone other than God. In fact, it is the confirmation of prior revelations [the Psalms, Torah, and Gospel] and fully explains the Holy Books [the prior scriptures]; there is no doubt in this fact that it is [revealed] from the Lord of the Worlds. (Qur'an 10:37)

How does this relate to the Qur'an's acceptance of the revelations of Moses, David, and Jesus? By negating much of the Bible, we are not negating the *original* messages of those prophets. Any Christian or Jewish scholar will readily tell you that much of the Bible was written by unknown people and that some of it is even spurious. The Bible, as a book, didn't even exist in Jesus' time. The so-called Gospels in the New Testament are really *biographies* of Jesus written by spectators and not the Gospel *of* Jesus.

Muslims believe that it is precisely because the Holy Book of Jews and Christians is faulty that they have deviated from God's universal way as enshrined in the Qur'an.

So the premise that Muslims live by is that those who follow the Bible cannot help but make errors in doctrine. The original teachings of their prophets have been lost. The Qur'an was revealed to appeal to their sense of logic and faith. All true Christians and Jews, asserts the Qur'an, will have *eyes overflowing with tears* when they hear God's last revelation read to them, recognizing the truth of it.

The Least You Need to Know

- Islam accepts all the major biblical prophets (and prophets not mentioned in the Judeo-Christian tradition) but explains their life and mission in a unique way.

- Prophets are sinless but can make honest mistakes.

- All true religions originated from God, and Muslims are taught to be tolerant of others' beliefs because of it.

- Muslims do not accept the Bible as the word of God but do believe that it is based on what was once authentic revelation from God.

Chapter 16

Jews in Islam

In This Chapter

- ◆ Learn about the special status both Jews and Christians occupy in Islamic thought
- ◆ Bring to light the influence of Judaism on pre-Islamic Arabia
- ◆ Find out how Jews and Muslims interacted in the early days of Islam
- ◆ Know what the Qur'an says about Judaism
- ◆ Discover the Golden Age of Judaism in the classical Islamic Empire

The Qur'an and the hadiths both make frequent mention of Jews. They discuss in detail the beliefs and practices, as well as the merits and drawbacks, of the Jewish religion. Whereas the earliest revelations of the Qur'an concern the evils of idolatry, later revelations spend more time on interfaith issues. This change in emphasis is the result of the conditions that Islam underwent. When Muhammad began preaching in Mecca, his audience consisted mainly of Arab idolaters. After he moved to cosmopolitan Medina, 13 years later, the audience expanded to include not only idolaters, but also three well-settled Jewish tribes (and a few scattered Christians).

Although Muslim-Jewish relations endured much strain in the waning years of Muhammad's rule in Medina, this hostility soon abated. In fact, Jews never had anything to fear from the rise of Islamic civilization. While Christians in Europe were busy persecuting Jews all throughout the last thousand years, culminating in the Holocaust, Jews who lived in the Muslim world enjoyed tolerance, peace, and prosperity. The Qur'an mentions with reverence the major Jewish prophets and even calls the founding of ancient Israel an act of righteousness.

In recent times, however, political conditions have cast a pall over Muslim-Jewish relations that never existed before. The tension of the Arab-Israeli conflict has divided Muslims and Jews irreparably, it seems. However, recent efforts have been made to heal some of the mistrust, and tentative steps toward peace may yet restore amicable relations between the followers of the world's two purest monotheistic religions. In this chapter, I will be exploring the place of Judaism in the Qur'an, Muhammad's interactions with Jews in Arabia, and the long history of mutual tolerance that came to an end in 1948.

The People of the Book

The Middle East, the crossroads of the world, is the birthplace not only of Islam but also of Judaism and Christianity. Because the Qur'an was first revealed in the Middle East, it is only natural that the majority of its contents reference people and places found there. Islam, then, has certain similarities with Judaism and Christianity, arising from the fact that they share the same basic geographic and historical background. This makes all three religions cousins of sorts. Islam is even classified as a Western religion.

Translate This

Ahl al Kitab means People of the Book. It is the term used to describe Jews and Christians in the Qur'an. It refers to the fact that God revealed books to their ancestors.

Given that Islam recognizes that Jews and Christians received authentic prophets and revelations in the past, the Qur'an uses a special title to separate them from mere idolaters. This term is *Ahl al Kitab*, or People of the Book. It is an allusion to the fact that Jews and Christians received Holy Books from God long before and can be counted on to have certain ideas and concepts that are similar to Islam's.

The People of the Book have such an elevated status that, according to Islamic Law, a Muslim man is allowed to marry a practicing Jewish or Christian woman. (And he is not allowed to force her to convert or curtail her religious freedom.) In addition, meat prepared by Jews and Christians based on their religious dictates (the kosher standard) is permissible for Muslims to eat. (Think of the great boom kosher delis will experience as the Muslim population in the West continues to increase!) Thus, Islam considers Jews and Christians to be co-religionists after a fashion.

Judaism and Islam

Over the centuries much misinformation has surfaced concerning the concept of Judaism in Islam. Some of it can be traced to long-held prejudices and historical mis-understandings, and some of it is because the current state of relations between Israel and the Muslim world leaves a lot to be desired. Sadly, in modern times, the misin-terpretation of historical events and the use of Qur'anic verses out of context have allowed some Western writers to contribute to the problem. Nevertheless, except for a rocky start and the unfortunate enmity prevalent today, the history of Jewish-Muslim coexistence has been remarkably friendly.

With that said, we can take a closer look at how Islam really perceives the Jewish peo-ple. To unravel this issue we have to look at three areas:

◆ The interaction between Muslims and Jews in Medina at the Prophet's time

◆ The perception of Judaism in the Qur'an

◆ The relationship between Jews and Muslims throughout the succeeding centuries

When Islam began in Mecca in the year 610 C.E., no Jews inhabited the city. Muham-mad was dealing with an Arab society steeped in idolatry and tribal custom. There was no police force or central authority governing the city. At best, a council of rich tribal heads dictated local policies, and these decisions were usually guided by self-interest. Public drunkenness, prostitution, infanticide, spousal abuse, the worst form of abject slavery, and robbery and banditry were the order of the day. Consequently, we find that the Qur'anic revelations were mainly directed against these and other vices. After Muhammad and his followers migrated to Medina (which was formerly called Yathrib) to escape the persecution of the Meccans, Muslims found themselves in a city that was divided among three factions. One consisted of a group of the following three Jewish tribes who lived in and around the city:

◆ The Banu Nadir

◆ The Banu Qaynuqa

◆ The Banu Quraiza

The other two factions consisted of two Arab tribes who frequently fought wars with each other. They were known as the Aws and the Khazraj. The Jewish tribes often played one Arab tribe against another and thereby exercised a certain amount of dominance in city affairs, even though their numbers were small compared with the rest of the population. Jews also exerted a sort of moral authority over the Arabs by pointing out that monotheism was better than the idols they worshipped. This helps to explain why the Arabs of Medina were more amenable to Muhammad than the Arabs of Mecca. The citizens of Medina were already primed for religious discussion. (Jewish leaders often predicted to the Arabs that a new prophet would come and destroy them and their idols and ally himself to the Jews.) This was the political and religious makeup of Medina in 622 C.E.

Just the Facts

During the first 15 years of Islam, Muslims were told to pray in the direction of Jerusalem. After a year and a half in Medina, a revelation instructed them to pray in the direction of the *Ka'bah* in Mecca.

Just the Facts

The longest chapter of the Qur'an is called Al Baqarah, which means the Heifer. It refers to the golden calf made by the freed slaves while Moses was attending a meeting with God on Mount Sinai.

Muhammad had been invited to live in Medina by representatives of both Arab tribes, who were tired of the constant warfare. This united decision on the part of the more numerous Arabs had the effect of limiting the influence of the Jewish tribes in the city. When Muhammad first arrived, though, the Jewish tribes acquiesced peacefully and accepted his civil leadership. Why did they do this? The answer lies in shared religious concepts.

The Jews had learned that Muhammad was preaching against idolatry and thus felt something of a common cause with him, for Judaism was also critical of this Arab custom. In addition, the Qur'an, as it was being revealed, spoke respectfully of Jewish prophets, and this had the effect of causing many Jews to sympathize with Islam. Moses, Job, Saul, David, and Solomon all had a revered place in Islamic theology. Many Jews thought that Muhammad would actually convert to Judaism and increase Jewish power throughout central Arabia.

Many were even further impressed when Muhammad demonstrated his considerable political acumen by drafting a constitution for Medina, spelling out the rights and responsibilities of all groups resident within the municipality. This lengthy constitution included the following terms:

- Everyone must live in peace within the city.

- No side will make any alliances with an enemy of any other party in the city.

- All citizens of Medina have the right to be secure and have their economic rights respected.

- If the city is attacked, all parties will join together in its defense.

In addition, Muhammad made a separate treaty of friendship between the rapidly growing Muslim community and the three Jewish tribes. The treaty bound each side to respect the other and also reiterated the illegality of forming alliances with outside parties against one another. Its acceptance by both sides demonstrated their willingness to accept the legitimacy of Muhammad's authority in Medina.

Tension soon arose, however, after several Jewish families converted to Islam. Among them was a prominent Jewish rabbi named 'Abdullah ibn Salam. He kept his conversion a secret at first but then declared it publicly in a meeting of Jewish clan leaders. Add to the situation the fact that Muhammad was *not* converting to Judaism and that the Qur'an was not particularly supportive of certain Jewish beliefs, and you can see the beginning of a rift. Some Jews began to charge that Muhammad could not be a true prophet because he was an Arab and not one of *God's chosen people.* They also began quizzing him at every opportunity about arcane facts concerning the prophets of old in order to trip him up. As the months went by, the situation went from bad to worse.

Just the Facts

Muhammad's city charter for Medina is considered the world's first constitution.

It Is Written

O children of Israel! Remember My favors to you; fulfill your covenant with Me and I will fulfill My covenant with you. And you should fear none but Me. Believe in My revelation [the Qur'an], which is confirming your scriptures; do not be the first one to deny My revelation, and do not sell them for a petty price, fear Me and Me alone. Do not mix the Truth with falsehood, or knowingly conceal the truth. (Qur'an 2:40–42)

The Qur'anic revelations received by Muhammad painted a picture of Judaism, as it was then practiced, that was extremely unflattering. The Qur'an accused the Jews of practicing racial discrimination and hypocrisy. It said that they were not following the teachings of Moses and that their customs had no authority from God. But the worst of it, from the Jewish point of view, was still to come. When Muhammad first arrived in Medina, the Jews had been hopeful that he would denounce Jesus as an impostor. (Judaism holds that Jesus is a false rabbi.) But instead of rejecting Jesus, the Qur'an called him the Jewish Messiah and a messenger from God who was sent to call the wayward Jews back to true faith! Such a view was totally unacceptable to the Jews, and the situation deteriorated from there.

Muhammad had been engaging in dialogues with Jewish leaders over religious issues and had succeeded in making some more conversions. However, after six months in Medina, the Jewish clan leaders began a vicious propaganda campaign against Muhammad, and much slanderous talk was directed against the Muslims. Some Jews actually pretended to convert just so they could gain entry into Muslim meetings and ask confusing questions to sow doubt into the minds of recent converts. The Aws and Khazraj tribes, who had almost all converted to Islam, were soon engaged in a war of words with their Jewish neighbors. The breaking point would soon be upon the city.

The Qur'an on Judaism

Let's digress for a moment and discuss what Islam was saying about Judaism. When we look into the numerous verses of the Qur'an that comment on Jewish practices, we must remember that they were mostly directed toward the customs of the three Jewish tribes in Medina. Those tribes were not examples of the best in Judaism, being as much involved in the shady life of rough desert merchants as any idolatrous Arab tribe. We must note here that the Qur'an does praise true Jews and Christians who have sincere faith and try to lead virtuous lives. In Chapter 2 you read:

> Rest assured that [Muslims], Jews, Christians and Sabians—whoever believes in God and the last day and performs good deeds—will be rewarded by their Lord; they will have nothing to fear or regret. (Qur'an 2:62)

The Qur'an even refers to synagogues as places where God's name is mentioned:

> If God didn't check one set of people by means of another there would surely have been pulled down monasteries, churches, synagogues and mosques in which the name of God is commemorated in abundant measure. (Qur'an 22:40)

Just the Facts

Yahudi is the Arabic term for any Jewish person who is born after the fall of the ancient kingdom of Judah. Anyone before that time, all the way back to Moses, is labeled as *Bani Isra'il.* Thus Islam divides Jews into two main historical periods.

So it is not the concept of being *Jewish* that the Qur'an calls into question. It is the application of religion or the lack thereof that is being highlighted. According to the Qur'an, the shortcomings of the Jewish community include the following:

- Jewish Law is overly harsh without sanction from God. (Qur'an 16:118)

- Jews assert that Abraham and his immediate descendants were Jewish, but that is rejected in the Qur'an. The Jewish identity came much later. (Qur'an 2:140)

- God did not make an all-time covenant with the Jews. The conditional agreement He did make with them was broken by the Jews later on. (Qur'an 2:83)

- The Jews of Medina engaged in slander and misinformation in their intrigues against Islam, and they publicly taunted and were disrespectful of the Prophet Muhammad. (Qur'an 4:46)

- Many Jews do not keep God's laws about the Sabbath, kosher, and other things. (Qur'an 4:47)

- The Jews in Muhammad's time said they were God's chosen and would never be harshly punished by Him for their sins. (Qur'an 2:80)

- Rabbis have not done a good job of influencing their people to lead moral lives. (Qur'an 5:78–81)

Just the Facts

There is a surprisingly steady stream of conversion from Judaism to Islam. There is even an organization called "Jews for Allah."

These are some of the many charges that the Qur'an makes against the worldwide Jewish community, and it calls on Jews to take a look at Islam and accept it as the best expression of the messages of Abraham and Moses. By accepting Islam, the Qur'an states, the Jewish people can perfect their faith and bring themselves back under the terms of the covenant between Moses and God, as called for by both Jesus and Muhammad.

The Only Muslim-Jewish War

The Jewish tribes of Medina grew increasingly hostile to the Muslims as a result of the major doctrinal disputes and the clash of cultures. One by one each tribe engaged the Muslims in battle (even though they had signed peace treaties). The first tribe to pick a fight with the Muslims was the Banu Qaynuqa. After declaring war on the Muslims, they were surprised to find that their neighborhoods were immediately blockaded. They surrendered under the terms that they would have to pick up their belongings and leave Medina forever. That tribe moved into northern Arabia and eventually settled in Palestine.

The second tribe to fight the Muslims was the Banu Nadir. They were the most active in intriguing against the Prophet and even tried to assassinate him. Again, when actual fighting broke out, the Muslims surrounded the fortresses of the Banu Nadir and forced their capitulation. The Banu Nadir were then ordered to pack up and leave as well. Most went to Palestine, but a contingent went to live in a Jewish community called Khaibar in northern Arabia.

The third tribe, the Banu Quraiza, avoided all conflict with the Muslims, and its leaders were determined to abide by the terms of their treaty with the Muslims. But the leaders of the Banu Nadir wanted revenge and thus sent ambassadors to Mecca, which was the center of idol worship. They convinced the Meccan leaders to arrange a grand coalition of dozens of Arab tribes in order to destroy the Muslims in Medina. The astonished Meccans asked the Jewish ambassador whether the Banu Nadir considered idol worship superior to Islam and its emphasis on one God. The envoy said that the Arab's idols were better.

A force of over 10,000 Arab warriors assembled and laid siege to Medina for about a month. Never had the Muslims been in such danger before. They feared that if the idolaters breached the great trench, hastily dug around the city by the Muslims, the Arabs would show no mercy. The worst danger, though, lay in the Muslims' rear line. The Banu Nadir, after much hard negotiating, brought the Banu Quraiza into the war and extracted promises from them to attack the Muslims from behind when they least expected it. Muslim women and children were sheltering in the buildings closest to the Banu Quraiza's fortress, and if they were attacked then the Muslim line would crumble from within. Muhammad got wind of the intrigue, however, and skillfully used an undercover agent to cause dissension among the besiegers. He then sent a few soldiers to cover their newly exposed rear, which was now facing another enemy.

It took a fierce sandstorm to break the ranks of the Arab forces, and after they had retreated in disarray, the Muslims attacked the traitors. After a hard-fought battle, the Banu Quraiza agreed to surrender on the condition that their fate be judged by the chief of the Aws tribe, with whom they had always had good relations. After the Banu Quraiza's warriors were taken into custody, the Aws chief asked the clan leaders what their punishment should be for betrayal according to the Torah. The answer was capital punishment, of course, and the clan leaders were then executed by the verdict of their own religion. (The remaining men, women, children, and other noncombatants remained unharmed and were forced into indentured servanthood. All their property was also seized.)

As can be expected, the Qur'an grew increasingly stern in its tone as all the aforementioned events unfolded. However, the Qur'an still maintained that all people were equal in God's sight and that it was only in the strength of their faith that they could be

> **Ask the Imam**
>
> Muhammad ordered Muslims to be kind to their Jewish neighbors and to share their food with the Jews. He also had business dealings with Jews and never failed in his end of the bargain. Jews continued to live in Medina throughout Muhammad's rule and even for many centuries after his passing.

judged. Muhammad kept his end of the treaty at all times, and many Jews converted to Islam of their own free will. He never forced any conversions nor did he act in an unjust manner. One of his wives, Safiya, was also a Jewish Muslim; although some people grumbled and accused her of being duplicitous, Muhammad publicly defended her honor and silenced the detractors.

The expulsion of the three organized Jewish tribes was due to their own duplicity and treachery. Western writers have recognized this reality and have not spent much time weaving a false web. There were still many Jews living in the city of Medina afterward, and religious toleration was the order of the day. The only burden Islamic law laid upon non-Muslims is what is known as the *Jizyah*. This is a tax that non-Muslims must pay to the government as compensation for not being drafted into the army in times of need. (All Muslim men are eligible for the draft, and non-Muslims are forbidden to join the army in an Islamic state.) Even as Muslims pay *Zakah*, non-Muslims must pay their fair share as well.

Jews in the Muslim Empire

The history of Islam from Muhammad's time until the advent of the twentieth century is one of remarkable tolerance toward Jews and Judaism. Even as Jews were persecuted in Europe during the Middle Ages, they almost always enjoyed political and religious freedom in Islamic societies. The greatest example of that is found in the period known as the Golden Age in Spain. From the eighth century until the fourteenth century, Muslims ruled nearly all of Spain and a small sliver of France. (The last tiny Muslim stronghold of Granada was overrun by Christians in 1492.) During that time, Jewish citizens of the state had rights nearly equal to their rights in America today. Jewish historians refer to the time their people lived in Muslim-ruled Spain as the Golden Age of Judaism.

Jews were also prominent in the courts of Baghdad, Cairo, Istanbul, and elsewhere, being palace physicians, finance officers, and even *viziers*, or government ministers. The Islamic *Millet*, or Sectional system, operated to the benefit of religious minorities by setting up an official board of people from every religion who ruled over their co-religionists according to their own religious laws. (Non-Muslims are exempt from following Islamic Law.) Important synagogues dot the major cities of the Middle East and, save for the modern Arab-Israeli conflict, relations between Jews and Muslims have been quite fair for more than a thousand years.

As you can see, Islam is not an anti-Jewish religion. It recognizes the legitimacy of the Jewish prophets and the right of Jews to follow their own religious beliefs. Islam merely points to what it considers the collective failure of the Jewish people to live up to the best ideals contained in God's revelations. In this regard, Islam is no different from Christianity, which believes exactly the same thing. Jesus is quoted in the Christian New Testament as calling Jewish religious leaders "Whited Sepulchers," "a generation of vipers," and many other strong epithets to emphasize how he felt they had warped God's true teachings for personal gain. What must be remembered is that Islamic history is filled with general tolerance for Jews while Christian history, sadly, is a tragic record of forced conversions of Jews, massacres, discriminatory laws, and even genocide. This is a reality that is often not emphasized by both sides in the Middle Eastern conflict but can be a source for revived mutual respect and tolerance.

Just the Facts

Islam does not teach its followers to discriminate against Jews. When a Jewish funeral procession was passing by him in Medina, Muhammad stood up in respect for the deceased. When asked about it, he remarked that we're all equal in death.

Islam teaches that the true message of the Jewish prophets found its fulfillment in the person of Muhammad and that he is the most like Abraham in his life and example. It is unfortunate that political strife has interrupted the dialogue between Islam and Judaism, but that may change in the future if the conflict in Palestine finds a successful resolution. All of the demagoguery and inflammatory rhetoric on both sides is not because of religion, but because of each side feeling that it has been wronged in some way.

The Least You Need to Know

- Islam does not teach its followers to be anti-Semitic. The intractable Arab-Israeli conflict, which has festered since 1948, is a political condition that is often unfairly cloaked in religious rhetoric.

- Islam accepts all the major Jewish prophets, including Moses, David, Solomon, and Job.

- Many Jewish teachings are compatible with Islam, such as monotheism, kosher standards, angels, and prophets.

- The Qur'an contains more than a hundred verses that discuss Judaism, Jews, and issues related to the ancient Israelites.

- Jews lived peacefully in the Muslim world for more than a thousand years and did not suffer persecution in any comparable way that their co-religionists did in Christian Europe.

Chapter 17

Christianity and Islam

In This Chapter

- ◆ Learn about the historical ups and downs of Muslim-Christian relations
- ◆ Discover Jesus and Mary through the lens of Islam
- ◆ Take a look at Muhammad's experiences with Christians
- ◆ Know what the Islamic position is on all the major Christian doctrines

The two largest religions in the world today are Islam and Christianity. They also happen to be historically separated by only 600 years. Given that both religions began with charismatic leaders, it's not surprising that their relations would be equally charged with emotion, fervor, and sometimes conflict. Islam accepts the founder of Christianity, Jesus Christ, as a true prophet from God, while denying that he is a god or God Himself. The Qur'an even devotes whole passages in commenting on the Christian religion. Christianity, which came before Islam, has not yet accepted the validity of Muhammad's message and consequently Christians know little of this rival faith.

The situation is changing, however, with the growth of more diverse multicultural societies in the West. With more Muslims than ever either moving to the West or converting from among the Western population, people here have had to take a closer look into their neighbors' beliefs. The growth of interfaith dialogue, long the province of Jews and Christians, has recently expanded to include Muslims as regular participants. In this chapter, I will explain the long and fractious history of relations between these two world giants and show the efforts that both traditions are making toward living together in harmony and mutual tolerance.

Setting the Stage

The history of Muslim-Christian relations has followed a thorny pattern of shifting political realities. Both religions, being missionary oriented, have been the big boys on the block, fighting in every arena for land, dominance, converts, and influence. Whereas Muslims and Jews got off to a rocky start but then settled into a tolerant relationship (until very recently), Muslims actually had good relations with Christians in the early days of Islam. The Qur'an even looks fondly upon them and predicts a certain amount of mutual goodwill:

> You will find that the closest to you in love are those who call themselves Christians because there are priests and monks among them who do not behave arrogantly. (Qur'an 5:82)

It was only after the initial spirit of tolerance abated on both sides that centuries of conflict ensued (culminating with the era of Colonialism when Christian European powers completely dismantled Islamic civilization). The so-called Islamic Resurgence that is much maligned in the West today is really nothing more than the Islamic world trying to right itself after the last knockout punch it received. Islam can recover because it has a definite explanation of what happened and a sense of certainty to propel it forward again. Muslims, when their nations were being dominated by direct European rule, never felt that their religion was to blame or that Christianity was superior. Instead of blaming God for their malaise, they turned inward and began blaming themselves and their own shortcomings.

Muslims consider Islam to be a perfect way of life, no matter what political situation they are in, so the urge to tell others about their beliefs is alive and well. Indeed, to this day, the war for converts between Christianity and Islam is a daily struggle, with more people converting to Islam from Christianity than the other way around. What gives Islam a certain measure of insulation that protects its followers from accepting Christian dogma? The answer lies in the explanation of Christianity given in the

Qur'an itself. Just as the Qur'an contains a full discussion of Judaism and its merits and drawbacks, it also has a complete analysis of Christianity. So while the average Christian might be completely in the dark about Islam, the Muslim is already well versed in both faiths. Talk about a home-court advantage!

Muhammad and the Monk

Muhammad grew up in the city of Mecca in Arabia. Only a handful of people who claimed to be Christians lived there among the thousands of Arab idolaters, and there was no organized church or place of worship. Indeed, a generation before Muhammad was born Christianity was all but made illegal by the reigning idolaters, who feared the loss of their religion. And what of the closet Christians of Mecca, or the few Christianized tribes in northern and southern Arabia? As many writers have lamented, the Christians of Arabia were not known as paragons of virtue, being a part of the lifestyle and grit of a rough and tumble environment. Furthermore, there weren't any centers of Christian learning or repositories of centuries-old knowledge. The main centers of Christianity were far to the north in the Byzantine Roman Empire or across the Red Sea in Egypt and Abyssinia. Arabia was a land virtually untouched by the Gospel.

What were Muhammad's first contacts with Christians? As I discussed before, he rejected idol worship from an early age and grew up as a poor orphan in the care of relatives. When Muhammad was about 12 years old, however, he had his first foreign adventure. He accompanied his uncle on a business trip to Syria, an event that in those days was like a rite of passage for young men. Caravans made up of dozens of horses and camels snaked their way through northern Arabia and into Syria, heading for the great trading bazaars where everything from Chinese silk to Germanic metalwork could be had.

> **It Is Written**
>
> According to Muhammad, "Every Prophet sent by God has been a shepherd. Moses was a shepherd, David tended animals, and before I became a Prophet, I also was a shepherd."

Just inside the southeastern region of Syria lived a Christian monk named Bahira. His usual habit was to watch the roads during the day, and when he saw this particular caravan coming in from the Arabian road, he noticed some strange portents. Clouds seemed to be following overhead, shading the travelers. He sent a boy to invite the weary merchants to his monastery. The young Muhammad was also brought to the dinner prepared for the men, though at first he had been left to tend the camels.

Bahira was fascinated by the boy and, after interviewing him, predicted privately to the boy's uncle, Abu Talib, that his nephew would be a prophet one day. The practical uncle dismissed the idea, and the next day the caravan went on its way. After a few weeks spent in the bazaars of Syria, the group returned uneventfully to Mecca, where Muhammad continued his normal routine of tending his uncle's flocks of sheep in the scruffy hills around the city.

An Interesting Proposal

When Muhammad turned 25 years old, he received an offer of employment from a 40-year-old Meccan widow named Khadijah. She wanted the young man to lead her next caravan to Syria. (His uncle, Abu Talib, had put in a good word for him.) He agreed, and the trip was very successful financially. This was Muhammad's second and final business trip to Syria. Khadijah was impressed by Muhammad and soon offered her hand in marriage to him. He accepted and for the next 15 years lived the life of a quiet family man.

But years later, as he neared his fortieth birthday, Muhammad grew restless and wanted to connect with his spiritual side. He would often retreat to a mountain cave to meditate. One night, while meditating in his usual spot, he was visited by the angel Gabriel, who announced to him that he was chosen to be the last prophet of God. Understandably, Muhammad was shaken, and he ran home and hid under his bed sheets. The next day his concerned wife took him to meet her old, blind cousin, Waraqah. He was a Christian and knew how to read and write, though he was forbidden by Meccan law from spreading knowledge of his faith. (Christianity was outlawed in Mecca before Muhammad was born because it was perceived as a threat to idolatry.) Waraqah listened to Muhammad's account and then told Muhammad that the angel who had come to him was the same one who had gone to Moses. He then said that Muhammad was going to be a prophet and would be opposed by his people. A few months later Waraqah passed away.

These two people, Bahira (whom he met one time at a banquet as a boy) and Waraqah (an old reclusive cousin of his wife with whom he was never known to associate), represent all of the contacts Muhammad had with Christians for the first 40 years of his life. Christian evangelists have often charged that Muhammad was instructed by closet Christian scholars in the ways of religion and that he simply took it from there and made up his own faith. This simplistic view, however, is unsustainable when one considers the depth of Islam and the fact that Muhammad had only the most limited contacts with Christians. There were no wandering evangelists or seminaries in Mecca, and Muhammad's enemies never seriously pursued such a charge against him because they knew him from childhood and they knew his circle of friends and acquaintances.

In fact, Muhammad had no significant interaction with Christians until he and his followers moved to Medina after 13 years in Mecca. A few Christians lived in Medina, and farther to the north were Christian Arab tribes. Muhammad spent a great deal of time setting up dialogues with these people and succeeded in converting several visiting delegations of Christians to Islam. Not all Christians who came converted, but Muhammad still showed them great respect. He even allowed a group of Christians to use the main mosque of Medina for their Sunday worship services.

Translate This

In the Qur'an, the term for a Christian is **Nasara** (lit. helper), which is loosely related to the word *Nazarene*. This is a reference to the childhood home of Jesus in Palestine. The name for the Disciples of Jesus in the Qur'an is *Hawariyoon*.

As he did with the Jews, Muhammad made a treaty of peace with the closest Christian community. These were the Christians of Najran, a small area hundreds of miles away in central Arabia. In that treaty, both sides agreed to respect the rights and beliefs of the other. During the time that Muhammad lived in Medina, there were no conflicts between the Muslims and Christians. There would eventually be a war with the Byzantine Romans to the north, but it would be a war for defensible borders and not a fight over religion.

Just the Facts

The original name of Medina was Yathrib. When Muhammad moved there, people started calling Yathrib "the City of the Prophet," or *Medinat un Nabi*. It quickly became known as *Medina*, or city, for short.

Christianity and Jesus in the Qur'an

The Qur'an describes the state of Christianity and its doctrines as they were in the seventh century, long before the Protestant Reformation. Beyond disagreement with a few particular Christian concepts, the Qur'an accepts and promulgates many teachings that are accepted in Christianity. What must be remembered here, as we take a survey of what Islam says about Christianity, is that Muhammad never went to a School of Divinity, he never read the Bible, and he never had access to any books or traveling evangelists. In fact, he couldn't even read!

Just how does Islam explain Christianity and what it stands for? You will find that Christianity is given as much coverage in the Qur'an as Judaism. In fact, the first nine chapters of the Qur'an contain hundreds of verses related to these two topics. Perhaps the best place to start is with Islam's concept of Jesus and where he came from. Jesus holds a particularly high place in Islam, and he is honored in many verses in the Qur'an. For example, we read, "And We made Jesus, the son of Mary, and his mother a sign for mankind." (Qur'an 23:50) Let's see how the Qur'an narrates his life.

The Islamic view of Christianity begins before the birth of Jesus. According to the Qur'an, the Jews of Roman-ruled Palestine had reduced their religion to mere rituals that had little effect on people's moral lives. They also were following practices that had no sanction from their ancient prophets. In these difficult times, a recently widowed woman prayed to God and offered her unborn child to God's service. She had in mind that her son would become a rabbi. God heard her prayer, but she gave birth to a girl!

Jewish law forbade female rabbis, so the mother was perplexed. The Qur'an notes her surprise and mentions that there is blessing in children of any gender. Because of her status as a widow, her male relatives were forced to draw straws to see who would have to support the orphaned girl, whom her mother named Mary, or *Maryam*. Zechariah drew the small straw and was charged with her upbringing. This is an amazing turn of events because, unbeknownst to Mary's mother, Zechariah was a prophet of God.

> ### Ask the Imam
>
> The Islamic name for John the Baptist is *Yahiya*, which means life. The significance is that God created a life in a womb that could bear none.

As the girl grew older, Zechariah taught her about God, religion, faith, and Jewish law—all subjects that girls normally didn't learn about. She grew into such an obedient and pleasant girl that her old uncle began to wish for a child of his own. But he was advanced in years and his wife was old and barren. He took a chance and prayed to God, and his prayer was answered. His wife became pregnant and gave birth to a son they named *Yahiya*, or John.

John and his cousin, Mary, were to have different paths. John later became a prophet (John the Baptist) and began preaching to the Jews about the coming Messiah, while Mary continued with her studies well into her late teens. Realizing that all the hustle and bustle of her family and the town was distracting her, Mary packed her bags and journeyed east into the wilderness to be alone. She set up a small tent and continued her meditations and studies. One day while she was studying and praying, the angel Gabriel came to her and announced:

> "O Mary! God gives you the good news of a word from Him. You will be given a son: his name will be the Messiah, Jesus, the Son of Mary. He will be noble in this world and in the Hereafter. He will be among those who are closest to God." (Qur'an 3:45–46)

The frightened girl gave the famous reply, "My Lord, how can I have a son when no man has touched me?" The angel answered, "So it will be. The Lord creates what He wills. He need only say, 'Be' and it is." Soon Mary became pregnant, and after the baby was born she returned to her people.

When her relatives saw her returning after a year or more of self-imposed exile, and carrying a baby as well, they became enraged and started accusing her of infidelity. They called her a loose woman and crowded around her menacingly. Mary froze and couldn't find the words to speak in her defense, so God caused the baby Jesus to speak. He told the relatives that he was a special miracle from God and would become a prophet. The people backed off and left Mary alone from then on. (There is no Joseph in the Islamic version of Jesus' life.)

Jesus is mentioned in the Qur'an as a dutiful boy who always obeyed his mother. When he reached manhood, his mission of prophethood began. He attempted to teach his people, the Jews, about true faith in God. He taught that the corpus of Jewish law was filled with unnecessary rules, though some of it was valid. He wasn't teaching a new religion; he was mostly trying to reform the old one. But no matter where he went, he had a hard time getting people to listen. This is when he called for disciples to follow him. He recruited a dedicated cadre of people who assisted him in his mission. The Qur'an neither mentions how many he found nor their names. The immediate effect, however, was that many new converts to Jesus' way were gained.

Just the Facts

Chapter 19 of the Qur'an is entitled "Maryam," in honor of the mother of Jesus.

Ask the Imam

Muslims accept the virgin birth but do not say it is a sign of divinity. Rather Islam teaches that God created Jesus with a mere command as a miracle for people to ponder.

Jesus was granted several miracles to get the people's attention. Among these were the curing of blindness, healing of lepers, revival of the dead, and knowledge of surplus goods that people tried to hide in their homes and not use in charity. But even his disciples doubted him on one occasion and asked for a miracle to be performed in front of them. They were hungry after many days of hard missionary work and asked Jesus to make a table full of food appear. Jesus complied with their wish, though he warned that anyone who disbelieved after that would be hopelessly lost. Chapter 5 of the Qur'an—*Al Ma'idah*, or "The Table Spread"—takes its name from this incident.

The Qur'an records that fierce opposition to Jesus came from the leaders of the Jewish community. They called him an impostor and contrived a plot against him. After they succeeded in having him arrested, they tried to get him executed. Here is where the story gets interesting: The Qur'an claims that Jesus was not killed or crucified, but that it was *made to appear so to them.* Certain early Christian sects also believed Jesus escaped death. Islam is uncompromising on this issue. God saved Jesus and took him to Paradise until the hour would come to complete his mission in the end of time.

It Is Written

O Jesus! I will take you and raise you to Myself and clear you [of the falsehoods] of those who blaspheme. I will make those who follow you superior to those who reject faith until the Day of Resurrection, then you will all return to Me and I will judge between you in the matters wherein you differ. (Qur'an 3:55)

So from the point of view of Islam, the Christian doctrine that Jesus is God is moot, because Jesus didn't die anyway, and certainly not for the sins of humanity. Who was crucified on that fateful day? If anyone was executed, it may have been the man who betrayed Jesus. If he looked sort of like Jesus, in the confusion the Caucasian Romans may have grabbed him and killed him, thinking all Semites looked alike. In any case, Islam says the method of deception is unimportant. What matters is that people thought that Jesus died, when he didn't.

Original Sin and All That

Islam gives a rebuttal to every major Christian doctrine. Many of these I have discussed before. The Qur'an recognizes that Christianity has many different sects, each with slightly different teachings, and thus addresses many issues without regard to the uniqueness of each Christian group—"The [Christians] have divided their religion into sects between them." (Qur'an 21:93) Here is a summarized version of what Islam says about each cardinal teaching of Christianity:

♦ **Original sin**   Islam says Adam and Eve were forgiven by God after eating from the tree and passed on no taint of sin to their descendants.

♦ **Atonement**   God doesn't need to sacrifice Himself to atone for the sins of mankind because He can forgive anything He wants, anytime He wants.

♦ **Trinity**   Islam says that God is not divided into parts. The Nicene Creed is unacceptable to Muslims.

♦ **Marriage prohibition**   The Catholic Church forbids priests to marry, but the Qur'an calls this an invented practice.

♦ **Monasteries and convents**   The Qur'an says God never authorized this lifestyle.

♦ **Confession**   Islam requires people to ask God for forgiveness directly. No man can act as an intermediary or facilitator.

♦ **The Holy Spirit**   Islam says that there is no Holy Spirit other than the angel Gabriel who has that nickname. Speaking in tongues or laying on of hands to heal sickness is not known or accepted in Islam.

Just the Facts

Islam has influenced many Europeans to question the validity of the Trinity theory. Michael Servetus, a Spaniard who wrote *On the Errors of Trinity* in the sixteenth century, observed that "Trinity has, alas! been a laughing stock to Mohammedans. Only God knows. The Jews also shrink from giving adherence to this fancy of ours and laugh at our foolishness about the Trinity."

♦ **A Begotten Son**   The concept of God having children or being born on Earth is completely rejected in Islam.

♦ **Salvation and redemption**   Islam says our sincere faith and virtuous actions get us into heaven, not just a one-time conversion moment.

♦ **Mary as Mother of God**   The Qur'an addresses this issue by pointing out that expanding the trinity to a quartet is as foolish as the three-in-one god idea to begin with.

♦ **The Bible** Muslims hold that it does not contain the authentic writings of the prophets and that it is full of errors and contradictions.

Will there be Christians and Jews in Paradise? According to Islam the answer is yes. The Qur'an states that any follower of those religions who "believes in God and the Last Day and does what is right will have nothing to fear or regret." Does this mean that Islam accepts Christianity and Judaism as valid paths to salvation? Yes and no.

The Islamic principle is that you will be judged by what you knew. If a person only knew about Christianity or Judaism or whatever and never heard of Islam, then God will take that into account on Judgment Day and judge the person fairly by it. If a person finds out about Islam, then it becomes incumbent upon him or her to accept it and leave behind the former religion. This is because Islam is considered to be God's last and, therefore, most complete message to the world.

Interfaith Dialogue

The Qur'an is very enthusiastic about interfaith dialogue. Muhammad himself often engaged in this practice with Jews, Christians, and idolaters. The Qur'an even encourages Muslims to invite people to such meetings by saying, "Come! Let us gather together our sons and your sons, our women and your women, ourselves and yourselves: then let us earnestly pray and invoke the displeasure of God on those who are deceitful!" (Qur'an 3:61)

The history of interfaith contacts has often been intimately tied to the political circumstances of the day. For most of Muslim history the dialogue was between parties of equal strength, that is until 1918 (the end of the First World War). Prior to that year there still remained a unified Muslim Empire consisting of an appreciable amount of territory. With the dismantling of the Ottoman Empire, however, interfaith dialogue has taken on the tone of conquered and conquerors. The five nations that have done the most harm to the Muslim world—Britain, France, Italy, the Netherlands, and Russia—suppressed the teaching and practice of Islam and went to great lengths to set up missionary schools and other forms of institutional Christianity in the lands they controlled.

> **Ask the Imam**
>
> Muslims do not accept Saint Paul as an authentic interpreter of the teachings of Jesus. He is never mentioned in any Islamic source.

Muslim civilization, on the contrary, from its earliest years until the thirteenth century has almost always encouraged the equal participation of non-Muslims in religious debate and inquiry and rarely attempted to suppress the religious rights of others. Although one can always find aberrations, Muslims have respected freedom of conscience in others. Succeeding Islamic Empires (like the Ottomans) have even paid for the construction and upkeep of churches and synagogues, considering the maintenance of religion for all citizens in an Islamic state to be a duty of the government!

With this diversity of religion in the classical Muslim world, one finds that a great amount of dialoguing went on. On closer scrutiny we find that the great Muslim caliph, Harun ar Rashid, for example, who ruled in Baghdad in the late eighth century, kept a staff of scholars representing Muslims, Jews, Christians, Hindus, and Buddhists who routinely held regular debate sessions on each other's religions. He even sent a delegation to Charlemagne (along with an elephant as a gift) and opened the lines of communication between Europe and the Middle East.

Translate This

Futuwwat was the Muslim chivalric code by which a Muslim soldier would give quarter to an injured opponent, protect women and children, and fight with honor at all times. The Crusaders brought these ideas back to Europe and thus European chivalry was born. Hail King Arthur!

The Crusades also presented ample opportunities for dialogue. Although the initial onslaught of the European invasion of Palestine was violent and merciless, as the Crusaders settled on their conquered fiefs all along the Mediterranean, daily life and trade brought them into contact with Muslim ideas and values. The whole concept of chivalry, for example, was adopted by European knights from Muslim warriors who practiced *futuwwat*. Prior to this time few rules existed in Europe about fair play and gentlemanly conduct in battle. King Richard the Lion-Heart once met in a truce with Saladin, the great Muslim hero, and, over a game of chess, they talked about issues between their religions.

The Activist Popes

Perhaps no one has been more instrumental in reviving interfaith dialogue in modern times than Popes Paul VI and John Paul II. It was the defining statements enshrined in the Second Vatican Council of 1962–1965 that opened the door for Christians to have open fellowship with Muslims. This council declared that Christians should accept and respect Muslims as followers of God and of the example of Abraham. The major document of church policy, the *Lumen Gentium*, had this to say:

> The Plan of salvation also includes those who acknowledge the Creator, among whom are, in the first place, the Muslims. These profess to hold the faith of Abraham, and together with us they adore the one, merciful God, judge of humankind on the Last Day. (*Lumen Gentium*, 16)

Following these and other extremely conciliatory statements, Pope Paul VI embarked on a short tour of the Muslim world and engaged Islamic scholars in ecumenical dialogue in places as diverse as Jordan and Uganda. But it was the efforts of Pope John Paul II that opened the doors to full-blown regular dialogue. Not only has he been an extremely prolific traveler among Muslims, but he has also apologized to Muslims for the conduct of Christians during the Crusades. He made history as the first pontiff to visit a mosque in Syria and has allowed the construction of a small mosque in Vatican City. His vision has given rise to a spirit of Muslim-Christian toleration that has not been seen for over a thousand years.

Saint Francis of Assisi traveled to Egypt and met with the Muslim ruler Al-Malik Al-Kamil in 1219. They had an amicable dialogue.

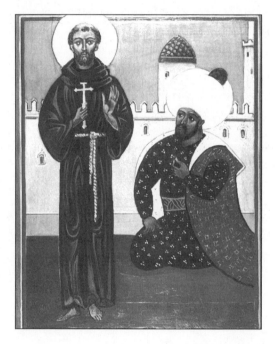

Protestant sects have also gotten into the act. Most notably the Presbyterians and Lutherans have begun to include Muslims in their national interfaith conferences. A decade ago the organization known as the National Council of Christians and Jews took steps to draw Muslim representatives into their regular meetings in several cities around the United States. As a participant in several of these sessions, I can attest to the great spirit of ecumenicity and fellowship that exists there.

This vast progress in multifaith tolerance and understanding is hampered somewhat by the efforts of several fundamentalist Christian groups who still hold medieval attitudes toward Muslims. They equate Muhammad with the anti-Christ or attempt to spread misinformation about Islam to slander its teachings. Many Christian bookstores are filled with books written by people whose only objective is to denigrate and insult Islam. Several Muslim organizations have been set up to promote authentic Islamic teachings to counter this slanderous movement and thus far have succeeded in a limited but important fashion.

The history of Muslim-Christian-Jewish dialogue is a rich tapestry with many colorful threads of thought. In the coming years such activities should become more public, and greater tolerance among the people of all three religions in the West can only benefit our societies. As the Second Vatican Council wrote:

Just the Facts

Great Christian theologians such as Thomas Aquinas and Albert the Great were heavily influenced by the writings of three Muslim philosophers: Al-Farabi, Ibn Sina (Avicenna), and Ibn Rushd (Averroes).

> Over the centuries, many quarrels and dissensions have arisen between Christians and Muslims. The Sacred Council now pleads with all to forget the past, and urges that a sincere effort be made to achieve mutual understanding: for the benefit of all, let them together preserve and promote peace, liberty, social justice and moral values. (*Nostra Aetate*, 3)

Just the Facts

The first public dialogue between Muslims and Christians happened after Muhammad sent a refugee column to Abyssinia in Africa to escape Meccan persecution. The Meccans sent ambassadors to the king there to ask for their arrest, but in a public interview the Christian king, Najashi, ruled that the teachings of Islam were closer to Christianity than to idolatry. He allowed the Muslims to stay and later converted to Islam, himself.

Build More Churches!

An Islamic government is charged with supporting all religions equally. It is a twist on the American ideal of separation of church and state, which forbids government from having any role in religion. In contrast, Islam says the state *must* support *all* religions! The Islamic government is forbidden to seize the churches, synagogues, or temples of any group, nor can the government meddle in the appointment of religious leaders by each group. The treaty Muhammad made with a local Christian community is very clear: No bishop can be removed from his office and no church can be confiscated.

From the time of Muhammad through to the last Muslim Empire of the Ottomans, Muslim rulers have been particularly concerned with the welfare of their non-Muslim subjects and their religious needs. For example, in the year 1076, the Muslim ruler of Bejaya, in present-day Algeria, wrote to Pope Gregory VII about the desire of the Christians in his land for a certain priest to be promoted to bishop. The pope was so overjoyed at this expression of religious respect that he wrote a beautiful letter in response, which concluded with the words: "We pray with heart and mouth that, after a long sojourn in this life, the same God may guide you to the bosom of happiness of the holy patriarch Abraham."

Many Americans in particular would be surprised to learn that a large portion of the current American constitution is compatible with the Islamic political vision. Concepts such as elected officials, congress, a judiciary, civil and criminal laws, equal political rights for women, and the rights and duties of citizens find their echoes in real-life applications in the history of Muslim civilization. Has Muslim history had its share of despots and kings? Sure it has, but so has the Christian world. What is to be judged are the principles and not how faithfully they are applied.

The Least You Need to Know

- Islam accepts the virgin birth of Jesus and his role as Messiah to the Jews. The Qur'an, however, denies that he is God or the Son of God, rather considering him to be a prophet.

- Muslims do not believe that Jesus was crucified nor that the Romans killed him in Jerusalem. Muslims hold that God answered Jesus' prayer and removed him from the physical world to await the end-of-time and a triumphant return to Earth.

- Christianity and Islam have had many centuries of interfaith dialogue interspersed with wars and periods of mutual fear and mistrust.

- European Christians completely occupied the Muslim world during the era of Colonialism and targeted Islam for elimination. The Islamic resurgence today is merely an attempt by Muslims all over the world to regain their religion.

- The secular governments of most Muslim countries suppress the meaningful practice of Islam by their populace.

Part 5

Regulating Life Within the Laws of Islam

Muslims consider Islam to be a complete way of life. It touches upon every aspect of our personal, familial, and social lives. The foundation of Islamic guidance comes from two main sources: the Qur'an and the sayings of Muhammad. How did both of these come into existence, and how do Muslims use them to guide their lives? In this part, I will explore both sources in detail so you can understand why Muslims do what they do.

18

Exploring the Sources of Islam

In This Chapter

- Learn about the Islamic scripture, the Holy Qur'an
- Discover the place of the *hadiths*, or prophetic sayings, in formulating Islamic teachings
- Find out who the companions of Muhammad were
- Meet the traditional scholars of Islam
- Discover the world of Islamic Law and how it is created

Every religious tradition has, as its foundation, a body of knowledge from which each successive generation can draw the fundamentals of their faith. Christians have their Bible and the works of countless theologians stretching over a thousand years. Judaism, Hinduism, and Buddhism have similarly ancient sources combining both scripture and a process of doctrinal development by their luminaries. Islam, on the other hand, is derived from only two main sources, both of which passed through one man and were completed in less than 25 years.

The *Qur'an*, which is considered to be the literal Word of God, forms the basis of Islamic teachings. The *hadiths*, or sayings of the Prophet, are considered a commentary on how to apply the Qur'an to daily life. The *companions* of the Prophet, those people who knew him and learned directly from him, are taken as a further source for elucidation and interpretation. Finally, throughout the centuries many great scholars have applied themselves to codifying, investigating, simplifying, and explaining the details of Islam for the common person. They did not introduce any new precepts or practices *per se*, however, because Islam has a strong tradition against making new additions. Thus, Islam holds a unique place among the religions of the world in that it is the only faith whose doctrines were not created centuries after the death of its founder.

A Closer Look at the Qur'an

Iqra. This command, meaning "Read," was the first word revealed of the Qur'an to Muhammad in the year 610 C.E. He was sitting in a mountain cave, just outside the city of Mecca, thinking about the meaning of things, when a brilliant flash of light overcame him. A hidden voice commanded him to *read.* Its tone was both frightening and compelling. But Muhammad was an illiterate. He never learned how to read, so he meekly answered, "I can't read."

Suddenly, he felt himself being squeezed so that the very breath seemed to rush out of him. When he could bear it no longer, the commanding voice repeated once more, *"Read."* Confused about what to do, Muhammad protested, "But I can't read!" The same crushing feeling overwhelmed him, and he could hardly stand it when the pressure was released and the voice ordered a third time, *"Read."* Muhammad, not wanting another bout with the pain, answered, "What should I read?"

The voice began to recite melodious-sounding words: "Read in the Name of your Lord Who created humans from a clinging [zygote]. Read for your Lord is the Most Generous. He taught people by the pen what they didn't know before." (Qur'an 96:1–5) Muhammad ran home scared and begged his wife, Khadijah, to comfort him. But the revelation was no apparition or evil omen, as he had thought. Khadijah told him that God would never let harm come to him on account of his honesty and generosity. She didn't know how right she was.

Just the Facts

The name of the mountain where Muhammad received his first revelation is called the *Jabal un Nur,* or Mountain of Light.

For the next 23 years he would receive revelations from God, carried by the archangel Gabriel. These revelations constitute the Qur'an, a name that literally means the *Reading* or the *Recital.* The Qur'an was given orally to Muhammad, and he would ask people to write down the verses as he dictated them. The Qur'an was, therefore, not revealed all at once. In fact, it grew larger over time until the last month of Muhammad's life when it took its final form of 114 chapters called *surahs,* each *surah* of varying length. The *surahs* comprise over 6,600 verses called *ayahs* that cover a wide variety of subjects. Sometimes whole *surahs* were revealed together; other times groups of *ayahs* would come, and Muhammad would tell people in which *surah* to include them. (Muslims believe that he made the arrangement of all chapters and verses under the direction of the archangel Gabriel.)

The revelations usually concerned issues at hand. When Muhammad was in Mecca, where his new followers were struggling to develop a strong foundation for their faith, the content revolved around monotheism, virtuous living, and the eventual triumph of Islam, even though it was a persecuted religion. Later in Medina, when Islam had become settled into the life of the city, laws and social dictates were the core of the message. Sometimes non-Muslims would challenge Muhammad to talk about arcane subjects that they knew he wouldn't know anything about, and suddenly a revelation would come explaining the matter. For example, a group of people in Medina asked him about Joseph and his adventures in Egypt, trying to stump him. An entire chapter of over a hundred verses (called *Surah Yusuf*) was revealed right there in answer.

Muhammad described four ways in which he received revelations from God. The first was through dreams at night, when the verses of the Qur'an were implanted in his mind. The second was through instantaneous revelations in his heart during the day.

The third way, which he said was the hardest to bear, was foreshadowed by a loud ringing sound in his ears and then the verses would flow. The last way involved the archangel Gabriel appearing as a man, sometimes visible to other people and sometimes not, who would then instruct Muhammad in what to say. God never appeared to Muhammad, for Islam says that God is too exalted to show Himself to us as if for our inspection.

> **It Is Written**
>
> You, [Muhammad,] never read a book before this nor have you ever written one with your own hand. Had you done either of these then the quibblers would have had legitimate reasons to suspect it. (Qur'an 29:48)

Style and Content

One of the many features of the Qur'an that Muslims consider miraculous is its style. Muhammad was not known to be a man of poetry before the Qur'an began to flow from his lips. He also never participated in the oral poetry contests that were a mainstay of life throughout Arabia. Yet this same man suddenly began to recite what is still considered today to be the greatest book in the Arabic language. The use of lucidly phrased metaphors, the flow of the text, and the engaging syntax are held up as the highest standard for Arabic lexicographers, and no other book is so highly esteemed from a grammarian's standpoint.

How is the Qur'an's unique style expressed? To answer this question, we need to look at two areas: presentation and content. The Qur'an employs a variety of literary mechanisms, from straight line-by-line or metered rhyming to flowing prose and passionate essays. Through a skilled mixture of the different techniques, the listener is taken on a rapturous ride through feelings, thoughts, emotions, and dreams. The opening verses of Chapter 36 of the Qur'an provide an example. In this *surah*, entitled *Ya Seen*, we read the opening verses in transliteration. The underlined words show the repetition of sounds:

> *Ya Seen. Wal Qur'anil <u>Hakeem</u>. Innaka lamin al <u>Mursaleen</u>. 'Alaa siratim <u>Mustaqeem</u>. Tanzilul 'azeezil <u>Raheem</u>. Le tunzera qawman ma unthera aba-uhum fa hum <u>ghawfiloon</u>. La qad haqqal qawlu 'alaa ak tharihim fahum la <u>yu-minoon</u>.*

Just the Facts

The Arabic alphabet is not written in Latin characters and contains sounds which have no equivalent in English such as "gha," "kha," and "qa." Transliterations, or writing the literal sounds of one language in the letters of another, is necessary to understand how Arabic sounds are pronounced.

Just the Facts

One of the most adept poets of the Arabs, Tufayl ibn Amr Ad-Dawsi, wanted to investigate what he had heard about Muhammad and the Qur'an, so he went to Mecca and asked Muhammad to recite some of it to him. After listening to it he exclaimed, "I swear by God, I have never heard such beautiful words before."

If you noticed the transition from one rhyme to another, you can see how the Qur'an can continually engage the ear of its listeners with something fresh and new. For this reason, Muslims never consider a translation of the Qur'an as equal to the Arabic text. The Qur'an itself makes a note of this unique style and its purpose when it declares that it is a book that is easy to remember. In longer passages you will find quite a lot of transition in style over the course of many different topics. (Although some Western scholars have criticized this literary technique, it is in fact one of the strengths of the Qur'an, distinguishing it from all other Holy Books.) When the Qur'an is recited out loud by a skilled reader, its beauty can move listeners to tears. (Qur'an reciting contests are held every year all over the Muslim world with the most important ones being in Malaysia and Saudi Arabia.)

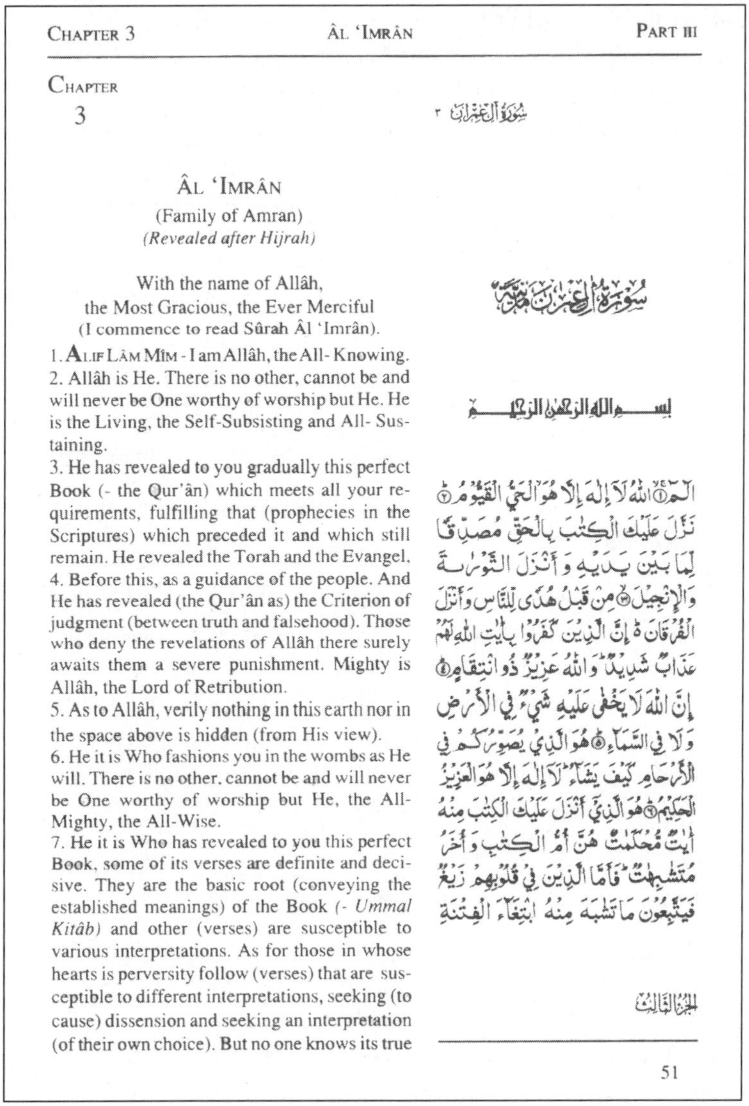

CHAPTER 3 ÂL 'IMRÂN PART III

CHAPTER 3

سورة آل عمران ٣

ÂL 'IMRÂN
(Family of Amran)
(Revealed after Hijrah)

سورة آل عمران مدنية

With the name of Allâh,
the Most Gracious, the Ever Merciful
(I commence to read Sûrah Âl 'Imrân).

بسم الله الرحمن الرحيم

1. ALIF LÂM MÎM - I am Allâh, the All-Knowing.
2. Allâh is He. There is no other, cannot be and will never be One worthy of worship but He. He is the Living, the Self-Subsisting and All-Sustaining.
3. He has revealed to you gradually this perfect Book (- the Qur'ân) which meets all your requirements, fulfilling that (prophecies in the Scriptures) which preceded it and which still remain. He revealed the Torah and the Evangel,
4. Before this, as a guidance of the people. And He has revealed (the Qur'ân as) the Criterion of judgment (between truth and falsehood). Those who deny the revelations of Allâh there surely awaits them a severe punishment. Mighty is Allâh, the Lord of Retribution.
5. As to Allâh, verily nothing in this earth nor in the space above is hidden (from His view).
6. He it is Who fashions you in the wombs as He will. There is no other, cannot be and will never be One worthy of worship but He, the All-Mighty, the All-Wise.
7. He it is Who has revealed to you this perfect Book, some of its verses are definite and decisive. They are the basic root (conveying the established meanings) of the Book *(- Ummal Kitâb)* and other (verses) are susceptible to various interpretations. As for those in whose hearts is perversity follow (verses) that are susceptible to different interpretations, seeking (to cause) dissension and seeking an interpretation (of their own choice). But no one knows its true

الٓمٓ ۝١ اللَّهُ لَآ إِلَٰهَ إِلَّا هُوَ الْحَيُّ الْقَيُّومُ ۝٢
نَزَّلَ عَلَيْكَ الْكِتَٰبَ بِالْحَقِّ مُصَدِّقًا
لِّمَا بَيْنَ يَدَيْهِ وَأَنزَلَ التَّوْرَىٰةَ
وَالْإِنجِيلَ ۝٣ مِن قَبْلُ هُدًى لِّلنَّاسِ وَأَنزَلَ
الْفُرْقَانَ إِنَّ الَّذِينَ كَفَرُوا بِآيَٰتِ اللَّهِ لَهُمْ
عَذَابٌ شَدِيدٌ وَاللَّهُ عَزِيزٌ ذُو انتِقَامٍ ۝٤
إِنَّ اللَّهَ لَا يَخْفَىٰ عَلَيْهِ شَيْءٌ فِي الْأَرْضِ
وَلَا فِي السَّمَآءِ ۝٥ هُوَ الَّذِي يُصَوِّرُكُمْ فِي
الْأَرْحَامِ كَيْفَ يَشَآءُ لَآ إِلَٰهَ إِلَّا هُوَ الْعَزِيزُ
الْحَكِيمُ ۝٦ هُوَ الَّذِيٓ أَنزَلَ عَلَيْكَ الْكِتَٰبَ مِنْهُ
آيَٰتٌ مُّحْكَمَٰتٌ هُنَّ أُمُّ الْكِتَٰبِ وَأُخَرُ
مُتَشَٰبِهَٰتٌ فَأَمَّا الَّذِينَ فِي قُلُوبِهِمْ زَيْغٌ
فَيَتَّبِعُونَ مَا تَشَٰبَهَ مِنْهُ ابْتِغَآءَ الْفِتْنَةِ

الجزء الثالث

51

A standard English translation showing the Arabic text, commentary, and meaning.

The second miraculous aspect of the Qur'an concerns its content. The Qur'an covers a variety of subjects, including religious doctrine, law, social values, morality, history, prophets and their struggles, philosophy, and science. Without containing a single unified narrative on any of those subjects, the Qur'an skillfully weaves components of each into self-contained chapters that reference one and then the other to provide coherent essays appealing to a variety of listeners.

Muhammad never went to school. During his life, he never read a book, nor was he ever tutored or engaged in learning of any kind. Then suddenly, when he turned 40 years old, the epitome of eloquence flows from his tongue? This is quite inexplicable. Only a century ago, Western scholars of Islam were claiming that Muhammad had epilepsy (which is not true) and that the Qur'an came during seizures. Do epileptics conjure rapturous poems and essays in such states? Other Westerners have charged that Muhammad made up the Qur'an, though they can't explain how. But as Dr. Maurice Bucaille observed, in refuting those who have suggested that Muhammad wrote the Qur'an himself, "How could a man, from being illiterate, become the most important author, in terms of literary merits, in the whole of Arabic literature?" Muslims would say that it is no less than direct revelation from God.

> **Ask the Imam**
>
> Before touching the Qur'an, a Muslim must make sure that he or she is in a ritually pure state. This is accomplished by washing the hands, face, and feet with water. There is no prohibition against women reading and handling the Holy Book as there is in some other religions.

Meccan and Medinan Revelations

The verses of the Qur'an are divided into two main categories based on the period of the Prophet's mission in which they were revealed. The first 13 years of prophethood were spent in Mecca, a hostile environment for the Muslims in which the reigning idolaters made life miserable for the new religion and its followers. The second period began with the *Hijrah*, or migration to Medina, when Islam became the dominant force in city politics and thus was no longer directly under fire.

Meccan revelations, as they are called, center on two main themes: confronting backward Arab tribal customs and pointing out the foolishness of idolatry. Some of the customs that the Qur'an spoke out against are as follows:

- ◆ Burying unwanted baby girls alive (infanticide)
- ◆ Believing in superstition and practicing witchcraft
- ◆ Men inheriting their widowed mothers as wives of their own
- ◆ Blindly following tradition for its own sake

The campaign against idolatry was especially urgent because the Qur'anic revelations were making it increasingly clear that the shrine of Abraham, the *Ka'bah*, was no place to store 360 tribal idols. Mecca was so decadent that idolaters often circled the *Ka'bah* naked, paying homage to their idols. The Qur'an mentioned specifically three gods that the Arabs worshipped and called such practices idiocy. Instead of praying to lesser gods for daily benefits and luck, Islam asserted, why not pray to the only true God, Allah?

Understandably, the Meccans didn't take kindly to Muhammad's preaching and teaching, and they began to harass the Muslims daily. Muhammad was often punched and shoved in the streets. Once he was almost strangled to death by an irate Meccan near the *Ka'bah*. Other Muslims were brutally tortured, and a few were murdered. (The first martyr of Islam was a woman who refused to go back to idol worship.) Consequently, Meccan revelations also contain the stories of past prophets who suffered hardships; this was a way to show Muhammad and his followers that others also endured rough times, but God's help eventually saved them.

Medinan revelations, or those delivered to Muhammad after he and his followers escaped Mecca, were concerned with how to build an Islamic society. The values and manners of Islam and the particulars of Islamic Law grew in importance and application. Verses regulating inheritance, marriage and divorce, the conduct of statecraft, civil laws, and criminal punishments made an appearance. An extensive collection of verses on relations with Jews and Christians was given as well. It was also during this period that alcoholic beverages were made illegal. But by this time Muslims were so staunch in their faith that they had no problem in smashing their wine vessels in the streets. This is one *Prohibition* that didn't fail.

The Compilation

The Qur'an was an oral message given to Muhammad through the archangel Gabriel. Muhammad himself couldn't write, so he asked his literate followers to be his secretaries. Even in the earliest days of Mecca, the Qur'an was being recorded. Paper was unknown in Arabia at that time, so the materials used consisted of Egyptian parchment, leather scrolls, and the shoulder blades of camels (which were sort of like large slates). During the Medinan period, the entire collection of written *surahs* was kept in a large leather bag in the possession of the Prophet. At one time the Prophet had over 20 secretaries writing down his words.

There was no need to put everything together in book form because the tradition established by the Prophet was for people to memorize as much of the Qur'an by heart as possible. By the time of the Prophet's death, hundreds of people had memorized the entire book in its properly arranged order. Nearly everyone else knew at least significant portions by heart. And with the Prophet's emphasis on literacy, more people than ever before were learning how to read and write, so written pages of Qur'anic verse began to circulate far and wide.

During the rule of the first Muslim caliph, Abu Bakr, a rebellion arose in southern Arabia, and during one battle more than 70 of the most prominent memorizers were killed. Umar ibn al Khattab, one of the top companions of Muhammad, prevailed upon Abu Bakr to prepare the Qur'an in a single book form so that its proper order and reading would never be lost. This was done under the meticulous supervision of the Prophet's chief secretary, Zayd bin Thabit, who was able to utilize newly introduced paper products from China. The book was kept in the care of one of the Prophet's widows and no more thought was given to the issue.

Later on, during the rule of the third Muslim caliph, Usman ibn Affan, non-Arab converts began arguing about the proper way to pronounce the verses of the Qur'an as well as the meanings of the words contained within. They even began writing personal copies, incorporating their own variant spellings, arrangements, and pronunciations of words. The problem became so serious that some of the old-time companions of the Prophet thought the Qur'an might be lost in a sea of competing versions. Usman acted decisively and ordered that the official edition, prepared in the time of his predecessor, Abu Bakr, be verified, duplicated, and one copy of it sent to every major Muslim city. Again, Zayd bin Thabit was given the responsibility for this task, and he headed a team of four who had committed the Qur'an to memory to ensure the utmost veracity. From the five or seven copies that they prepared, scribes in the far-flung regions of the Empire could make further copies, so all controversies and disagreements would be laid to rest. All the faulty copies people had made themselves were to be burned so that only the authenticated edition would circulate.

Translate This

A *Hafiz* is a person who has committed the entire Qur'an to memory. The name literally means a *Guardian*. The Holy Qur'an is the most memorized book in the world.

Two copies of those *Usmani Qur'ans*, as they are called, exist to this day in museums in Turkey and Tashkent. They have exactly the same text as any Arabic Qur'an today. To those who have suggested that the Qur'an we have today is not completely in line with the one Muhammad recited, the reply is simple: All of the people who were involved in recording the Qur'an both during and after Muhammad's time were memorizers of the book. In addition, there were hundreds of other such people who would have noticed any alterations in the text. Among Muhammad's thousands of surviving companions, there was never any controversy on this issue.

Major Themes of the Qur'an

The three major themes of the Qur'an are as follows:

1. The absolute authority of God

2. The accountability of humans for their deeds

3. The impermanence of this life

Each theme is expressed in a forceful way using parables, examples, references to past peoples or prophets, and logic.

Fully one third of the verses of the Qur'an relate to issues concerning the next life and what people will find after death. Another third of the verses deal with prophets, interfaith issues, and the human experience, while the final third cover subjects ranging from law to personal and social obligations. All of these different themes appear at different places throughout the whole scripture.

The Teachings of the Prophet

"O You who believe," the Qur'an exhorts, "obey Allah and obey the Messenger." In another verse we read, "You have a beautiful pattern to follow in the Messenger of Allah." These are just two of the many *ayahs*, or verses, that tell Muslims to follow the teachings of the Prophet Muhammad. But isn't the Qur'an one such teaching? The Islamic answer is no. The Qur'an is God's literal Word merely transmitted through the mouthpiece of Muhammad. The Prophet's teachings are something else entirely. This is why the *Shahadah*, or Islamic Declaration of Faith, has two parts—in order to remind people of this.

Muhammad's life example, called his *Sunnah*, or Way, represents his own interpretation of how to live by the dictates of the Qur'an. One often-used example concerns the five daily prayers of Islam. The Qur'an tells Muslims simply to pray at fixed times, but it doesn't tell them how to pray. It mentions nothing about reciting *surahs*, bowing at the waist, saying certain phrases, and so on. These the Prophet taught in his own words. The archangel Gabriel, Muslims believe, was providing Muhammad with guidance on this and all other issues, but the knowledge was filtered through Muhammad's speech, experiences, and actions. Thus the *Sunnah* of Muhammad is considered to be the second most important source of Islam.

> **It Is Written**
>
> Muhammad, during his last major public address, said, "I'm leaving you with two things. If you hold fast to them you will never go astray. They are the Book of Allah and my Sunnah."

How Are Hadiths Different from the Qur'an?

The Qur'an contains verses that have their own style. From rhymes to prose, there is a certain way that the information is presented and certain types of grammar constructions. Muhammad's own sayings, or *hadiths*, which form the basis of the *Sunnah*, are what he said on a daily basis in the course of normal life. When he spoke to people of his own volition, he neither rhymed nor recited in a melodious voice. Here is an example of the difference in style. The first selection is a verse from the Qur'an. The second two selections are well-known hadiths of the Prophet, taken from the collection of the ninth-century scholar Imam Bukhari.

Qur'an:

O You who believe, shall I lead you to a bargain that will save you from a painful doom? It is that you believe in Allah and His Messenger and then strive in His cause with your wealth and your persons. That is best for you if you only knew. (61:10–11)

Hadiths:

The older a person gets the more his desire for two things increases: wealth and longevity. (Bukhari)

Learning is a duty on every Muslim, male and female. (Bukhari)

Translate This

A *hadith* is classified as anything the Prophet Muhammad said, did, or gave silent approval to.

As you can see, the Qur'an contains a distinctly religious tone while the hadiths are more like statements or pronouncements such as an orator might make or a teacher might say to his or her students.

Who Recorded the Hadiths?

During the Meccan period and early Medinan period, Muhammad used to forbid his followers to write down his personal sayings for fear that people would mix them up with the Qur'an. Near the end of his life, however, when the sanctity of the Qur'an was secure and lots of people knew the entire Qur'an by heart, he relaxed this prohibition. Many of his followers began to write down what they had learned from him on a variety of topics.

One of the earliest collections of Muhammad's sayings to have survived to this day is called the *Muwatta of Imam Malik,* which was written in Medina within 80 years of Muhammad's death and draws on many firsthand witnesses and the children of those who lived and worshipped in the Prophet's time. Given that most early Muslims could still not read or write, though, a large majority of the Prophet's sayings were passed on orally from parent to child for several generations. As the population increased and the movement of people became more pronounced, many of those who knew or who had learned the oral hadith traditions became scattered.

Starting in the late seventh century, but gaining real momentum by the eighth, scholars who wanted to collect these elusive sayings and preserve them for later generations began traveling all over the Muslim Empire looking for people who had these hadiths or who had learned them from others. One of the early Caliphs, Umar ibn Abdul Aziz (who ruled from 717–720), actually commissioned a historian to compile the Prophet's sayings in an official public record. He was just one of many Muslims who began to look seriously into this task.

Because there are always dishonest people and forgetful ones, these early scholars developed a system for sifting through the collected data to determine whether a hadith was authentic or fabricated. This process involved a grueling investigation into the genealogy of the person giving the hadith, focusing on the moral character of the narrator and whom he or she had heard it from, and so on. If any discrepancy was found, the hadith would be labeled as not fully reliable or even false. All of this information is recorded as a chain (called an *isnad*) going back to the original person who heard the hadith from the Prophet. Here are some common designations in evaluating hadith literature:

 Just the Facts

Imam Bukhari (d. 870), the most famous collector of hadiths, gathered more than 600,000 hadiths but included only 2,602 in his official book because the rest he could not prove with sufficient certainty that the Prophet said them.

- ◆ **Sahih**   A sound and accurate report

- ◆ **Hasan**   Probably true but with less certainty

- ◆ **Dhaif**   A weakly proven report that needs corroboration

- ◆ **Saqim**   Probably false and without much proof

- ◆ **Ahad**   The chain of narrators is reduced to one individual at a certain point and thus confidence may be lacking

- ◆ **Mutawatir**   The hadith has been narrated by so many people in so many places that it is undoubtedly authentic

---

Ask the Imam

Imam Bukhari, considered by Sunni Muslims to be the foremost authority of hadith who ever lived, heard that there was a man in a far-off land who had a unique hadith. The Imam traveled for weeks to reach the man's city and asked where this person could be found. When the Imam approached the man's house, he saw him trying to coax his donkey to move by pretending he had food in his hand. The Imam concluded that the man was a liar and left without ever speaking to him.

Another area of criteria concerned the harmony between the hadith and the Qur'anic text. Muhammad predicted that many people would attribute false sayings to him in the future, so he gave the instruction that any hadith that contradicts the Qur'an does not come from him; therefore, it should be rejected. These were just two of the methods employed by the early hadith scholars in ensuring the accuracy of the prophetic traditions. The bulk of the work was completed within 200 years of the Prophet's death.

The major hadith scholars, whose works are named after them, are Imam Bukhari, Imam Muslim, At-Tirmidhi, Ibn Majah, Abu Dawood, and An-Nisa'i. All of their collections are available widely. The hadiths are classified by topic and cover everything from how to perform the five pillars and how to treat neighbors to what to do in war, how to treat your family, what to do if you want to go on a journey, and so on.

Hadith Literature: A Snapshot

Here is an example of a hadith with the full chain of narrators going back to the Prophet. This hadith comes from the collection of Imam Bukhari and is classified as proven (*Sahih*). (The voluminous biographical material on each narrator is omitted here.)

On the authority of Abu Al Nauman, who said he heard it from Said ibn Zayd, who heard it from 'Ali ibn Zayd, who said he heard it from Jabir ibn 'Abdullah, who heard it from the Prophet: the Prophet said, "Whoever has three daughters, cares and provides for them, and shows them mercy, will enter paradise."

The Companions of the Prophet

A companion of the Prophet is classified as anyone who heard, saw, or spent time with the Prophet Muhammad. These people, who are called the *sahaba*, are considered to be authorities on Islam because they learned about Islam directly from the source. In terms of numbers, there were over a hundred thousand *sahaba*, though if you count only the ones who spent meaningful time with the Prophet you're actually looking at only a few hundred noteworthy men and women.

Muslims frequently quote a saying of Muhammad's in which he compared his companions to guiding stars: Whichever one is followed, a person will be

> **Ask the Imam**
>
> The *sahaba* were not like the disciples of Jesus. It was a more inclusive grouping that included all Muslims. Although he had something of an inner circle, Muhammad never specifically made a separate grouping of people with a special status.

rightly guided. Muhammad's companions are considered the best generation in Islamic history, with each succeeding generation being a little less noble than the one before it. The *sahaba* were truly amazing people from a certain standpoint. Most of them were converts to Islam who were transformed from a variety of lifestyles into the unified tradition of Islam. They encompassed all races and social standings but came together in mutual communion as brothers and sisters in faith. Each had his or her own talents, and Muhammad was able to utilize the abilities of each to the advantage of the community as a whole.

Early Meccan Converts

There are certain *sahaba* who stand out because of the hardships they had to endure. Among these are the earliest Meccan converts to Islam. They converted when conversion could mean being ridiculed, shunned by their own families, or even killed. The following list introduces some of the best-known *sahaba*:

- **Khadijah bint Khuwaylid**   Muhammad's first and only wife for over 25 years, who was the first convert to Islam.

- **Abu Bakr As-Siddeeq**   Muhammad's best friend and the first caliph of Islam after he passed away.

- **Umar ibn al Khattab**   A convert who later became the second caliph.

- **Sumayyah bint Khubbat**   An early convert who was tortured to death by the Meccans. She is traditionally known as the first martyr of Islam.

- **Bilal ibn Rab'ah**   A black slave who suffered terrible torture at the hands of his idolatrous master. Abu Bakr bought his freedom and later Bilal became the first *muezzin*, or prayer caller, in Islam.

Prominent Women

Many people would be surprised to learn that women played very prominent roles in the rise of Islam. From the first night when Khadijah consoled her husband after his first revelation, through to the end of the Prophet's life, women supported Islam as fiercely as men. For women, Islam provided a way out of the stifling Arab customs of the day. From female infanticide to unrestricted violence, women before Islam had a very hard time. Islam brought them equal status, rights, and a voice in the community that they had never had before. I will be discussing more about this in Chapter 20.

Some of the most prominent women, other than those already mentioned, include …

♦ **Umm Salamah**   She had to endure immense pressure from her family, even losing the custody of her child for a time. She never faltered and eventually escaped to Medina.

♦ **Umm Ammarah**   During a fierce battle in which the Meccans attacked the Muslims from behind, she stood over the wounded Prophet and fought off a crowd of attacking men with arrows, a spear, and finally a sword and shield.

♦ **A'ishah**   The daughter of Abu Bakr and a wife of the Prophet. She was a leader of women and a teacher to both men and women.

♦ **Barakah**   She was an African woman who was Muhammad's caretaker when he was a boy. After Muhammad attained prophethood, she carried secret messages, at great danger to herself, between the hidden Muslim meeting places around Mecca.

The 'Ulema: Scholars of the Faith

The body of Islamic knowledge is quite extensive. Areas of study can include Arabic grammar, the Qur'an, the hadiths, Islamic Law, biographies of the *sahaba*, philosophy, interfaith dialogue, the life history of Muhammad, and political and economic theory. Most people don't have the time to delve very deeply into these subjects, so religious scholars fill the gaps in knowledge. The difference between Islam and other religious traditions, however, is that Muslim scholars (the *'Ulema*) are not charged with formulating new doctrines. Rather, they organize and interpret the data given in the Qur'an and the hadiths.

The only areas in which new additions to Islamic Law can be made are those involving an unexpected issue that confronts the Muslim community. For example, how does Islam view test tube babies or cryogenic freezing or even organ transplantation? Islamic scholars, who often work independently of each other under little to no regulation, consult a descending order of sources to arrive at an answer that is within the general spirit of Islam. This is called the science of *Fiqh*, or deducing legal positions. The four sources consulted are …

♦ The Qur'an (the word of God).

♦ The hadiths (the basis of the Prophet's *Sunnah*).

♦ The consensus of the *sahaba* on an issue (*'Ijma*).

♦ Independent reasoning or analogy (*Qiyas*).

In the last source, the scholar himself or herself tries to come up with an answer from his or her own logic and ability to reason. Sometimes scholars have to get very creative to provide answers for the community. The word *Ijtehad* is the name for this process of coming up with definitive rulings that rely on a lot of independent thought. It is through this process that the corpus of Islamic Law is a living, breathing institution that can adapt to any age or circumstance. Recent legal rulings, called *fatwas*, have declared that it is allowed to say the call to prayer over a loudspeaker, to perform prayers in a spacecraft, to donate organs, and to trade stocks that are not connected with vice.

> ### Ask the Imam
>
> There is no prohibition against women being scholars in Islam. Throughout Islamic history until this day, many famous *'Ulema* have been females revered for their learning and sagacity. Because there is no clergy in Islam, only a society of scholars, the certifying authority is widespread from recognized Islamic colleges.

Early Theologians

Not everyone is qualified to issue fatwas or engage in *Ijtehad*. Although no central hierarchy exists among Muslim scholars, such as in the Catholic Church with its ecclesiastical structure, there are certain recognized qualifications for being accepted as a religious authority in Islam. A person has to study in an accepted Islamic university or with a graduate who has been given permission to teach higher studies. Such independent teachers are often called *shaykhs*, an old Arabic term that means chief or leader. People who complete programs of study, which usually last about five years, are given a certificate called an *'Ijazah*, the equivalent of what we would call a Master's degree in Islamic studies.

Some of the most famous *sahaba* of the past and their students are still remembered by Muslims. Names like *Hassan al Basri* and *A'ishah bint Abi Bakr* are spoken of with reverence. It was during this early generation that the teachings of Islam were systematized and made more comprehensible to the masses. All of the major Islamic sciences from *Fiqh* to Arabic lexicography were initiated within the first two centuries of the Islamic expansion. The foundation of this knowledge still defines traditional Islamic education today.

The Five Imams

The science of *Fiqh* was initiated by a variety of concerned scholars in the first centuries of Islam. They often worked together at first but then formulated their legal processes of *Ijtehad* independently. Each scholar attracted numbers of students who carried on the work after their founder's passing. These growing legal traditions attempted to explain the teachings and application of Islam to the masses.

This service was necessary because many verses of the Qur'an can be interpreted in different ways. In addition, some of the hadiths are vague or even confusing for the average person to understand. Because people see things differently, each of these schools of thought, or *madh-habs*, varied slightly in its findings. When talking about issues of *Ijtehad* where no clear-cut Islamic answer is available, the amount of disagreement can increase. For example, the Qur'an declares that Muslims are allowed to eat "flesh from the sea." Some scholars thought this meant only fish, while others included clams, crustaceans, and anything else that lives under the water. Although the *madh-habs* agree on more than 80 percent of the issues related to Islamic beliefs and practices, it's over the peripheral issues that disagreement and controversy sometimes ensue.

Each of these schools of thought began to be known by the name of its founder. The four *Sunni* and one *Shi'a* (for an explanation of the differences between these two major sects of Islam see Chapter 27) *madh-hab* that have survived to this day are as follows:

- ◆ **The Hanafi**   Founded by Abu Hanifa (700–767). He emphasized reason and analogy in the development of Islamic Law.

- ◆ **The Shafi**   Founded by Muhammad Al Shafi'I (767–820). He was the first to classify the four main sources of Islamic Law ranging from the Qur'an and *hadith* to *Ijma* and *Qiyas*.

- ◆ **The Maliki**   Founded by Malik ibn Anas, the author of Al Muwatta (716–795). Imam Malik emphasized the importance of following the legal traditions of Medina.

- ◆ **The Hanbali**   Founded by Ahmed ibn Hanbal (780–855). This is the most conservative of the surviving four schools of Sunni Islamic Law. Ibn Hanbal crafted his understanding of Islam in response to a new Muslim ideology based on rationalism. The Wahhabi movement, which has governed Saudi Arabia for almost two centuries, favors this stricter school of Fiqh.

- ◆ **The Ja'fari**   Founded by Imam Ja'far as Sadiq (699–765). This is the principle Shi'a school of Islamic Law and is not recognized as valid by more conservative scholars of the Sunni tradition. A majority of its principles conform to those of the other schools of thought, though there are significant differences.

Muslims everywhere generally adhere to one of these five schools of thought, taking all of their questions about how to follow Islam to the scholars and manuals produced by each. Most Muslim countries have areas of concentration in which the majority of the people follow one or the other. The modus operandi that has prevailed for centuries between the adherents of each legal tradition has been that all are valid legal paths to being a good Muslim, so no one should criticize another's *madh-hab*. Muslims commonly identify themselves by the legal tradition they follow.

Activist Scholars

Islamic scholars have played a key role in protecting and promoting Islam. It was they who often put their own lives at risk in confronting the excesses of the political rulers. When external enemies threatened the Muslim world, the scholars called upon the people to defend themselves. During the era of Colonialism, men such as Muhammad Abdu, Jamal Uddin Afghani, and Uthman Dan Fodio explained to the community why they had been conquered by non-Muslims and what they could do about it.

Given the complete absence of an Islamic political structure uniting Muslims throughout the world, as is called for in the Qur'an, scholars have today replaced the sultans, caliphs, and khans of the past as the protectors of Islam. This practice can lead to abuse, of course, and one dangerous trend today is the growth of the "instant shaykh." People who have little Islamic knowledge suddenly set themselves up as authority figures and attract gullible followers. Muslims routinely discuss this issue and look for ways to curtail the ambitions of people who don't have the patience to undergo a traditional course of study.

There are many prominent (and authentic) Islamic scholars in the West today. They provide guidance to Muslims who are trying to negotiate life in a non-Muslim society that is often seen as hostile to religious values. Some of the more well known are Jamal Bedawi, Hamza Yusuf, Siraj Wahhaj, Ahmad Sakr, Jamal Zarabozo, Ruqqaiyah Waris Maqsood, Mukhtar Maghroui, and Muzzamil Siddiqi.

In the last decade numerous Islamic colleges have been set up, from California to Maine, and they are now graduating scholars who were born in the West and educated in the Islamic traditions of the East. Both houses of the United States Congress have had opening invocations performed by Islamic scholars, and the White House is now the frequent scene of visits from Muslim leaders. The U.S. military has been certifying Islamic chaplains for years in association with several important American Islamic institutions. A new chapter has opened in the world of Islam, and its first page begins with the new generation of Muslim *'ulema*, or scholars, from North America.

The Least You Need to Know

♦ Muslims consider the Qur'an to be the literal Word of God dictated to Muhammad by the archangel Gabriel.

♦ The sayings of the Prophet are considered secondary in status to the Qur'an. The details of how to practice Islam are given in the *hadiths*.

♦ The companions of the Prophet are those who carried the message of Islam forward both before and after Muhammad's death. Muslims revere them as examples of strong faith.

♦ Islam is interpreted for everyday Muslims by scholars. A scholar in Islam is similar in status to a theologian in Christianity and Judaism, with the exception that a scholar does not create doctrines.

♦ Muslim scholars are considered to be the authorities on Islam but are not considered holy in the same way a priest or rabbi is. Women can become scholars in Islam as well.

Chapter 19

Living Islam

In This Chapter

- ◆ Learn about the Islamic view of family and marriage
- ◆ Step into a mosque and look around at what's inside
- ◆ Discover the ceremonies that mark the passage of life for Muslims
- ◆ Mark the holidays of Islam and discover their significance
- ◆ Find out what Muslims can and cannot do
- ◆ Learn about the dietary restrictions that affect every aspect of Muslim life

Islam is not just a religious or spiritual discipline. It also provides guidance for every aspect of a person's life both at home and out in society. The very basis of a healthy community, after reforming one's own self, is the family. "Save yourselves and your families," declares the Qur'an, and this theme encompasses a large part of a Muslim's life. Islam holds that the best places to be are in the home or in the mosque; when out in the world at large, one had better avoid the many snares and traps of *Shaytan*.

But Islam is not a dowdy religion, consigning its followers to just praying, fasting, and staying out of trouble. It is also a community experience, and wholesome activities to celebrate life are not only encouraged but religiously mandated. People should come out to mingle and build stronger bonds among themselves. For this reason Islam promotes public ceremonies to mark the passage of life-changing events. There are also two annual holidays for people to come together in joy and merriment. In this chapter I will show you the familial and social aspects of Islam.

Islam and the Family

Islam has a definite conception of the ideal family life. The Qur'an describes the relationship between a husband and a wife as "two garments that protect each other." Both have equal status as adults, and neither is encouraged to lord it over the other. With that said, Islam also assigns the husband the role of the head of the family. It doesn't mean that the husband is to be the dictator of the family, though, but rather the caretaker of everyone's safety and well-being. Consequently, on Judgment Day a man will have to answer for how he shepherded, cared for, guided, and provided for his family.

> **Ask the Imam**
>
> Although there are patterns of discrimination against women evident in some conservative Muslim societies, according to longstanding Islamic legal theory, women are allowed to work outside the home, are required to get an education, and can hold positions of authority over men in the workplace. The only caveat is that a mother is encouraged to put her family first before a career, but this is not a legal requirement in Islamic Law. During the rule of the second Caliph, Umar ibn al Khattab, the chief officer overseeing the merchants of Medina was a woman.

As the Qur'an itself explains: "Men are the appointed protectors and maintainers of women because Allah has given them more responsibility than them." (Qur'an 4:34) Never are men called smarter, more deserving, or more capable than women. They are simply given the responsibility to work (and the added physical strength to go along with it) so that women have a greater freedom to make choices that will ensure they don't need to sacrifice their family life for the sake of supporting themselves. Looked at from a certain angle, God has eternally doomed men to work for women!

Muslims take Muhammad's experiences with his extended household as examples of how interfamilial relationships can be conducted. Muhammad's marriage to Khadijah lasted for over 20 years, and he had no other wife during this time. Khadijah is held up as the ideal wife—caring, supportive, and compassionate. With her prowess in economic affairs, she helped to fund the Prophet's activities. A year after her death, Muhammad's companions encouraged him to marry again, so he married an older widow who had no support. He would later take more wives, widows mostly, for the same charitable and kindly reasons. During those years people frequently asked his wives about how he treated them and what he did around the house. Besides praying quite often, they reported, he was always friendly, kind, helpful, and never overbearing or demanding. Thus, ample opportunity existed for people to see how a prophet coexisted with his family.

The Ties That Bind

Islam envisions a society in which people are connected on many levels. Families are united, and divorce is rare. Communities are made up of settled people who look out for each other, and everyone attends the mosque regularly. As such, the ties of neighbors are continually strengthened. If one household is in need, others step forward to assist. Crime is rare, and the citizens are literate and thoughtful. Has such a utopian vision ever existed? Actually, for a large chunk of Islamic history, many communities functioning around the world have come close to this ideal.

When Muslims look at modern society with all of its problems, they sometimes get the urge to become insular. Issues such as abortion, teen pregnancy, rampant promiscuity, dating, drug addiction, violent youth culture, and alcoholism were virtually unknown in the traditional Muslim world until recently. One of the reasons for the growth of Islamic parochial schools in North America is the alarming trends that seem to be tearing apart American society. Do Muslims claim that Islam has the answers to these problems? Yes, but in the meantime, few Muslims are willing to allow their families to assimilate into the more negative aspects of modern culture.

The Ideal Muslim Home

In an Islamic home the father is a responsible man who works hard for his family. He is neither arrogant nor cruel and shows tender kindness to his family. Toward his wife, he is loving, and he caters to her sexual needs through caressing and tenderness. These symbols of intimate affection were described by the Prophet as the *ambassadors*, which must come before intimate relations. He is never alone with another woman, even at work, and he consults his family on all major decisions. He does not physically or emotionally abuse his wife because he knows the Prophet Muhammad never hit or disrespected a woman in his whole life. The children are obedient and respect their father completely. Their greatest shame is to cause their father to become angry.

The wife is cooperative with her husband in all things that require a team effort. She is not a slave, a servant, nor a second-class citizen. She is her own person with her own financial assets, hobbies, and interests. The Qur'an describes the relationship between a man and wife as that of helpers to each other. The Prophet Muhammad said that mothers deserve three times the respect as that given to fathers, and this is on account of the sacrifices women make for their families. With that said, the wife understands the grave responsibility upon her husband's shoulders, for on Judgment Day the father will bear the blame for any failures to protect his family.

It Is Written

According to Muhammad, "Indeed, Allah has made it forbidden for you to disobey mothers."

She doesn't refuse his sexual advances so as not to alienate him, and she doesn't have any friends that he dislikes. She upholds his reputation and doesn't spill his secrets in public. Though she may work if she wishes, her money is her own. She would never sacrifice her children's moral, physical, and emotional needs, however, solely for the sake of personal goals. She doesn't wear much makeup in public or dress specifically to attract other men's eyes, and she looks forward to Paradise, which is promised to those women who are sincere helpmates to their husbands.

Spare the Rod

How should a child be raised according to Islam? The answer is best expressed in the words of the Prophet Muhammad, who said that when children are under the age of 7, we should be easy with them. From the ages of 7 to 14, we should be strict with them, and after 14 we should be their friend. This three-stage developmental process takes into account every level of intellectual and emotional capacity. Small children don't always understand what they're doing, so punishment must be withheld as much as possible. Teenagers are prone to trouble, so a firm hand is in order; after puberty, Islam considers a person an adult.

It is the responsibility of the parents to rear their children properly and to teach them manners, religious obligations, and worldly knowledge. Abu Bakr, a famous companion of the Prophet, once noted that the child who is taught to be good at an early age has an easier time being virtuous later on in life. Another famous companion, 'Ali ibn Abi Talib, once counseled, "Raise your children differently from how you were raised because they are meant for a different time than you."

The Prophet Muhammad, whose *Sunnah* is considered the ideal model for all Muslims, used to hug and kiss his children and grandchildren and always made time to

play with them. He also did not complain
about what they did. Anas bin Malik, who as
a boy came to serve the aged Prophet, later
remarked, "I served the Prophet for 10 years
and never once did he say, 'Why did you do
this?' or 'Why did you do that?'"

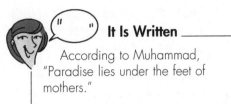

It Is Written

According to Muhammad,
"Paradise lies under the feet of
mothers."

Welcome to My Mosque

The mosque, or *masjid*, is the focal point of the Islamic community. It is open for the
five daily prayers, and Muslims routinely congregate there for prayer, meditation, and
reflection. In the Prophet's day, the main mosque of Medina was used for community
meetings, planning sessions, and even as a homeless shelter for the poor people who
embraced Islam and needed a place to stay for the night.

In North America today, the mosque still retains many of its traditional functions.
Community dinners are usually a monthly occurrence. Weddings and funeral prayers
are often performed there as well. A new innovation that is common mostly to
mosques in the Western world is the addition of a weekend school for the children of
the congregation's members. On Saturdays or Sundays, children attend the school to
learn about the fundamentals of their religion and to socialize with other children of
similar backgrounds.

There are currently over 2,000 mosques spread all across Canada, the United States,
and Mexico. Most have congregations numbering less than a thousand, but a few
serve several thousand people annually. Most mosques are operated by an elected
body whose terms are limited. Unlike most Christian churches or Jewish synagogues,
however, the public leadership of a mosque usually lies with a president, director, or
chairman of the board while the post of Imam (a traditional title for a prayer leader) is
limited to leading prayers, performing weddings and funerals and teaching religious
classes. In the past most Imams were imported from overseas but with the rise of an
indigenous number of Islamic scholars and activists one can find increasing numbers
of American-born Imams in our nation's mosques.

What Happens in a Mosque?

The main activities one finds in a mosque are prayer and teaching. The most attended
prayer, of course, is the Friday service called *Salat ul-Jumu'ah*, or the prayer of gathering. It is an obligation on all Muslim men over the age of puberty to attend. Women
are allowed and encouraged to attend as well, though there is no sin recorded for

them if they pray at home. This is a mercy owing to the fact that many women have child-rearing responsibilities, such as breast-feeding and the like.

Hyper-spiritual Muslims, who are known as *Sufis*, sometimes sit in large circles in mosques and chant Islamic phrases and the names of God in unison. Other Muslims simply go to the mosque to read and study the Qur'an in a quiet atmosphere. Loud shouting and calling out are frowned upon, and men are encouraged to apply scented cologne when they arrive. (Women are asked to wear more-muted perfumes that do not surround them in an envelope of scents so as not to attract undue male interest.)

Just the Facts

Although non-Islamic backward cultural practices in some Muslim countries result in women being discouraged from attending public religious services, Muhammad said, "Do not prevent the female servants of Allah from going to the mosque."

When the time for any particular prayer arrives, the *muazzin* gives a shortened version of the prayer call and people arrange themselves in straight rows behind the Imam. Men line up in the front rows, followed by rows of children, and finally the women line up behind. There is no gender discrimination here, as was explained in Chapter 11. With all the bowing and prostrating that goes on, it is best that the sexes are not mixed together.

No Shoes Allowed!

Shoes are not allowed in the main prayer area of a mosque. This tradition has its roots in ancient customs of which Judaism and Christianity used to partake. The main hall where the actual prayers are performed is called the *musallah*, or prayer place. There are no aisles of pews or chairs inside, just carpeting, often with parallel lines marking the rows to help people line up straight. Non-Muslim women are not required to wear head scarves before entering the mosque, but some mosques have a policy asking visitors to don a scarf for reasons of modesty or respect.

Friday, the Day of Gathering

On Fridays, Muslims all over the world attend a half-hour service in which they listen to a two-part speech, which is then followed up by a group prayer. The service is held in the early afternoon, and many Muslims in North America are forced to ask their employers for an extra long lunch break on Fridays. This is because *Salat ul-Jumu'ah*, as it is called, is classified as a religious duty upon men. The Qur'an states:

> O you who believe! When the call for prayer is made on Friday, hasten to the remembrance of Allah and cease your business. That is better for you if you but knew. (Qur'an 62:9)

Friday is not considered like a Sabbath day or a day of rest. Muslims are asked to stop working and come together as a community for less than an hour, and then they can go back about their business. It's really quite interesting that in some Muslim countries where there are large Christian populations, the governments usually designate Friday and Sunday as weekend days, with Saturday being a workday. Other nations keep the traditional Western days of Saturday and Sunday for rest and merely mandate that for the time of Friday prayers workers can get a break in the workday.

Friday is also significant for Muslims because of the following saying of the Prophet Muhammad:

> The best day on which the sun rises is Friday. On it Adam was created, on it he was expelled [from the garden], on it his repentance was accepted, on it he died, and on it the Last Hour will take place. On Friday every animal is on the lookout from dawn to dusk in fear of the Last Hour, but not jinn and men, and it contains a time at which no Muslim prays and asks anything from Allah but He will give it to him.

The Features of a Masjid

Every *masjid*, or mosque, has the following features:

1. A *musallah*, or main prayer hall, usually carpeted

2. A minaret from which the *muazzin* makes the call to prayer five times a day, though mosques built in the West often omit this nonrequired feature in favor of an internal sound system

3. An area for people to do *wudu*, or ritual washing for prayer

4. A small inward curved niche in the front wall indicating the direction of Mecca

5. A *minbar*, or raised pulpit with several steps leading to a small platform

6. Usually, some type of dome as part of the traditional architecture, but a dome isn't required

7. Separate prayer areas for men and women marked off in some way

8. A collection of Qur'ans and books of the Prophet's sayings for worshippers to use in between prayers.

Many mosques also incorporate a community hall and classrooms for weekend religious schooling. The education curriculum will vary from simple Qur'an memorization to more formal classes in Muslim theology and tenets.

A typical mosque has a dome and a minaret.

What Is an Imam?

An *Imam* is a person who leads the prayer in the mosque. It is a term sometimes applied to the leader of the community, as well. Basically, an Imam serves a function similar to that of a priest or rabbi. He conducts religious services, performs marriages and funerals, gives counseling, and teaches adult and children's classes. An Imam gains his position by first completing a course of study in a recognized Islamic college. Then he is hired by the mosque's board of directors and retained on salary.

It Is Written

According to Muhammad, "On every Friday the angels take their stand at every gate of every mosque to write the names of the people who enter chronologically and when the Imam sits [on the pulpit and is ready to begin] they fold up their scrolls and get ready to listen to the sermon."

Imams are not considered holy men, nor are they ordained in official ceremonies like functionaries in other religions. Their status is based on their learning and piety and nothing more. There is no concept of a priesthood or hereditary class of godly folk in Islam. Any man can become an Imam if he chooses to pursue this career path. Women can also be Imams, though only of women congregants. Generally, women bypass this stage and become full-fledged scholars, or *'Ulema*, and serve the community through providing religious guidance and legal rulings. Islam does not prohibit women from teaching men, as the New Testament of the Bible does.

Ceremonies for Life

Islam provides a way for people to mark the passage of time with rites and ceremonies. No one would deny that significant events require special recognition, and neither does Islam. The traditions for marriages, births, and funerals were all taught by Prophet Muhammad and personally conducted by him for the community on numerous occasions. This section introduces the three ceremonies that Islam recognizes.

Nikah: Marriage in Islam

Nikah is the word for marriage in Islam. It is considered a civil contract between a man and a woman for the purpose of forming a family and engaging in marital relations that are allowed and wholesome. It is not considered a religious sacrament. The Prophet encouraged people to get married as soon as they were financially able so that the "raging hormone syndrome" that drives people to date and become promiscuous can be avoided. Ideally, young men and women should get married any time between the completion of puberty and their late twenties.

No dating in the traditional sense is allowed in Islam, so how do prospective partners meet? This question often comes up in public presentations of Islam. It may surprise you to learn that dating was unknown in America just a hundred years ago. Prior to the modern anything-goes era, people used to be paired up by relatives and matchmakers and through contact at social functions or in school. Islam has a similar mechanism for getting people together.

> **Ask the Imam**
>
> Contrary to popular myth, Islam does not allow a girl to be forced into marriage. Even though this reprehensible practice is prevalent all over the world, including in some Muslim countries, such a marriage is considered invalid in Islam and Muhammad, himself, annulled one such marriage when it was brought to his attention.

Pairings take place through contacts from relatives, online matchmaker services, or can even be initiated by a person who wants to get married. Islam allows prospective mates to meet only in chaperoned circumstances. Never are two unmarried people to be alone together on account of the dangers of temptation. Every woman who is seeking a husband is required to have what is known as a *wali*, or advocate, who will act on her behalf and for her benefit. This is most often a father, brother, or uncle, though a *wali* does not have to be related. Basically, the *wali* has the job of telling prospective suitors to give it up if the woman decides against further contact with them. The *wali* also sees to it that unscrupulous men are kept at bay.

Meetings in chaperoned settings or in public can go on for as long as both sides like, so they can get to know each other better over coffee, at a museum, or wherever. The chaperone can be of either sex and is usually someone connected to the girl. If the two people decide to end their personal explorations, there is no shame on either party. If they decide to go forward and get married, then a public announcement of engagement is made and a formal wedding date is set. There is no concept in Islam of living together first or having intimate relations as a way of testing the worth of a match.

The woman then sets a dowry for the man to give that is called a *mahr*, or marriage gift. She can ask for as much or as little as she desires, whether it be money, a house, or even merely a ring. If the amount is very high, she may give her bridegroom a timetable to pay it off after marriage. This monetary gift to the woman is sort of like an insurance policy for her, giving her some financial muscle just in case the marriage doesn't last long.

When the day of the wedding ceremony arrives, people gather either in a big hall or in a mosque. The pair of soon-to-be newlyweds sits in the front, facing the Imam, who is seated as well. The Imam asks the *wali* if the woman has agreed to the wedding, and then he asks the man if he agrees. The amount of the *mahr* is publicly announced.

Next, the Imam asks each party to exchange and sign a wedding contract. This document spells out the rights, duties, concerns, and obligations that each side wants the other to obey. When this is done, the Imam reads the sermon of marriage, which begins by invoking God and then extols the merits of a loving relationship. Following this, the opening verses of Chapter 4 of the Qur'an are read. The subject matter is God's creation of men and women and how they are supposed to join together in marriage. The Imam announces the marriage complete, and the joyous gathering erupts in a flurry of congratulations and hugging of the newlyweds. There is a reception afterward, called a *walima*, in which the wedding party celebrates with food, fun, and gift-giving.

Aqiqah: Welcoming Baby

The arrival of a new baby brings joy to any family. Islam has a way to cement that joy in a ritual called the *Aqiqah*, or Welcoming Consecration, which is held seven days after birth. When a baby is first delivered, the father or mother whispers the Islamic call to prayer in the newborn's ear, welcoming the baby into the life of the world where the responsibility to respond to Allah's call is greatest. A bit of mashed date is then lovingly fed to the baby by custom, and a beautiful supplication for its good fortune in life is made.

Next, the selection of a name is made that reflects the values of Islam. The name can be overtly religious in nature, such as 'Abdullah (Servant of God), or it can be more mundane, like Aliyyah (elevating) or Jameelah (beautiful). Many Muslims name their boys after prophets or famous companions, while girls are often named after members of the Prophet's household or from terms derived from the Qur'an that call goodness to mind.

Circumcision of male babies usually happens within the first few days after birth. It is not considered a religious sacrament in Islam. Rather, it has a more practical function related to good hygiene and cleanliness. Female circumcision, contrary to popular imagination, is not at all encouraged or required in Islam, nor is there any benefit in doing so from a religious or practical standpoint. The practice is virtually unknown in most of the Muslim world except in parts of Africa where it is a pre-Islamic tribal custom. In that case, local Christian natives engage in the practice as well. Muslim organizations have been in the forefront trying to abolish this practice, though long-standing local customs are difficult to change.

On the seventh day after birth the actual Aqiqah ceremony takes place. Families gather for a special dinner. A sheep or goat is ritually sacrificed (usually at a butcher shop), and the meat is cooked and served to the guests. A portion is also donated to the poor. The baby's hair is shaved off, and its weight in silver is given in charity. People congratulate the parents on their newborn and give gifts for the baby of either money, toys, or clothes.

Janazah: Muslim Funerary Rites

The Muslim funeral procedure is conducted with a unique frame of mind. Islam teaches that death is merely a doorway into the third stage of life, our time in the grave until Judgment Day. Consequently, the traditional condolence to the bereaved is, "To God we belong and to Him we return." While sincere crying and sorrow are allowed for the mourners, loud wailing and the tearing of clothes is forbidden.

The body is usually brought to a mosque for the special funeral prayer, known as the Janazah, but it can be performed anywhere. The people line up in rows, with the coffin on a stand in front of them. They begin the prayer in the usual fashion; however, there is no prayer call, no bowing, nor any prostration during this ritual. The entire procedure is conducted standing up. It takes about five minutes to perform, and the words that the mourners recite silently to themselves center on asking God to forgive the deceased and all those who have passed away before him or her.

The rule in Islam is to bury the body as soon as possible. Long drawn-out wakes and showings are not a part of Islamic tradition. The body, which was washed with water and then wrapped in white sheets, is carefully raised over the shoulders. A funeral procession to the graveyard is conducted, and the body is laid to rest in the grave while verses of the Qur'an are read. Wooden coffins are allowed, but steel ones are frowned upon. It is best to have no container at all so that the earth can reclaim our physical bodies as quickly as possible. It is customary for people to bring gifts of food and to visit the survivors for several days after the funeral. Tombstones that rise above the ground are forbidden, though many Muslims disregard this rule. Occasionally a tree is planted over the grave.

> **Ask the Imam**
>
> A deceased person is supposed to be buried within three days according to Islamic Law—the quicker the better.

Completing the Qur'an

There is a very common unofficial ceremony practiced throughout most of the Muslim world called Khatmi-Qur'an, or Sealing the Qur'an. This is a celebration to mark a child's completion of their first full reading of the Qur'anic text in Arabic. It usually takes up to two years under the guidance of a teacher for children to master the proper pronunciation and to read the text clearly from the first verse to the last. Most children complete the Qur'an between the ages of four and seven. This celebration is called an Ameen Ceremony in Southeast Asia. The ceremony usually involves a dinner and presentation by the child who is being honored.

Islamic Holidays

There are two main holidays in Islam. Each comes after an important Islamic ritual and is supposed to remind the celebrant of the meaning and joy of what was just accomplished. The first holiday comes after the end of Ramadan, and the second after the *Hajj* is completed.

Ramadan and *'Eid ul Fitr*

The after-Ramadan celebration known as the *'Eid ul Fitr* (Festival of the Fast Breaking) is the most popular holiday in Islam. For obvious reasons, being released

from a month-long, dawn-to-dusk fast can
make people quite happy. The first day of the
'*Eid* begins in the mosque with a special
morning prayer service, which consists of a
short congregational prayer followed by a
two-part sermon reminding people of the lessons they should remember from Ramadan
for the rest of the year. The '*Eid* festivities officially last for three days, and Muslims hold parties on each of the days. In some places
carnivals are held. Special '*Eid* sweets are prepared, and children are given gifts.

Just the Facts

Muslims in Iran celebrate
the Persian festival of the
New Year (*nawruz*). This is
a pre-Islamic custom that
currently incorporates com-
memorations of ancient Persian
rulers and their accomplishments.

After the Hajj: '*Eid ul Adha*

The second official holiday in Islam is known as '*Eid ul Adha*, or Festival of the
Sacrifice. It comes at the end of the *Hajj* ritual in Mecca. No special religious rites
connected to the *Hajj*'s events are held in the rest of the Muslim world, as the rituals
are confined to Mecca, so this holiday is usually more muted in tone. The lesson of
the *Hajj* is about sacrificing what we love for God's sake, and sermons in the mosques
usually relate to this theme. The special prayer service and three-day celebration are
carried out in the same fashion as for the other '*Eid*.

Other Holidays of Note

There are only two official holidays in Islam based on the clear pronouncement of
Muhammad. However, Muslims have adopted other holidays and celebrate them in
different regions. Here are two of them:

- **Maulid un Nabi**   The birthday of the Prophet. Although birthdays are not
  celebrated in Islamic tradition, Muslims in the early centuries of Islam began
  commemorating the Prophet's birth, which is said to fall in the Islamic month
  of *Rabiul Awwal*. People sing songs and chant and hold conferences and give
  speeches extolling his life and virtues. Most of the world's Muslims participate
  in such festivities.

- **'Eid ul Ghadir**   A festival peculiar to a sect of Muslims known as the *Shi'a*.
  It commemorates what they say was Muhammad's supposed announcement
  that his nephew, 'Ali ibn Abi Talib, would be his immediate successor. Sunni
  Muslims, the other major Muslim sect, dispute this claim. *Shi'a* Muslims also
  commemorate the death of the Prophet's grandson, Hussein, during a battle
  with imperial Umayyid forces in 680 C.E.

Halal and *Haram:* What Can a Muslim Do?

Islam classifies all actions by their merit or sinfulness. The rule in the *Shari'ah*, or Islamic Law, is that everything is allowed except what is expressly forbidden. Allowed activities for a Muslim are called *halal*, while prohibited ones are labeled *haram*. In keeping with the Islamic spirit of planning for all eventualities, there are two other main categories by which actions can be judged. These are things permissible, though not encouraged; and things disliked, though not sinful. In this section I will explain many of these types of deeds and what Islam says about the performance of each.

The Muslim Kosher Standard

Food is one of the most important elements of our daily lives. Islam is concerned with both what we eat and how much we consume. Some types of food are *haram*, and thus Muslims, like observant Jews, must watch what they eat. Although the Muslim *halal* food standard is not nearly as strict as the Jewish kosher requirement, it is, nonetheless, quite rigorous. The main features of Muslim dietary restrictions are as follows:

- A Muslim can eat anything that is not forbidden.

- Animals must be ritually slaughtered by either the Muslim *zabiha* or the Jewish kosher standard.

- Pork products are forbidden.

- Animals with fangs are forbidden.

- Seafood is generally allowed.

- Intoxicants are forbidden.

- Ingredients derived from animals such as gelatin and enzymes must be *zabiha* or kosher.

- Blood and carrion are forbidden.

Islam Forbids Intoxicants

Islam is famous for forbidding its followers all alcoholic beverages. Wine, beer, whisky, and the like are off-limits. There is a reason for this, and the evidence is all around us in our families, communities, and nation. Drunkenness leads to violence, ill health, recklessness, family breakup, and despair. Drunk driving is one of the leading causes of death today, and a large portion of domestic violence, rape, and crime is due to the scourge of alcohol. But it doesn't stop there. Islam takes a stand on drug abuse as well.

Once a companion asked the Prophet if people were allowed to chew a certain narcotic leaf found in southern Arabia. Muhammad asked about its effects on people, and when he was told them he declared that anything that intoxicates the mind is *haram* for a Muslim. Consequently, Islamic scholars are unanimous in declaring mind-altering drugs prohibited.

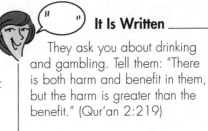

It Is Written

They ask you about drinking and gambling. Tell them: "There is both harm and benefit in them, but the harm is greater than the benefit." (Qur'an 2:219)

To go even further, Muhammad explained that anyone who buys, transports, sells, carries, serves, or stores intoxicants is equally as guilty as the consumer and is cursed by God. Even glasses specifically made for alcohol such as wineglasses and brandy bottles are illegal. Muslims are the only people in the world who can proudly state that prohibition does work if you change the hearts of the people first.

Gambling

Islam forbids all forms of gambling and games of chance in which monetary rewards are at stake, equating them with being a trick from *Shaytan* to keep people's minds off God. Any winnings are considered funds gotten unfairly, while any losses are held to be foolish setbacks that should have been avoided. Lotto, betting, poker, and all other forms of gambling are labeled as sins. Other types of activities, such as games of skill, are allowed. So go for that ring toss at the carnival in confidence, but avoid the slot machine at all costs!

Music and Islam

There is quite a lot of debate in the Muslim world today about the permissibility of music and singing in Islam. Given the rise of pop music in the last several decades, almost to the status of a religion among teenagers, you can well imagine the conversation in most Muslim homes at night. ("Why can't I go to that concert, Mom?") The reason that music is a concern at all in Islam has to do with its

Just the Facts

Cat Stevens, the popular British singer of decades past, embraced Islam after reading the Qur'an. Today, as *Yusuf Islam*, he writes religious songs for children.

effects on people. When a person is caught up in a song, he or she is oblivious to most everything else. Songs also teach, and the lessons may not be the most proper ones to learn.

The Prophet Muhammad forbade public dancing and the solo performances of women singers. He also declared certain types of instruments off-limits, such as flutes and stringed pieces, equating them with having the ability to make people forget God and to get lost in the passions of the flesh. He predicted that in the end of time female singers would be popular, and people would be more into music than religion. The problem with female singers is that some male listeners might begin to lust after them. This creates disharmony in the home as men begin to compare their wives with the flashy singer, and their eyes may start to wander. Women can become influenced to emulate the singer's lifestyle and revealing mode of dress as well, and soon you have a maddening circle of adultery and promiscuity that is out of control. Few people would deny that certain singers become raunchier (and less clothed) year after year. The music business sometimes seems to border on being a purveyor of sex and pornography. Islam tries to nip it all in the bud.

Drums and other percussion instruments are allowed, and group singers, especially children, are encouraged. Traveling songs, poetry, celebration music, and the like are all allowed. The basic rule is that music should not be suggestive, immoral, or lewd. If it meets a wholesome standard, as defined in Islamic morality, then sing as much as you like! Just remember that the best music of all, for a Muslim, is the voice of a skilled recitor of the Qur'an putting his heart and soul in the recitation of its musically inclined, rhythmic chapters.

Animal Rights and Islam

God created animals and other living things for the benefit of humanity. But this does not mean that we have been granted license to do as we please. The Holy Qur'an teaches that every animal has its own communal life and its own way to worship God, and thus our dealings with them must be on that footing. We have been created with a greater intellect than animals and so have a special responsibility to be fair, just, and kind to all other living things. The Blessed Prophet Muhammad once said that every injustice will be paid back on the Day of Judgment; even if one goat hits another with its horns, it will be taken account of. Therefore, in our use of animals for our own survival we must do justice.

God gave us the free use of the plants and animals of this Earth. He said, "Eat and drink of the good things of the earth." He also said, "It is God Who has provided you with livestock of every kind. You can ride some and others you eat ...." (Qur'an

40:79) But we must balance our use of animals and plants with our primary role as caretakers on the earth. For example, we are not allowed to harm animals or plants for no reason. The Blessed Prophet forbade people from capturing baby birds, burning anthills, and whipping animals cruelly. All the people he stopped from doing these things were just having "fun." Well, as the Prophet pointed out, it wasn't fun for the animals. Muhammad said, "If someone kills a sparrow for sport, the sparrow will cry out on the Day of Judgment, 'O Lord! That person killed me in vain! He did not kill me for any useful purpose.'" So hunting for sport is forbidden in Islam. You must eat what you hunt.

If we use animals for our work, we must feed them and not overwork them. If we eat animals, we are supposed to slaughter them according to humane rules that prevent all cruelty and suffering; and if we have them as pets, we are to feed them and care for them properly. The Prophet once told a story in which he noted that a woman who starved her pet cat to death would be tormented by that cat on Judgment Day by way of revenge. We thus have a responsibility to all living creatures around us, and even though many non-Muslims assert that animals have no rights or feelings, Islam says otherwise.

> **It Is Written**
>
> He is the One Who sends the winds as heralds announcing His Mercy and sends down pure water from the sky, so that with it We may give life to a dead land, and quench the thirst of countless animals and humans that We have created. We distribute this water among them so that they may glorify Us, yet most people refuse to do anything except show ingratitude. (Qur'an 25:48–50)

Monetary Restrictions

Islam regulates economic affairs with the same thoroughness as other areas of life. Free trade, fair competition, contractual rights, and compassionate capitalism are the hallmarks of Islamically based finance. The main features that guide Muslim financial life are listed as follows:

- Muslims are forbidden to engage in interest-based borrowing or lending. This is because interest brings a hardship on the borrower and gives the lender easy gains that were not earned.

- Muslims are required to make written contracts for any and all business dealings.

- Muslims are exhorted to be honest in all financial exchanges. God will punish dishonest business people and reward the upright with paradise.

♦ Stock trading is allowed in companies that do not deal in forbidden substances or interest. Futures contracts are forbidden because no one can foresee what conditions will be like tomorrow and to lock someone into such a contract is unfair. Mutual funds are allowed with the same attention paid to the items individual companies deal in.

♦ Muslims are allowed to be business partners with non-Muslims.

The Least You Need to Know

♦ Men are the head of the family in the Islamic family structure, but the wife has the status of an equal adult who must be consulted in family affairs.

♦ The mosque is considered a sort of all-purpose community center where people can worship, hold meetings, and discuss community affairs.

♦ The birth of a baby is celebrated in a special ceremony called an *Aqiqah*. It is customary to give gifts for the baby on that day.

♦ Muslims have a kosherlike standard that restricts what they can eat and consume.

♦ Islam forbids gambling, alcohol, drugs, and suggestive music.

Chapter 20

Looking at the Status of Women in Islam

In This Chapter

- ◆ Learn about the role and concept of women in Islam
- ◆ Discover what it means to be Muslim and female in Muslim society today
- ◆ Find out what rights and duties Islam confers upon women
- ◆ Read up on divorce, polygamy, and Islamic Law
- ◆ Find out why Muslim women cover their hair in public

Women have always had to struggle for equality and acceptance in male-dominated societies. Sometimes local or national customs are to blame for women's woes, while other times religion (or its misapplication) is responsible. Every nation has had to deal with this issue, and some have been more successful at finding equitable solutions than others. Over the last hundred years, women in Europe and America have been able to garner such rights as inheritance, equal education, and even voting privileges, but women in much of the rest of the world seem to have lagged behind.

The perception in the world today is that Muslim women have the fewest rights and liberties of all. This view is strengthened by decrees from many Islamic groups and Muslim governments that range from mundane things such as requiring segregated classrooms to more serious indignities such as forbidding women to work, go to school, or even drive a car. But are these restrictions rooted in religion or in long-held local customs and prejudices that have nothing to do with Islam? In fact, the real story of women in the early days of Islam is one of progressive liberation and elevation of status. It was for this reason that women were the staunchest supporters of Muhammad's mission. If women in some countries today are not enjoying the full rights theoretically bestowed upon them by Islam, it is not the fault of the religion, but of chauvinistic men who use religion selectively to maintain their dominance.

Does Islam Teach Inequality?

Many Westerners believe that Islam teaches that women are second-class citizens. Commentators often point to the many backward customs prevalent in the Muslim world as proof that religion is to blame for this sorry situation. Women who have escaped the stifling lifestyle of their home countries are held up by women's rights groups as paragons of bravery who stood up to their culture and were liberated. An episode of the *Oprah Winfrey Show* centered on one such woman, a princess from Bahrain who wanted to marry an American Marine. She had to leave her country to do it because her family forbade her marrying a non-Muslim. Unfortunately, the show's unintended side effect was to make it look like the Muslim world was the new *Iron Curtain* that women had to escape from!

Beyond Stereotypes

The stereotyping doesn't stop there! The popular family show *Seventh Heaven* aired an episode in which the plight of women in Afghanistan under Taliban rule played a central role. Several emotional tirades about the alleged barbarism and cruelty followed one after another. The subtle message was clear: Islam is bad for women.

 It Is Written

According to Muhammad, "Women are the twin halves of men." In other words, neither is complete without the other.

Perhaps the most damaging film of all has been *Not Without My Daughter*, in which Sally Fields plays an American woman whose husband goes berserk on a trip to his native Iran. The violence and abuse, interspersed with prominent images of mosques and Muslim clerics, gave many Muslims the impression that this film was designed specifically to attack Islam.

Even as the Nazis made all Jews seem sinister, even as American cowboys were seen as heroes battling the savage Indians, and even as blacks are often portrayed falsely in the media as criminals, Muslims believe that the religion of Islam is getting a bum rap with regard to the role and status of women. High-profile cases are held up as the norm, and the status of women in some Muslim countries is blamed on religion when the real culprit is poverty and lack of education for both men and women. (In fact, most Muslim women lead very normal lives!) Islam does not teach that women are inferior to men, nor does it call upon its followers to suppress them. What is the evidence to support this counterclaim?

The Holy Qur'an lays out the case for women's equality in several ways:

> O people! Reverence your Lord Who created you from a single soul and created of like nature its mate and from those two He scattered countless men and women. Reverence Allah through Whom you demand your mutual [rights] and [reverence] the wombs [of mothers that bore you] for Allah ever watches over you. (Qur'an 4:1)

For centuries, European Christians debated whether or not women had souls or even if they went to heaven. Islam never engaged in such nonsense. The Qur'an, quite contrary to pre-Islamic Arab beliefs, called women the equals of men in all aspects of religion:

> For believing men and women, for devout men and women, for truthful men and women, for patient men and women, for humble men and women, for charitable men and women … for them has Allah prepared forgiveness and a great reward. (Qur'an 33:35)

Ask the Imam

Islamic Law considers women to be equal with men in all respects. Men and women have the same religious and moral duties, and the economic rights of women are identical to men. Husbands do not acquire the property of their wives upon marriage. Women have full right to vote in Islam and can hold positions of authority over men. All of these principles have had their examples in Islamic history.

Muhammad himself established the equal suffrage rights of women by including them in the oath-taking practice, which was the equivalent of voting in Arab society. Islam has never taught that women should be denied a political voice, and in those Muslim countries that are not ruled by kings (which is forbidden in the Qur'an, by the way) one finds that women vote freely. Iran, which is often held up as the epitome of chauvinism, actually has more elected women in government than the United States!

Islam does not teach that women are inferior in religion or in political rights. The only caveat, as was noted in Chapter 19, is that men are called upon to be the protectors and primary providers of the family. This doesn't mean that women are weak or incapable of defending or supporting themselves, for Islamic history is full of wealthy, strong, and martial women. Rather, it elevates women by freeing them from a lot of drudgery that God has said men are primarily responsible for. According to some Islamic scholars, women are not even obligated to do the housework! (Any work they do is considered a charity on their part.) The Prophet Muhammad worked around the house as much as any other member of his family. Men are the undeclared servants of women, in an ideal Islamic sense.

The Struggle for Equal Rights

In most Muslim countries, few people have any rights, men or women. Remember that the Islamic civilization was virtually wiped out during the era of Colonialism, and thus what is left is a confused jumble of customs, religious ideas, imported ideologies, political turmoil, and poverty. The very fact that most Muslim countries are under the sway of dictators, presidents for life, kings, and other tin-pot leaders is an indication of just how serious the problem is.

In most places, the struggle for women's equality is carried out under a backdrop of governmental oppression of the men. Whether it's Syria, Algeria, Uzbekistan, or Tunisia, the average citizen must be mindful of secret police, arbitrary arrest, torture and imprisonment, cronyism, and bribery as a fact of life. In such conditions, it may be easier to understand a backlash against the advancement of women in society. The men may feel they are losing control of another sphere of life. This is, of course, no excuse to justify unrestricted male dominance; it is merely a way to try and make sense of the struggle women must go through.

Remember that the women's rights movement in the United States encountered such stiff opposition that it took over a hundred years for meaningful equal-protection laws to be enacted in the late twentieth century. Early pioneers like Susan B. Anthony and Elizabeth Cady Stanton were ridiculed by American men as rebellious, scandalous, and downright anti-Christian. Although several important rights were eventually achieved, many American women would argue that the status of their gender still needs much improvement. Indeed, this brings up the point that Muslims are consistently trying to make: Even as it is unfair to look at crime statistics against women in America and conclude that Christianity is oppressive to women, so too, Muslims would say, it is equally unfair to blame Islam for what are essentially abuses against women by men who either falsely use their religion to justify their actions or are ignorant of religion and are just criminally minded or abusive.

Just the Facts _____

Many Christian leaders of the past advocated the inferior status of women. The apostle Paul called for women to keep silent in the presence of men and forbade them to be teachers of men. One of the main architects of the Protestant Reformation, Martin Luther, in trying to explain why girls developed faster than boys, equated girls with being weeds, which grow faster than good crops that take a longer time to mature!

How can the lot of women in the Muslim world be improved? Education coupled with political reform is the key. Contrary to what may be immediately assumed, a more thorough religious education for men and women in which the rights of women in Islam are given prominent coverage is the best course of action. To be very frank, there is quite a lot of misinformation and faulty ideas about Islam in the Muslim world. The status of women is just one of those areas where great improvement is necessary. On the second issue, political reform, based on an Islamic model, would guarantee the safety and security of the population at large in a similar way that the American Constitution protects the rights of the average American. Despite the occurrence of the high-profile Iranian Revolution of 1979, the proper implementation of Islam in a nation is not rooted in chaos or barbarism.

Islam does not encourage the oppression of women. In fact, the teachings of Muhammad call upon men to respect the rights of women. Islamic Law contains dozens of laws for the protection of women's rights. Among these are the following:

- A woman's property cannot be seized by her husband.
- Women cannot be denied the right to an education.
- Ruining a woman's reputation is a criminal act.
- Forced marriage is prohibited.
- Women can file legal suits in court and provide sole testimony.
- Women can initiate divorce.
- Women get automatic custody of young children after divorce.
- Alimony and palimony are mandatory.
- Women can enter into contracts without interference or permission from a man.
- Spousal abuse is a punishable offense.
- Women receive equal pay for equal work.
- Women can vote and stand for civil office.

The list goes on further and covers so many areas that it rivals current Western laws regarding women's status and rights. So from the Islamic standpoint, the liberation of women is not accomplished by rejecting their religion but by actually implementing it. Replacing the current regimes in Muslim countries with Islamic governments that will rule according to the traditional understanding of Islam as it was practiced during its Golden Age (from about the ninth to the thirteenth centuries) is also essential. This is how Muslims look at the issue among themselves.

True liberation for women cannot be achieved by rejecting religious or moral dictates, Islam claims. Wearing skimpy clothing, becoming promiscuous, and abusing addictive substances as much as men do does not make one equal nor is it healthy. Many Muslim women have taken on this issue and have asserted that it is the modern Western woman who needs liberating from the sexual control of men. In America and elsewhere, women are presented as sexual objects with no value beyond their physical attributes. Popular movies, music, books, and advertising messages force women to compete with each other in dressing up (or down) to vie for the attention of men. Rape, pornography, wife abuse, and other forms of violence against women have been called epidemic in official U.S. government reports. Islam, these Muslim women say, would end all of that. So the way to help women in both the Eastern and the Western worlds, Muslims humbly offer, is to apply the principles of modesty that most of the world's religions teach in our modern society.

Just the Facts

Every year thousands of women in North America and Europe convert to Islam, equating it with liberation in the true sense of the word. Author Carol Anway, whose own daughter converted, wrote a book called *Daughters of Another Path* in which she chronicled the journey to Islam of women from many different backgrounds.

Translate This

The name **Ottoman** is derived from Osman I. He was the first ruler of the Turkish tribe that invaded and conquered Anatolia in 1281. The Ottoman Empire lasted until 1918.

Myths About Muslim Women

Perhaps no other issue has influenced people's imagination more than the status of women in Islam. In the Middle Ages, when Europeans were engaged in warfare with Muslims in Palestine, the focus was on painting a picture of Muslims as minions of the Devil. But with the powerful *Ottoman* Empire holding sway over much of southeastern Europe from the fifteenth century until 1918, many Westerners began changing their views of Muslims as invincible conquerors and instead focused on the exotic excesses of Ottoman court life.

Europeans began to view the typical Muslim family as a licentious man lording over a harem of beautiful, nubile women. Many French, Italian, and British painters created fanciful images that fueled this notion and gave rise to the myth of the harem. The word *harem* itself does not mean in any way a pleasure room full of compliant women. It literally means *forbidden space* and is the term Muslims used for that area of the house where male visitors were not allowed to go. In the same way that it is considered bad etiquette to walk into the bedroom of another person's house while you are a guest for dinner, Islam also has an etiquette regarding private areas of the home.

A typical harem scene as envisioned by John Frederick Lewis, a nineteenth-century European painter.

(Courtesy of the Laing Art Gallery)

The harem of any house was the area where women could be assured of privacy, where they could lay aside their head scarves and relax without feeling the pressure of men around. The bawdy imagery, unfortunately, comes from the un-Islamic practices of some Ottoman rulers who would literally collect women as concubines and cordon off whole areas of their palaces as pleasure gardens. These are the harems that Europeans have taken as representative of the normal state of Muslim women. (The later Ottoman sultans were the guiltiest purveyors of this practice.) Islam, as it was understood in its first centuries, did not foster or condone this type of extreme sensualism, and except for a few high-profile cases, this practice has been virtually unknown in the Muslim world.

How are Muslim women viewed today? Surprisingly, the myth of the harem is no longer as much in vogue among Westerners. Instead, it has been replaced by an equally damaging myth, that of the Muslim woman as a victim of fanatic religious zealots. This stereotype has taken off in recent years due to three main factors:

♦ The issue of arranged marriage.

♦ The decrees about women in such places as Saudi Arabia and Afghanistan during Taliban rule.

♦ Cultural oddities in some Muslim lands.

We'll examine each in turn.

Arranged Marriages

Many women are wary of marriage because of the danger of being stuck with a bad man. The prevailing wisdom in our time is that dating helps people to make more informed choices by letting them see another person intimately before taking the vow of marriage. The concept of an arranged marriage, then, would seem like the antithesis of this approach. "How can you love somebody you don't even know?" is the big question.

It may surprise many to learn that arranged marriages are not an Islamic requirement. There is no teaching in the Qur'an or in the hadiths that calls for this practice. It is, rather, a cultural phenomenon that exists in many Muslim countries even as it exists in much of the non-Muslim world from Zimbabwe to China. In fact, it is really the institution of *dating* that is the new practice which much of the world is struggling to accept. Islam merely regulates the conduct of people who want to form a marriage, whether arranged or by themselves. The three main points to know about Islam and arranged marriages are as follows:

♦ Islam does not require it.

♦ A woman cannot be forced into a marriage she doesn't want to have.

♦ The arranged pair can have an extended engagement and can break it off if either party wishes to do so.

Are women sometimes forced into arranged marriages? Yes, but this abuse goes against the teachings of Islam and is not limited to Muslim populations. Forced marriage is alive and well among Hindus, Buddhists, and Christians in many parts of the developing world and elsewhere. In a story about the Prophet Muhammad, a woman who had been married against her will went to the Prophet and complained about it; he annulled the marriage on the spot. If people fail to follow their religion, it is not the fault of the religion. The Bible forbids people to get drunk, yet alcoholism is one of the most serious national challenges facing Christian countries everywhere. So before people blame Islam for something that appears oppressive, they must learn what the religion teaches about it and then condemn the hypocrites who fail to follow their professed beliefs (or the ignorant who follow cultural patterns not knowing they are contrary to their religion's teachings).

 Just the Facts

Recent studies have shown that arranged marriages actually last longer than those that result from dating or living together first. If the facts are to be believed, the divorce rate, which now stands at around 50 percent in the United States, has shot up dramatically since the advent of the sexual revolution. How has the advent of dating contributed to life-long commitments then?

Arranged marriages work for most people, and they help to take some of the pressure off those who are looking for a mate without a lot of heartache and hassle. The growth of online dating services, personals ads and matchmakers in the West over the last few years is merely a throwback to the best elements of the arranged marriage system which was the norm in the West up until relatively recently. The companions of the Prophet demonstrated many different ways of finding a mate. Some married for love and sealed their commitment without intermediaries, others were matched by friends, and still others agreed to arranged marriages brokered by relatives.

The Taliban and Women

Turning to the Taliban, the student-founded group that brought a certain kind of order to warlord-plagued Afghanistan in the closing years of the twentieth century, there are two problem areas with regard to women's rights. The first involves some accounts by the Western press that distorted the motives of the rulers. The second concerns the misrepresentation of the actual conditions that existed in Afghanistan.

To begin then, some news reports had given the impression that the Taliban was at war with women. Specifically, after taking power, the Taliban banned most women from working and from going to school, and required that they wear large robes called *burqas*. Initially, their logic was that conditions were unsafe for women (hence the all-enveloping robe) and that they had to rebuild society from scratch (by keeping women at home to raise their children correctly).

Despite their trying to sound reasonable, however, most educated Muslims around the world were as outraged over these pronouncements as non-Muslims, for no one can make forbidden what Islam allows, even if for a seemingly good cause. But Muslims were made to cringe even further when some Western media sources linked these pronouncements directly with Islam itself. Hearkening back to the days of the Iranian Revolution in the late 1970s, they made it seem as if Islam equaled women's oppression. But none of the Taliban's decrees concerning women were rooted in authentic Islamic Law. The Taliban leadership admitted as much when their representative in the United States remarked in 1999, "We are following Afghan customs that go back thousands of years." They are a product of their national experience, and their policies show that their culture takes precedence over their religion.

This brings us to the facts of life in Afghanistan. It was actually the Soviet invasion of the country in 1979 that turned this peaceful nation upside down. While there, the Soviets laid waste to most of the countryside and committed some of the worst atrocities against simple villagers that the world has ever seen. War and social dislocation have shaped every generation there since. When Ronald Reagan began covert American support for the *mujahideen*, the Afghan rebels, he inadvertently helped in the creation of a new political reality in the country.

After nearly 10 years of all-out war, the victorious *mujahideen* finally drove out the Soviets. But instead of laying down their arms and building a new society, these groups began fighting amongst themselves, further exacerbating the poverty of the nation. Individual warlords carved out their own private fiefs, and banditry and chaos were the order of the day throughout much of the early 1990s. Kabul, the capital, was routinely shelled by all sides, adding to the misery of the nation. Enter the Taliban in 1996. They were a group of students from refugee religious schools who were asked to rescue some girls kidnapped by a local warlord. They overwhelmed his forces and committed themselves to ridding the country of wicked rulers. They quickly organized and recruited other Afghans who were also sick of the suffering, and eventually the Taliban steamrolled over most of the rest of the warlords. By 2001, the Taliban controlled nearly 90 percent of Afghanistan.

> **Ask the Imam**
>
> The Taliban was not considered politically legitimate in most of the Muslim world. Only two Muslim nations ever bothered to recognize their governmental authority in Afghanistan.

They inherited a country where people were starving, cities were in ruins, and the economy was of Stone Age proportions. Women were just as poor and desperate as the men were. Getting back to their ideas for reform, they believed that husbands and fathers had to first become stable with steady work and then women could claim their place in public society at a later date. Unfortunately, their logic backfired, and the lot of women worsened while that of men failed to improve. Islam certainly did not condone their miscalculations or methods. They simply implemented policies as their simple minds saw fit. In their devastated land probably nothing they could have done would have worked. It also didn't help that there was still civil war, a famine was gripping the countryside, and the international fugitive, Osama bin Laden, was running camps full of gun-toting anarchists masquerading as Muslim freedom fighters. Under such circumstances, can any reform work for men or women? Indeed, as of this writing, the situation of women in Afghanistan after the United States ousted the Taliban in early 2002 has not improved in any appreciable way. The warlords have returned and the security situation is consistently unstable.

Anomalies in the Muslim World

Practicing Muslims often discuss the primitive (un-Islamic) cultural values prevalent in certain parts of the world. To be fair, most Muslim women in the world are not oppressed or held back. In fact, women in such places as Malaysia, Tanzania, America, and Bosnia are highly educated and mobile. It is the utter inexplicability of a few lingering cultural values, however, that people tend to take the most interest in.

The first anomaly I will examine is the so-called honor killings that sometimes occur in Palestine, Jordan, and other nearby places. The logic is that if a girl brings dishonor on the family by either dating or being promiscuous, then a family member must kill her to protect the family's reputation. There is no sanction in Islam for such a horrible practice, and Muslim scholars in those countries have issued *fatwas* against it. But people cling to odd notions of macho culture more strongly than to religious dictates. This is a worldwide phenomenon, as other ethnic and religious groups also engage in negative cultural practices.

The second anomaly is that of female circumcision. This practice is mainly found in a few isolated regions of Africa and is not sanctioned or required by Islam. It is a pre-Islamic cultural relic that Christians, Muslims, and animists engage in equally. When the issue first came up among women's rights groups in the West, their initial response was to blame Islam. However, after news reports found that African Christians were as likely to engage in the practice, Islam was no longer mentioned as the cause. When the Prophet Muhammad heard about this practice, he tried to diminish its effects by restricting its application and in no way did he ever teach that it should be done. Female circumcision is absolutely not endorsed in Islam.

Women's Rights in Islam

The Qur'an says: "Women shall have rights similar to those of men." There are, however, some specific issues of difference that are often misinterpreted in the West. People have charged that in Islam a woman's testimony is only half of a man's, that women are cheated out of half of their inheritance, that the Qur'an allows wife-beating, that men can divorce on a whim and have four wives, and that Islam promotes unfair segregation.

These charges are usually bandied about to "prove" that Islam is an unfriendly and chauvinistic religion toward women. When each is looked at in context and with accuracy, not false hype, then even these objections melt away. Let's examine each of them separately.

Are Women "Half" of Men?

The charge that a woman's testimony is only half of a man's arises from a Qur'anic verse (2:282) that talks about business contracts. A woman is asked to have a friend come along when she negotiates a business contract. Later on, should the other party to the contract try to cheat her, her friend can remind her about the details in a court situation. Does this sound all that bad? (Note how the second woman does not need anyone to back her up. Her word is taken from only her.) In seventh-century Arabia, aggressive men routinely cheated women and this Islamic rule leveled the playing field. Even today, such advice is still valid. A witness who will see to it that fairness is maintained is a good idea. In this and all other testimony, a woman's word is accepted as equal to that of a man. The second witness for business contracts is merely a safeguard for the woman. In any other court business there is no requirement for a woman to have a second witness.

> ### Ask the Imam
>
> If a woman feels her husband is not providing enough financial resources for her use on the family, Islamic Law says she can secretly take money from him because she is only taking what is rightfully hers.

Why Only Half an Inheritance?

The Qur'an is very specific about who gets what after a person dies. In fact, the verses that deal with this topic (4:11–12) are so detailed that it takes a lawyer to apply the formulas for all of the heirs. One of the dictates is that a female will inherit a share that is only half that of the man's. This seems unfair on the face of it, but remember the role of men in an Islamic family. The man has to support the family as a matter of religious obligation while the woman is not obligated to spend a dime unless she wants to.

When a man marries, he must pay to the woman a dowry that can be as much as she wishes. The man is supposed to pay mandatory alimony and palimony, while no such requirement is upon women. A woman cannot be forced to share her fortune with her divorced husband. A man also must support his unmarried sisters and his mother if his father dies. So a woman gets half an inheritance to keep for herself but a man is obligated to spend on all those around him. Even the extra inheritance share may not always be enough!

Does Islam Allow Wife Abuse?

Domestic violence is one of the most important issues for women. In the West, this scourge has been called the invisible crime because of its widespread but underreported nature. Men in every society and every culture can become abusers. It is not promoted in any religion on earth, yet Islam is sometimes falsely charged with allowing it because of one misrepresented verse in the Qur'an:

> As to those women from whom you fear defiant sinfulness, first admonish them, then refuse to share your bed with them, and then, if necessary, slap them. Then if they obey you, take no further actions against them and do not make excuses to punish them. (Qur'an 4:34)

Islam never gives any man the right to strike his wife for any reason except the one listed in this verse, namely, the wife is engaging in some type of evil activity such as drinking alcohol, abusing the children, or other really bad behavior. Given that most women are not of this nature, physically punishing a wife should never arise in 99 percent of all Islamic marriages. Now, let's take a closer look at this verse. If you will notice, two steps for reform and correction are mentioned first: talking with the woman; and if that doesn't work, the man sleeping on the couch to express his displeasure. Islamic scholars have ruled that these two steps could be carried out indefinitely.

But what if a woman is so bad that she refuses to listen and doesn't care if her husband is not sleeping with her (and she is still engaged in the sinful activity). The last recourse is for the husband to slap her. Now this is where Islam gets interesting. Muhammad, who was brushing his teeth at the time, was asked by a man, "What should we slap them with?" He answered, "With this." And he held up his toothbrush. Look at that! Muhammad interpreted this verse in such a way as to make the physical punishment laughable. (Some Islamic scholars have ruled that a handkerchief can be substituted.)

The symbolic meaning of the slap with the toothbrush, then, is that the man has reached the end of his patience. An alternative meaning to the Arabic word, *daraba*, that is often translated as "slap" or "beat," is *to go away from*. In other words, the symbolic tap of the toothbrush means he is about to leave the marriage.

So actually, if you look at the verse in context, and use the mandatory interpretation of the Prophet, there is never any reason for a man to hit his wife in any way that would harm her. Are there Muslim men who disregard this teaching and abuse their wives, and for no reason? Yes, and when Muhammad heard about some men like that in his time he said, "Those men who beat their wives are not the best among you." (In prophetic language that means they are the worst people, sinners.) On another occasion he remarked that it was insane for a man to beat his wife and then try to sleep with her later. The golden rule, aptly stated by Muhammad, is: "The best among you are those who are best to their families, and I am the best to my family." He never laid a hand on a woman in anger.

To restate, Islam does not allow a man to beat his wife; it merely provides a way for the man to symbolically express his displeasure when his wife is committing a grave sin that threatens the stability of the family. Divorce may be the man's next step. Have some Muslims not understood this and engaged in abusive behavior? Undoubtedly, but this is again where the educated Muslim would say that Muslims need to be reacquainted with the actual teachings of their religion so they can create harmony both in the home and in society.

Polygamy in Islam

The Qur'an allows a man to marry up to four wives. Before Islam there was no limit in Arabia to the number of wives a man could have. The Qur'an restricted this to a maximum of four. But at the same time the Qur'an gives a rule to any man considering multiple marriages: If you can't treat each wife fairly in all things, then marry only one, as it is more just (4:4). This disqualifies most men immediately. In practice, 99.99 percent of the marriages in the Muslim world are with a single woman. What could be the reason for this seemingly licentious privilege for men, and why is it so rare?

Just the Facts

John Cairncross in his book *When Polygamy Was Made a Sin* proves that early Christians routinely engaged in plural marriages with the sanction of the church.

Islam is a faith that boasts a solution to every problem. If one is not immediately recognized, then the scholars can do *ijtehad* (independent reasoning) and come up with an Islamically inspired answer. *Polygyny*, which is commonly mislabeled as "polygamy," is the practice of having multiple wives or female partners. It is an often misunderstood solution to certain unique problems. (Both Judaism and Christianity allowed men to have multiple wives, though this practice has fallen out of favor since the Middle Ages.)

What do you do if there is a shortage of men, say, because of war? Only a limited number of women would find husbands. What about the rest? Multiple marriage is better than having unattached women become the secret mistresses of married men. What about women who for whatever reason cannot find a suitable match, especially if they suffer from a debilitating condition? What if a woman is barren? Should she be divorced and cast aside in favor of a fertile wife? What about those women who want careers and don't necessarily want a full-time man to look after?

> **Ask the Imam**
>
> A man with more than one wife is required to treat them equally in all respects. Each wife gets her own house or apartment, and the husband must divide his days equally between them. Any money or gifts he gives to one he must give to the other as well. If he is unfair, on the Day of Judgment God will cause half of his body to be paralyzed.

Polygyny is the answer to all of these problems. It actually works in women's favor by tying the man to each wife so much so that he is more aware of his responsibilities, trying to earn enough to support his extended family. Of course, polygyny is not for every woman, and there are those who will not have any part in it. (It is illegal in the United States and even some Muslim groups attempt to discourage the practice.) Islam says that's fine, too. For other women it is a way to get a part-time husband rather than having no husband at all. Is this allowance ever abused? Yes, but as I explained before, people have shortcomings that the religion should not be blamed for.

Divorce in Islam

Islam envisions marriage as the bedrock of a healthy society. But it also recognizes that two people may not be compatible. The Qur'an calls for men and women to make every effort to resolve their marital differences, and it even makes suggestions for mediators. However, if the discord is too great an obstacle, then divorce is the best option so that people can move on with their lives. Muhammad said, "The most hateful thing that God has created and allowed is divorce." It is not a step to be taken lightly because it affects children and the community in many negative ways. Islam provides a way for the man to initiate divorce and, contrary to popular opinion, there is a method for female-initiated divorce as well.

Talaq: Male-Initiated Divorce

The procedure for divorce in Islam is relatively easy. If two people have resolved to end their marriage, then why should there be a long drawn-out and bitter fight in court? The male-initiated divorce is called *talaq*, or divorce. The man must pronounce to his wife three times the word *"Talaq!"* and then the first phase of the divorce procedure begins. From this point, all sexual relations must stop for a period of three menstrual cycles to see if the woman is pregnant. (If she is, they may try harder to reconcile.) During that time, the Qur'an forbids the man to force the woman out of the house or to emotionally abuse her. He still has to pay all the bills as well.

If the couple has sexual relations at any time during this waiting period, then the divorce pronouncement is null and void. If the time expires and they wish to remain married, the man needs to propose and another wedding must take place all over again. To emphasize to the man that divorce is no light matter, this system of *talaq* pronouncement and a waiting period can be done no more than three times. If the man initiates the *talaq* for the third time, he is forbidden to remarry the woman unless she has been married and divorced by another first. So the male-initiated divorce has a built-in cooling-off period with a maximum number of times that *talaq* can be done. All of this serves to make people think twice, literally, before they act.

Khul': Female-Initiated Divorce

Women are not forever bound to men they want to leave. Islam provides a way for women to initiate divorce called *Khul'*. Basically, a woman can file papers with a religious or civil court or with a recognized scholar, asking to divorce her husband. Although she doesn't need the permission of her husband, she does need to offer a reason. (Muhammad once granted a divorce to a woman who said she couldn't stand any longer to look at her husband's ugly face.) She must agree to give up all or part of her dowry in compensation to the soon-to-be divorced husband, the amount being determined by the importance of her reason for wanting to leave the marriage. Men are encouraged in the Qur'an, however, not to take any of it back on account of once having had a relationship with their now former wife. The waiting period of three menstrual cycles applies as well, after which the divorce is final.

Alimony and Palimony in Islam

Islam requires that a man pay both alimony and palimony. He must support his children in all aspects while they are under the care of his divorced wife. The mother gets automatic custody of her children, but fathers also have rights in Islam. When sons reach the age of seven or daughters pass their puberty, the father can ask that custody be reverted to him. Thus, the mother has the children when they need her the most and the father can also take his turn to raise them when they need the parenting style only fathers can provide. The parents can also practice joint custody if both parties agree; otherwise the formula noted above is enforced.

Islam and the Dress Code

Images of veiled women and turbaned men in flowing robes permeate Western conceptions of Muslims. Fashions in the Islamic world actually vary from place to place. Arabs dress differently from Pakistanis, who in turn dress differently from Muslim Filipinos. There are certain requirements that Islam places on both men and women in dress, however, and I will explore them here.

On Veils and Turbans

Men have the following dress requirements that can be expressed in a variety of fashionable ways:

♦ No tight clothes allowed.

♦ Men must allow a beard to grow if they can do it. (There is no sin or stigma on men who cannot grow a beard.)

♦ A turban or a kind of hat called a *kufi* is proper formal attire.

♦ The area from the knees to the navel must be covered in public at all times.

♦ Long pants or a loose gown and a shirt are considered an appropriate outfit.

Women have a slightly different dress requirement. The idea is that women are so alluring to men that males may judge them only by their looks or may try to accost them sexually. To protect women from this type of abuse and degradation, and also to make them aware that God judges them by their hearts, and not their looks, Islam asks them to cover their hair and wear loose-fitting clothes so that their full beauty is concealed. (Of course, the Qur'an tells men and women to lower their gaze and not to ogle each other.)

It should be noted that traditional Christianity and Judaism also require women to wear veils as well. The sight of Orthodox Jewish women wearing long skirts and berets, wigs or hats to cover their hair is a common occurrence in many American cities. The Bible calls for veils in I Corinthians 11:3–13, though modern interpretations have downplayed the significance of these verses.

Translate This _____

Hijab is the common name of the veil Muslim women wear over their hair. It literally means to screen off from view. Opinions vary among Muslims as to its necessity, though most Muslims believe it to be a requirement of the religion based on a direct saying of Muhammad to that effect and one verse of the Qur'an in which it is mentioned.

By the way, Muslim women don't need to wear their veils at home or when only women or their close family members are present. Proper dress for Muslim females includes …

◆ A veil to cover the hair in public (called a *hijab or Khimar*).

◆ Loose-fitting clothes.

◆ Long pants or a dress to the ankles and a shirt, gown, or blouse that covers to the wrists.

◆ Excessive makeup and perfume are frowned upon.

The hijab, *or head scarf, is a requirement for Muslim women to wear in the presence of men they are not married or related to.*

Some Muslim women follow dress customs that are not specifically required in Islam. These include wearing a veil over the face (*niqab*), wearing an all-enveloping robe called a *burqa*, and wearing socks and gloves in public. These women seek a greater level of piety and thus try to conceal from male view as much of their bodies as possible. Again, there is no requirement for all women to cover the face or wear a burqa, though some Muslim cultures promote these practices vigorously.

Purdah and Islam

Some Muslim cultures practice a form of female seclusion called *purdah*. This word originates from the Persian language and describes the system whereby women are not allowed to leave their homes except for the direst emergencies. This is not an Islamic custom but was picked up by some Muslims who settled in Iran and India where it was an established pre-Islamic tradition designed to showcase the wealth of a family (in other words, we're so rich our women don't have to leave the house and work in the fields). Many people in the West have the misconception that this practice is widespread. The fact is that most Muslim women in the world are not locked away in their homes. Purdah is practiced mostly in the Indian subcontinent and in Saudi Arabia.

The Least You Need to Know

- Islam views women as equal partners with men in life as well as in religion. Islam does not teach that women are inferior to men.

- There are many misperceptions about the status of women in Islam that are fueled by a few high-profile cases. The vast majority of Muslim women live normal lives and face normal challenges.

- Poverty and illiteracy in general, not religion, are the root cause for the plight of women in some developing nations.

- A Muslim man can marry up to four wives only if he can treat each equally. The norm is monogamy in the Muslim world.

- Islam does not allow wife beating. If abuse occurs in some Muslim homes, it is due to the same reasons that cause men to abuse their wives in the West.

- Islamic Law relieves women of all financial responsibility for the family and instead places the entire burden on the man.

- There is a definite procedure for divorce in Islam that can be initiated by the husband or wife. It includes a cooling-off period so that there is a chance for reconciliation.

Part 6

The History of Islam

History textbooks often mention the rise of Islam in a summarized fashion, as if it wasn't as important as the Vikings, the pharaohs, or the Reformation. Very little space is given for describing the land of Arabia before Muhammad's advent, for analyzing the events of his life, or for describing what happened after his passing. This oversight in our education is unfortunate and inexcusable, for Muhammad changed the course of human history in a dramatic way. Just who was he, and what did he accomplish and how?

After Muhammad's passing, Islam produced a world-class civilization that many scholars feel was more vibrant, long-lived, and vivacious than many of the civilizations that arose in the wider world. Great dynasties arose and fell in the Muslim heartlands, and the landscape from Morocco to China was dotted with fabulous cities containing many of the modern conveniences that we take for granted today. Although there were setbacks, Islam always seemed able to absorb any challenges that came before it. In this part, I will provide a survey of Muslim history from the time just before Muhammad to the events that are affecting Islam to this very day.

Chapter 21

Muhammad in Mecca

In This Chapter

- Learn more about ancient Arabia, the land where Islam began
- Discover Muhammad's early childhood influences and upbringing
- Meet the people who formed Muhammad's inner circle
- Find out what Muslims believe about Muhammad's ascension to heaven

Throughout the course of this book I have made many references to the Prophet Muhammad and his role as the central personality in Islam. Who was he, and how did he come to have enough courage to complete a mission that oftentimes seemed doomed to failure? In this chapter, I will finally take a thorough look at the life of Muhammad, from the conditions of the society he was born into until his migration from Mecca to Medina. It is interesting to note that this one man, who has done so much to change the course of human history, was actually a thrice-orphaned child from a poor clan who grew up tending sheep. As you learn more about his early life, you will gain a greater appreciation for both the man and the simple directness that Islam is famous for.

Arabia: The Birthplace of Islam

Arabia—the name conjures up images of sand dunes and desert oases. Bedouins on camels, groves of frankincense and myrrh, and the ruins of the Nabateans compete in our imagination with modern clichés about oil and mysterious princesses in forbidden desert palaces. This contrast of the rare and exotic, and the harsh and surreal, is not far from the reality that has permeated much of this peninsula's history. But while it is true that vast deserts fill most of the land between the Red Sea and the Indian Ocean, there are also scattered fertile valleys, oases, and sleepy coastal cities. Arabia is by far a land of many contrasts. Think of Arizona or New Mexico, and you'll have a pretty good idea of the nature of the land there. In addition, the people are not as unknown to the West as one might think. Since before the Roman Empire the inhabitants of that strategic plot of land have been the middlemen in the trade of many of the spices and other goods that our modern world now takes for granted.

One Arabian city, in particular, that has been of great importance is Mecca. This dusty oasis town was a main stop on the East-West trade route and has always been considered one of the main centers of Arabian culture. It owed its financial existence to the spending habits of the frequent travelers who passed through its otherwise barren valleys. Religion, also, was a form of big business, with hundreds of idols from tribes all over central Arabia being housed and venerated inside the *Ka'bah*. In return for housing their gods in a place of honor, the tribes that inhabited western Arabia gave generous guarantees of protection to the caravans that issued forth from Mecca twice a year. To the Meccans, religion equaled money, so the more gods the merrier.

There was no king in Arabia nor a central government. Arabian civilization in the sixth century centered on the concept of the tribe as one's nation. A tribe was a collection of loosely related individuals living in a certain territory. The tribal leader was called a *shaykh*, and he was usually the oldest member of the most important family. Although subclans existed within the tribe, internal differences were usually suppressed for the greater good of the whole. Wherever you were, your tribe was your passport and status. A complex series of alliances maintained some semblance of order but petty tribal wars and a culture of raiding each other's property kept the land in a constant state of flux. Though a well-developed concept of bravery was in force, and guests were treated like the members of one's own family, beyond these two virtues it was in many respects a land gripped in the worst of security situations. Think of the wild, wild West in American history and double its severity and you'll get some idea about what life must have been like for those who lived there.

Translate This

Shaykh is the term for any leader or chief of a group or organization. It has both religious and secular connotations.

Meet Muhammad's Parents

Abdullah was a handsome young man of the Hashim clan, a subgroup of the dominant Quraish tribe of Mecca. He had been married to a young woman named Aminah for only about six months when he decided to join a caravan heading for Syria, where he hoped to make a quick fortune in the lucrative trade fairs of Damascus. By this time, his wife was pregnant and she tearfully bade her husband farewell. Little did she know that on his return journey, Abdullah would catch a fever and die in Yathrib, a city far to the north.

A few weeks after Abdullah had left, Aminah confided in her servant, an African girl named Barakah, that she had had a dream in which a voice told her to name her unborn child "Muhammad." This was an odd name and had never before been used among the Arabs. It meant highly praised. The baby was born in about the year 570. News of the tragic death of the father reached Mecca just before the baby's birth, and the sorrowful grandfather, 'Abdel Muttalib, comforted the newly widowed young wife by saying, "He will be like a little Abdullah to us."

Thank God I'm a Country Boy!

The custom in those days was for city mothers to send their babies to foster mothers from the countryside for a few years so that the infants would grow up in a challenging environment. Every year women would come from the hinterlands and go door-to-door offering their services. No one went to Aminah's door because they knew she was a widow and couldn't pay much. At the same time, there was a frail-looking foster mother named Halima, who couldn't seem to find a baby to take. 'Abdel Muttalib brought the pair together, and the baby Muhammad was taken to be raised by the tribe of Sa'ad in the open desert.

Muhammad spent several years with the tribe—longer than was customary because of fears about a plague in Mecca—learning the life of a nomadic herder and picking up good manners from the rough but simple folk. His primary playmate was Halima's daughter, just a few years older than he, who helped Muhammad adapt to the harsh ways of Bedouin life. When he was five years old, he was finally returned to his grateful mother in Mecca. His manners, rugged constitution, and good grammar impressed many. His mother wanted to show him off to her distant relatives in Yathrib and to visit her husband's grave, so she took him and Barakah on the 10-day journey northward. She spent two weeks there in the oasis town, bunking with relatives in the night while weeping most of every day over her husband's grave. Muhammad, still quite young, spent his time playing with his cousins.

On the return trip, about halfway to Mecca, Aminah fell ill with fever and couldn't travel any further. Her condition continued to worsen, and as she lay dying in her tent by the side of the caravan trail, she made Barakah promise to always look after Muhammad. The tearful servant and child buried the departed lady soon afterward, and the pair returned to 'Abdel Muttalib's home in sorrow. A couple of years later, this loving grandfather would also reach the end of life. But before he died, he asked his son, Abu Talib, to look after Muhammad as if the boy were his own. Thus, Muhammad and Barakah went to live in his uncle's already poverty-stricken household. Muhammad had been orphaned three times before the age of 10.

War and Trade in Mecca

Abu Talib put Muhammad to work tending his small flock of sheep in the hills above the city. For most of his teen years this was Muhammad's only occupation. Thus he was not able to carouse with the other boys his age in the city, who spent their youth drinking, visiting prostitutes, and fighting or on raids. The only excitement in Muhammad's young life came when the Quraish tribe fought a battle against a rival tribe. Muhammad, along with the other teenage boys, had the dangerous job of retrieving any enemy arrows that fell on the battlefield. Muhammad didn't actually engage in any of the fighting himself.

Muhammad: Citizen of Mecca

Muhammad soon grew into a well-respected young man, and by his early twenties he had developed a reputation for honesty and integrity. He even had two nicknames: "the truthful" and "the trustworthy." Having been inadvertently sheltered for most of his youth from urban values, he was known to be more mature than other young men his age.

Muhammad remained a poor man, however, with limited opportunities until a lucky break came. A wealthy widowed woman named Khadijah was looking for someone to lead her caravan to Syria and conduct business on her behalf. Muhammad's uncle got him the job, and he was so successful and honest that when he returned, Khadijah soon fell in love with him and asked him to marry her. He was 25, and she was 40. He agreed to the match, which one of Khadija's friends arranged, and the couple would eventually have four daughters and two sons. (The sons would both die in infancy.)

After 15 years of blissful married life, however, Muhammad became restless. He never participated in idolatry because his established frame of reference (owing to his occupation as a shepherd) was the vastness and grandeur of nature. He saw right through the gods made of sticks, stones, and severed animal heads. He wanted to know where he could find the answer to the mystery of life. By his late thirties he began retreating to a lonely mountain cave that he had found earlier as a young man tending his uncle's flocks. There he could think without interruption.

A Prophet Is Chosen

In Chapter 18, I related the entire episode about the angel who came to Muhammad and revealed the first verses of the Qur'an. It was quite a spiritual experience, and as Muhammad ran home from the cave he looked up and saw the angel's face, filling the space between the earth and the sky. "Muhammad, you are the messenger of Allah," the angel said, "and I am Gabriel." When Muhammad burst in through the front door, he frantically called to his wife, "Cover me! Cover me!"

While her husband shivered feverishly through the night, Khadijah went to consult her old cousin, Waraqa, who was something of a gnostic Christian, though he was forced to keep his beliefs to himself because of an edict from Mecca's ruling council some years before that outlawed the open practice of that faith. When the frail blind man heard what had happened, he told her that if Muhammad's story was really true, then that was the same angel who had talked to Moses. Meanwhile, the angel came again to Muhammad, this time in his dreams: "You, who are wrapped up, get up and warn people! Glorify your Lord and keep your clothes pure! Avoid the idols. Don't give in charity expecting anything in return. For your Lord's sake be patient." (Qur'an 74:1–7)

When Khadijah returned home, she found her husband sitting up in bed. She asked him to rest further, but he replied, "Khadijah, the time for resting is over. Gabriel has asked me to warn people and to call them to Allah and His service. But whom shall I call, and who will listen?" Khadijah thought for a moment, and then told him she would be the first to listen. Thus, a woman became the first convert to Islam.

What Would Islam Ask of the Meccans?

The religion that the Meccans would soon learn about would be based on monotheism, which was a radical idea in a society that depended on idolatry for its financial health. Tourism, connected with the attraction of a *Ka'bah* filled with idols, fueled the local economy and gave a measure of authority to the dominant tribe of Quraish, which had custody of the holy sanctuary. But the many changes that Islam would be asking of people would run far deeper than mere theology.

The Arabs did not believe in an afterlife or in a Day of Judgment, and the Qur'anic revelation as it grew in scope and content would propose both. In addition, the concept of accountability for one's own actions before God would be unnerving in a society where literally anything was allowed. "What!" the Qur'an records the idolaters as later saying, "When we're dust and bones we're going to be raised up again? That would be a lousy re-creation." The Qur'an will answer, "Yes, indeed, your ancestors and everyone who came after!" (Qur'an 56:48–49)

The moral and ethical codes of Islam would also emphasize honesty, charity, mercy, respect for others' rights, and an elevated conception of the female gender. Muhammad would even pronounce that animals had rights and could not be beaten or overworked. Perhaps the straw that would break the camel's back, however, would be Islam's attack on blind tribal loyalty. The community of believers was a more important bond than who your relatives were. All of these ideas, as they would come to light, would soon begin to upset the Meccan leadership, especially as more and more people would start converting to this new way of thinking.

How Was Islam Received in Mecca?

When Muhammad began to preach his message publicly, (after about three years of private preaching to family members and friends) the Meccans didn't know how to respond at first. Muhammad was a member of the Hashimite clan, a poor but respected arm of the Quraish tribe. Many people from this clan were converting, and some of them were relatives of powerful people. After a few months of hoping the problem would go away by itself, however, the Meccan leaders decided to respond.

Their first tactic was to try to bribe Muhammad, offering him money, a beautiful girl of his choosing, a free visit to a witchdoctor to cure him of his "demonic visions," or even a prominent seat in the tribal council of Mecca, but he refused all offers. Next, they called upon the venerable Abu Talib to convince his nephew to stop his newfound occupation. Muhammad gave this famous reply in answer to his uncle's entreaties, "Uncle, by God, if they put the sun in my right hand and the moon in my left, and asked me to give up my mission, I wouldn't do it until either Allah made His way succeed or I died trying."

The angry Meccans began to harass any Muslims who came near the *Ka'bah* to pray. It was after a steady stream of converts from other clans began to join Islam that the real abuse started. Clan leaders, finding that they were losing control of some of their own members, began a policy of old fashioned discipline to reinforce their authority. Thus sons and daughters who converted were subject to hazing, corporal punishment, and loss of livelihood. Soon thugs began to attack converts from the fringe elements of society, slaves, immigrants, and those who had few family connections, bullying and beating them in the streets while the citizenry turned a blind eye. The slaves, in particular, had it rough. Those who accepted Islam were tortured by their masters more mercilessly than ever before. One woman burned her slave's forehead with a hot poker, and another slave owner staked out his slave in the hot desert sand and rolled heavy stones on his chest.

The poets of the city began weaving slanderous prose and reciting it in the market-place. When Muhammad went out of the city to greet incoming caravans to call them to Islam, these poets would follow behind, shouting, "Here is a madman. Don't listen to him." Because Muhammad and his followers were verbally abused wherever they went, many people who wanted to convert to Islam were forced to keep their choice a secret. (Three of Muhammad's own daughters were divorced by their idolatrous husbands and sent home in disgrace because they had converted as well.)

After two more years, the Meccans decided to expel Muhammad's entire clan to a barren valley a few miles outside the city. Hundreds of men, women, and children were rounded up by armed Meccan warriors and marched into a steep-walled valley with nothing but the clothes on their backs. This was the Muslim "Trail of Tears." Muhammad and the people of his clan were forced to live there for three long years with only limited food supplies that were smuggled in from sympathetic relatives and friends. The deprivation during the Boycott, as it was called, was so bad that Muhammad's beloved wife, Khadijah, fell ill and died. The virtual prisoners were released only after some visiting Arab delegations shamed the Meccans into lifting their cruel and unusual policy.

> **Ask the Imam**
>
> Muhammad used to get depressed about the constant verbal and physical abuse he and his followers suffered. The Qur'an contains several passages in which God is basically telling him, "Hold on, things will get better." This focus on hope during hardship is a primary theme in Muslim mental health practice.

> **It Is Written**
>
> When commenting on the banishment of his followers and their families for three years by the Meccans, Muhammad remarked, "Those were the hardest years of my life." His wife passed away during that time.

The African Migrations

Although they were able to return to their homes, the situation remained precarious. Muhammad forbade his followers to fight back, even though he himself had to endure people throwing garbage at him and putting thorns in front of his door. Any resistance on the part of the Muslims would have been seized upon by the Meccans as an excuse to wipe them out in one blow. Muhammad was, nevertheless, heartbroken to see such insane violence directed against his followers, so he prayed for guidance and made a plan of escape (at least for a few of his followers). He would send the most vulnerable members of his community across the Red Sea into the Christian kingdom of Abyssinia. One group of a dozen made it safely and without notice. Soon thereafter Muhammad sent a larger group of about 80 men and women. Such a large departure wasn't without notice, however; and the Meccans, concerned that Muhammad was trying to open up a new base of strength, sent two of their most skilled ambassadors to petition the Abyssinian king to return the refugees as criminals.

The wise king brought the representatives of the Muslims before him and asked to know more about Islam. The Muslim leader, Ja'far, explained the details of the faith. After a heated exchange with the Meccan ambassadors involving the Muslim concept of Jesus, the king decided to allow the Muslims to stay in his country.

Muhammad's Night Journey and Ascension

After 11 years in Mecca, the Muslims numbered over 200 men, women, and children. Daily, Muhammad and his followers endured violence at the hands of the Meccans, and it seemed that the situation would never improve. But one morning, Muhammad emerged from a relative's house, in which he had spent the night, and made a public announcement so dramatic that some new converts to Islam threatened to renounce their faith. Muhammad said that he had been taken to Jerusalem, had ascended from there into Heaven, and then had returned to Mecca—all in the same night!

Just the Facts _____

Some Orientalists have charged that Muhammad's journey to Heaven could not possibly have been real. The Bible, upon which much of Western civilization is founded, contains more fantastic miracles than that. If one accepts the premise that there is a higher power, an overarching order to the universe, then believing in divine revelation is no more fantastic than believing in such an idea as multidimensional travel.

How did Muhammad explain all of this? He said that after he had finished his late-night prayer, the angel Gabriel came to him accompanied by a fantastic horselike creature called the *Buraq*, whose every stride took it to the furthest extent of its eyesight. Muhammad mounted the *Buraq*, and they reached Jerusalem within a few minutes. The spirits of the past prophets appeared, and Muhammad led them all in prayer in the darkness of midnight. Then Muhammad remounted the *Buraq*, and Gabriel ascended with him into the next realm and through the seven layers of Heaven.

Muhammad was able to see Paradise and all of its delights, and he was greeted by some of the prophets who dwelled within. He was taken to the furthest edge of the seventh Heaven beyond which Allah manifests His power. They could go only as far as the edge, and Muhammad reported seeing lights and sounds and sweeping streams of energy that he couldn't describe in words. When the tour was over, Gabriel took Muhammad back to Jerusalem and then back to Mecca.

The Meccans, of course, took this as proof that Muhammad really was crazy. That morning, the streets were abuzz with what Muhammad was proclaiming. Some Muslims rushed to Abu Bakr, Muhammad's closest friend, to get his opinion on the matter. Without hearing anything from the Prophet yet, Abu Bakr exclaimed, "By God! If Muhammad himself said it, then it's true. He tells us that the Word of God comes to him any time of the day or night, and we believe him. Isn't that a greater miracle than what we're doubting here today?"

Abu Bakr then joined the throngs in front of Muhammad and asked him questions about Jerusalem, the kinds of buildings, the main features, and other peculiarities, because Abu Bakr had himself stayed there once. Muhammad answered the questions accurately, and this caused even more confusion because everyone knew he had never been there before. Then Muhammad told of a caravan he had passed on the road back to Mecca. He described it in detail, and a few hours later it arrived. The idolaters backed off their claims of insanity and resumed their old line of attack that Muhammad was gaining converts by means of sorcery.

This event is considered noteworthy by Muslims and is celebrated every year with religious speeches, parties, and gatherings. The journey to Mecca is called the *Isra'*, and the ascension to heaven is called the *Me'raj*. Today the famed Dome of the Rock stands over the place where Muhammad made his journey into the next realm. For this reason, Jerusalem is considered the third-holiest city in Islam, after Mecca and Medina.

Just the Facts

There is an apocryphal story that Muhammad was willing to compromise and accept three Meccan deities in exchange for religious liberty. Both Western and Muslim scholars have proven that this report is completely untrue and out of character with Muhammad's life and work. The novel penned by Salman Rushdie, *The Satanic Verses*, is a loose reference to this fallacious story.

A view of the rock in Jerusalem upon which Muhammad ascended to heaven.

(Courtesy of Aramco)

The Great Escape!

Meccan attacks continued unabated, and Muhammad himself was no longer safe from their brutality. His uncle and protector, Abu Talib, passed away just as the cruel boycott was being lifted, removing the last facade of family support. Muhammad had to do something to save his beleaguered followers and himself. After unsuccessfully petitioning the leaders of the nearby city of Ta'if to accept him and his people, Muhammad chanced to run into a group of people visiting from Yathrib. He explained Islam to them over a campfire outside the city, and they accepted it! Two years later a larger group of 70 people, representing the Auws and Khazraj tribes, pledged their belief in Islam, all in secrecy at night lest the Meccans find out. Before leaving, however, they invited Muhammad to move northward and rule their civil war–prone city. A way of escape had opened up and not a moment too soon!

By the year 622, the Meccans, after 13 years of enduring a movement that challenged every facet of their tribal way of life, decided to end Islam once and for all. They intended to murder Muhammad, and to cover their murder they wove a carefully contrived plot in which a group of young men, one from every major tribe, would sneak into his house at night and all would stab him (so that Muhammad's clan would be powerless to take revenge on anyone).

Muhammad got wind of this devious scheme and ordered his followers to pack their bags and leave for Yathrib in small groups over several days so as not to attract any undue attention. When nearly every one of the Muslims had left, Muhammad and Abu Bakr made their exit as well under the cover of darkness. Muhammad's cousin, a young man named Ali, was to stay behind and sleep in Muhammad's bed, making it look like he was home. The six assassins sent by the Quraish discovered the ruse and soon the alarm was sounded that Muhammad had escaped. The Quraish set a huge bounty on Muhammad's head, and soon Meccan warriors were combing the country-side. After eluding their pursuers through a circuitous route, first heading southward and then northward towards Yathrib, Muhammad finally made a triumphant entry into the city that would be his home for the rest of his life. In his honor the name Yathrib was quickly be dropped in favor of *Medinat un Nabi*, *the City of the Prophet*, or Medina for short.

The Least You Need to Know

◆ Arabia was one of the many crossroads of civilization. Caravan routes linking Asia with Europe traversed much of that desert land.

◆ Muhammad had developed a reputation for honesty and trustworthiness in his youth and earned nicknames to that effect.

◆ The Arabs of Mecca opposed Muhammad's preaching and persecuted his followers.

◆ Muslims believe that Muhammad was given a tour of Heaven by the archangel Gabriel. This is the famous ascension of Muhammad from Jerusalem.

Chapter 22

The Victory of Islam

In This Chapter

- ◆ Learn about the battles fought between the Muslims and the Idolaters
- ◆ Find out how Muhammad defeated the Meccans
- ◆ Discover why Muhammad was married 13 times
- ◆ Understand Muhammad's life in its totality

Islam was a persecuted religion in its earliest years. At any moment it could have been eliminated because the Muslims in Mecca were a scattered and vulnerable lot. Conditions became so unbearable that Muhammad had to send some of his followers to Africa to escape the wrath of the Meccans, and Muhammad himself had to flee for his life to Medina. But even as the Muslims regrouped in Medina, the Meccans initiated armed attacks against them to keep them under pressure.

Over the next several years, the Meccans would mount three invasions of the north that almost succeeded in vanquishing the fledgling religious movement. But the Muslims, though vastly outnumbered in every battle, had an unshakable faith in their cause. The Meccans had no such motivating factor, only blind, unfocused hatred. Muhammad led his community through these and other crises and continued to organize his followers and train them in the ways of Islam. By the time he passed away, the movement he started was poised and ready to challenge the superpowers of the world.

The First Islamic State

Muhammad and Abu Bakr entered Medina to great fanfare. Everyone, Arab and Jew alike, lined the streets to see this man of Mecca who claimed to be a prophet. As he wound his way through the streets, shouts of "Come stay in my house!" echoed from many lips. Muhammad, however, knowing that to disappoint anyone on his first day would be unwise, dismounted his camel and announced he would stay wherever the camel stopped. It wandered for a few minutes, paused briefly in front of one man's house, and then moved on until it sat down in a vacant lot near the city center. Muhammad would lodge in the lucky man's home where the camel had paused while his quarters (along with the great mosque of Medina) would be built.

Before construction started, however, there was a serious problem to attend to. The Muslims who had fled Mecca came with little more than the clothes on their backs. Muhammad mobilized the good-natured converts in Medina to the benefit of the hundreds of destitute Meccan refugees. He asked the people of Medina to "adopt" their fellow believers from Mecca and share half their goods with them. Every family adopted one of the newcomers, and the immediate problem of poverty was alleviated.

Just the Facts

Two terms were coined as a result of the Muslims's flight to Medina: *muhajirun,* meaning "immigrants" to signify those Muslims who fled Mecca; and *Ansar,* meaning "the helpers," to identify those Medinans who offered assistance to the refugees.

It took seven months of hard labor to build the mosque and an attached apartment for the Prophet. But after it was finished, the simple brick building with a palm leaf roof provided a focal point for the Muslim community. It was there that Muhammad would conduct meetings and accept new converts from surrounding tribes. The mosque became a kind of community center, city hall, classroom, prayer area, and homeless shelter for the steady stream of destitute new Muslims who needed a place to sleep at night.

Muhammad wrote a city charter, guaranteeing the rights of all citizens, and he also had his secretaries draft treaties of friendship with the local Jewish tribes and with other communities in central Arabia. Within Medina, members of the two main Arab tribes were rapidly converting, and Muslims were preaching and teaching Islamic brotherhood on a constant basis. New verses of the Qur'an were continually being revealed, with new social rules, civil and criminal laws, and doctrines to live by. This was the first

Islamic state, and it is to this time that Muslims today hearken when they talk of re-establishing Islam as a political system.

The Desperate Times

The Meccans greatly feared the growth of Muslim power in Medina. The main cara-van route to Syria passed within range of that city, and they thought that Muhammad might try to interfere with their trade. (After all the Meccans had done to him, it was only natural to fear retaliation.) In the tradition of raiding one's neighbor, the Mec-cans began to carry out a sort of guerilla warfare against the Muslims. Small groups of Meccan warriors would frequently attack the outskirts of Medina, as well as any travelers and farmers in the area. This forced Muhammad to organize regular patrols, and frequent clashes in the hills became common.

The Battle of Badr

A particularly large caravan was returning to Mecca from Syria. It was laden with trade goods, and the people of Mecca anticipated it eagerly. The master of the cara-van, Abu Sufyan, became afraid that the Muslims of Medina might try to intercept it in revenge for the raids that the Meccans had been making. He sent a message ahead with a fast rider telling his Meccan compatriots to come to his aid if need be.

The Meccans, who were looking for any opportunity to galvanize their populace against the Muslims, decided to raise an army and attack Medina. They recruited a thousand warriors who were well equipped with horses, camels, armor, and supplies. Abu Sufyan had said in his message that he was going to stop at an oasis called Badr, so that's where the Meccan army decided to march first.

Back in Medina, Muhammad found out about the caravan and the massive threat. He man-aged to cobble together a dedicated, though poorly equipped, force of 313 men. The Muslims, thinking that the Badr oasis would be the likely location for the caravan to go, made their way there in all haste. After a couple of days of hard marching, they arrived at the wells first. Muhammad ordered his men to fill in the wells with sand and to take up positions on a small ridge.

Just the Facts

The Battle of Badr took place in the month of Ramadan in the year 624. The Muslims were observ-ing their dawn-to-dusk fast yet despite their thirst and vastly smaller force, they prevailed over the Meccan idolaters.

Abu Sufyan decided to avoid the wells altogether and was safely on his way back to Mecca, but the Meccan army disregarded his written pleas to retreat. The thirsty horde arrived at Badr only to find the water blocked and a force of men ahead of them standing under a black flag. The idolaters, seeing that they vastly outnumbered the Muslims, engaged them in a fierce battle. The Muslim ranks never wavered, however, and they turned back the tide, forcing the Meccans to retreat in disarray.

The Muslims won a splendid victory and suffered only minimal losses, while the defeated Meccans returned home in shame. They lost several of their top leaders, and nearly 100 men were killed or taken prisoner. Later, after much discussion in Medina as to what to do with the many captives, Muhammad decreed that any captured soldiers who could teach 10 Muslims to read would be freed. Any detainees who were illiterate could be released upon payment of a fee from their families. The Qur'an explained that this tremendous victory was due to God's favor and the staunch determination of the true believers.

The Battle of Uhud

The Meccans were not at all content with their defeat. In Arabia personal and tribal honor were among the most sacred concepts, and to be defeated by a weaker foe was shameful indeed. The famed poets of the Arabs began to recite verses lamenting the Muslim victory and calling for revenge. A year later the Meccans managed to organize an even larger army consisting of 3,000 men and set out to challenge the Muslims once again. Their destination was a small mountain called Uhud, which stood just outside of Medina.

When Muhammad was informed about the devastating force that was about to challenge his community, he called a council of war and asked for his companions' opinions about what to do. The consensus was to go out and meet them in battle, rather than fight them within the city. Accordingly, Muhammad organized a force of 1,000 men and marched them to the far side of Mount Uhud.

When the Meccan forces arrived on the field of battle, a treacherous commander on the Muslim side pulled out and took 300 of his men with him. He was what was known as a hypocrite: someone who pretended to accept Islam in Medina just to appear trendy but who secretly worked against it whenever possible. The disheartened Muslims now had only 700 troops to meet 3,000. Muhammad, thinking quickly, placed 50 archers on a side pass to prevent any Meccan cavalry from launching a rear assault and placed the main body of his forces into a frontal defensive position.

The onslaught of the Meccans was swift and fierce, but the Muslim lines held. At one point, Muhammad ordered a charge and the Meccans began to flee in confusion. It began to look as if the Muslims would achieve another stunning victory, but the archers on the hill, seeing their chance at participating in the war (and perhaps collecting the booty left on the battlefield) begin to diminish with every yard the Meccans retreated, left their posts and ran down into the battlefield to join the mad rush. This was the worst mistake they could have ever made.

The commander of the Meccan cavalry, Khalid ibn Walid, saw his chance, and he raced his mounted warriors behind Uhud and through the pass and attacked the surprised Muslims from behind. The Meccan infantry, seeing the new development, arrested their retreat and attacked anew; thus, the Muslim forces were caught in the middle. In the confusion, dozens of Muslims were killed and the Prophet was knocked down and slightly wounded.

Just the Facts

The hypocrites of Medina were people who pretended to be Muslims. They gave such trouble to Muhammad and the real Muslims that the Qur'an devotes dozens of verses to their description and their negative effects on the Muslim community.

The Muslims hastily retreated up toward the steep mountainside and took up positions there as the elated Meccans postured and then finally began to comb the battlefield, looking for dead and wounded Muslims to mutilate and torture. The Meccans withdrew later that day, and the Muslims returned to Medina, chastened that some of their number had disobeyed orders, causing the battle to be lost.

The Battle of the Ditch

As you learned in Chapter 16, the Muslims and Jews of Medina eventually engaged in civil war. The two Jewish tribes of Banu Qaynuqa and Banu Nadir both broke their treaties in turn and were consequently expelled from the city. The last Jewish tribe, the Banu Quraiza, still lived peacefully with the Muslims.

Representatives of the Banu Nadir tribe, which was now settled in a northern city named Khaibar, traveled to Mecca and roused them to end Islam once and for all. Under their guidance, the Meccans became allies with numerous tribes all throughout Arabia, and a force of over 10,000 warriors was assembled—the largest Arabia had ever seen! This massive horde converged upon Medina with the goal of destroying Islam and enslaving any Muslims who might survive its brutal assault.

The Muslims had precious little time to organize a proper defense or court allies. A Persian convert named Salman al Farsi suggested that a wide and deep trench could be dug all along the exposed front section of the city, while the walls in the rear of the city could be blocked and fortified. The Prophet and his companions agreed to this plan, and the trench was finished just before the enemy arrived. The Muslims who watched the approach of the horde were awestruck with terror. The Meccans, however, halted their advance when they espied the trench and were confused about what to do. It was a tactic unknown in Arabia, so their momentum was interrupted. After a few unsuccessful infantry assaults, a kind of stalemate ensued.

For almost a month the frustrated Meccans tried to breach the trench, but their men were beaten back every time under a furious rain of arrows. The cavalry was, of course, useless because the chasm was too wide to jump. The Muslims inside the city were running low on food, but their spirits were high. The Banu Nadir, however, succeeded in getting the Banu Quraiza to join the alliance. They held the rear flank of the city and could attack the Muslims from behind.

It Is Written

When the enemy attacked you from above and from below; when your eyes were petrified due to fear and your hearts leapt up to your throats, and you began to entertain all sorts of doubts about Allah, there, the believers were put to a severe test and were shaken with tremendous apprehension. (Qur'an 33:10–11)

The Meccans' strategy was to initiate an all-out assault from the front and rear of the city, and it would have succeeded except for the fact that Muhammad used a double agent to sow doubts in the minds of the alliance's leaders. He was able to make the Banu Quraiza hesitate and to split the Meccans from their Bedouin allies with false rumors and reports. A fierce desert sandstorm blew over the plains the next night, and the alliance broke apart. The once proud coalition dissolved and quit the siege.

The Conquest of Mecca

The Muslim victory over the Meccans and their allies elevated their status among the tribes of Arabia. Numerous tribal chiefs were converting, and it seemed as if the Muslims would become strong enough to rival Mecca. But the following year, during the annual pilgrimage season in Arabia, Muhammad organized a group of 1,400 pilgrims to march to Mecca for religious rites. They were virtually unarmed!

When the Meccans found out about the Muslim pilgrims, they were alarmed. They sent their cavalry to prevent the Muslims from entering the city, but the Muslims took a different route and set up camp just outside Mecca. The stunned idolaters sent representatives to Muhammad, and the two sides hammered out a 10-year-long peace treaty called the *Treaty of Hudaibiyah*. Both sides agreed to halt any hostilities and to rein in their allies. Although the Meccans stipulated that the Muslims could only begin making pilgrimages the following year, the Muslims returned to Medina with a new sense of security.

But the peace treaty was to be short-lived. A tribe allied to the Meccans attacked a tribe allied to the Muslims and massacred a large number of their people. This violated the treaty, and when news reached Mecca of Muhammad's displeasure, the Meccans at first publicly repudiated the treaty. Abu Sufyan, however, who was the Meccans's most influential leader, saw that Muhammad's power had grown too great for them to handle. He rushed to Medina to plead for the reinstatement of the treaty, but Muhammad refused to see him. A couple of weeks later, a force of over 10,000 Muslims marched upon Mecca. They arrived at night and made camp all around the hills above the city. Muhammad ordered each group of soldiers to light several campfires so that it would look as if their already overwhelming numbers were much greater.

The Meccans sent Abu Sufyan to Muhammad's camp to surrender peacefully that night. Abu Sufyan even converted to Islam in an audience with the Prophet. As per the terms of capitulation, the next morning Muhammad led the victorious Muslims in a triumphal march into the city. After his soldiers took up positions throughout the town, he led a column toward the *Ka'bah* and found a large throng of Meccans standing there. These were the people who had tortured him and his followers for years. By any standard of justice he could have had them punished. They called out to him, "What are you going to do with us?" He replied, "You are all forgiven today. Go back to your homes. You are all free."

Muhammad showed the utmost mercy, and Mecca was taken without a fight. Western scholars have long praised Muhammad for this act of wise clemency, calling it a coup of intelligent strategy, but for Muslims it is a sign of Muhammad's character: He was long-suffering and tolerant. Within days nearly the entire population of the city decided to convert under no coercion. The main task that Muhammad called for was to remove the idols from the Ka'bah, and the Muslims joyfully executed this duty, turning the venerated gods of the Arabs into a pile of rubble in the street. Muhammad spent the next few weeks in Mecca so he could organize its administration, after which he returned to Medina, the recognized seat of the Islamic State.

Confronting the Superpowers

The Byzantine Roman Empire and the Persian Empire were the two superpowers of the day. Muhammad had sent letters of introduction and invitation to the emperors of both countries; the Byzantines seemed undecided about Islam, but the Persians declared their hostile intentions. Nevertheless, it was the Byzantines who first threatened the Muslims. Their emperor, Heraclius, ordered his troops to menace the allies of the Muslims in northern Arabia. To counter this threat, Muhammad marched an army all the way to the borders of Syria. Mysteriously, the Byzantines backed down and withdrew their army. No battles took place, and Muhammad succeeded in cementing several important alliances with local tribes and political leaders. This expedition would mark the end of Muhammad's active participation in any defensive or military endeavors.

> **Just the Facts**
>
> Muhammad sent letters of invitation to all of the known rulers of the world. Copies of many of these letters still exist in museums.

Taking Another Look at Muhammad's Marriages

Some Western scholars have charged that Muhammad was licentious on account of the many marriages he contracted. Popular myth has maligned the Prophet and cast a shadow over an otherwise universally accepted great leader. But what was the nature of these marriages, and do they demonstrate a weakness for pleasure? Let's examine this issue more closely.

> **Ask the Imam**
>
> How could Muhammad marry more than four wives when the Qur'an established a limit? The verses prohibiting more than four wives were revealed after the last of Muhammad's marriages.

When Muhammad married Khadijah in Mecca, he was 25 years old and she was 40. He lived with her monogamously for almost a quarter of a century (23 years). He didn't take another wife until after she died, and he was over 50 years old. If he was licentious, the time to have married multiple women would have been in his youth, not when he was an old man charged with the endless duties of being a prophet. (He spent most of his days in meetings and a portion of every night in the mosque praying.)

He remarried while still in Mecca only at the insistence of his companions, and his first new wife was an overweight widow whom none of Muhammad's other companions wanted to marry. His next marriage was to the daughter of his friend Abu Bakr. Muhammad had had a dream that he was supposed to marry her, and when he approached his friend, he found out that A'ishah was already engaged to someone else. Abu Bakr succeeded in getting that engagement cancelled and then engaged his daughter to the Prophet. The controversy surrounding this marriage is that A'ishah was very young. She was somewhere between the ages of six and nine at the time of engagement. Although the actual marriage and consummation would not take place for at least three to five more years, (after the Muslims migrated to Medina), looked at from today's standards the age difference is often deemed inappropriate. This has led to the baseless charge that Muhammad was, in the words of Pastor Jerry Vines (and defended by Jerry Falwell) "a demon-possessed pedophile."

Setting aside the insulting nature of the comment, what must be remembered is that in seventh-century Arabia there was no social stigma attached to marrying someone dramatically older or younger, even if the age difference was extreme. A'ishah was engaged to Muhammad while still a child, but she did not join the Prophet's household as his wife until after she attained puberty (somewhere between the ages of 9 and 12). Neither A'ishah nor her parents had any objection to the marriage, and she, herself, always expressed her love and affection for the Prophet even into the many decades that she outlived him. (A'ishah became one of the most important early scholars of Islam and was the teacher of many of the greatest leaders in the early Islamic Caliphate.) If Muhammad were a pedophile, he would not have waited for A'ishah to reach puberty before completing the marriage, nor would he have stopped at only one marriage to a young girl.

All the rest of Muhammad's marriages occurred in Medina and were spread out over 10 years. After the 3 wives already mentioned, he married 11 other women. With the exception of one divorcée, all of them were widows or freed captives of war (whose fathers were most often chiefs of tribes, thus allowing a political alliance to be cemented). Muhammad asked their consent before marrying each, and they readily agreed. Muhammad divided his time with each equally and helped with the housework in each wife's apartment. Again, if he was addicted to sex, he would have married all young women. Instead, they were mostly old and/or widowed and he rarely had time to spend with any member of his family, because of the strong demands on his time as both a temporal and spiritual leader.

Each wife had a special status in the community. They were known as the *Mothers of the Believers* and people deferred to them as respected members of the Prophet's family. After the Prophet passed away, his nine surviving wives took up the task of being teachers and social activists. Many Muslims today name their daughters after the Prophet's wives.

The Passing of a Prophet

Muhammad conducted one final pilgrimage to Mecca when he was nearing 63 years of age. He delivered a famous address, known as his Farewell Speech, and then retired to Medina where he tried to continue with his duties as best he could. By this time, however, he was frail and weak, owing to age (and possibly also due to an unsuccessful poisoning attempt directed against him years before by a woman belonging to the Banu Nadir). He became progressively reflective and introspective in the eyes of those around him and made more frequent visits to the graveyard to commune with his thoughts. When he became too ill to lead the congregational prayers in the mosque, he chose Abu Bakr to stand in for him. Finally, after suffering through several days of an intense fever, Muhammad raised his eyes to Heaven and called out, "Better the next world on high." With his head resting in his beloved A'ishah's lap, Muhammad passed away. The date was the 8th of June in the year 632. He was buried in the place where he breathed his last. Today the famous green dome of the Prophet's Mosque in Medina marks the spot where his grave lies.

His life and mission touched upon the hearts of a people who were living in superstition and idolatry. The teachings he promoted uplifted the status of women, gave rights to the poor, regulated the moral and social life of his followers, and provided a path to salvation for millions. Michael Hart, in his book *The One Hundred Most Influential People*, ranked Muhammad as the most important person who ever affected our world because of his example, success, and enduring message. He was able to successfully fuse the tenets of religion and politics on a level no one has been able to do since. Writers from Washington Irving to Mahatma Gandhi have praised him for his sincerity and noble character. Such was Muhammad, the Messenger of Allah:

> Philosopher, orator, apostle, legislator, warrior, conqueror of ideas, restorer of rational dogmas, of a cult without images; the founder of twenty terrestrial empires and of one spiritual empire, that is Muhammad. As regards all standards by which human greatness may be measured, we may well ask, is there a man greater than he? (Lamartine, Historie De La Turquie, vol. II, pp. 276–277, 1854)

The Least You Need to Know

- The Muslims were attacked three times by the idolaters of Mecca, and each time they survived.

- Muhammad made a treaty with the Meccans, but they broke it. The Muslims then marched to Mecca in force, and the city surrendered without a fight.

- Muhammad forgave all the people who had persecuted him and let them go free after his conquest of Mecca.

- Muhammad was born in the year 570 in Mecca and died in the year 632. He is buried in Medina.

Chapter 23

The Rightly Guided Successors

In This Chapter

- Know what the ideal Islamic government is really like
- Learn about the men who ruled the Muslim community after Prophet Muhammad's passing
- Understand the challenges that Islam faced after the Prophet was gone
- Find out why the first generation after Muhammad experienced two civil wars and numerous political assassinations
- Retrace how the political system of Islam changed from a democratic tradition to a dynastic dictatorship

The Muslim community had to deal with a temporary crisis of faith after the death of Prophet Muhammad. For 23 years Muhammad had guided his followers, teaching them a completely new tradition and acting as their spiritual, legal, and moral focal point. What would become of Islam without him? Drawing upon the Qur'an, the answer became clear:

"Muhammad is no more than a Messenger." "Many were the Messengers who passed away before him. If he dies or is killed, will you turn and run?" (Qur'an 3:144)

The Muslims not only didn't give up their faith, they quickly elected a leader and quelled several internal uprisings as well as confronted dangerous external threats. The first four rulers of the Muslim world were so faithful to Islamic precepts that the period of their rule is known affectionately as the *Khulafa ar Rashidah*, or the Period of the Rightly Guided Caliphs. However, within the space of 30 years the political structure came under such pressure that the egalitarian democratic system of elections gave way to a hereditary monarchy that forever changed the Islamic political tradition until the fall of the Ottomans in 1918. How did this happen and what were the major events that transpired?

Islam on Government

The government of the Prophet Muhammad was unique in that he was the sole authority because of his position as the spokesman of God's will. He appointed governors in many cities and territories throughout Arabia and gave them tremendous leeway in how they carried out their duties. His only stipulation was that they abide by the Qur'an and his *Sunnah*. The people of any locality, if they felt their governor was unjust or slack in his religious character, could petition the Prophet, who would investigate and appoint a new governor if necessary.

Just the Facts

The Qur'an promoted a political system highly suggestive of representative government in which the people should be consulted on all affairs not connected with clear religious dictates. In other words, representative democracy, of sorts.

Non-Muslims had the basic legal status of free citizens, and their religious liberties were respected. By the decree of the Prophet, further backed up by the Qur'an, forced conversion was forbidden, and any non-Muslim who felt wronged by a Muslim could be assured of a fair hearing. The most prominent companions of Muhammad formed the core of the informal administration, and their sincere belief in the truth of Islam emboldened them to work tirelessly at the many tasks at hand. No real structure of government existed beyond that, and as long as Muhammad was there, none was needed.

One practice that Muhammad established early on was a regular schedule of public meetings with the community members to get their advice on political actions, alliances, governors, and other mundane affairs. These meetings were held in the Mosque of Medina for the most part, and they presented a chance for all members to speak their minds on the issues that faced the community. Muhammad never silenced anyone nor took action against those who expressed differing opinions. Moreover, he often concurred with the majority consensus. This process was called the *Shura*, or Tradition of Consultation, which forms the basis of the representative political structure in Islam.

After Muhammad passed away and was buried, one such Shura was called to determine what the Muslims should do next. The main issue on the table was, of course, who should lead the community now that the Prophet was gone. (It was understood that this new leader would not be a prophet and would assume only a political role.) Muhammad himself had given numerous instructions to his companions on the functions and responsibilities of the future head of state. The top position would be an elected post, and the tenure of that leader would last as long as he abided by the tenets of Islam. Thus, an Islamic government consists of a *khalifa*, or caliph, and a representative council that can override or remove the caliph if he oversteps his bounds.

The Caliphate of Abu Bakr As-Sadeeq (632–634)

The meeting to choose a caliph, or successor to the Prophet's political function, got under way quickly and was attended by all of the prominent companions of Muhammad, except for those in other cities who could not arrive in time. The Medinan converts proposed that one of their number should be elected as the leader, but after heated debate it was decided that Abu Bakr, who was from Mecca, was the most qualified to lead. He had been Muhammad's closest friend and had been given the job of leading the prayers in the main mosque when the Prophet lay ill. Abu Bakr stood before the citizens of Medina and gave an acceptance speech, which included the following:

> O people, I have been chosen to be your leader, even though I'm no better than any of you. If I do right, help me. If I do wrong, correct me. (Rafi Ahmed Fidai, *Concise History of Muslim World*, page 68)

The only real dissent to Abu Bakr's election came from the Prophet's cousin, Ali ibn Abi Talib, who voiced his opinion that he should have had a say in the meeting. (At the time he was busy making the funeral arrangements for the Prophet.) Ali withheld his pledge of support for some months but later relented. Some of Ali's more ardent supporters, however, became disenchanted from the start with the argument that Ali, being a close relative to the late Prophet, had more right to rule. As we shall see, this nascent group of dissidents would eventually grow into the breakaway sect of the Shi'as.

Getting back to Abu Bakr's immediate challenges, it must be noted that not everyone who had become a Muslim in Arabia was sincere or particularly enthusiastic. Some Arab tribes, especially those far away from the area of Mecca and Medina, accepted Islam only because it seemed to be the trend. This fact became immediately clear when several of these tribes rebelled and declared that they would no longer pay their *zakah* and do other Islamic duties. To make matters worse, several claimants to prophethood arose seeking to create their own religions and political fortunes. Soon Arab Bedouins led by these false prophets began raiding Muslim outposts even as far as Medina and creating all sorts of trouble for the Muslims.

Abu Bakr had few troops left in Medina, since he had just sent a large army to Syria to guard against the Byzantines and their allies, who were menacing some tribes allied to the Muslim state. That large army was under the command of a teenager named Usamah bin Zayd, whom the Prophet himself had appointed for that task. Even with most of the army deployed in Syria, Abu Bakr was still able to gather a small force to defend Medina against the increasing Bedouin attacks.

Translate This

Riddah means apostasy, or renouncing your religion. It is a major crime in Islam and can result in capital punishment if the apostate turns into an enemy of the community.

Ask the Imam

After a battle, all of the captured weapons and baggage are distributed equally among the soldiers by their commander, except for the one fifth that goes to the Islamic government. The proceeds from that are to be spent primarily on orphans, freeing slaves, and relieving the poor.

After securing the capital, he ordered his small but tough army to subdue the Arab rebellions in the hinterlands. Before beginning the battle, however, the Muslim generals invited the rebels to return to Islam, and many tribes gave in without a fight. Still, a few unruly groups were hungry for a war and engaged the Muslim forces. But in battle after battle, the Muslims were victorious over the rebellious Bedouins and made them sign treaties of peace. This series of minor wars was known as the Wars of the *Riddah* and lasted only about a year.

The two great empires of the day were the Byzantines and the Persians. As noted in the previous chapter, the Prophet had sent letters to the rulers of both lands inviting them to Islam, and they had both refused, even to the point of starting to fight against Muslim communities in northern Arabia. The Persians were supplying arms and money to the rebellious Bedouins in an attempt to bring about the defeat of Islam. In the interests of self-defense, the Muslims felt compelled to go on the offensive.

One Muslim leader, who lived near the border of Persian-controlled Iraq, came to Medina to ask for protection for his people from constant Persian threats and attacks. Abu Bakr sent an army of 8,000 men in the year 633 to engage the Persians in battle. With a series of stunning victories, the outnumbered Muslims captured huge areas of prime real estate. Within one year, most of the lands of southern Iraq were firmly in the control of the Muslims.

On another front, Muslims in southern Syria were under constant danger of attack from the Byzantines. Abu Bakr ordered the army to shift into Syria to meet the new threat. After a few important battles, the Muslims drove out the Byzantines and secured the entire northern frontier of Palestine. In one battle, a group of Muslim women, who were acting as the medical corps for the Muslim army, were surrounded and attacked by the Byzantines. The women picked up their tent poles and used them as spears to fight the raiding enemy soldiers. The short swords of the Byzantines proved worthless against the women's long poles. The women held the enemy away and killed many of them.

Umar ibn al Khattab and Persia's Defeat (634–644)

Two years and three months had passed with Abu Bakr as caliph, but he was very old and eventually fell ill. Just before he passed away, he called a council of the most important companions of the Prophet and discussed with them who should rule after him. He suggested that Umar ibn al Khattab should lead the Ummah, or community, and everyone agreed that he was the best choice. A few days later Umar was confirmed in a public vote as the new caliph.

Umar had no time to rest. Pressure from the Persian army on the Iraqi front was increasing, and action was called for. A new army was sent from Medina to a place near the Euphrates River called Qadisiyyah. The people who lived in the area threw in their lot with the Muslims and rebelled against their Persian overlords who had always treated them harshly. After a fierce battle, the badly outnumbered Muslims defeated the Persian army and took control of almost all of the land west of the Euphrates River.

Just the Facts

Most of the cities that the Muslims laid siege to in Palestine and Syria surrendered under the Muslim promise that no harm would come to the population. Muslim soldiers did not engage in looting or plundering when they took a city. Tax rates from the new Muslim governors were also lower than what the people were used to paying.

Meanwhile, in the West, the Muslim forces facing the Byzantines in Syria were winning battle after battle. In almost every case, the Muslim army had only to surround a city, cut off its supplies, and ask the people to surrender, promising them that they would not be harmed. Nearly every city in Syria fell to the Muslims this way, and almost no actual fighting occurred.

Just the Facts

When Umar entered Jerusalem to accept the surrender of the city's leaders, he was asked to pray in a prominent church. He refused, saying he feared that people would turn it into a mosque after him.

After the Muslims captured the key city of Damascus, the Byzantine emperor, in far away Constantinople, decided to organize an army of 250,000 men to fight the Muslims. At a place called Yarmuk, in the year 636, an army of 40,000 Muslims defeated the Byzantines and forced them to retreat. In that same year the patriarch of Jerusalem agreed to hand over control of his city to the Muslims, and Umar himself came (at the patriarch's request) to accept the surrender of the city. The strategic regions that bordered northern Arabia were in Muslim hands for good.

Umar helped to further organize the national Muslim government. The expanding Muslim world was divided into eight provinces, each ruled by a governor appointed by the caliph. He also reorganized the system of tax collection and the treasury. The Muslim calendar was also fixed, tying the year zero to the Hijra, or migration, of the Prophet in the year 622 of the Western calendar. Other achievements are as follows:

♦ Egypt, Syria, Palestine, and a large part of present day Iraq were captured from the Byzantines and Persians.

♦ Umar garrisoned Muslim armies in separate camps and military towns, rather than quarter them in conquered cities. The major city of Basra in southern Iraq began as one such town.

♦ Umar reiterated Islam's tolerant nature towards Jews and Christians, assuring them of their rights and forbidding forced conversions. Many administrators in the lands taken from the Byzantines and Persians were, in fact, non-Muslims who were retained in their positions.

Umar ruled as caliph for 10 years until a Persian assassin stabbed and killed him. As he lay dying from his knife wound, he appointed a committee of important Muslims to choose a new caliph within three days of his death. After a few days of debate, the choice fell upon Uthman ibn Affan, who was a trusted companion of the Prophet.

Uthman ibn Affan and the Great Conspiracy (644–656)

Uthman became the leader at a time when Muslims were making strides on all fronts. To add to this progress, Uthman ordered the building of the first Muslim navy. He also made sure that an official copy of the authorized Qur'an was available in every main Muslim city to pre-empt any dispute about its contents in the expanding (and increasingly non-Arab) empire. Everything seemed to be going well for the Muslims, but some new problems began to arise. Uthman was not as strict in taking subordinates to task as Umar and was often hesitant about confronting corruption. People loved the gentle character of Uthman, but when it became known that some of the governors in the provinces were corrupt or incompetent, people began to complain that Uthman wasn't taking strong enough action against them.

Part of the problem was that the Muslim administrators in the new territories relied heavily on the system of local government that the Persians and Byzantines used. The Arabs were still not skilled at governing large cities and lands, so they often left in place whatever city workers and tax collectors they found there. Financial abuse and mismanagement were rampant, and oversight was lacking. Uthman removed some of the inept governors, but others, such as those in Syria and Egypt, became so powerful that they sometimes simply ignored the caliph's written orders. A third problem was that Uthman seemed to have appointed several of his relatives to governorships early on, and this fueled charges of nepotism. Opposition and dissatisfaction soon spread throughout the empire.

A group of people came to Medina from Iraq to complain about their own unjust governor. Uthman listened to them and promised that he would take some sort of action, and this seems to have mollified them. As they were returning to their own province by caravan, however, a non-Muslim saboteur planted a fake letter in the baggage ordering all the people who complained about their governor to be killed when they returned home. He signed the letter with a forged name reading: "Uthman." When the people in the caravan found this letter, they believed that Uthman intended to murder them.

Accordingly, they returned to Medina, surrounded Uthman's house, and demanded he come out. When they showed him the letter they had found, Uthman said the letter was a fake and that he didn't have anything to do with it. The mob refused to believe him and, later, some of their men killed him while he sat reading his Qur'an in private. To make matters worse, they wouldn't flee the city and instead stayed to publicly press their case. The Muslims in Medina were shocked and in grief. Uthman was loved by all for his gentleness and kindness, and now he had been cruelly murdered.

Ali ibn Abi Talib (656–661)

Ali was selected as the next caliph of the Muslims by a vote of the people in the main mosque in Medina. Soon, people from all over Arabia came to give him their pledge. But the immediate problem that faced him was the same one that had faced Uthman: what to do about the rebellious governors in Iraq, Egypt, and Syria. In addition to this, a large number of Muslims began demanding immediate punishment for the killers of Uthman.

Ali was in a difficult situation. He decided to delay his investigation into the murder until the situation could be better understood and addressed. This was in keeping with his cautious nature. He was always against hasty decisions made through enflamed emotions. But some people took this delay the wrong way and thought that Ali was refusing to bring the killers to justice. When A'ishah, the widow of the Prophet, heard about this, she joined with a group of like-minded people who decided to take drastic action against the caliph to force him to punish the killers.

It Is Written

Muhammad said, "Don't become disbelievers after me by fighting against one another and killing each other."

Just the Facts

The caliph, Ali, had to contend with two major civil wars during his rule. A rebel group known as the *Kharajites* (seceders) later assassinated him. Rule by elected caliphs gave way to dynastic succession in the world of Islam after his time.

Meanwhile, Ali was doing his best to address the political problems before him and decided to make a clean break from the scandal-tainted rule of the governors appointed by his predecessor. Consequently, he sent written messages to all the recalcitrant governors, asking them to step down from their posts. For the most part his orders were ignored, as the issue of Uthman's murder and the lack of justice meted out against the perpetrators galvanized the powerful elite to stall. Most importantly, Mu'awiya of Syria refused to even read the caliph's letters.

The Battle of the Camel

A'ishah and a group of companions intent on taking revenge for Uthman's murder decided to travel to the new Muslim garrison city of Basrah to raise an army to confront Ali. They found some of the killers of Uthman along the way and executed them. Then they defeated Ali's supporters in the region. They soon gathered a huge army that was large enough to march against Medina itself. When news of this reached Ali, he organized an army of his own and marched to Basrah to stop A'ishah and her supporters. He didn't want A'ishah, or anyone else, to take the law into their own hands. Accompanying Ali's army was Abdullah ibn Sabah, a treacherous man who may have been behind the forged letter that resulted in Uthman's death. When Ali asked Abdullah and his men to leave, knowing that they were suspicious characters, the provocateur thought of a daring plan. As you will see, it would be the cause of a great disaster.

The two armies met outside of Basrah in the year 656. Ali and A'ishah met face-to-face between the two armies and negotiated a peace agreement. After they returned to their camps, Abdullah ibn Sabah made his move. Before anyone could stop them, a few of his men, who were hiding behind the front lines of both armies, charged out, swinging their swords and pretending that the battle had begun. In the confusion, the men of both armies rushed to fight each other, thinking that they had been ordered to do so.

Thousands of Muslims were engaged in battle against each other, and the slaughter was fierce. Upon seeing the fighting begin, however, A'ishah became alarmed and tried to stop it. She mounted her camel and rode out into the melee trying to tell her men to hold, but her own army thought she had come to encourage them to fight even harder, so the battle went on for hours.

When Ali saw that A'ishah's presence was making the situation even hotter, he ordered some of his soldiers to rush her position and cut down her camel so that none of her men would be able to see her. After Ali's men had carried out the order, they escorted her off the battlefield. Ali's army defeated the rebels and peace was restored. The affair was known as the Battle of the Camel, after A'ishah's daring ride into the battlefield. She returned to Medina in sorrow and resumed her activities as a teacher.

The Struggle for Power

To save Medina from any more political trouble, Ali moved the capital of the Islamic empire to the new Muslim city of Kufah, near the border with Iraq. With the immediate trouble solved, Ali again turned his attention to the rebellious governors. He decided to replace every governor ever appointed by Uthman, thinking that they were weak and untrustworthy. But Mu'awiya of Syria again refused to step down and instead gathered an army to defend his position. He also launched a propaganda campaign against his rival.

In the year 658, Ali marched his army to a place in Syria named *Siffin*. There he found Mu'awiya's army ready to face him. Ali tried to start peace talks with Mu'awiya, but his foe refused, saying that he would never negotiate until the issue of Uthman's killers was settled once and for all. A three-day battle followed, and Ali's army made steady progress against Mu'awiya's forces. When it looked like he was going to lose, Mu'awiya ordered his cavalry to hang pages from the Qur'an on the ends of their spears to make Ali pause. The trick worked, and Mu'awiya and Ali began negotiations.

A radical group of Ali's men were angry that their leader didn't pursue total victory against the rebels. Known as the *Khawarij*, or Kharajites, they deserted and returned to Kufah to prepare an army to attack Ali's forces. Meanwhile, Ali and Mu'awiya pulled back their armies and returned to their own lands while the negotiations went on. Ali put down the revolt of the Kharajite fighters when he returned and then worked to strengthen his position in Kufah.

A Compromise with Syria

After several months of sending messages and proposals back and forth, both Ali and Mu'awiya agreed that they would each step down, pending arbitration by a three-man committee, and that neither one of them would campaign for the office. But this was a trick on Mu'awiya's part. In a large public gathering, after Ali's representative declared that Ali would step down as caliph, one of Mu'awiya's supporters then stood up and said that Mu'awiya would now be the new caliph! Confusion and turmoil engulfed the meeting.

This blatant double-cross and political brinkmanship angered many, and the angriest people of all were the few remaining Kharajite men who had gone into hiding or who had pretended to make peace. They decided to kill both Mu'awiya and Ali and then find a new caliph. While they wove their schemes, Mu'awiya and Ali's armies began moving against each other from Egypt to the Hijaz region of Arabia. Mu'awiya's forces even briefly attacked and occupied both Mecca and Medina!

Finally, one lone Kharajite assassin was able to sneak up on Ali and stab him. He died in the year 661, just after his morning prayers. The last of the true caliphs who had lived by Muhammad's precepts was gone. (The Kharajite agent sent to kill Mu'awiya failed to assassinate his target.) Under Mu'awiya's undisputed rule from Damascus, the Islamic Empire would become a monarchy. Although the religious aspects of Islam would still continue to be promoted vigorously, the political system enshrined in the Qur'an would never again function the way it did in Medina. The first Islamic dynasty, centered on the tribe of Umayyah, was thus born. Known as the Umayyad Dynasty, it would last for less than 100 years but would soon itself give way to a more vigorous dynasty which would oversee the true flowering of Islamic civilization.

The Least You Need to Know

♦ The first four caliphs, or leaders, after Muhammad are considered by Muslims to have been "rightly guided," or sincere to their religion in their governance style.

♦ The Muslim community was forced to fight the Byzantines and the Persians in Palestine, Syria, and Iraq; they won many stunning victories.

♦ The first caliph died of old age, but the next three were all assassinated for political reasons.

♦ Islam was not spread by the sword. This is a popular myth that was cultivated by propagandists in the Middle Ages. Forced conversion is forbidden in the Qur'an.

♦ The Islamic political structure began as something akin to a representative democracy but was transformed into a hereditary monarchy by ambitious men 30 years after Muhammad passed away.

Chapter 24

Islamic Civilization: The Dynastic Period

In This Chapter

- ◆ Learn about the Umayyads, the first Muslim dynasty
- ◆ Discover the wonders of Baghdad and its Abbasid flavor
- ◆ Step into the world of Muslim culture, art, literature, and architecture
- ◆ Find out why the Muslim world fragmented into several competing states

Islam produced a civilization that in many ways far surpassed Rome at its height. From the time of Muhammad's famed Hijrah, or migration, to Medina in 622, until the year of the fateful destruction of Baghdad in 1258, a single Muslim government ruled over most of the ever-expanding world of Islam. Although civil wars and dynastic feuding would engulf the political tier, life for the average Muslim citizen was far better than in Europe, which was a land of mud huts and illiteracy. In the Muslim world, vibrant cities teeming with artists, scholars, merchants, and rogues provided endless opportunities for enrichment and intellectual advancement.

Muslim rulers were patrons of the arts and learning, and they set up such public services as hospitals, primary schools, colleges, and even rest stops on the caravan trails. Any Europeans who could afford to do so made their way to the great universities in the Muslim world; there they could study and learn what no Christian school could offer. But this upward growth was rudely interrupted by invasions that left much of the Muslim world occupied by either heathen Mongols or fanatic Crusaders. Rising out of the ashes, the unitary Muslim state that had disappeared in the year 1258 was supplanted by a fragmented jigsaw puzzle of competing kingdoms and sultanates. In this chapter, I will be taking you on a grand tour through this period in Muslim history.

The Umayyads

After the death of the fourth caliph, Ali, in 661, his son, Hassan, declared himself eligible to be the next caliph. As the grandson of Muhammad and the son of Ali, Hassan had a lot of support in Arabia and Iraq. (Many people around the area of Kufah had developed a kind of hero-worship toward Ali that would later result in the formation of the distinctive *Shi'a* sect of Islam.) But Mu'awiya, the governor of Syria, also laid claim to the title of caliph. Another protracted civil war might have ensued except for the fact that the pious Hassan quickly retracted his claim and retired to private life before the situation spiraled out of control. Mu'awiya was then able to anoint himself the caliph of the entire Muslim world.

The *Umayyads*, as this dynasty was called, would rule for the next 90 years from Damascus. During their tenure, the borders of the empire expanded in all directions, from China to France. Islamic learning flourished, and the major traditions of Islamic Law began to be established. Hundreds of books were written every year on every subject imaginable, from gardening to politics. Free public hospitals and schools were set up in every city and town, and Muslim scientists and philosophers were busy making new discoveries and organizing the knowledge they had acquired from their subject nations.

Translate This

The name *Umayyad* comes from *Banu Umayyah,* a clan that falls under the umbrella of the Quraish tribe of Mecca.

How the Caliphate Became Hereditary

Mu'awiya broke an important Islamic rule about choosing new leaders. Instead of letting the Muslims form a committee to elect a new caliph after his death, Mu'awiya decreed that his own son, Yazid, would be the caliph after him. This outraged many Muslims because Yazid was known to drink wine and to live a wasteful lifestyle—two indulgences that were forbidden in Islam. The hereditary question also was a problem because the Prophet was very clear about choosing people on merit and not on birth.

Mu'awiya died suddenly in the year 680, and Yazid promptly declared himself the caliph. Many religious scholars and the few surviving companions of the Prophet openly opposed him, including Ali's other son, Hussain, who refused to accept the worldly minded Yazid as the new sovereign and instead assumed the title himself.

Hussain was able to gather a small group of supporters and began to set up his government in Kufah. Yazid meanwhile sent an army of 4,000 to crush this challenger, and when word of the approaching invasion reached Iraq, most of Hussain's men deserted him. At a place named Karbala, the Syrian army surrounded Hussain's forces, which now numbered less than a hundred, and killed them all to the last man and woman. It is this episode of cruelty that Shi'as commemorate every year in the first month of the Islamic year.

Just the Facts _____

Every year, Muslims from the Shi'a sect of Islam hold passion plays to commemorate the martyrdom of Hussain at Karbala. Some go to extremes and cut their foreheads or beat themselves with whips to express their sorrow at his cruel murder.

After Yazid's death, many caliphs of his line came and went. Some were effective administrators, while others were lackluster. One of the most famous of the later Umayyad rulers was Umar ibn Abdul Aziz, who ruled from 717 to 719 C.E. He was known as an excellent Muslim and earned the nickname "the Second Umar," after the famed early head of the Islamic state. He ruled with justice and fairness. He even sent Muslim missionaries as far away as Tibet and China. Umayyad rule would last until 750, when internal dissent brought the second and last great dynastic house in the unified world of Islam to power: the Abbasids.

An inside view of Jerusalem's famous Dome of the Rock, built during Umayyad rule. Muslims call it Al Quds, or the Holy Place.

(Courtesy of Aramco)

The Abbasids and the Mongol Invasions

A group known as the Abbasids overthrew the Umayyads after a series of wars and internal rebellions. The caliphs of this line, who claimed to be descendants of the Prophet's uncle, Abbas, were to rule for the next five centuries, and it was under their auspices that the greatest progress was made in the arts, sciences, literature, and medicine. In Abbasid cities, libraries and schools jostled for space with bazaars and the mansions of the wealthy. The city of Baghdad, known as the jewel of the world, was founded by the second Abbasid caliph as a unique fortress city built in the shape of a wheel, with all roads leading to the palace in the center.

The Abbasid Empire gradually declined, however, in its later years, owing to bad government practices and a weakness for foolish spending among many of the nobles and leaders. Some of the caliphs were more interested in constructing palaces, holding expensive pageants, and drinking alcohol than in upholding the banner of the Islamic way of life. One notable exception was the famed Harun ar-Rashid, who is the caliph mentioned often in the famous collection of stories entitled *The Thousand and One Nights.*

In the dynasty's waning years, local warlords and charismatic leaders carved several semi-independent states out of the empire, actions that further weakened the central authority. By the year 1000 North Africa was completely lost to a Shi'a dynasty known as the Fatamids, named after the Prophet's youngest daughter. The most important new force to weaken Abbasid power, however, was that of the Seljuk Turks. They were recent converts to Islam whose military prowess came to be a vital support to Abbasid authority. Eventually they got smart and realized they could usurp power for themselves, and they succeeded in reducing the power of the caliph to that of a ceremonial head. The last Abbasid ruler spent all of his time in vain ceremonies and refused to act when word of an impending invasion reached him. As history would show, the invaders would not spare his beloved city, as he had hoped, and the Muslim world was soon going to find itself on the verge of annihilation.

Abbasid rule and the city of Baghdad were wiped out in 1258, when vicious invaders called the Mongols swept into Muslim lands like a tidal wave. They conquered all of Muslim Persia and Iraq and unleashed a reign of terror against the populace that is eclipsed only by Adolph Hitler's Nazi war machine. It is estimated that over 16 million people were massacred in Persia and Iraq alone. (It took the Mongols 40 days to execute the entire population of Baghdad.) Libraries were burnt, cities were razed, and the practice of Islam was forbidden under Mongol decree.

Eventually, however, after several generations of life off the harsh Central Asian steppe, the grandchildren and great-grandchildren of the original Mongols converted to Islam. It took nearly a hundred years but they were finally able to appreciate and learn about the teachings of the faith and the civilization it bore. Soon the Mongol rulers were restoring mosques, reopening schools, and adopting the cultures of the lands they lived in. They even went on to conquer nearly all of Hindu India and a large part of southern Russia and Eastern Europe for Islam. But the power and might of the Abbasids would never again be achieved by any other Muslim empire.

The Golden Age of Islamic Civilization

Islam as a religion promotes study and learning. Contrary to popular opinion, Islam is not against modernity or scholarship. In fact, for most of the last thousand years it was the Muslim world that was advancing on all fronts and the Christian world that was lagging behind in the arts and sciences. During the Abbasid caliphate, Muslim cities were the largest in the world, with well-established social services and a cultural vibrancy that caused Europeans to marvel. Free public hospitals, universities, local public health inspectors, even paved roads were everyday parts of life for citizens in Muslim lands.

The Islamic world was a cosmopolitan mix of people of all races and colors who spoke dozens of different languages (Arabic was the *lingua franca*, being the religiously sanctioned tongue). The mighty caravan routes were much like superhighways are today and were filled with traffic and congestion. International business was booming, and for the first time, merchants could rely on writing checks that would be honored at banks throughout the Muslim world. Travel was easier than at any time in human history, and the practice of medicine was no longer a quack's profession, with aspiring doctors required to pass exams. The Islamic world, in short, was much like modern America with the exception of the technology available today.

> ### Ask the Imam
>
> Non-Muslims were welcome in Islamic regions because the Qur'an contains a built-in acceptance toward other religions. It prescribes tolerance and mutual respect and forbids pressured conversions. In some Islamic universities in Spain and North Africa, non-Muslim students of the sciences numbered almost as many as Muslim students!

Islamic Art Forms

Muslim artists often quote a maxim attributed to the Prophet: God is beautiful, and He loves beauty. The Muslim world produced many different art forms, even as Muslim artists continue to ply their trade today. But there is a prohibition in Islam against painting or drawing people or animals that appear *too* lifelike. This is in keeping with the anti-idolatry trend in the faith. But beyond this there are few other curbs on free artistic expression. The following list presents the main art forms that the world of Islam produces:

◆ **Calligraphy** Writing the Arabic script in a fancy and artistic manner. Primarily, Muslim calligraphers have used verses of the Qur'an as their subject matter. There are several styles of writing the Arabic script, much like the different fonts on today's word processors; and the flourishing strokes of a good calligrapher are highly prized in the Muslim world.

Muslims have used calligraphy to adorn the verses of the Qur'an. Here is Chapter 1 of the Qur'an expressed in a highly artistic style.

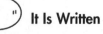 **It Is Written**

According to Muhammad, "Those who make pictures (of animate creatures) will be punished on the Day of Resurrection, and it will be said to them, 'Bring to life what you have created.'"

◆ **Geometric design** Tessellations, as they are called, are repeating geometric designs. Muslim mathematicians made this type of artwork possible with the development of algebra and trigonometry. Most mosques in the traditional Muslim world have some element of this art form in their construction.

◆ **Arabesque** A distinctive combination of floral design and artistic patterns. Europeans copied many of these motifs during the Renaissance, and Muslim influences can be seen in cathedrals throughout France, Germany, and Italy.

♦ **Persian miniatures**   Small paintings by Muslim artists of scenes that depict a variety of subjects from kings to peasants. This style of painting spread over several regions of the Islamic world.

Architecture

Public buildings have always had a special place in Islam. The mosque, which has to hold large crowds every day, was often the largest and most beautifully constructed edifice in any Muslim city. Architectural monuments such as the Taj Mahal and the Blue Mosque in Istanbul stand out as stunning achievements. Palaces, colleges, and libraries also received grand treatment and rival the great castles and palaces of Europe in their beauty and complexity.

Literature

Every civilization is judged by the knowledge it leaves behind. Although the world of Islam is by no means gone from world affairs, its greatest period of intellectual and cultural achievement occurred during the Abbasid caliphate, with later contributions by the various Muslim states that broke away. It was during this time that papermaking was adopted from China, enabling the publication of books on a large scale.

For the first time, authors writing in Arabic, Farsi, and other languages were actually able to make money from their efforts. Because of the religious commandment in Islam that Muslims must learn to read and write, the tremendously large literate populations of the teeming Muslim cities were fertile ground for a steady stream of books, manuals, and letters. The main library in Baghdad had thousands of titles that people could borrow, and bookstores made an appearance for the first time as well. Some of the best-known authors from this period were the satirist Al Jahiz, the philosopher Al Ghazali, and the adventurer Ibn Batutta. A fictional practical joker named *Goha* who stars in a collection of stories was also quite popular.

Famous works of literature include …

♦ *The Arabian Nights*   A collection of stories, from Sindbad and Ali Baba to Aladdin and Ma'ruf the Cobbler, that have entertained people for centuries.

♦ *The Mathnawi*   Poetry from Jalaluddin Rumi. Currently, his poems about faith and life sell more books in America than any other poet's.

♦ *Layla and Majnun* The classic Romeo and Juliet tale by Nizami that predates Shakespeare by centuries.

♦ *The Conference of Birds* Farid ud-Din Attar's story of the quest to find the king of the birds and what the weary travelers really find.

♦ *The Musings of Rabi'a al-Adawiya* Passionate, intense, and moving verse from Islam's most famous female mystic.

♦ *The Adventures of Seyd bin Dhi Yazan* Sort of like a Muslim Robin Hood and Prince Charming rolled up into one.

♦ *The Island of Animals* A fable about the animals of the world taking man to court for mistreating them.

♦ *The Ghulistan* An engaging collection of poems, social commentaries, and stories by Sa'di Shirazi.

♦ *The Rubbaiyat* Poetry of Omar Khayyam. Irreverent and often philosophical verse that begs the reader to love life.

The Beginnings of Rival Muslim States

As I mentioned earlier, the strength of the Abbasid caliphate weakened to such an extent that entire regions were able to break away and achieve de facto independence. After the Mongol invasions, the permanent dismemberment of the unitary Muslim state was complete. Even though the Mongols eventually converted, they merely remained the lords of their own nations. From the thirteenth century onward, several large Muslim empires competed amongst themselves. These included the Persian Empire, the various Turkish states, the Mamlukes of Egypt and Syria, and the Mughals of India. (In those territories where Islam was spreading through missionary efforts, these areas developed political realities of their own, such as in western Africa and southeast Asia.)

Although the Ottoman Turks would eventually unify much of the Muslim heartland in a state that would last until the twentieth century, they were never able to extend their sway over the eastern half of the Muslim world. Thus, a distinctive western and eastern Islamic flavor could be seen for the first time. Ironically, even though the Muslim world became so fragmented, it survived, albeit in truncated form. By contrast, when the Roman Empire collapsed in the fifth century, its civilization disappeared. Islam did not suffer the same fate because it is more than a culture and a civilization; it is also a religion offering spiritual guidance.

Islam and Spain: A Unique Blend

When the Abbasids seized power from the Umayyads in 750, they ordered the execution of every member of the Umayyad ruling elite. (They didn't want some prince to pop up and rally the people against them in the future.) But one member of the Umayyad household managed to escape, and he made his way across north Africa and into Spain, where he founded a new branch of the Umayyad house. Muslims had already conquered Spain, as early as the year 711, when Tariq bin Ziyad, the famous Muslim general, crossed the Strait of *Gibraltar* at the invitation of a Spanish Christian chief.

Translate This

Gibraltar comes from the term *Jabal Tariq,* or the Mountain of Tariq, after the place where General Tariq bin Ziyad landed in Spain.

Spain was quite easy for the Muslims to take, given that the populace was in a constant state of dissatisfaction with their king, Roderick the Visigoth. During the first major battle, two flanks of his army, which were commanded by his rivals, actually switched allegiances and joined the Muslim side, resulting in the defeat of the despised ruler. By 718 the Muslims were in possession of nearly the entire peninsula.

For the next 800 years, the Islamic government in Spain worked to build a civilization so advanced that its influence helped to bring Europe out of the Dark Age and resulted in the Enlightenment. The fabulous Muslim cities of Cordoba, Seville, Toledo, and Granada boasted paved streets lit by oil lamps, hospitals, universities, endless bazaars, libraries, and public gardens. Europeans flocked to these great cities and returned home with new ideas and a burning zeal to make backward Europe as advanced as Muslim Spain.

Unfortunately, the unity of the Umayyad state in Spain was to be short-lived. Eventually it broke up into competing fiefdoms—more than 20 at one point—which became easy prey for the Christians in northern Spain who began reasserting their power. By the year 1492, the Spanish Catholics had conquered the last Muslim stronghold of Granada. They turned thousands of mosques into churches, burned mountains of books written in Arabic, and initiated the infamous Inquisition in which hundreds of thousands of Muslim civilians were rounded up and tortured to death by the Church.

Just the Facts

Jews in Islamic Spain had more rights than Jews anywhere else in the world. They lived generally in safety and prosperity alongside their Muslim and Christian neighbors. This period of intense Jewish cultural growth is often called the Golden Age of Judaism.

The legacy of Islamic Spain can be seen even today in the thousands of buildings that still stand and in the flavor of the Spanish language and the Spanish culture, which were heavily influenced by Muslims during their rule.

The Mughals

Muslim rule in India began in the year 712. Hindu pirates, acting under the authority of a local lord, attacked a ship carrying Muslim civilians. When the pirates refused to release them, the Umayyad governor of Iraq ordered an army to attack what is today Pakistan. But it wouldn't be until the sixteenth century that Muslim rule over nearly the entire subcontinent would be complete.

The famed Mughal dynasty, which ruled India from 1526 to 1857, produced many great works of art and architecture, most notably the Taj Mahal. However, the insidious designs of the encroaching British spelled the doom of Muslim rule in India. After a final major battle to drive the British out of his domain, the last Mughal emperor was captured and sent into exile. The British chopped off the heads of all of his sons and sent them to him on a tray as a "present."

Classical miniature painting was produced throughout the Muslim world from India to Spain.

(Courtesy of Aramco)

The Crusades

No other event has defined Muslim-Christian relations to such a great degree as the Crusades. These were a series of European invasions, lasting from 1095 to 1270, into the Middle East to capture the Holy Land for Christendom. The first of the eight expeditions was wildly successful from the Christian standpoint, but the rest were ill-organized and doomed to failure. The Muslim world was weak and divided, and the Abbasids held no influence in the region.

Europe's First Colonies

Although the Holy Land was under Muslim administration for over five centuries, Christian pilgrims were still allowed to visit and perform their religious rites. In addition, a large Christian and Jewish population lived in peaceful coexistence with their Muslim neighbors. Owing to the general lack of education among European Christians, however, pilgrims from that continent would often enter Jerusalem and create public spectacles with loud singing, dancing, and rowdy musical bands. When the Muslim authorities attempted to curtail the unseemly activities, Christian monks began spreading wild rumors and increasingly inflamed propaganda that the Muslims were interfering with their religious rights.

At the same time the emperor of the ever-shrinking Byzantine Empire was sending a passionate plea to the pope in Rome to save his kingdom from the Seljuk Turks. This event combined with the already tense situation in the Holy Land provided a rallying point. Pope Urban II called upon the petty kings of Europe to march to the Holy Land and capture it for their religion. He promised to forgive their sins and admit them to Heaven for their trouble. The kings of France, England, the German fiefdoms, and Hungary were the first to respond, though they just promised loot and fiefdoms to their noblemen.

The unprepared Muslims withered under the massive invasion force; on June 15, 1095, the victorious Europeans entered Jerusalem. They promptly got down to business and slaughtered the entire population of the city. A contemporary Christian writer reported that so much blood was spilled that the streets were filled with streams of it. (The phrase "Kill them all, God knows His own" was coined by a representative of the pope who was asked what to do

Just the Facts

Saladin was known for his great self-restraint, chivalry, and manners. He exemplified the Qur'anic ideal of the warrior-scholar. When Richard the Lion-Hearted lost his horse during the course of one battle, Saladin sent him a new one with the message, "It is not right that so brave a warrior should fight on foot."

about the Christian Arabs who looked just like the Muslims.) One by one, other Muslim cities fell, and the butchering of civilians went on. When the Crusaders ran out of steam, they established effective rule over a territory stretching from southern Turkey to the border of Egypt.

The End of a Dream

The Crusaders were disunited and constantly quarrelling amongst themselves. The fossilized feudal system they had carried with them from Europe made it nearly impossible for them to work together or to improve the lives of their subjects. Their demise was assured after a Muslim sultan named Saladin rose to power in Syria. He united several Muslim regions under his command and fought a furious campaign to liberate the conquered territories. The most decisive battle occurred in 1187 at Hattin in Syria. Saladin completely defeated the Frankish army, and nothing stood between him and Jerusalem.

In 1192 Saladin forced the surrender of the city and entered it under a peace agreement. In contrast to what the Christians had done, he did not punish the civilians or soldiers of the city but only took over the administration. This story was repeated throughout the rest of Palestine. Although the Europeans made many other attempts to retake the Holy Land, they failed. By 1270, the Christians had resigned themselves to Muslim control over Jerusalem and had resumed their pilgrimage customs under guarantee of safe passage from the Muslim authorities.

The Least You Need to Know

- The political structure of the Islamic state became a family dynasty 30 years after Muhammad's passing.

- The first dynasty, which lasted 90 years, was called the Umayyad dynasty.

- The second Muslim dynasty, the Abbasid, came to power in a violent uprising and further expanded the borders of the Islamic state. The Abbasids founded the city of Baghdad as their capital.

- Muslim civilization produced great painters, authors, architects, and calligraphers whose works are on a par with the artistic achievements of any other civilization.

- The Mongols practically wiped out Islamic civilization in their destruction of over half of the Muslim world.

- The Crusades were a series of European invasions into the Middle East. Muslim forces eventually drove them out but not until Muslims united under a determined leader named Saladin.

Chapter 25

Islam in America

In This Chapter

- ◆ Find out who really discovered America
- ◆ Learn the true identity of many of the millions of Africans who were kidnapped and sold into slavery
- ◆ Discover the links between the African American heritage and Islam
- ◆ Find out why so many Americans accept Islam
- ◆ Note the major Muslim organizations operating in America today

Over the last five centuries, two distinctive trends have been at work in the Muslim world: a decline in power and a rebirth. Beginning with a decline in state power, the Muslim world slid into such weakness that it became easy prey for the ambitions of Europeans who saw a chance for easy plunder. Beyond merely occupying foreign territories, however, these same Europeans actually began enslaving the inhabitants, mostly those of African heritage, and exporting them in the most brutal fashion to the new American colonies. Many of these unfortunate souls were Muslims. Under the slave master's whip, the lives of hundreds of thousands of Islam's adherents were wiped out.

Today a rebirth is sweeping the world of Islam, as many ordinary people begin to take a fresh look at the faith that has shaped their cultures in so many ways. So, too, have many African Americans in the United States begun to take a fresh look at their own heritage and to reach back to their religious and cultural roots as once practiced by their forefathers. For many, this means accepting the teachings of the Prophet Muhammad.

Curiously enough, people of other races in the West are also starting to take a look at this comprehensive and inviting way of life, and the number of white and Hispanic converts to Islam increases every year. As a sign of the growth of Islam through both conversion and immigration, Muslims in North America now enjoy the support of many organizations that work tirelessly to bring their hopes and concerns to the national forum. In this chapter, I will explore the growth and establishment of *American Islam*.

The Forgotten Religion of African Americans

When Christopher Columbus set sail from Spain in 1492, Catholic forces had just completed the capture of the last Spanish Muslim stronghold, Granada. There were now hundreds of thousands of Muslims under Christian control, and soon they would be the victims of intense persecution under the Inquisition. Most of these people were about to be forcibly converted to Christianity. A large number pretended to convert to save themselves from the torture chamber. (The Catholics contemptuously referred to them as *Moors* or *Moriscoes*, a derogatory term coined by Europeans to describe North African Muslims.) A small but significant number of sailors in Columbus's crew were of Muslim extraction. They, too, had to hide their faith.

Upon landing in the Americas, Columbus was stunned to find that some of the people he encountered were black-skinned and possessed clothing styles suspiciously akin to those of the Moors of Granada and West Africa. Other Spaniards also noticed similar peculiarities. Hernando Cortes, conqueror of the Aztecs, remarked that some of the natives had clothes that were "painted in the style of Moorish draperies." But it was Columbus's son, Ferdinand, who would later surmise what has been begrudgingly accepted by many modern scholars: Africans landed in the Caribbean long before Columbus. What's even more exciting is that they were mostly Muslims.

Ask the Imam
Muslims who fear for their lives on account of their religion can hide their faith and pretend to follow something else until the danger is over. It is better though, says the Qur'an, to stand up for your faith and die as a martyr.

Islam did not survive, however, and it appears that the early African voyages, dated mainly to the twelfth century, were not permanent forays but accidental discoveries. The sailors, mostly from the Islamic Mandinka tribe of West Africa, merely intermingled and assimilated into local Indian cultures. Their influence did alter native life, however. One of Vasco de Balboa's recorders wrote, "It is believed that such African Americans came long ago from Africa … and that, having shipwrecked, established residence in those mountains." (A. H. Quick, *Deeper Roots*)

The next great influx of Africans to the Americas—and it would number in the millions—happened shortly after the Spanish realized that the local native peoples of the Caribbean and of Central and South America were unsuited for the kind of abject slavery the Spanish were enforcing. Consequently, they turned to the Portuguese, who began selling captured Africans to them as slaves. This scheme worked well enough on the face of it, but soon the Spanish found that a large number of these African slaves were Muslims. Upon entering the New World, they began organizing themselves, revolting, converting the Indians to Islam, and otherwise making a nuisance of themselves to their Catholic masters. In 1550 the Spanish king issued the following warning:

> You are informed that if such Moors … should teach Muslim doctrines, or wage war against you or the Indians who may have adopted the Muslim religion, you should not make slaves of them whatsoever. (A. H. Quick, *Deeper Roots*)

However, the lucrative nature of the slave trade made such entreaties fall on deaf ears. Soon a new system developed whereby imported slaves would first be taken to special training camps in the Caribbean; there they would be so beaten and humiliated that they would accept whatever commands—and religion—their masters gave them. It is estimated that upwards of 20 percent of all Africans brought to the Americas were Muslims. Because of the brutal forced conversions they underwent, however, very few remained even remotely concerned with protecting their faith.

Millions of slaves were imported into North America from the late seventeenth century until the early nineteenth century. Some of them did manage to retain their knowledge of Islam, and a few even practiced it in secret. American slave owners occasionally marveled over this oddity in some of their slaves, as evidenced by surviving historical documents. Some slaves could write Arabic and recite basic Islamic phrases, though they took great risks in doing so. One slave, who had handwritten a Qur'an from memory, explained to his enraged master that he had done it *before* he became a Christian.

Some slaves who had managed to retain their Islamic faith desired to return to their homeland once more and took steps to achieve it. One such man was Abd Rahman Ibrahima, a West African prince who had been sold into American slavery in 1787. After futilely resisting his master for years, he eventually found a way to petition President John Quincy Adams for his freedom. In 1829 he was returned to his homeland, where he died in the faith of his fathers. The harsh treatment meted out to most slaves, however, caused even the staunchest Muslims to wither. By the early twentieth century, all that remained in their descendants were a few phrases and old dictates about not eating pork. These last vestiges of Islam survived well into the early twentieth century in isolated pockets along the coasts of Georgia and the Carolinas.

The Rise of African American Islam

The quest for civil rights in America began shortly after the end of the Civil War. But opposition from many segments of white society effectively put this movement on ice. In the early twentieth century, however, many African Americans began to reassert their identity. Some looked for a way to better integrate themselves into American Christian society, while others, most notably Marcus Garvey, called for African Americans to look back upon their heritage as Africans and gain strength through their own traditions.

This ideology was taken up by a young African American man from North Carolina named Noble (Timothy) Drew Ali. He began to preach a message that mixed Islamic symbols with self-help slogans. He made up his own small book, which he called *The Holy Qur'an of the Moorish Science Temple of America*, and told people he was a prophet of God sent to redeem African Americans and to return them to the religion of their forefathers, the Moors. Of course, his message had little to do with authentic Islam, and his Qur'an was not actually a real Qur'an; but he gained many converts and set up Moorish Science Temples in several cities, the first being established in 1913 in Newark, New Jersey.

Just the Facts

Marcus Garvey's most influential mentor was a man named Dues Muhammad Ali. He established the Universal Islamic Society in 1926 in Detroit.

Upon his death in the 1930s, his followers divided and went in different directions. This was not the end of the nascent quasi-Islamic movement among African Americans, though. In 1930 a mysterious merchant named Wallace D. Fard made an appearance in Detroit and began preaching a message directed toward what he called "the lost-found tribe of Shabazz." (There is no such word in the Arabic language.) He mixed a few elements of Islam with mysticism and African American separatist philosophy and opened a temple for use by his growing following. In 1933 he formally established the Nation of Islam.

Fard's most ardent convert was Elijah Poole, who later took the name Elijah Muhammad. He carried the movement further after Fard's mysterious disappearance in 1934 and developed an ideology that mixed Islam and Christianity. He had moved to Chicago in 1932 and was named chief minister of the rapidly expanding Nation of Islam. Under his leadership, the organization proselytized aggressively and was able to open temples and businesses in several cities throughout the country.

Were the teachings of this group Islamic? Actually, no. They were quite far from authentic Islam. Beyond symbolism, Elijah Muhammad taught a number of doctrines that are incompatible with Islam. These include ...

> **Just the Facts**
>
> Wallace D. Fard is thought to have been an immigrant from Iran or Turkey, though his true identity has never been discovered.

- ◆ Wallace D. Fard was a divine, Christlike savior.

- ◆ Elijah Muhammad is a messenger from God.

- ◆ All whites are evil.

- ◆ Intermarriage between the races is forbidden.

- ◆ An evil scientist named Yacub created the Caucasian race in a spiteful fit of rage.

- ◆ The Bible is as valid as the Qur'an.

- ◆ The practices of Islam do not need to be learned in their orthodox form.

Malcolm X: Martyr of Islam

Malcolm Little, a small-time crook who was serving a prison sentence, came to know of the Nation of Islam. In 1947 he converted and became one of the group's most enthusiastic members. Upon his release in 1952, he entered the spotlight and became the Nation's national spokesman. Soon he began a coast-to-coast speaking tour that eventually caught the notice of the American press. In 1959 he was interviewed by Mike Wallace and created quite a stir among white Americans with his message of righting the injustices done against African Americans and of white culpability in the oppression.

Malcolm X, as he took to calling himself (to emphasize that his slave name was not his real identity), eventually began to feel uncomfortable with some of the actions of his spiritual leader. Elijah Muhammad was accused of having affairs, and this breach of personal discipline troubled the reformed criminal, who relied on Elijah's example to bolster his own inner strength. In addition, some members of the Nation were jealous of Malcolm's position as the unconfirmed successor to the now-ailing leader. They began to spread rumors about him, and his prestige began to suffer. It didn't help that Malcolm also began questioning the validity of the group's teachings on a variety of subjects.

Just the Facts

Cassius Clay, whom Malcolm X had befriended, accepted Islam in 1964 after a major boxing match. He changed his name to Muhammad Ali.

By 1964 Elijah Muhammad had removed Malcolm as an official minister of his organization. It was then that Malcolm X's life would take a dramatic turn. He set out for a pilgrimage to Mecca, and along the way he found that he really didn't know anything about Islam. The Nation of Islam, he realized, was *not* teaching the religion of Islam. Malcolm had to learn how to say Islamic prayers and for the first time became aware of the true teachings of Islam. He also discovered that Islam was against racism and irrational hatred of whites. Upon his return to the States, he promptly resigned from the Nation of Islam and began a national crusade to bring true Islam to African Americans. He was assassinated (some say by his former colleagues) in 1965. His autobiography, published shortly before his death, still inspires people to confront injustice passionately.

Islam Among African Americans Today

Elijah Muhammad's son, Wallace, also questioned the validity of his father's teachings. He was variously silenced and even excommunicated at one point from the Nation of Islam. When Elijah Muhammad died in 1975, Wallace was chosen as the new leader in a controversial decision that shocked many of the Nation's longtime members. Wallace, whose name had been changed to *Warith Deen* Muhammad, immediately began to dismantle large elements of his father's religious empire: dozens of temples, stores, farms, and other businesses that had been designed to fund the movement.

Translate This

Wallace Muhammad's Muslim name, **Warith Deen,** has an extra significance to it. It literally translates as *Inheritor of the Faith.*

The changes ran deeper than structural modifications, however. Under Warith Deen Muhammad's leadership, the old racially charged doctrines of hatred were removed. Followers were instructed in authentic Islamic beliefs and practices, and temples were converted into traditional mosques where Islamic-style prayers began to be held regularly. Even the name of the national organization was changed several times until it was known as (most recently) "The World Community of Al-Islam in the West."

Of course, opposition to such radical modifications in a long-standing movement was sure to come. A faction led by Louis Farrakhan, one of Elijah Muhammad's close associates, broke away and resurrected the old Nation of Islam. Much to the chagrin of Muslims all across America, Farrakhan's message of racial hatred against whites and Jews has given a bad name to a religion that doesn't teach either of those tenets. Whenever Farrakhan or one of his ministers speaks, Americans are unfairly given the impression that it is Islam speaking. Muslim-American organizations have routinely denounced the false teachings of the Nation of Islam for years, but this criticism by orthodox Muslims has received little coverage in the American press.

Recently, Farrakhan, who is reported to be ailing, has softened his tone. In a momentous ceremony held in the year 2000, he even declared his allegiance to Warith Deen Muhammad's community and has taken steps to integrate his followers into true Islam. The success of this move has yet to be seen. Mainstream Muslims were both surprised and pleased at such a move and now watch with anticipation, hoping that this embarrassing chapter is finally rehabilitated. As for Warith Deen Muhammad, he resigned and retired from his organization in 2003 after serving tirelessly for nearly 30 years.

Other Islamic movements have cropped up in the African American community that had nothing to do with the Nation of Islam or the Community of Al-Islam. These were often started through the propagation efforts of immigrant Muslims who took their duty to convey Islamic teachings seriously. With more than one million African American Muslims in America today, Islam is the fastest-growing religion among a population whose Islamic roots go back on this continent over five centuries.

Muslim Immigrants and the American Dream

In addition to African Americans, other immigrants have also brought Islam with them to this continent, albeit they came freely and were not forcibly converted. These are primarily people who emigrated in four great waves from various parts of the Muslim world, starting in the late 1800s. Each influx of Muslim immigrants can be summarized as follows:

- ◆ 1875 to 1912: Syrian, Lebanese, and Jordanian laborers migrate and become factory workers and peddlers.

- ◆ 1919 to 1921: Arabs from across the Middle East arrive (as laborers).

◆ 1947 to 1960: Palestinians, Egyptians, and Eastern European Muslims arrive. Many were well-educated and moved into the professional mainstream quickly.

◆ 1967 to 2001: Muslims from Asia (primarily the Indian subcontinent), the Arab world, and Africa arrive. Most are educated professionals or come as students and remain.

Most mosques, like this one in Queens, New York, were built by the latest wave of immigrants from the Muslim world.

The Muslims from the first two waves were rapidly assimilated, and nothing is left of their presence save for a few town names and abandoned mosques in scattered places. The third wave built many of the older mosques that are still in use in the great urban centers of the United States and Canada. The fourth and most recent wave has been active in political and social affairs in their communities and in the nation at large. Most of the mosques and Islamic parochial schools on this continent were built as a result of their efforts. For more information about the history of Islam in America, visit the most complete summary of the topic at www.amperspective. com/html/islam_in_america.html.

Just the Facts

The first designated mosque in the United States was established in Cedar Rapids, Iowa, in 1934. The earliest recorded Muslim congregation to meet regularly used a borrowed building in Ross, North Dakota, around the year 1900.

Caucasian Converts to Islam

There is nothing new about Caucasian converts in Islam. In the Prophet Muhammad's time, people of all races and ethnic groups were accepting Islam. The Ottoman Turkish caliphate ruled over much of Eastern Europe for centuries, and many groups, most notably the Bosnians, Albanians, and some Bulgarians joined the Islamic faith. The earliest-known Caucasian American convert to Islam was Alexander Russell Webb, the U.S. ambassador to the Philippines in the late nineteenth century. He published a book in 1893 titled *Islam in America.* Today an estimated 100,000 Caucasian Muslims live in North America and Europe.

Hispanic Muslims

There are no firm estimates of the numbers of Latinos who have accepted Islam in North America. Figures range from 10,000 to as high as 35,000 depending on whose study one consults. Although it may sound strange to talk about an Islamic movement among people of Latin American heritage, with its staunch Catholic image, Hispanics are not trapped by the Church, and many are looking for something more than they are experiencing. For many, Islam is seen as part of their heritage because the Spanish language and culture were influenced by the centuries-long rule of Muslims in Spain.

> **Ask the Imam**
>
> A prominent part of the annual United Muslim Day Parade held yearly in New York City is a very large contingent of Puerto Rican Muslims, who also boast a mosque of their own in Brooklyn.

Muslim Organizations in North America

Several national Islamic organizations operate in North America today. Far from being the insidious dens of terrorism that some so-called experts on Islam make them out to be, they are merely forums for Muslims to come together to talk about the challenges of, and solutions for, living as Muslims in the West. Every year, the five largest organizations hold conventions in one part of the nation or another. These gatherings follow a standard format with lectures, shows, bazaars, exhibits, and mutual fellowship.

Each of the Islamic organizations has its own unique history, and their relevance to the lives of Muslims in North America is great. They distribute information on Islam to politicians; organize prayer times; advocate on behalf of Muslim concerns; educate Muslims and non-Muslims about Islam; and publish books, pamphlets, and magazines that guide the faithful in their daily lives. The major Islamic organizations are as follows:

- ◆ **The Islamic Society of North America (ISNA)**   This is the most well-known Muslim organization, founded in 1981. It acts as an umbrella group for many local mosques and associations. (www.isna.net)

- ◆ **The Muslim Student's Association (MSA)**   Founded by foreign students in 1963, it has since grown to be the most important indigenous Islamic student organization, with chapters in nearly every college in North America. It tackles issues related to campus life for Muslims. (www.msa-natl.org)

- ◆ **The World Community of Al-Islam in the West (WCIW)**   Warith Deen Muhammad's transformed group, which adheres to Muslim orthodoxy. W. D. Muhammad resigned from this organization and retired in 2003. It has since splintered into several groups, each claiming inspiration from W.D. Muhammad's example. (www.muslimjournal.com)

- ◆ **The Islamic Circle of North America (ICNA)**   An offshoot of the MSA founded by immigrants from the Indian subcontinent in 1971. It has chapters in many major cities and engages in charity work and missionary efforts. (www.icna.com)

- ◆ **Muslim American Society (MAS)**   A relative newcomer to the scene (founded 1992), this multicultural Muslim organization strives to provide all types of services ranging from youth activities and sports programs to school curriculums and voter registration. (www.masnet.org)

Other Muslim organizations work to confront discrimination, influence politics, distribute charity, improve women's rights, and educate people about Islam. In short, Muslim groups have the same goals and follow similar methods in their approach as major Christian and Jewish religious organizations.

The Least You Need to Know

- ◆ Many Africans who were brought to the New World as slaves were Muslims. Most were forcibly converted, but a few tried to practice Islam in secret.

- ◆ Islam began growing in the African American community in the early 1900s. It was not authentic Islamic teachings they were learning, however, but a mixture of Islam, Christianity, and Black Nationalism.

◆ The Nation of Islam has never adhered to standard Islamic teachings; its doctrines about racial hatred and new messengers from God are against Islam.

◆ Most modern African American Muslims follow orthodox Islam.

◆ The number of converts to Islam among African Americans, Hispanics, and whites continues to grow each year.

Part 7

The Legacy of Islam

Great civilizations have often passed on a considerable legacy before being extinguished. Although Islam is far from extinct, its greatest influences occurred at the same time that Europe was sunk in the Dark Ages. Greek learning and the discoveries of other nations were rapidly assimilated into the growing Muslim scientific community, where they were refined and added to. Indeed, Islam produced some of the finest scientists that humanity has ever seen, and they made discoveries that laid the groundwork for modern technological knowledge.

Islam continues to evolve in today's world. Through its many forms, sects, and trends, the influence of Muslims upon the economic, political, and moral life of the world is considerable. Muslims are trying to make sense of the fast-paced world just like everyone else. The global Islamic revivalist movement, which is often quite misunderstood, is one way in which Muslims are struggling to regain their rightful place as equal members in today's rapidly changing world. In this part, I will answer the question: What do Muslims want?

Chapter 26

Discover the Influences of Islam

In This Chapter

- ◆ Learn how the knowledge of the ancient Greeks was saved by Islamic civilization
- ◆ Discover the Muslims's involvement in the European Renaissance
- ◆ Meet some influential Muslim philosophers and scientists
- ◆ Find out how the legacy of Muslim civilization has shaped the modern world

The rapid expansion of the Muslim world in its first thousand years encompassed more than just the acquisition of territory and converts. Islamic civilization absorbed the learning, ideas, books, and philosophies of the Greeks, Romans, Indians, and Persians, thus making a new synthesis of knowledge possible. But Muslims went even further; they built upon this knowledge with new discoveries of their own, inventing algebra, ophthalmology, trigonometry, historiography, and many other sciences.

Islam created a multicultural, vibrant transnational society more diverse and productive than Rome ever was. Europeans, whose feudal nations were backward and undeveloped until five centuries ago, fed off of Muslim achievements and found their desire for advancement was ignited in the translated books they acquired from the universities and libraries of Islam. Nearly every aspect of modern society, whether something as mundane as writing a check or as lofty as astronomy, has been influenced by Islamic discoveries, refined and honed in the great civilization brought about by the Qur'an. As I take you on a tour through the legacy of Islam, think of how Muslim achievements have made life easier for all of us today.

Charting the Muslim Influence on Europe

Muslim rulers took it as an act of piety to construct mosques, hospitals, schools, and universities. Consequently, in every major Muslim city there are numerous examples of each. Perhaps the greatest era of advancement in education took place during the Abbasid caliphate (750–1258). As a multiethnic society, the Abbasid rulers enjoyed wide access to the ideas and discoveries of many previous civilizations. This in turn led to the widespread availability of manuscripts for use by both scholars and students.

Just the Facts

The oldest continuously functioning college in the world is Al-Azhar University in Cairo, Egypt. It was founded in the year 970 and has achieved the status of the most authoritative school of Islamic sciences in the Sunni Muslim world.

The expansion of knowledge in Muslim civilization can be divided into three phases. The first phase was inheritance. Ancient writings from the Greeks and others were collected and translated into Arabic. The availability of paper made duplication of these manuscripts possible, so universities as far away as Spain or Timbuktu could have their own copies on hand.

The most famous institution for the collection and translation of ancient books was known as the *Baytul Hikmah*, or House of Wisdom. Established by the Caliph, al-Ma'mun, in 830, this think tank was staffed by Muslims, Christians, Jews, Hindus, and Buddhists and was given the task of making all the knowledge of the world available in the Arabic language. The works of Plato, Socrates, Aristotle, and Ptolemy were preserved for future generations through the medium of the Arabic language. (These were later translated from Arabic into Latin for Europe's consumption.)

In the second phase, Muslim scholars and scientists synthesized the diverse areas of knowledge into organized bodies of thought whose premises could be tested and proved or disproved. Muslims developed the scientific method of formulating a hypothesis and testing it to see whether it is correct. Visiting European students marveled over this process, which was unknown in dogma-plagued Europe. Adelard of Bath, a prominent Christian scholar of the Middle Ages, wrote: "Indeed, I have learned from my Arab masters to follow reason as a guide."

This figure shows a twelfth-century model of the solar system from Baghdad.

(Courtesy of Aramco)

In the last stage, Muslims began adding to this store of knowledge with new discoveries of their own from the ninth century onward. The list of sciences either refined or invented by Muslims is dizzying: algebra, chemistry, astronomy, medicine, cartography, botany, and navigation, to list just a few. (The term *Greco-Arab science* was coined to label this synthesis of learning styles.) Given the religious impetus to learn to read and write, Muslim populations were generally literate enough to provide a steady stream of students, both male and female, to the great lecture halls of Islamic universities. By way of contrast, during this same period in Europe few could read beyond a scattering of priests and nobles.

The major conduit for Muslim learning into Europe was through the great colleges of Muslim Spain. Christians flocked to Cordoba, Toledo, Seville, and Granada to study subjects that were unknown in the rest of Europe. One contemporary Christian priest lamented, "All our young men are vying with each other to learn Arabic." This is no small statement. As much as English today is the international language of science, art, and technology, if you can imagine it, Arabic was that language from the ninth to the fifteenth century. New words such as *astrolabe, algorithm, soda, syrup,* and *zenith* were adopted into European languages, and Christians read the voluminous writings of Muslim scholars with enthusiasm.

Just the Facts

The main library in Muslim-ruled Cordoba had 400,000 books. The ninth-century rulers of Cairo maintained a public library with two planetariums, numerous reading rooms, and a collection of 1,600,000 different manuscripts.

Illuminating the Science Hall of Fame

Throughout the height of Muslim civilization, great Muslim thinkers represented every field of learning. Many of them were religious authorities, poets, and novelists in addition to being top scientists. Omar Khayyam, for example, who is best known for his risqué collection of poetry, *the Rubbaiyat*, was also an accomplished astronomer who produced a solar calendar far more accurate than the Gregorian calendar used in Europe. The following list summarizes some of the most famous Islamic thinkers and scientists:

♦ **Mohammad al-Khawarizmi (d. 840)**   He is the founder of algebra, and he also laid the foundation for trigonometry.

♦ **Hasan ibn al-Haitham (d. 1040)**   He established the science of optics and linked algebra with geometry.

♦ **Abu Raihan al-Biruni (d. 1048)**   He correctly established the circumference of the earth and studied the difference between the speed of sound and the speed of light.

♦ **Ibn Sina (d. 1037)**   Known as Avicenna in the West, this one man produced a textbook on the practice of medicine (known as the *Canon*) that was so comprehensive it was the main medical guide in Europe for more than five centuries. In another book he classified all known pharmaceuticals and their uses. He also determined that the speed of light was constant.

It Is Written

Muhammad said, "Acquire knowledge. It enables its possessor to distinguish right from wrong. It lights the way to heaven. It is our friend in the desert, our society in solitude, our compassion when friendless. It guides us to happiness. It sustains us in misery. It is an ornament among friends and an armor against enemies."

♦ **Ali Ibn Rabban at-Tabari (d. 870)**   He wrote the first encyclopedia of medicine that collected together all known medical knowledge. This work spanned seven volumes.

♦ **Jabir Ibn Haiyan (d. 803)**   He is considered the father of modern chemistry through his work in classifying the elements and experimenting with their properties.

♦ **Abu Abdullah Al-Battani (d. 929)**   Like many other scientists in the Muslim world, Al-Battani knew the world was round. He was the first to correctly identify the length of the solar year to the second. He also made many discoveries in astronomy and mathematics.

- ◆ **Mohammad al-Razi (d. 930)**   His accomplishments in medicine were enormous. His 10-volume encyclopedia dealt exhaustively with Greco-Arab medicine. He correctly identified the source for smallpox and was the first to classify substances into organic and inorganic compounds.

These are just a few of the great minds who revolutionized their areas of expertise. Visiting Europeans learned voraciously and returned to their lands to found colleges and universities such as the famous academies in Chartres, France.

Sadly, all of this vitality and progress in the sciences came to an end by the close of the fourteenth century. In the East, the Mongol devastation, the Crusades, and civil wars among the surviving rulers effectively ended the influence of the *'ulema*—the Muslim scholars and scientists—over the elites. The result was a decline in support for institutes of higher learning. Although important colleges remained opened, never again would there be that high level of intellectual activity.

In the West, the Catholic reconquest of Spain from Muslim rule resulted in massive mountains of Arabic-language books being burned by the church, under the suspicion that they might be Qur'ans and were thus a threat to the state. The universities were closed, the scholars dispersed throughout the rest of the Muslim world, and the torch of Islamic inquiry was put out permanently—though not before Europe had been dragged out of its Dark Ages and into a new era of enlightenment. This was the legacy and the gift of Islam to our modern world today: the preservation of Greek knowledge and the great discoveries that made modern science possible.

Muslim astronomers at work charting the movement of the stars and planets in this painting from the twelfth century.

(Courtesy of Aramco)

Speaking in a Familiar Tongue

Islamic colleges in Spain were the most advanced in the world all throughout the Middle Ages. Every year hundreds of Europeans, eager to learn, enrolled and then later took their knowledge back to their home countries. They also eagerly translated books into the Latin language and circulated them widely. As they worked, they encountered many new terms and, having no other word for them, simply modified them for use in their own languages. Through this process, several European languages adopted thousands of words of Arabic origin, much like foreign languages today incorporate many English words, such as *computer*, *jeans*, and *okay*. Spanish has an estimated 6,500 Arabic words. English has nearly 10,000!

Uncovering the Unique Features of Islamic Civilization

What was life like in Cordoba, Cairo, or Baghdad during the height of Islamic civilization? Whether you were a commoner or a noble, chances are you would have been able to go to school and have a comparable level of education. Free schools for the less fortunate were established as early as the Umayyad caliphate, in accordance with religious dictates that Muslims must learn to read the Qur'an.

Every society needs a police force and other government officials to keep order and look out for the welfare of the population. In the Muslim world, this job was allotted to the *Muhtasib*, or Inspector General of Weights and Measures. These men and women were given wide powers to act on behalf of the public welfare. They regulated food production, fined polluters of rivers and streams, oversaw the sale and transport of milk, inspected restaurants and bathhouses, and strictly enforced a series of medical exams before any prospective doctor could begin to practice. One of the many surviving *Muhtasib* manuals included the following regulations:

- ◆ #109 No seller of fruit or vegetables is to weigh his own merchandise by picking up his scales himself; on the contrary, they are to be hung at a fixed point.

- ◆ #139 No one should be allowed to claim mastery over an art which he does not possess, above all in the practice of medicine, since this can lead to the loss of human lives: in truth it is the earth covering the tombs of dead men which hides the mistakes of the physician … Each artisan's activities should be limited to the exercise of his own trade; only those whose experience is recognized may claim to have mastered a skill.

♦ #195   A beast of burden should not be left standing in the bazaar, because it blocks the road and hinders people from passing and it might … kick someone walking by.

♦ #213   Metal workers and brass beaters must be made to stop the noisy part of their work during the required prayer times.

In addition to a reasonable amount of regulation in society for both hygiene and business, citizens of a typical Islamic city enjoyed paved streets lit by oil lamps at night. Spacious homes competed for space with apartment flats, and jobs were plentiful. The poor or homeless could count on public welfare from the *Zakat* officer in the town hall, and those who felt wronged could hire a lawyer, called a *hakeem*, and bring suit in court. Even the ruler could be sued. A man claiming that his animals were unlawfully sold to him once sued Saladin, the Muslim hero of the Crusades. Saladin sat in court with his lawyer and argued his case and was cross-examined at length. (The plaintiff later dropped his case after evidence was presented to prove him wrong.)

Muslim judges, called *Qadis*, could be male or female and were either appointed by the government or chosen by local communities. Following the dictates of the Qur'an to judge in all fairness, the Qadis also had to be masters of the Islamic legal sciences and honest individuals as well. Detailed records of actual court cases spanning the last thousand years of Islam have survived to this day.

Another benefit people enjoyed was the safety of depositing their money in institutions called *al bank*, which is the forerunner of the modern banking system. Venture capitalists could borrow money from the banks with an agreement to share a percentage of their profits with the lending institution. (Charging interest on loans is forbidden in Islam, so banks were picky about whom they loaned money to.) The much-publicized Islamic banking system today operates in much the same way.

> **Ask the Imam**
>
> Muslims are allowed to live in non-Muslim lands provided they promote their religion to those around them. They must also respect the local laws of their adopted countries as long as the laws don't contradict the laws of Islam.

Travelers could count on safe roads, patrolled by the caliph or sultan's troops; and frequent rest areas, called khans (caravansaries), dotted all major roads. If travelers were short on cash, government offices would make non-interest loans to the truly needy ones or give a gift of funds outright. Checks could be written that would be honored by banks in other cities. Hotels, butlers, and the ever-present shopping mall known as the bazaar made shopping a snap.

A detailed map of the world prepared by Muslim geographer al-Idrisi in the thirteenth century.

(Courtesy of Aramco)

The features of Islamic civilization sound suspiciously similar to many of the facets of modern life in the West. Now can you understand what the world of Islam lost? Muslims want that back, but they are saddled with fragmented states, outside interference, poverty and illiteracy, and bad governments. If American civilization were to come to an end and be replaced with something like that, wouldn't the descendants of today's citizens dream of what we have now?

The Least You Need to Know

- Muslim civilization preserved the knowledge of the ancient Greeks and others and passed it on to Europe.

- While Europe was in the Dark Ages, the Islamic world was the center for learning, inquiry, and science.

- The foundations for modern science and the scientific method were laid by Muslim researchers from the ninth to the thirteenth century.

- Muslim scholars invented algebra, made astounding astronomical discoveries, systematized chemistry, developed the practice of medicine to the highest standards in the world at that time, and made great strides in many other fields.

- Islamic civilization left a legacy upon which modern civilization is built. The western Europeans who studied in Muslim universities took what they had learned and built upon it.

Chapter 27

Meet the Islamic Sectarian Movements

In This Chapter

- ◆ Learn about the different sects that existed in the early centuries of the Islamic Empire
- ◆ Understand the position of the Qur'an regarding religious diversity within the Muslim community
- ◆ Investigate the main differences between the majority Sunni sect and the minority Shi'a groups
- ◆ Discover the Sufi path and how it relates to Islam

Diversity is often praised as an essential component of the human experience. This diversity extends through all aspects of life, and many people would assert that pluralism in religion, both within and without a particular faith, is desirable and indicative of the overall health of the belief system. In this regard, all religions are divided into sects, though whether they coexist in harmony is another matter. Christianity, Judaism, Hinduism, and Buddhism each contain myriad diverse branches that all took root from the same tree. The same is true of Islam. There are currently about two dozen different sects in the Muslim world. Some have ancient roots, whereas others are really quite recent.

The two largest sects that have survived to this day are the Sunnis and Shi'as. Together they account for more than 95 percent of the world's Muslims, with the Sunnis being in the vast majority. Other smaller groups continually compete for breathing space around the periphery of these two monoliths. What does Islam say about sectarianism? While the Prophet Muhammad did tolerate and even praise some differences of opinion, he did not approve of outright division. This sentiment is echoed in the Qur'an, which expressly forbids ideological conflict within the same religion to the point where overall unity is endangered. Why did the unity of the Muslim religion become compromised, and what are the reasons for each major split? This is the issue I will be exploring in this chapter.

Sectarianism and Islam

The Qur'an accepts that preceding religious communities have broken up into sects. Although Islam calls upon its followers to be tolerant of people of other religions, it does not mention favorably the existence of sects within them. The Prophet Muhammad is quoted as saying, "The Jews have broken up into seventy-one sects. The Christians have broken up into seventy-two sects and my community will break up into seventy-three, and all of them will be in hellfire except one." When he made this pronouncement, the Muslim community was a single entity, centered on Medina, and no one could have conceived that Muslims would become so divided. One man asked, "Which sect will go to paradise?" Muhammad answered, "The one which I and my companions belong to."

Translate This

The term *Shi'a* literally means partisan of something, and thus is a descriptive name for Islam's second-largest sect, whose founders were ardent supporters of the Prophet's cousin, Ali, in the struggles for power in early Islamic history.

This prediction contains the caveat that only one Muslim sect will be correct, and as a consequence, every different Muslim party, from Sunnis and Shi'as to Sufis and Salafis, vehemently claims that it is following the *authentic* tradition of the Prophet and his immediate followers. So which Islamic sect is the true one? As in the case of Christianity and Judaism, it depends on whom you ask. What I can say is that Islam is very explicit when it calls sectarianism a fault. The Qur'an warns Muslims, "And don't be like those … who split up their religion and became mere sects, each rejoicing in what it claims it has." (Qur'an 30:31–32)

Without attempting to discuss the merits or drawbacks of any particular sect, I will explore some of the most important ones and show how they have influenced the Muslim community through the years until the present time. For the record, the beliefs and practices of Islam, as outlined in this book thus far, are from the majority Sunni position, unless otherwise noted.

A Quick Look at Early Sects

How did sectarianism begin in Islam, and what were the first sects? To answer this question we need to look at events during the period of the first four caliphs (632–661), for the decisions made within that time frame resulted in most of the sects we have today. The first two groups to break off from the mainstream majority were the *Kharajites*, which you read about in Chapter 23, and the *Shi'a* (sometimes spelled as *Shiite*). A third group arising a few centuries later attempted to blend Islam with Greek philosophy. Although each of these early sects resulted from complicated political feuding, only the Shi'a have survived as a viable force to the present day.

Beliefs of the Kharajites

The Kharajites were originally just a political faction in the army of the fourth caliph, Ali (d. 661), who was struggling for control of the empire with a rival named Mu'awiya. When Ali entered peace talks with his foe, the Kharajites took it as a sign of weakness and *seceded* in their loyalty to him (thus the meaning of their name). The members of this group, however, soon began looking beyond politics and started delving into theology. Being outside the mainstream effectively meant there was no check on their activities.

The Kharajites focused almost exclusively on issues related to fate and the nature of sin. They had the uncompromising belief that if a Muslim committed a major sin, he was no longer a believer. Another issue they tackled was entry into Islam. Was a child born automatically into the fold of Islam, or did each individual have to choose Islam after attaining the age of puberty? The Kharajites opted for the latter. (Think of the Protestant/Catholic debate on when a person should be baptized and you'll understand the significance such questions had in early Islam.) Their main contribution, however, was in calling attention to

> **Ask the Imam**
>
> The Qur'an and the sayings of Muhammad are the main sources from which Islam is derived. The controversy caused by the early sects lay in interpreting what that data actually meant and how it applied to religious ideology.

the practice of unfairly assigning new converts to the role of junior members in existing Arab tribes. This sect, which never gained a large following, is now relegated primarily to the country of Oman where it is called 'Ibadiism.

The Greek Rationalists

A new sect arose a short time later called the *Mu'tazilites*, or Moderate Withdrawers. They sought to create a middle position between the extremes of the Kharajites and the feuding companions of the Prophet. Hassan al Basri, an influential scholar who is credited with inspiring this movement (d. 728), laid out the position that a sinning Muslim was merely a hypocrite and not an unbeliever, and that everyone had the free will to choose. Other scholars soon began blending the newly introduced methodologies of Greek philosophy with traditional Islamic learning to further elucidate the true meaning of God's power versus humankind's freedom of action. Thus, the science of Islamic theology known as *kalam* (or didactic discourse) was born.

This was a useful development because Muslims hadn't yet created the terminology necessary to debate such issues as the subtleties of Christian Trinitarianism, faith versus reason, or the many thorny issues raised by the ancient Greek sophists. There would be other uses for this learning as well. Throughout the ninth and tenth centuries especially, popular religion in the Muslim world began incorporating elements of pagan religions, such as dualism (a belief in a god of good and another of evil) and even anthropomorphism (deifying elements of nature).

These rationalist-minded scholars used their newfound language of theology to combat such damaging trends and succeeded in causing a revival of orthodoxy in much of the Muslim world. Traditional Muslim scholars, however, who relied more on uniquely Islamic sources such as the Qur'an and the *hadiths*, rejected this reliance on Greek learning and opposed the new theology vigorously. A synthesis of both trends was achieved in the writings of Al-Ash'ari (d. 935), a prominent scholar of the tenth century, who showed that both intellectual reasoning and traditional scriptural interpretation were compatible.

The Sunnis and Shi'as

It has been estimated that Sunnis make up approximately 85 percent of the world's Muslim population, with Shi'as accounting for much of the rest. When people talk of sectarianism in Islam, these two names, which are rooted in the earliest days of the Islamic caliphate, are the most often mentioned. It may be tempting to make a passing comparison here with the great Protestant-Catholic divide in Christianity.

However, whereas that division didn't occur until well over a thousand years into the life of the Church, the great Sunni-Shi'a break came within the lifetime of the surviving companions of the Prophet Muhammad and was not originally centered on doctrinal disputes, but on politics and succession.

The main reason for the existence of the Shi'a sect is directly related to the election of Abu Bakr as the first caliph of the Muslim community in the year 632. The Prophet had just passed away, and the leaders of Medina gathered to choose a political successor to keep the fledgling Muslim nation united. There was no question about doing this because the Prophet had spoken about it so often. After a heated debate, Abu Bakr was chosen to lead. Ali, the cousin and son-in-law of Muhammad (he was married to Muhammad's favorite daughter, Fatimah), was not present at that meeting, and he later protested that he should have been given a fair shot at being selected the caliph.

Just the Facts

The largest sect of Muslims, comprising around 85 percent of the world community of Islam, is known as the *Ahl as Sunnah wal Jamiah,* or the *Sunnis* for short. Their philosophical base is that allegiance to the Prophet's example and that of his companions is the defining mark of a true Muslim.

Although Ali refused to swear allegiance to Abu Bakr for a few months, eventually he caved in and both he and his supporters took the oath. The stage was set for bad blood, however; and as each new caliph was elected, Ali's friends stood by in anger, watching other men being given the nod while their beloved leader was passed over (hence the name Shia't Ali, or Party of Ali). Finally, in 656 when Ali was finally elected the fourth caliph, his group felt vindicated. Ali's rule was short-lived, though; and the Shi'as (as his followers came to be known), who were still just a political faction at that time, felt that the clan of Banu Umayyah had unfairly snatched away the caliphate through war and deception. That the victorious Mu'awiya would decree his own son to be the caliph after him was an especially impious affront.

The die was soon cast for permanent division as the sons of Mu'awiya and Ali carried on their fathers' rivalry for the caliphate. Hussain, the son of Ali, gathered a small number of supporters to oppose the rule of Yazid, the son of Mu'awia, who, in turn, raised his own army to crush this impetuous challenge to his widely unpopular elevation as caliph. In the year 680, Yazid's army was able to intercept Hussein near the city of Kufa in Iraq, and his men completely decimated their badly outnumbered quarry. Hussain's head was sent to Damascus in a bag as a trophy, much to the consternation even of many of Yazid's followers. Another son of Ali, known as Ali Zayn al Abideen, who was not present at the battle, was allowed to live unmolested until his death in Medina in 713. It is from this child of Ali that the line of Shi'a authority would descend through the generations.

The Shi'a Under Umayyad Rule

During Umayyad rule there were occasional uprisings of Shi'as, mostly in Iraq and Iran, but they met with little success. The Shi'as became more aware of themselves as a separate reality, however, and allegiance to their leader, or Imam, became much more strict, thus by the waning years of Umayyad rule Shi'as became an identifiable political party of sorts whose ultimate authority rested in a descendant of Ali. By the fifth generation, however, there was a split in loyalty between two half-brothers named Zayd and Al Baqir. Those who followed Zayd's leadership halted the direct line of spiritual succession with him and thus became known as the "Fivers." They believe any descendant of Ali from that point forward can be the Imam regardless of the directness of his family tree. Today the Zaydis, as they are called, reside mostly in Yemen where they make up over 40 percent of the population. Their rituals and beliefs differ little from the majority Sunni population, and they even accept the caliphate of both Abu Bakr and Umar, though they are divided as to the legitimacy of the third Caliph, Uthman.

> **Ask the Imam**
>
> How do Shi'as and Sunnis feel about each other? While there is animosity and suspicion on the popular level, top-level scholars from both camps have been remarkably conciliatory from the very beginning.

> **Translate This**
>
> The *Shi'a Imams* are a line of men whose ultimate ancestor was Ali. Different groups of Shi'as stop at different Imams in the line of the family tree and consider their chosen man to be the last and most authentic final guide. There are *Fivers, Seveners,* and *Twelver* Shi'as. Each group has diverse religious doctrines.

Al Baqir, however, engendered the lion's share of support. His son (and subsequently the sixth Imam), Ja'far as-Sadiq (699–765), is credited with formulating the basis of Shi'a legal and religious concepts. Being of such prestigious lineage, he was able to wield a great amount of influence over his flock and he chose to concentrate his time on organizing and systematizing what had, up until that point, been a movement focused on the narrow issue of succession. He crafted a School of Islamic Law, or *madh-hab*, that differs little from the four major Sunni schools and is generally accepted as legitimate by them. Today the Ja'fari Madh-hab, as it is called, is the official legal reference for the majority of Shi'as worldwide.

After Ja'far's death in 765, the Shi'a divided into two separate sects, each following one of his two descendants, Musa and Isma'il. The Isma'ili sect, as it is called today, stopped the line with the latter and went on to develop its own doctrines further. This group held that the Imams were part of a grand cycle of history. In place of a ruling Imam, however, temporal leaders who could speak for a future-awaited savior would govern. (The Aga Khan is currently considered the worldwide head of one of the two existing Isma'ili branches of Shi'aism.) This group was active in missionary work and converted many peasants and people on the frontiers to its cause. They even succeeded in establishing several Isma'ili dynasties at different points in Muslim history.

From Political Movement to a Separate Sect

Near the end of Umayyad rule in 750, when the Abbasids (who were descendants of the Prophet Muhammad's uncle, Abbas) were gathering their supporters to stage a coup, the Shi'as joined the cause, thinking that the new rulers would hearken to their call and choose a descendant of Ali to be the caliph. When the Abbasids chose one of their own instead, the Shi'as withdrew their support and began looking inward. Periodic persecution followed by periods of neglect by the central authorities defined much of their early evolution into a distinct religious sect. Indeed, by the end of the eighth century, they had started to develop doctrines of their own that were quite specific and unique.

Accordingly, the Shi'as began to compile their own books of prophetic traditions and Qur'anic interpretation centering on what they considered to be the correct view of Islam. Many of the traditions they recorded were different from the ones assembled by the majority community during and shortly after Muhammad's passing. A major text was also prepared called the *Nahjul Balagha* (Path of Eloquence) in which the attributed sayings and sermons of Ali are collected. Variations in how the five pillars of Islam were practiced crept in also. For example, many Shi'as today combine certain prayers so that they actually pray at only three points during the day, not five. The Shi'a call to prayer adds lines in which Ali is praised, and extra holidays commemorating events in the life of Ali and his descendants have been added, such as the Eid ul Ghadir and the passion plays surrounding Hussain's martyrdom. In addition, a kind of historical revision took place in which most of the Prophet's companions were vilified and considered unfaithful to Islam.

Another area of difference with the majority Sunni community occurred in the province of leadership. While Sunnis have always taken a more relaxed view toward the selection of a leader (the most qualified adult male), Shi'a doctrine came to teach that Ali and his male descendants have a secret, almost prophetic, knowledge that is passed on from father to son. They are sinless and infallible and are therefore the only choice to rule over the community of believers. The first Shi'as followed Ali as their leader based on his association with Muhammad, though he sometimes disapproved of their excessive emphasis of his role. Succeeding generations rallied around his descendants, whom they called their *Imams* (leaders).

The main group of Shi'as, whom we now know as the "Twelvers" went on to follow four more descendants of Ali and were united as a group in Baghdad all throughout the Abbasid caliphate. The Abbasid caliphs generally tolerated their existence (barring a few periods of suppression) so long as the Shi'a never involved themselves in politics. Consequently, the community again turned inward and began refining its doctrines and unique perspective on Islam even further. Five important Shi'a concepts and doctrines (which are not shared by Sunnis) are summarized as follows:

◆ **Imamate**   Only a descendant of Ali can legitimately guide the Muslim community. Imams are sinless and suffer persecution willingly on behalf of all sincere believers. On Judgment Day, they, along with the Prophet's daughter, Fatima, will have the power to intercede on behalf of the sincere. Their knowledge and power to govern on Earth comes from God.

◆ **Taqiyya**   Given that the Shi'a community has often been the target of persecution, individual Shi'as are allowed to hide their true beliefs when among those who would harm them. By extension, those Imams who compromised or submitted to the authority of the Umayyads or Abbasids are absolved of their acquiescence.

◆ **Taqlid**   This is a concept that developed among both Sunnis and Shia's, and it means to imitate or model oneself on the example of a pious scholar. But whereas it is much maligned in Sunni thought today, in Shia'ism it is considered essential that every believer choose a scholar whose legal rulings, practice of daily rituals, and understanding of the faith they will imitate.

◆ **Khums**   Shi'as are required to pay one fifth of their yearly earnings to their local mullah or religious authority above and beyond the annual *zakat* payment. This control over funds has enabled Shi'a clerics to remain independent of governmental control throughout their history.

◆ **Mutah**   The practice of *mutah*, or temporary marriage, was initially allowed in Islam's earliest years as a concession to soldiers who may have had to travel for weeks or months from home. Before he passed away, Muhammad outlawed the practice, according to Sunnis, though Shi'as dispute this and allow its practice. A man who enters into a *mutah* marriage pays an agreed amount of money to a woman with a marriage contract that has a set expiration date after which the marriage is no longer valid.

With the death of the eleventh Imam in 874, who apparently left no heirs, the Shi'a developed the concept of a twelfth *Hidden Imam*, who was taken as a baby into another realm of existence. A prominent Shi'a family of Baghdad, the Banu

Nawbakht, called themselves the agents of the Hidden Imam and claimed they had contact with him and spoke his will. After 941, this contact was declared closed. The next phase of leadership for the Shi'a community then passed into the hands of men who were charged with speaking on behalf of the twelfth Imam, who communicated his will through dreams. This arrangement was to go on indefinitely until some future date when the Hidden Imam would return as a Messiah to liberate the Shi'a from the oppression heaped upon them by the usurpers of Ali's rightful office. He would also usher in a period of righteous rule over the earth.

The Twelver Shi'as gradually developed a new hierarchy of leadership consisting of an infallible pope-like figure to lead the community. This person would rule the masses through a temporal priesthood consisting of men with such titles as *Ayatullah*, *Mullah*, and *Hojatulislam*. (The late Ayatullah Khomeini, who participated in the Iranian Revolution in 1978, achieved the highest rank in the eyes of many of the worldwide Shi'a community and was considered infallible.) After the United States conquered Iraq in 2003, it soon found out how much allegiance ordinary Shi'as gave to their religious leaders, with the top Shi'a cleric in the country, Grand Ayatullah Sistani, playing the role of deal maker and breaker on a variety of issues ranging from elections and security to influencing the contents of the country's new constitution. (By way of contrast, Sunnis have no similar priesthood or identifiable religious structure.)

Translate This

Ayatullah, the Shi'a term for a top-level cleric, means Sign of God.

The Shi'a differ with the majority Sunnis on many issues related to leadership, doctrine, practice, and scriptural selection. Competing Shi'a and Sunni political factions have struggled for power all throughout Muslim history. While some Shi'a dynasties were formed, most notably the Fatimid dynasty of Egypt (910–1171), it has pretty much been a Sunni party for most of Muslim history.

In recent times there has been a resurgence of Shi'a identity, especially in Lebanon, Iraq, Iran, Pakistan, and elsewhere. Iran, in particular, is governed as a Shi'a theocracy with democratic overtones. Sunni movements ranging from the benign to the puritanical have also enjoyed a renewed period of growth, and this has sometimes led to tensions in various parts of the Muslim world. One small puritanical movement in particular, known as Wahhabism, which began in Saudi Arabia in the late eighteenth century, has declared its opposition to Shi'aism in no uncertain terms, labeling Shi'as as apostates and unbelievers. (They also label most traditional Sunnis as unbelievers as well!) Unnoticed by many in the West, there has been something of a low-level war ongoing between the more radical followers of each group in such diverse places as

Pakistan and Iraq, often consisting of small-scale attacks on each other's mosques and leaders.

With tensions high throughout the world, considering the ongoing fight against global terrorism, the situation may get worse before it gets better. What must be realized is that Islam, as taught by Prophet Muhammad and lived by his companions, cannot be blamed for passions and extraordinary events any more than Jesus can be blamed for the long list of unfortunate events that have happened in Christian history. One positive thing that has occurred recently in the Muslim world is that many have begun to question the illogical and un-Islamic teachings that have been put forward by oddball extremist groups for years. One would hope that something of a reformation back to authentic original Islam would soon make its appearance, giving hope once more to those who dream of a world based on justice and sincere devotion to the best in humankind. This describes the goal of the majority of all people of faith everywhere.

The Sufi Path

Sufis are perhaps the most well-known Muslims in the world. *Gentle, introspective,* and *highly spiritual* are the words that come to mind when Sufis are mentioned. However, *Sufism* is not really a sect of Islam; rather it is the name of a spiritually oriented trend that is promoted within any given existing sect. For example, you can have Sunni or Shi'a Sufis. Sufism implies a very esoteric, spiritual emphasis in one's practice of Islam (*tasawwuf*). The Sufis seek to bring the experience of faith deep within their hearts to attain a state of inner ecstasy. The famous poet Jalaluddin Rumi expressed it best when he wrote: "What God said to the rose and caused it to laugh in full-blown beauty, He said to my heart and made it a hundred times more beautiful." (*The Mathnawi*, vol. III, couplet 4129)

The Sufi movement didn't begin with a single founder, nor are all Sufis united in one organization. It was the culmination of many social trends that first arose in the Umayyad dynasty. With the rapid growth of the empire, wealth began pouring in from all corners of the world, and a lot of otherwise faithful Muslims began to overindulge in worldly pleasures. (Islam, on a very basic level, is against overindulgence, and Muhammad's personal example was one of frugality and self-denial of most of life's pleasures.) In addition, as the legal schools of thought, or *madh-habs*, were being formulated by the scholars of Islamic Law, some people felt there was too much emphasis on the rules and not enough on the spirit behind them.

Conscientious individuals began to see the rise of opulence, legalism, and pageantry among the Muslim community as a kind of deception. The dangerous life of the world was about to engulf the pure message of Islam and leave nothing but an empty shell in its wake. These spiritually minded people started to renounce the world and live very simple lives to promote an example for others to follow. The very name *Sufi* comes from the Arabic word for wool, which became the preferred clothing of these people (who shunned silk and other fineries). This train of thought was not something invented out of thin air, however, for the Qur'an often spoke of the deception inherent in the life of the world. It also emphasized God's love and the importance of making His remembrance the focal point of one's life.

In time, as the dynastic struggles of the Umayyads and Abbasids wore on, intellectual and spiritual geniuses arose throughout the Middle East who attracted followers and students seeking to emulate the Sufi state of self-enlightenment. This ever-increasing association of individuals eventually gave rise to Sufi orders, or *tariqas*, from the twelfth century onward, which maintained headquarters and missions in many Muslim and non-Muslim lands. A *shaykh* would act as a kind of chief abbot and had absolute authority over his or her disciples. The basic foundation that Sufi shaykhs used to legitimize their power was the life of the Prophet Muhammad himself. They called him the exemplar of the God-oriented lifestyle and suggested they were merely continuing the tradition with their followers. The primary ideas of Sufism can be summarized as follows:

Just the Facts

The Whirling Dervishes are Sufis who follow the teachings of Jalaluddin Rumi (d. 1273). They spin rhythmically while chanting the 99 names of God in elaborate ceremonies called *semas*.

It Is Written

This thing we tell of can never be found by seeking, yet only seekers will find it.
—*Bayazid Bustami, d. 874*

◆ Faith in God can be experienced by the devoted believer through a program consisting of meditation, chanting, selfless love for others, and self-denial.

◆ Worldly possessions, if not kept to a minimum, can corrupt a person's soul. Frugality is the key to spiritual wealth.

◆ The path of Sufism requires its followers to develop patience, thankfulness to God, and a complete reliance on God's knowledge of the future.

◆ In addition to the Qur'an and *hadiths*, another body of wisdom is contained in the teachings of the great Sufi masters. These consist of poems and wisdom stories that have hidden meanings.

A new generation of Sufi literature soon arose that attempted to explain, often through allegory, the path of the sincere seeker and what pitfalls one may expect to find. Two of the most famous works from the twelfth century were *The Story of Layla and Majnun* and *The Conference of Birds*. The first is basically a Romeo and Juliet story whose sub-text is meant to show how lost we are from God and what a hellish life we will have to endure until our ultimate reunion is achieved, while the second book is a Muslim-style *Canterbury Tales* in which a group of seekers is ushered on the path to their Lord and encounter a series of obstacles, each resolved with a story or allegory, until they ultimately learn that the path to God starts within themselves.

While most Sufis have generally remained within the pale of Islamic Law, starting during the Abbasid caliphate and beyond, some have gone to extremes. Bizarre rituals involving *jinns*, sword swallowing, numerology, and other stunts have become common fare in folk Sufism; and a few Sufis have even come to deny some very basic Islamic dictates, such as the prohibition against drinking wine, praying at the tombs of the dead, and self-flagellation. Many Sufis have also engaged in music and singing, much to the chagrin of the religious purists. This behavior has resulted in Sufism getting a bad reputation among the traditional *'ulema* (scholars), and many modern Muslim leaders look upon Sufism as suspect even to this day, despite the popular support of the masses in much of the Islamic world.

There were attempts to reconcile Sufism and orthodoxy in the Middle Ages. Several prominent theologians, especially Imam Abu Hamid Al Ghazali (1058–1128), worked tirelessly to formulate a grand synthesis of law and spirit. While schooled in the prevailing legal approach to Islam, he adopted Sufism into his own personal practice of Islam later in life, after realizing that legalism was not very spiritually satisfying. While the gaps were closed significantly through the efforts of him and others, and Sufis came to enjoy a renewed wide acceptance in the Muslim world, there are still notable exceptions. For instance, the Salafis, an ultraconservative Sunni movement, consider Sufis to be misguided at best and outside the fold of Islam at worst.

The Sufi movement has actually benefited the Muslim world in many ways. During the centuries of political and economic decline (1500–1900), Sufi orders took up the task of teaching Islam to the general masses. While traditional scholars largely were absent from Muslim society, preferring to study and debate within closed walls, it was the Sufis who traveled as missionaries, operated charities, and provided spiritual guidance in the countryside. Islam was introduced to places such as Indonesia and central Asia almost wholly in this way. Another area in which Sufis excelled was in organizing Muslims to participate in their own self-defense. During the period of Russian expansion into Ottoman territories, it was Sufi orders who were at the forefront of resistance, especially in the Caucasus Mountain region. In places as diverse as West Africa and China, Sufi-led revolts stayed the hand of invading armies for centuries.

The distinctive dress of the Sufis consists of a turban and a robe.

(Photo by Luke Powell)

Sufi poetry, which tackles major religious and philosophical questions, is the source for inspiration for millions of Muslims—and now non-Muslims. In fact, poetry, story-telling, and verse have been the primary teaching tools for passing on Sufi knowledge. Perhaps the best-known poet in the world at this time is *Rumi*, whose anthologies of poetry now sell more copies than any other poet in North America.

Common Sufi practices for achieving enlightenment consist of the following:

◆ Chanting God's names and praises in unison (*zikr*) while seated in a circle or standing and turning slowly. This ritual can be done singly or in great performances with dozens, or even hundreds, of others. Music often accompanies such large gatherings.

◆ Fasting, Qur'an reading, and meditation in remote, natural places, especially in the early morning.

◆ Prolonged prayer at night and frequent supplications for knowledge and forgiveness.

◆ Sitting at the feet of a shaykh, listening to his or her teachings and stories, and then contemplating their meaning. Combined

Just the Facts

Some of the main traditional Sufi *tariqas* (orders) that have established branches in the West are the *Naqshabandi,* the *Chisti,* the *Tijaniyya,* and the *Qadiriyyah.*

with spiritual rituals, over time the initiate can rise in the ranks to become a member of the inner circle.

- ◆ Pilgrimage to the shrines of past Sufi masters (who are known as *saints)*.

- ◆ The use of aromatherapy to heighten awareness.

- ◆ Selfless devotion to the poor and needy to emphasize the true intent of religion.

Sufism has enjoyed rapid growth in the West since the 1960s. Sufi orders are being established by Muslims and even by non-Muslims who don't necessarily want to convert to Islam, but who desire to participate in the spiritual discipline. The most organized order in the United States and Europe seems to be the Naqshabandis, whose activities can be perused on the web at www.sunnah.org. Although there is a vast difference in each Sufi group's adherence to basic Islamic teachings, there is no doubt that this spiritual trend found in Islam has found a new home and is now a part of the American religious tradition.

The Least You Need to Know

- ◆ Islam is officially against sectarianism, though Muhammad foretold its appearance among Muslims.

- ◆ The earliest sects of Islam were formed over political and doctrinal issues. The main areas of conflict concerned who should rule and what was the extent of humankind's free will.

- ◆ The Sunni sect is the largest single body of Muslims, consisting of approximately 85 percent of all the world's followers of Islam.

- ◆ The Shi'a sect of Islam began because Ali was not elected the first caliph. It would later develop its own unique doctrines.

- ◆ Sufism emphasizes spirituality and self-discipline as a way to achieve enlightenment. Sufis often chant and meditate on God and live lives devoted to frugality and charity.

Chapter 28

Islam in World Affairs Today

In This Chapter

◆ Learn about the global Islamic revival and how it relates to world events

◆ Discover the real story behind the Iranian Revolution

◆ View the Arab-Israeli conflict through Muslim eyes

◆ Find out how Muslims felt about September 11 and its perpetrators

◆ Know what Muslims are thinking about America's new role in the Middle East

Islam is a religion, a civilization, a state, a social system, as well as a philosophy. Muslims have always looked upon their faith as an integral part of life and have tried to order their societies upon a holistic model that unites both the temporal and spiritual spheres of life. Political miscalculations, willful negligence on the part of the religious establishment, and the laxity of the general populace resulted in Islamic civilization becoming so weak that it was eventually given a sound thrashing by the Mongols. (Genghis Khan *did* taunt Muslims saying he was a punishment from God upon them!) What was left of the Islamic world came to be dominated by the

Christian West during its era of global expansion. Like the phoenix, however, Islam will never be permanently vanquished, and a growing consciousness among worldwide Muslims has resulted in a startlingly tenacious revival.

Muslims are seeking to negotiate a rebirth of their civilization under extremely difficult conditions, and sometimes the growing pains seem insurmountable. The consensus among Muslims is that, until they regain their self-respect and a balance in their lives between authentic Islam and the dictates of the modern world, they will never truly be able to integrate themselves into the global village. We will look at some of the issues and unresolved conflicts that are important to Muslims today in the hopes that equitable solutions may be found to bring about an age of peace and harmony among the world's religions.

The Death and Rebirth of Islam

When did the death knell sound for the independent world of Islam? Many Muslims say that it was Mu'awiya who ruined a good thing by usurping the caliphate from Ali way back in the seventh century. Others postulate that the real damage was caused by the Mongols, who destroyed half the Muslim world in the thirteenth century. What about the abolition of the Ottoman caliphate in 1924, at the hands of Turkish secularists? Although any of these would give sufficient reasons for a decline, Muslim writers of the last two centuries have generally looked beyond politics and war in crafting an explanation and have instead focused on the fickleness of the human soul. It wasn't external events that caused a decrease in Islamic independence, they argue; rather it was a weakness of faith in the Muslim community at large.

This unique way of interpreting the devastation of the past is rooted in Islamic theology. "This book will raise some communities [if they are faithful to it] and bring down others [if they disregard it]," Muhammad said of the Qur'an. Muslims stopped evolving in all areas of life, from piety and religious devotion to education and technology, and wound up having a stagnant civilization at the same time European civilization was on the rise. Europe's Enlightenment (due in part to Muslim scholastic influence in prior centuries) occurred simultaneously with Islam's slow but steady decline.

It Is Written

If Allah helps you, then there is none who can overcome you. If He forsakes you, then who else is there other than Him who can help you? Therefore, in Allah let the believers put their trust. (Qur'an 3:160)

Muslim scholars such as Jamaluddin Afghani (1839–1897) and his student Mohammad Abdu sought to reverse this intellectual, political, and cultural slide by attempting a grand synthesis of religion and progressive values. They taught that Islam could be revived only when Muslims stopped opposing the introduction of modernity. Islam, they argued, could assimilate any noble ideal, and these ideals would only add to the strength of the community. This philosophy carried over into the twentieth century with such writers as Syed Abul A'la Maududi, Sayyid Qutb, Rashid Rida, Muhammad Iqbal, and others.

Interestingly enough, a split later occurred between these reformers and the traditional religious establishment, which wanted to maintain the status quo out of fear that Islam would be changed or altered rashly. Fierce debates were held in such places as India, Egypt, and Syria in the last century. The result was a kind of unspoken division between revivalists and traditionalists that is still apparent to this day. Ironically, both sides have developed a live and let live attitude for the most part, and one can see the followers of each trend freely borrowing from each other when the need arises.

Certain trends in the revivalist or reformist movement are, to be sure, very good for Muslims and Islam as they mirror the best in our faith. For example, Islam is unfairly criticized for its attitudes about women's status and rights; and the chauvinistic nature of some traditional societies, which often is completely at odds with the progressive Islam of the Prophet's day, does nothing but reinforce this unfortunate view. Reformers point out that Muhammad overturned many prevalent social customs that were demeaning and even dangerous to women. To revive true Islam, they say, we must return to that spirit of progressivism in women's rights. These are the kinds of changes in attitude that are often opposed by traditionalists, who counter-argue that it is dangerous to attempt change in a society because once it is done, there is no telling what direction it will go. You would not believe how often these types of topics come up among Muslims everywhere from the banquet hall to the college classroom. This kind of lively intellectual debate is just the thing our community has needed for a long time.

Why Has God Let Muslims Fail in War?

On the military front, the Muslim world has been fairly hopeless in the last three centuries. Russia, the Netherlands, France, and Britain have among themselves collectively divided the Muslim world into a great jigsaw puzzle. The last significant vestiges of foreign domination were removed only in 1992 when the Central Asian Republics declared their independence from the Soviet Union. Why were European powers able to inflict such a defeat upon Muslims? It wasn't that Muslims weren't skilled in the arts of war, the modern line goes, but that they ceased to fight for God's sake. Verses such as "The believers must win if they are true in faith" give a kind of antidote to what would have otherwise engendered disillusionment and despair.

Muslims take setbacks as a sign of God's punishment for their spiritual laziness. It doesn't matter that there is no caliphate in the world, or that the West has weapons of such power that it can destroy the planet, or that anti-religious zealots govern Muslim nations. If the believers have become hypocrites, then a just chastisement from above is needed to wake them up. When Muslims start being true to their faith, they can regain their role as representatives of God's last religion on Earth. Under this philosophy, the cause of Islam can be promoted anew anywhere in the world by sincere believers, and success or failure are both instructive for future generations.

> ### Ask the Imam
>
> Nuclear chemical and biological weapons are actually forbidden in Islam because they cause indiscriminate destruction of civilians and wildlife. Islamic Law forbids harming women, children, the aged, noncombatants, and the environment in a wartime situation. Any Muslim government that is pursuing programs to invent such weapons is theoretically engaging in sinful conduct.

The Rebirth of an Ideal

The Islamic revival that has been sweeping over the Muslim world is akin to the great revival promoted by Christians in America in the early nineteenth century. The difference is that much of the Islamic revival is going on in tandem with liberation movements. Oppressed Muslims in Chechnya, Communist China, or the southern Philippines have as much fervor for this trend as do Islamist parties in Algeria, Iraq, and Turkey. Ironically, technology developed by Western nations has aided in the growth of religious consciousness among Muslims. The modern communications revolution has made Islamic teachings more available to the masses than ever before. Millions of Muslims who never really knew much about their faith are now as educated in their religion as some of the companions of the Prophet were.

In the last five decades, five ostensibly Islamic states have been established, consisting of the Sudan, Pakistan, Afghanistan, Iran, and Somaliland. (At least on paper they claim to be Islamic, though each is far from the ideal.) Numerous movements in other countries are trying to accomplish the same thing, both through peaceful and violent means. When secular governments happen to allow free elections in the Muslim world, Islamist parties invariably come out on top, such as in Turkey, Egypt, Jordan, Tajikistan, and Algeria. (The secular militaries in some of these countries promptly make Islamic parties illegal, often resulting in a violent reaction from the people.)

Although there have been many challenges to the global Islamic movement, such as a lack of coordination and faulty methodologies, the hidden progress in making people aware of what their religion is all about has been enormous. The simple fact of the matter is that a large chunk of the world's Muslims are Muslim in name only. They have minimal or even nonexistent knowledge of Islam and do not practice its precepts beyond a few cultural expressions in clothing or family law. With the current rise of Islamic awareness, the direction of the Islamic revivalist movement is continuing to evolve into grander themes. Could a new Islamic caliphate emerge uniting several Muslim nations into one federal entity? Time will tell. An extremely large number of ordinary, peace-loving Muslims hope so.

Who Are the Extremists?

Unfortunately there is a third force at work in some parts of the Muslim world right now that has taken the spotlight away from the mundane arguments of the traditionalists and revivalists/reformers. Whereas the former two engage in philosophical and ideological dispute and look for generally peaceful change, the third force is made up of what has come to be known as *Jihadis*. These are people who believe passionately that the only way to regain Islamic ascendancy is through violence or warfare, which they mislabel as *jihad*. I say mislabel because they often seem to have such an unrealistic approach to their cause and methodology that there is little resemblance to the real Islam that so many millions know and love.

The modern manifestation of this movement began in central Arabia in the mid-eighteenth century with a Muslim preacher named Muhammad ibn Abdul Wahhab (d. 1791). He gained some knowledge of Islamic Law, mostly from the books of a very conservative medieval scholar named Ibn Taymiyya, and began to notice that the Arabs of his land were quite lax in their adherence to Islam as he understood it. Polytheism and superstition were rampant and personal piety among his people was negligible. His plan to cure all of this was to follow a very puritanical approach to faith that was so austere and rigid that even the traditional religious scholars of his day were quite horrified.

Ibn Abdul Wahhab called for a rejection of the traditional, urbane Islamic codes, for a thorough reevaluation of the hadith literature's authenticity, for the complete abolishment of local customs he thought were accretions to religion, and for a kind of never-ending campaign against infidels and even other Muslims who were deemed to be backsliders. These other Muslims (pretty much all the rest of the Muslims in the world!) were placed on the level of unbelievers and wrongdoers and, according to Ibn Abdul Wahhab's theory, all such people could be subjugated or killed and their property taken by the victors.

That sounds like a frightening ideology, and it is. It is not the way Prophet Muhammad lived and taught. Quite the contrary, a thorough examination of the primary sources of Islam will bring the reader to the inescapable conclusion that Prophet Muhammad was a tolerant and fair man who fought only for self-defense and never harmed innocents. The Islam he lived was practical and spiritually satisfying, not brutal and devoid of zest and mercy. (Keep in mind that Islam is a convert-driven religion so it must be appealing in a wide sense.) So how did such an aberration come to survive in the Muslim world? (Keep in mind very few Muslims anywhere subscribe to this kind of ideology.) The answer lies in a three-way conjunction between religion, naked politics, and oil wealth.

In the same region that Ibn Abdul Wahhab was preaching and gaining converts, there lived a small tribal group under the leadership of one Muhammad ibn Saud. Ibn Saud and the cleric put their heads together and decided to form an alliance: what is God's would belong to the Wahhabis and what is Caesar's would belong to the House of Saud. To make a long story short, the Wahhabis, with the power of their allied tribal militia, the Saudis, instituted a reign of terror in Arabia, pillaging cities, destroying religious shrines, and committing the usual mayhem of zealots toting guns and swords. After a few run-ins with the Ottomans and other more local setbacks that almost crushed the movement, the Saudis (and their religious backers) were able to establish an enduring kingdom in Arabia from 1932 onwards. What did they name it? *Saudi* Arabia.

The system that was set up in the new kingdom tolerated no dissent from the official Wahhabi line. Shi'as and Sufis were persecuted, traditional scholars were replaced with Wahhabi-trained clerics, and loyalty to the House of Saud was tantamount to loyalty to Islam. So concerned were they with stripping away all vestiges of *bid'a*, or wicked innovation in religion, that they even demolished Prophet Muhammad's house in Mecca, saying it was becoming a shrine in itself. (They also filled in the wide trench that was dug around Medina by the Prophet and his men just before the Battle of the Ditch. Historic sites and buildings have no significance in their eyes.) The addition of petrodollars from the 1950s onward enabled the Saudis to promote their signature brand of ultra-purist Islam in many places around the world. Now you can understand what drove the Taliban of Afghanistan to destroy the large Buddha statues after they came to power. The founders of that movement studied in schools in Pakistan that were funded partly by the Saudis!

This doesn't mean that everything the Saudis fund is sinister or suspect; they have done a lot of good work around the world supporting refugees, building mosques and schools, and providing secular education to millions. It is the extremist views of Wahhabism on issues related to women, what constitutes purity of belief, and endless indiscriminate *jihad* that can have a negative effect if not taken with a grain of salt. This is no truer than in the realm of armed groups who have taken this new interpretation of Islam as a kind of liberation theology to right the wrongs they see in the world. If you take a look at some of the movements around the globe that have been labeled as terrorist by the West, you often see the hand of Wahhabism: the seeming wanton disregard for life; the rhetoric of anti-Jewish conspiracies; the imagery of the robe-clad warrior with a Kalashnikov slung over his soldier, riding to his glorious death and paradise—all of these are straight out of a mythical dichotomy created two centuries ago by one man and his puritanical inclinations.

The results are obvious: terrorist attacks, innocents killed, property destroyed by an enemy that is difficult to identify, neutralize, or understand. (Al Qaeda, by the way, hates America because of its overwhelming support for Israel, its support for dictatorships throughout the Muslim world, and its image as a promoter of vice and economic injustice.) What must be remembered is that not every Muslim group fighting for justice in the world necessarily subscribes to the ideals of Wahhabism. The sort of blanket condemnation by the West of any and all Muslims who want justice is unfortunate because, even as the American Revolution was a violent fight for justice, so, too, do some Muslims need the same kind of liberation from oppressors, invaders, or corrupt leaders.

As I have mentioned, the overwhelming majority of Muslims around the world do not agree with the tenets of Wahhabism. It is a controversial ideology that has been denounced by mainstream Muslim scholars ever since its founding. Recently, after several terrorist attacks rocked Saudi Arabia itself in 2003, the Saudi authorities have taken a fresh look at what some of their clerics are teaching and have begun to institute reforms in education. It is ironic that the call for a return to 'traditional' Islam is gaining ground in the heartland of Wahhabism.

Real Islam is not contained in the ideals of Osama bin Laden any more than Christianity can be summed up by the actions of abortion clinic bombers or other zealots throughout history. The one thing that has disappointed Muslims in the wake of the September 11 attacks (done by Wahhabi ideologues) is that it seemed that Westerners so overreacted, so blamed all things Islamic, that they pushed all Muslims into a corner without asking first if the hijacker's actions represented the authentic religion of Prophet Muhammad. The inflammatory anti-Muslim rhetoric that was filtering into the Muslim world became so bad that on a trip overseas in December of 2003, President Bush was so bombarded with complaints of

Just the Facts

It may surprise you to know that religiously minded Muslims do not support men such as Saddam Hussein, the late Hafiz Al Assad, or Yasir Arafat. These men are not known to be exemplary Muslims (just the opposite in fact). None of them were elected, as Islam requires, and all of them actually have worked to suppress the free practice of religion in their nations.

Western fear-mongering by *secular* Muslim leaders that he turned to an aide and asked, "Do they really believe that we think all Muslims are terrorists?" This was precisely the message Muslims around the world heard emanating from America. The Iraqi prisoner abuse scandal in which American military personnel were caught sadistically torturing prisoners (a story that broke in April of 2004) only confirmed in the minds of many Muslims that the West was interested in humiliating not only Muslims, but Islam itself. Thoughtful Muslims have found it ironic that American leaders from President Bush on down have pleaded for understanding and have asked people not to blame all Americans for the actions of a few. Aren't Muslims to be accorded the same level of understanding?

What Do Muslims Want?

It is often hard for Westerners to understand what Muslims in so many places are fighting for. This is understandable because Europe and North America have enjoyed an unbroken chain of peace that has lasted for half a century. Even though the two World Wars caused enormous destruction, especially in Europe, the wars were fought among nations that already were the most powerful in the world and they rebounded quickly. To know what Muslims want, you have to look at the reality of what the last several centuries have been like for them.

The Muslim world, which used to span an uninterrupted swath of territory running from Spain to China, was fragmented because of internal weakness and then set upon by external enemies. The once cosmopolitan, multiethnic melting pot of Islam, where local rulers were really just a footnote in the history of the civilization, was divided into mini-states by European interlopers. When the colonizers left, the fragmented states that they created were turned over to antireligious secularists, kings, or the like. Following the Western model of separating religion from politics, these unelected presidents, emirs, and dictators closed religious schools; arrested Imams; removed or warped religious instruction in the public school curriculum; imposed socialism, secularism, or communism on their people; and passed laws that were contrary to the Islamic legal tradition. All of this didn't happen over many centuries, but over 75 years.

Poverty, illiteracy, endless coups, and corruption have plagued most Muslim nations due to the estrangement between ruler and ruled. For example, in Nigeria, a country with billions of dollars in oil revenues, most of the population lacks basic education and medical services. As a result of the chronic mismanagement of the nation, an Islamic revivalist movement has succeeded in causing several northern provinces to declare the resumption of Islamic Law as the legal code of the territory. (Non-Muslims are generally exempted from Islamic Law, by the way.)

In other nations, such as India, Israel, the former Yugoslavia, and the Philippines, where Muslims live as persecuted minorities, the reality of life is harsh and oftentimes dangerous. Muslims point to the murder of 200,000 Bosnians by the Serbs, the Israeli usurpation of Palestine, the French-led genocide against the Algerians, and the Chinese Communist policy of forcibly settling non-Muslims in Muslim lands all as examples of grave injustices done against them. If Americans ever wondered why so many people around the world wanted to immigrate to their shores, they need look no further than the daily news with all its stories of tragedy in the developing world. (For all its foibles, America is generally a safe place to live, and Muslim Americans are very grateful!)

Just the Facts

The main hot spots that Muslims currently want to see resolved are Kashmir (independence from India), Palestine (a Palestinian state with at least part of Jerusalem as its capital), Chechnya (independence from Russia), the Sudan (an end to the foreign-backed southern rebellion), Azerbaijan (an end to the Armenian occupation), Iraq (the withdrawal of all foreign forces) and Xinjiang in China (independence or at least meaningful autonomy).

Most Muslim nations were not even created by the people living within them. European colonial powers decided the borders of those countries before they left, and this has created a legacy of conflict among these nations, which often fight for land or resources that in the past would have been communal property. (Winston Churchill once boasted, "I created Jordan one afternoon in the drawing room.") Recent wars pitting such diverse rivals against each other as Ethiopia and Eritrea, Pakistan and India, as well as the Arab-Israeli conflict over Palestine, illustrate this continuing problem.

Reformist Muslims aren't asking to conquer the world or to upset the global economic system. They just want what their ancestors had, another Golden Age of Islam with all its art, culture, economic opportunity, and self-respect.

There have been many positive and negative developments in the revival of Islam in the past century. Muslims have succeeded in establishing home rule in about 90 percent of their world. (Captive Muslim territories can still be found in parts of Russia, China, the Philippines, Africa, and Europe.) In addition, many new Islamic groups have been formed, bringing a vitality back to Islam that was lacking for a long time.

Major setbacks have occurred as well. Many wars, despotic governments, and losses of territory have caused the Muslim world to suffer tremendous hardship. (Think of the virtual partition of Bosnia, the decimation of Chechnya, the occupation of Afghanistan and Iraq by the United States, the excesses of numerous dictators, or the fate of occupied Azerbaijan.) In addition, Muslims feel that the United States has replaced Europe as the great suppressor of Islamic revivalism because of its overwhelming economic and military presence in the world. Most disturbing of all was the establishment of American military bases in Saudi Arabia in the late 1990s (a policy that has since been reversed), which is the proverbial heartland of Islam. Other events have also seemed to confirm for Muslims the suspicion that America will deny its own ideals in pursuit of its aim of global domination, most notably the invasion of Iraq while the American government shows tolerance for a long list of very nasty dictators from Central Asia to Africa. Even more in the mind of many Muslims, however, is the strangely one-sided nature of U.S. foreign policy regarding the Arab-Israeli conflict.

The Establishment of Israel

The existence of Israel is not actually an *Islamic* religious issue. The Islamic religion does not forbid the creation of nations or borders *per se*, nor does Islam teach hatred of Jews or any other ethnic group. On the contrary, Islam calls all people the descendants of Adam and thus holds to the ideal of basic human equality before God regardless of an individual's personal beliefs. What makes Muslims keenly interested in this situation can be boiled down to two things: injustice and Jerusalem.

From the Muslim point of view, the Arabs of Palestine were unjustly driven from their land in 1948 by a United Nations decision in which they had no say. The rallying cry of European Zionists—"A land without a people for a people without a land"—was, in fact, a patently false fiction for the very reason that, except for the driest areas of Palestine, the land was already filled with Arabs. Even though Arab countries made a feeble attempt to stop this alien imposition, the newly organized Israeli forces, which were equipped with superior weapons and training from supporters around the globe, were able to seize even more land than the UN partition plan allotted them.

The local Arabs, who in time came to be labeled Palestinians, were driven out of hundreds of towns and villages through terror campaigns and brute force. The hundreds of thousands of Arabs who remain today are still being oppressed by an Israeli government that routinely seizes people's homes and farms and engages in mass arrests and torture. Perhaps the most insidious plan of all, from the Muslim perspective, is the construction of Israeli settlements on appropriated Arab land. (That sounds suspiciously close to ethnic cleansing.) Although much talk has been made of the Arab desire to destroy the state of Israel, little coverage of the reasons why Arabs and Muslims are so angry has been aired. Unqualified American support for Israel hasn't helped America's image as an honest broker either.

Just the Facts _____

It may be surprising to learn that Arab Christians have actually been at the fore-front of the struggle for Arab rights in Palestine. The prolific writer, Edward Said, has brought this issue to the world through his compelling books. Hanan Ashrawi, who was one of the most well-known members of the Palestinian National Authority, was an international spokeswoman for her people's cause. On the opposite end, the most violent Palestinian terrorist group, the Popular Front for the Liberation of Palestine (PFLP), was actually run by a Christian named Ahmed Jibreel.

So how have Muslims from Malaysia to Gambia been brought into this conflict? Muslims all over the world are concerned about the fate of Israeli-occupied Jerusalem. Jerusalem is the third-holiest city in Islam, behind Mecca and Medina. The Prophet Muhammad had his miraculous Night Journey and Ascension from the holy rock on the Temple Mount there, and the first city that Muslims faced when prayers were originally established was this one. The Muslim response is clear: Jerusalem (at least the old city) must be either placed under Muslim control, shared, or given the status of an international city.

If the Arab-Israeli conflict were merely a struggle for land between Israelis and Arabs, then most Muslims might not feel so close to the situation—for Islam is not, after all, an Arab religion or centered on the concerns of any one racial or ethnic group. It's when you add a religious dimension that is central to Islamic sensibilities that the circle of concerned individuals is expanded. One of the reasons the famed peace talks that were first initiated in Oslo and that had almost succeeded in a breakthrough peace settlement broke down was because of the very issue of the status of Jerusalem. Yasir Arafat, the Palestinian leader, later remarked, "How could I go back to my people and show them an agreement without Jerusalem?" The controversial *separation wall* currently being constructed by Israel seemingly to wall off most Palestinians into small reservations is hardly helping prospects for peace.

To reiterate: It is not an article of faith in the minds of most Muslims to destroy Israel. If the issue of Jerusalem could be solved to the satisfaction of the world's Muslims, and the injustices done against the Palestinians resolved, then perhaps the modern state of Israel could exist in peace in the Middle East. (Muslim rulers during the Crusades often made long-lived peace treaties with the Europeans.) As of this writing, two Arab countries have already concluded treaties with the Jewish-dominated state of Israel. More might be willing to do the same if the Israelis would concede that wrongs were done and that Jerusalem should be the property of all the religions that claim it—or the property of none at all. Stay tuned.

The Iranian Revolution

In 1978 Americans saw Iranian students storm the U.S. Embassy and hold the American diplomats hostage for more than a year. Why did the Iranians engage in such an uncouth act? Why did they hate the Shah so much? To understand this situation, you need only look at the reasons for the American Revolution against the British monarch. Issues such as a lack of representation, unfair taxes, undue search and seizure, and despotic policies caused the American colonists to wage an eight-year war for their freedom. The Iranians had it worse than that with a forced program of modernization (fraught with corruption) foisted upon them, few civil liberties of any kind, secret police and torture chambers, and a ruling elite that was above the law.

In Iran, the position of *shah* (Persian for king) was that of an absolute dictator who had no check on his authority. The previous shah, Riza Pehlavi, decreed many laws against Islam, among which was one prohibiting the wearing of head scarves by Muslim women. His son, Muhammad Riza, who began his rule in 1941, embarked on an ambitious program to modernize the country. In his quest to bring Iran into the twentieth century, however, he relied on old-fashioned repression to quell any dissent. His secret police, known as the *Savak*, routinely arrested and tortured people. In addition, the Shah turned over control of the country's resources to foreigners, such as the Americans and British, and lived a lavish lifestyle while many of his subjects lived in abject poverty.

Just the Facts

Ayatullah Khomeini, the Shi'a cleric who declared that America was the *Great Satan*, did so out of frustration because the CIA had meddled in Iranian affairs for decades and because the U.S. government supported the Shah of Iran, who was a ruthless dictator.

When the excesses of the Shah's regime could not be tolerated by the populace any further, an exiled Shi'a cleric named Ayatullah Khomeini came to the forefront of the movement to topple the Shah. He used smuggled cassette tapes and booklets to rally ordinary Iranians against their king. Student-led protests began to swell into general strikes, and people all over Iran declared their desire for freedom from dictatorship. Even the Shah's army turned against him, and in 1979 Khomeini stepped off a plane in Tehran and was proclaimed the ruler of the newly founded Islamic Republic.

So why the hostage crisis? Unbeknownst to most Americans, in 1952 the people of Iran had carried out a successful revolution against the same Shah and tried to establish a democratic republic, but the CIA initiated a countercoup a year later, orchestrated from the American Embassy, that brought the brutal and sadistic Shah back to power. His revenge against the populace was terrible and bloody. (Another failed uprising by Iranian civilians was brutally crushed in 1963.) Iranians were afraid in

1978 that America would intervene again to bring the hated dictator back to power. As Mark J. Gasiorowski, a historian at Louisiana State University, said in an interview in the *New York Times* in November of 2003, "It's quite clear that the 1953 coup cut short a move toward democracy in Iran. The United States bears responsibility for this."

Just the Facts

Islam does in fact require that women past the age of puberty cover their hair with a veil of some type in the presence of men whom they would theoretically be eligible to marry. No other item of clothing has been so controversial. Traditional Christianity, Hinduism, Sikhism, and Judaism require the veil as well, but it is Islam that has been singled out for having its symbols banned. Recently, for instance, the French government banned all religious symbols from being worn in their schools. Though they included yarmulkes and *large* crosses as a curious kind of balance, it was clearly stated by French authorities that the Islamic *hijab* was the real target of the ban.

Was there chaos in the aftermath of the Iranian Revolution and a lot of unjust reprisals against the Shah's supporters? Undoubtedly, but the same occurred during the American Revolution when British loyalists were harassed, their property seized, and a few even hanged. Not to excuse the excesses committed by the new Iranian regime, this comparison merely serves to illustrate how any revolution can result in bloody disorder until things settle down. (The Iranian Revolution was no more messy than the French Revolution.) After the passing of two decades, life in Iran has settled down, and we see at least some type interplay of political forces, each using the ballot box to try to achieve its goals. The questions the Iranians still have to answer are how to best integrate Islam into the democratic process and what Islam requires of a person in their individual life.

The Satanic Verses

When Salman Rushdie published his novel poking fun at the Prophet Muhammad and his family, Muslims around the world were outraged. Islamic Law contains strict anti-defamation protocols. Even as Western nations have banned certain books and other types of speech (such as Nazi propaganda and hate speech), Islam also calls unjust slander a criminal offense. The punishment for slandering a woman falsely is 100 lashes; for defaming the Prophet of God, capital punishment is a possible legal sentence (unless the slanderer retracts his or her statements and seeks public forgiveness).

The late Ayatullah Khomeini of Iran leveled the death penalty against Rushdie unless he publicly withdrew his work. Given that Rushdie, an Indian expatriate, was living in

England at the time, he was in no immediate danger. Muslims looked aghast, however, as Western liberals rushed to his defense, even as they remained silent in the face of free speech violations carried out against Muslims in many parts of the world. In France head scarves are banned from most public institutions. Turkey goes so far as to restrict Qur'anic education for children, and China has numerous restrictions against the free teaching of Islam.

With the passage of time cooler heads have seemed to prevail and the Iranian government lifted the sentence imposed by the late cleric. There is little danger of any harm coming to him now, and he has since published other books and novels. Unfortunately, the whole affair was blown out of proportion, and again the broad brush was used to make all Muslims seem like they were crazed assassins ready to pounce. The very fact that Rushdie enjoys nearly complete freedom of movement, even though there are more than a billion Muslims in the world, proves that the vast majority of Muslims are just as thoughtful and reasonable as anybody else.

September 11 and What It Meant to Muslims

Like everyone else who lived through that terrible day, I will never forget where I was and what I was doing on the morning of September 11. I had just left my job to make a quick trip to Staples when I heard the news on the radio of the first plane slamming into the side of one of the two towers. I thought it was an accident at first, but on my way back to work the radio announcer gave the news of a second plane crash into the other tower. The first thought I, and every other Muslim, had in such situations was, "O God, please don't let it be Muslims who did it."

My next thought, after the initial shock passed, was of overwhelming concern for the people who were suffering through the catastrophe. I, as well as many other New Yorkers, knew people who worked in the area. (As it turns out, over 200 Muslims working in the towers perished that day as well.) That first day Muslims were in a state of shock as profound as that felt by other Americans. We had the added burden, however, of knowing what irrational reprisals would be directed at all of us, even though we had nothing to do with the attacks that were carried out by 19 men who belonged to an almost-unknown shadowy organization named Al Qaeda.

Within the first 24 hours Muslim organizations in the West were issuing condemnations of the attack. Muslims themselves refused to believe that anyone who shared their religion could have done such a thing. They came up with theories that it must have been an Israeli plot or something cooked up by the CIA or some other unknown anti-Muslim alliance. This kind of suspension of reality is a testament to the fact that Islam could never condone an attack on innocents. Muslims just refused to believe it.

While CNN was showing 10-year-old footage of Palestinians cheering and saying that this was the reaction from the Muslim world, real-life Muslims were shaking their heads in disgust and fearing for the future. As the Los Angeles riots have proven, Americans are not immune from communal violence. Thankfully, some rather forceful condemnations of anti-Muslim violence by President George W. Bush in the aftermath of the attacks helped to blunt the worst of the retaliation that began to surface. Still, Muslims have suffered and continue to suffer much discrimination and bias.

As was mentioned in previous chapters, Islam is not a vigilante religion where any clandestine group can make up its own rules, pick its own enemies, and disregard all norms and customs related to the legal conduct of warfare. Al Qaeda has no following among the Muslim community anywhere in the world. It has no base, no country to call home, and no voice in the world. It is a collection of disgruntled men, guided by Wahhabist philosophy, which has taken the fight against colonial Israel (and by extension its backer, America) to a new and unprecedented level. Their methodologies are squarely against even the most basic Islamic teachings about armed self-defense, and they have no other desire than to wreak havoc all across the globe for their own twisted ends. So flawed is their approach that they care not if they kill or harm fellow Muslims, whom they claim to be fighting for in the first place!

Sadly, Westerners were generally so uninformed as to what was going on in the Muslim world that after September 11 they automatically began to believe that the religion of Islam was to blame for the attacks. Without knowing the historical forces that gave rise to this militant movement of no more than a few thousand individuals, they broad-brushed all Muslims as terrorists, suspended the civil rights of their Muslim citizens to an unprecedented degree, and antagonized the very community they most needed to build bridges with. Authentic mainstream Muslims are the most important tool in discrediting the very flawed ideology that extremist groups subscribe to.

One positive note is that this tragedy has not only united Americans in a new sense of national purpose and consciousness, but it has also opened the way for a new dialogue between the followers of many faiths. Numerous Christian pastors and Jewish rabbis have come forward throughout the aftermath of September 11 to show their support for their Muslim neighbors, and Muslims themselves have begun to come out of their cocoon to take a more active role in their neighborhoods and countries. Muslims, for perhaps the first time, have realized that we can no longer ignore the rise of extremist movements that claim to speak for all of us. We need to be vigilant in learning about and passing on the vibrant, tolerant, and rational faith that has come down to us from the earliest days of our faith.

Blood and Treasure: America in the Muslim World

When the ultimatum was given to the Taliban late in 2001 to surrender Osama bin Laden and his henchmen, their reply was that America wouldn't have the guts to invade Afghanistan. Within two months the entire country was in the hands of the U.S. military. Al Qaeda was driven into exile, and a new Afghan government, backed by warlord militias, began to contemplate its new mandate. For Muslims it was a mixed bag of emotions and opinions.

On the one hand, believe it or not, most Muslims saw the Taliban as backward, reactionary, and generally without a good foundation in Islamic governance. Their many odd and even brutal policies, such as forbidding women to work, whipping people with sticks for minor offenses, and even forbidding kite-flying made them seem like simpletons in the Muslim world. For all the Taliban's talk of being the most Islamic, there was no stampede of religious Muslims to move into their mountain realm. On the other hand, the Taliban, for all their faults, was better than what existed before their ascension in 1996. Prior to that time brutal and sadistic warlords, funded by drug profits, had turned the country into some nightmarish gangland battlefield. The Taliban silenced the guns in most of the country and brought some normalcy back to the shell-shocked population.

Muslims knew, however, that after the United States fingered Al Qaeda as the perpetrator of the September 11 attacks, that Afghanistan was in a world of trouble. The Taliban, of course, did not organize or call for the terrorist strikes, but they had allowed Al Qaeda to operate freely in their country. (Al Qaeda was helping them to keep a coalition of diehard warlords in the northeast of the country at bay.) To this day almost every Muslim I meet agrees that the Taliban made the biggest mistake in the world by not handing over—or at least exiling—Bin Laden and his crew.

How do Muslims feel about the United States's and NATO's role in Afghanistan? That depends on who you ask. Although some Muslims decry the occupation of another Muslim country by non-Muslims, others are satisfied that the end results for the population will be better in the long run. Afghanistan, under its new leaders, has crafted a constitution and held off a resurgent Taliban underground movement and, as of this writing, has had mixed results in establishing a more just society. Ironically, and to the satisfaction of Muslims worldwide, the Islamic religion is still given a prominent place of honor in their new system. We can but hope that now real Islam will be allowed to flourish as the nation rebuilds yet again.

When turning to Iraq and the U.S. invasion and occupation, the consensus becomes a little clearer: Muslims in general are very happy to see the tyrant, Saddam Hussein, sitting in prison, but they also feel that the justification for the war (and subsequent dismantling of a large chunk of the infrastructure of the country) was based on false pretenses and colonialist designs. Critics point to the original case for war, Saddam's weapons of mass destruction (WMD) and his determination to use them, and are enraged that the propaganda and evidence put forth by the United States and Britain appears to have been faulty. The revised reasoning put forth by world leaders that Saddam was an abuser of human rights and thus was ripe for removal, while true, falls on incredulous listeners who still observe that the United States, in particular, turns a blind eye to human rights abuses committed by other dictators elsewhere.

Putting that issue aside, most Muslims have felt that the war in Iraq was really a war to remove a strong rival of Israel in the region. The subsequent vision as laid out by the Bush administration in 2002 and 2003 of bringing democracy to the region, then, was met with even greater skepticism given that a large population of Christian and Muslim Arabs were still living under military occupation by an expansionist Israel. How can these concerns be addressed, and how can the United States make its positions clearer? A good starting point would be in addressing the Arab-Israeli conflict and bringing a solution to fruition. This would do much to win the hearts and minds of the people of the region.

As of this writing the United States still has large military forces stationed in Iraq and, to a lesser extent, in Afghanistan. Is this the beginning of an American imperial presence in the Muslim world, such as the French and British experience of years past? This is the question Muslims are asking themselves. This is also a question that other Westerners must ask, too. For the way to defeat the power of extremists is to take away the very reasons that give rise to such movements in the first place. Time will tell if the American experiment of transforming the Middle East will succeed or fail.

Islam is compatible with democracy, with only a few caveats. Although it is fine to elect leaders and representatives and craft worldly laws, all Islam asks is that certain laws expounded specifically within the Qur'an and hadith be sacrosanct—the rest of our legal wrangling from traffic regulations to voter registration rules is fair game. In this, an ideal modern Islamic democracy would look something like Britain or Sweden, which have state religions and active electorates. As President George W. Bush said in November of 2003, "It should be clear to all that Islam—the faith of one-fifth of humanity—is consistent with democratic rule. Sixty years of Western nations excusing and accommodating the lack of freedom in the Middle East did nothing to make us safe, because in the long run, stability cannot be purchased at the expense of liberty."

Islam, the Next Chapter

So what happens next? After learning about the beliefs, practices, hopes, struggles, and aspirations of Muslims, where is the world of Islam going in the coming decades? Will it integrate fully into global society, or will it retreat back into itself? Is there going to be a great clash of civilizations in the near future, as some writers have suggested? The answer to all of these questions, from the Muslim perspective, is *only God knows.* We can, however, look at current trends both within and without the world of Islam and make some cautious predictions.

There will likely be an accommodation established between Islam and the West, if for no other reason than the fact that within a few more decades, significant portions of the population in Europe and North America will be made up of Muslims. Revolutionary struggles pitting Islamists against corrupt secular governments in the Middle East will likely continue for some time, and the Arab-Israeli conflict will probably be settled in the not-too-distant future. Muslim freedom fighters will continue their campaigns to liberate their occupied nations, and Muslims in the West will continue to press for equal religious rights enabling them to wear *hijabs* (head scarves), beards, and attend Friday congregational services.

We may see the emergence of a new, albeit symbolic, Islamic caliphate again. The new caliph may not actually have any state authority but will act as a sort of global Islamic spokesman in much the same way as the Catholic pope is seen as a representative of Christendom. In my humble opinion, the new caliphate will probably be located somewhere in east Asia and not the Arab world, but that is purely speculation based on my reading of the trends.

The Crescent and Star, which is often promoted as the emblem of Islam, is actually a Byzantine Imperial symbol that was appropriated by the Ottoman Turks. The Prophet Muhammad used black-and-white flags as his symbols; common alternatives are green flags with the Muslim creed written on them.

Muslims are, in general, peace-loving people who look to their faith to help solve the problems that confront us all in daily life. As you have learned, Islam is not a religion of hate or violence, but is a way of life that brings out the best in its sincere followers. My prayer is that as the future unfolds, Muslims and non-Muslims can gain a greater appreciation for what Islam is actually about. Taking the time to read this book is certainly a great place to start! May you go in peace and live a good life devoted to faith and helping your fellow creatures. *Ameen!* Let it be so!

The Least You Need to Know

- Muslims are looking for redress for a century of humiliation and oppression that has been directed against them.

- The two main issues that cause Muslims worldwide to oppose Israel are the injustice against the Arabs inherent in Israel's founding and the status of Jerusalem.

- Al Qaeda and other extremist groups follow a narrow puritanical reinterpretation of Islam developed in the eighteenth century that is discredited among the mainstream Muslim community.

- The Muslim world is in such turmoil as a consequence of the legacy of Colonialism.

- Islamic revivalism is not a danger to the West. Muslims are seeking mainly to gain responsible government in their countries.

- The future of relations between Islam and the non-Muslim world is bright with many positive possibilities.

Further Reading

Now that you have taken your first look into the world of Islam you might want to know more about a particular area or delve deeper into the philosophy, culture, or history of Islam. As you may have noticed, Islamic beliefs and teachings are not so complicated that it is impossible to gain a great amount of understanding. In fact, Islam has often been praised for its simplicity, directness, and explicability.

These qualities don't mean, however, that Islam is a lightweight subject or that there isn't a lot more to know and discover. On the contrary, within the pages of the Qur'an and Hadith are a myriad of themes, ideas, concepts, and meanings that invite further study. The history of Islamic civilization down to our present day is filled with hard-earned treasures of knowledge that make the Islamic experience even more rewarding and satisfying. In addition, Muslim folklore, fiction, philosophical essays, and religious commentary present a fascinating journey for the traveler thirsty for adventure, reflection, and challenge.

The Holy Qur'an (in English)

The best place to continue your journey, of course, is with the Holy Qur'an. While many translations of the Arabic text into English are available, some are more clearly translated than others. The most commonly accepted translations in the English world today are these:

The Meaning of the Holy Qur'an, translated by Abdullah Yusuf Ali. Beltsville, MD: Amana Publications, 1995.

The Holy Qur'an, translated by Muhammad F. A. Malik. Houston, TX: Islamic Society of Greater Houston, 1999.

The Message of the Qur'an, translated by Muhammad Asad. Chicago: Kazi Publications, 1980.

All three of these translations were made by recognized Muslim scholars and are widely available online. I don't recommend using most of the translations you'll find in your local bookstores, though. They are generally out-of-date translations, works done by well-meaning but unqualified Christian missionaries, or translations by people with Muslim names who do not follow Islam according to the standard mainstream. Can you imagine reading a Bible translated by an atheist or a Hindu?

The Hadiths

For books of the Prophet's sayings, or *Hadiths*, I recommend any of these:

An-Nawawi, Imam Yahya. *Riyadh us Saliheen*. Translated by S. M. Madni Abbasi. Karachi: International Islamic Publishers, 1986.

Arshed, Aneela Khalid. *The Bounty of Allah*. New York: The Crossroad Publishing Company, 1999.

Bukhari, Muhammad. *Imam Bukhari's Book of Muslim Morals and Manners*. Translated by Yusuf Talal DeLorenzo. Alexandria: Al-Saadawi Publications, 1997.

Khan, Maulana Wahiduddin. *An Islamic Treasury of Virtues*. New Delphi: Goodword Books, 1999.

Books About Islam

For excellent books about Islam, the Prophet Muhammad, and related topics, I recommend the following sources:

Ali, Tariq. *The Clash of Fundamentalisms: Crusades, Jihads and Modernity*. New York: Verso Books, 2003.

Al-Ghazali, Abu Hamid Muhammad. *Remembrance of Death and the Afterlife*. Translated by T. J. Winter. Cambridge, U.K.: The Islamic Texts Society, 1995.

Al-Ghazali, Sheikh Muhammad. *Journey Through the Qur'an*. London: Dar Al Taqwa, 1998.

Al-Qaradawi, Yusuf. *The Lawful and Prohibited in Islam*, Indianapolis, IN: American Trust Publications, 1999.

Anway, Carol. *Daughters of Another Path*. Lee's Summit: Yawna Publications, 1995.

Aswad, Barbara and Barbara Bilge. *Family and Gender Among American Muslims*. Philadelphia, PA: Temple University Press, 1996.

Bendinar, Elmer. *The Rise and Fall of Paradise: When Arabs and Jews Built a Kingdom in Spain*. New York: Barnes & Noble Books, 1983.

Boisard, Marcel. *Humanism in Islam*. Indianapolis, IN: American Trust Publications, 1979.

Bowman, Betty and Muzaffar Haleem. *The Sun Is Rising in the West*. Beltsville, MD: Amana Publications, 1999.

Bucaille, Maurice. *The Bible, the Qur'an and Science*. Indianapolis, IN: North American Trust Publication, 1978.

Dirks, Debra. *Our Choice: Portraits of Modern American Muslim Women*. Beltsville, MD: Amana Publications, 2003.

Dirks, Jerald. *The Cross & the Crescent*. Beltsville, MD: Amana Publications, 2001.

Doi, Abdur Rahman I. *Shari'ah: The Islamic Law*. London: Ta Ha Publishers, 1984.

Dunn, Ross E. *The Adventures of Ibn Battuta*. Berkeley: University of California Press, 1986.

Ebrahim, Abul Fadl Mohsin. *Abortion, Birth Control & Surrogate Parenting: An Islamic Perspective*. Indianapolis, IN: American Trust Publications, 1989.

Emerick, Yahiya. *Muhammad*. Indianapolis, IN: Alpha Books, 2002.

Faruqi, Isma'il. *The Cultural Atlas of Islam*. New York: Macmillan Publishing Company, 1986.

Feldman, Noah. *After Jihad: America and the Struggle for Islamic Democracy*. New York: Farrar Straus & Giroux, 2003.

Fernea, Elizabeth W. *In Search of Islamic Feminism*. New York: Doubleday, 1998.

Green, Joey. *Jesus and Muhammad: The Parallel Sayings*. Berkeley, CA: Ulysses Press, 2002.

Haddad, Yvonne. *The Muslims of America*. New York: Oxford University Press, 1991.

Haddad, Yvonne and Jane I. Smith. *Muslim Communities in North America*. New York: State University of New York Press, 1994.

Haddad, Yvonne and Adair Lummis. *Islamic Values in the United States*. New York: Oxford University Press, 1987.

Hariri-Wendel, Tanja. *Symbols of Islam*. New York: Sterling Publishing Co., 1999.

Khalidi, Tarif. *The Muslim Jesus: Sayings and Stories in Islamic Literature*. Cambridge, MA: Harvard University Press, 2003.

Lang, Jeffrey. *Struggling to Surrender*. Beltsville, MD: Amana Publications, 1994.

———. *Even Angels Ask*. Beltsville, MD: Amana Publications, 1997.

Lings, Martin. *Muhammad: His Life Based on the Earliest Sources*. Rochester: Inner Traditions International, Ltd., 1983.

Maqsood, Ruqaiyyah Waris. *A Basic Dictionary of Islam*. New Delphi: Goodword Books, 1998.

———. *After Death, Life*. New Delphi: Goodword Books, 1998.

———. *The Muslim Marriage Guide*. New Delphi: Goodword Books, 1999.

Moore, Keith L. *The Qur'an and Modern Science: Correlation Studies*. Makkah: WAMY, 1990.

Omis, Safi. *Progressive Muslims: On Justice, Gender, and Pluralism*. Oxford: Oneworld Publications, 2003.

Qadhi, Abu Ammaar Yasir. *An Introduction to the Sciences of the Qur'aan*. Birmingham, AL: Al-Hidaayah Publishing and Distribution, 1999.

Rahim, Muhammad Ata Ur. *Jesus: Prophet of Islam*. Riyadh: Pirip, 1984.

Rauf, Feisal Abdul. *Islam: A Sacred Law*. Putney: Qiblah Books, 2000.

Sarwar, Shaykh Muhammad. *The Complete Idiot's Guide to the Koran*. New York: Alpha Books, 2003.

Schimmel, Annemarie. *My Soul Is a Woman: the Feminine in Islam*. New York: Continuum, 1997.

Sells, Michael. *Approaching the Qur'an*. Ashland, OR: White Cloud Press, 1999.

———. *The New Crusades: Constructing the Muslim Enemy*. New York: Columbia University Press, 2003.

Stowasser, Barbara Freyer. *Women in the Qur'an, Traditions, and Interpretation*. New York: Oxford University Press, 1994.

Waugh, Earle. *Muslim Families in North America*. Edmonton: University of Alberta Press, 1991.

Wintle, Justin. *The Rough Guide History of Islam*. Rough Guides Ltd.: London, 2003.

Islamic Non-Fiction, Fiction, and Poetry

Leisure reading from the world of Islam is a not-to-be-missed experience! Here are some very enjoyable books, both classic and modern, to feast your mind on:

Ali, Tariq. *Shadows of the Pomegranate Tree*. New York: Verso Books, 1996.

———. *The Book of Saladin: A Novel*. New York: Verso Books, 1999.

Al-Ghazali, Abu Hamid Muhammad. *The Alchemy of Happiness*. London: The Octagon Press, 1983.

Al-Jahiz, Abu Uthman ibn Bahr. *The Book of Misers*. Translated by R. B. Serjeant. London: Garnet Publishing Limited, 1997.

Asad, Muhammad. *The Road to Mecca*. Gibraltar: Dar Al-Andalus, 1980.

Atiyeh, George N. *The Book in the Islamic World*. Albany, NY: State University of New York, 1995.

Attar, Fariduddin. *The Conference of Birds*. New York: Penguin, 1995.

Baig, Reshma. *The Memory of Hands*. New York: International Books and Tapes Supply, 1999.

Burton, Sir Richard. *The Arabian Nights*. New York: The Modern Library, 1932.

Hafiz, Shamsuddin Muhammad. *The Gift: Poems by Hafiz*. Translated by Daniel Ladinsky. New York: Penguin, 1999.

Haley, Alex. *The Autobiography of Malcolm X*. New York: Ballantine Books, 1978.

Helminski, Kabir and Camille. *Jewels of Remembrance*, *Poems of Rumi*. Putney: Threshold Books, 1996.

Irwin, Robert. *Night & Horses & the Desert: An Anthology of Classical Arabic Literature*. New York: Anchor, 2002.

Juyyusi, Lena. *The Adventures of Sayf Bin Dhi Yazan*. Indianapolis, IN: Indiana University Press, 1996.

Kemal, Yashar. *They Burn the Thistles*. Translated by Paul Theroux. New York: William Morrow and Company, 1977.

Munif, Abdul Rahman. *Cities of Salt*. London: The Octagon Press, 1994.

Shah, Amina. *Arabian Fairy Tales*. London: The Octagon Press, 1989.

Shah, Idris. *The Exploits of the Incomparable Mulla Nasrudin*. London: The Octagon Press, 1993.

Tufayl, Ibn. *Hayy ibn Yaqzan*. Translated by Lenn Evan Goodman. Los Angeles: Gee Tee Bee, 1996.

Wolfe, Michael. *One Thousand Roads to Mecca*. New York: Grove Press, 1997.

Glossary

Abbasid   The name of the second great Muslim dynasty. After the initial Muslim expansion, the Umayyids (661–750) fell afoul of these descendants of the Prophet's Uncle, Abbas. In 750, they revolted and seized power, creating one of the longest lived, and most dynamic, Muslim dynasties.

Adam   The first man on earth, according to Islam.

Ahl al Kitab   "People of the Book." Jews and Christians who received revelations (books) from God in the past.

Akhirah   The next life.

alim   A scholar in Islam. Plural: *'ulema.* This office is open to both males and females.

Allah   "The One God before Whom there are no others." It is linguistically related to the Old Testament Hebrew name for God, *Eloh* (pl. *Elohim*), and the Aramaic word, *Elah.*

Ansar   "Helpers." Converts to Islam who lived in Medina and assisted the Prophet and the Meccan refugees who came with him.

aqiqah   The ritual for welcoming a baby into the world.

Arabic   The name of the language spoken by the Arab people. Non-Arabs learn at least a small amount of it for religious reasons because the Qur'an was revealed in that tongue and also because Islamic prayers are recited in it.

Arkan al Islami   The famed Five Pillars of Islam, consisting of the declaration of faith, prayer, fasting, charity, and pilgrimage to Mecca.

Asma' ul Husna   "The Most Beautiful Names." A list of the 99 names of God through which Muslims understand what God's nature is like.

Asr   The late-afternoon prayer.

assalamu alaykum   "Peace be upon you." The Muslim greeting of peace. The reply is, "*Wa alaykum assalam,*" "And upon you be peace."

ataqullah   "Be conscious of God's presence in your life." A common exhortation among Muslims and in the Qur'an.

ayah   "A sign." The term for a verse of the Qur'an.

Ayatullah   "Sign of God." The title of a major Shi'a cleric.

azan   The Muslim call to prayer consisting of several religious statements.

Azra'il   The proper name of the angel of death, also known as *Malikul Mawt*.

Bani Isra'il   The Children of Israel.

Barzakh   "The partition." The time between death and the resurrection. The souls of the dead are in a stored state and are either dreaming pleasantly or being tormented, based upon their faith and deeds while in the world.

Baytul Hikmah   "House of Wisdom." A scholarly think tank established by Caliph Ma'mun in 830 in the city of Baghdad. Most of the major translations of Greek texts into Arabic took place here as well.

Baytullah   "The House of God." One of the alternate names for the *Ka'bah*.

Colonialism   The period from the seventeenth to the twentieth century when the major European powers conquered and occupied nearly every nation on Earth, most of them Muslim territories.

Crusades   A series of Christian invasions into the Muslim Middle East that began in 1099 and ended in 1270.

Dajjal   The anti-Christ. It literally means *the Liar*.

deen   Way of life.

dhikr (ziker)   Remembering God through repeating religious phrases. This is the Muslim version of the rosary.

Dhulm (zulm)   Transgression, going out of all bounds in moral behavior. One of the Islamic terms for sin.

du'a   Supplication, personal requests to God.

dunya   The world.

'Eid ul adha   The Islamic holiday at the end of the *Hajj*.

'Eid ul Fitr   The Islamic holiday at the end of the fast of *Ramadan*.

Emanul Mufassil   The seven main beliefs of Islam listed in detail.

Esa   The Islamic name for Jesus.

Fajr   The pre-dawn prayer.

fatwa   A legal ruling by a competent Islamic legal scholar. Fatwas can be challenged or overruled and are not automatically binding on the community.

fiqh   Understanding the application of the Islamic Law and how to formulate new rulings.

fitrah   The inner moral compass that all humans are born with. People can become influenced by it to seek God, or they can consciously bury it under a load of sin and denial.

futuwwat   The Muslim code of battlefield honor that Europeans copied and labeled chivalry.

Gabriel   The chief angel charged with the responsibility of bringing revelations to prophets and others. Also spelled *Jibra'il*.

hadith   "An account." Any saying by, or action attributed to, the Prophet Muhammad.

hafiz   "Guardian." A person who has memorized the entire Qur'an by heart.

Hajj   "Pilgrimage." The annual pilgrimage to Mecca, which takes place in the twelfth month of the Islamic lunar calendar. All Muslims must make this journey once in a lifetime if they are physically able and can afford to do so.

Hajji   "Pilgrim." The honorific title given to the person who has completed the Islamic pilgrimage ritual.

halal   Allowed food to eat or activity to engage in.

haram   Forbidden food to consume or activity to engage in.

Hawwa   The name for Eve in Islam.

haya   Life in general.

Hayat ad-Dunya   The life of this world.

Hidayah Guidance from God.

hijab The head scarf worn over the hair.

Hijrah The migration of Muhammad and his followers from hostile Mecca to friendly Medina in 622. The Muslim calendar was later given this year as its start.

houri Pleasure mates in Heaven who are soulless and programmed to please one's carnal desires.

hudood The legal limits allowed by Islamic Law.

Iblis "Frustrated." The proper name of Satan before he turned to evil.

Ibrahim The Islamic name for Abraham.

idda Before the finalization of a divorce, the waiting period for a woman to see whether she is pregnant.

ihtisab Self-reflection and assessment.

ijtihad Using independent thought to create a new Islamic legal opinion for an issue that has no clear answer in the two main sources of Islam.

Illiyun The register in which the people of paradise have their names written.

Imam "Leader." In Sunni Islam, it denotes primarily the person who leads the congregational prayers. In Shi'a Islam, it is the title of the supreme guides from God who were direct descendants of the Prophet through the marriage of his cousin, Ali, and his daughter, Fatimah.

Iman (Ee maan) The term for faith or belief. Sometimes spelled in English as *Eman* or *Eemaan*.

Injeel The Arabic name for the Gospel or *Evangel* of Jesus.

insan The Islamic term for humankind; adaptable creatures.

Isha The late-night prayer.

Islam (Iss laam) "Surrendering to God and attaining peace." The Arabic name for the religion taught by Muhammad.

Israfil The angel who will blow the trumpet, signaling the last day.

ithim A bad deed or sin.

I'tikaf The practice of spiritual retreat by living in the mosque during the last 10 days of *Ramadan*.

Jahaliya   "Ignorance." Refers to the time before the advent of Islam when superstitious and barbaric customs were a part of Arabian life.

Jahannum   The name for Hell.

Janazah   Funeral rites in Islam.

Jannah   "Garden." Heaven or Paradise.

jihad   "To struggle, strive, or exert." Often mistranslated as holy war, this term can apply to any exertion in God's cause. Examples range from going to school or a woman making the *Hajj* to fighting a just war or even giving up a bad habit.

jinn   "Hidden ones." The term used for a class of invisible spirits that inhabit another dimension. They can communicate with us only through our minds. There are good and evil jinn. The caricature of the genie is based on this creature.

Jum'uah   "Gathering." Friday, the day for the congregational prayer.

Ka'bah   The cube-shaped shrine in Mecca built originally by the Prophet Abraham. All Muslims pray in the direction of this shrine out of respect for Abraham and to affirm monotheistic unity.

kafir   "One who hides or covers the truth." Often mistranslated as unbeliever. Plural: *Kuffar*.

Kalimah   "Creed or word." The defining statement of the faith contained in the words: There is no god but God. "*La ilaha ill Allah*."

Khalifa   "Caretaker." The term for the supreme leader of the Muslim community after the passing of the Prophet. Spelled as *caliph* in English.

Kharajites   "The seceders." The ultra-purist faction that rebelled against the fourth Caliph, Ali ibn Ali Talib. Plural: *Khawarij*.

Khatmi Qur'an   The name of the ceremony celebrating a child's first completion of reading the entire Qur'an. Also called an *Ameen* ceremony.

khul'   A wife-initiated divorce.

Kiraman Katibeen   The two angels assigned to each person that record good and bad deeds in one's book of records.

Kiswah   The embroidered black cloth that covers the Ka'bah in Mecca. It is replaced with a new one each year.

Kitabullah   "Book of God." One of the titles of the Qur'an.

Laylat ul Qadr "The Night of Measurement or Power." The exact date on which Muhammad started receiving the Qur'an. It falls on one of the last 10 days of Ramadan.

Maghrib The sunset prayer.

Mahdi The awaited hero who will rally the oppressed Muslims of the Earth to victory in the end-of-time. For Shi'a Muslims, he is the savior who will make Shi'aism transcendent.

mala'ikah (Mala eeka) Angels, beings with power, message-bearers.

Malikul Mawt The angel of death.

Masih The Messiah. A term attributed to Jesus in the Qur'an. He was meant to be the Messiah for the Jewish people.

masjid "Place of prostration." The proper name for a Muslim house of worship in the Arabic language.

Masjid al Haram "The Restricted Mosque." Another name for the Ka'bah and the mosque that surrounds it. Many restrictions apply to a person who enters this mosque, such as the person must not kill any living thing, even a bug; and the person must be in a purified state.

Masjid an Nabawi The Prophet's mosque in Medina.

Mathnawi The name of the collected poems of Jalaluddin Rumi.

Maulid un-Nabi The birthday of the Prophet Muhammad. This widely celebrated holiday is controversial in some Islamic circles because it has no sanction from the main Islamic sources.

Mecca (Makkah) A city in southwestern Arabia founded by Abraham's wife Hagar and their son Ishmael. An important religious shrine is located there, and it is the birthplace of Muhammad.

Medina (Madeena) "City." Formerly known as *Yathrib*, this city became the first capital of Islam in 622, when Muhammad and his persecuted followers fled Mecca. Also spelled *Madinah*.

Mika'il The angel who can alter the weather by God's command.

minbar The pulpit on which the Imam stands to deliver his Friday sermon. Out of respect for the Prophet's position, the top step of this three- or four-step pulpit is not stood upon.

Muhammadanism The name Europeans gave to the religion of Islam in the seventeenth century, thinking that Muslims worshipped Muhammad as God.

mosque   The English term for an Islamic house of worship.

muazzin   The person who gives the Muslim call to prayer five times daily from the minaret of a mosque.

Muhajirun   The Meccan Muslims who fled to Medina during the Hijrah. Literally means *the immigrants*.

mujahid   A person who engages in *jihad*. Plural: *mujahideen*.

munafiq   A hypocrite.

Musallah   The actual place where a ritual prayer is held in a mosque.

mushrik   An idolater.

Muslim   "A person who is surrendering to God and finding peace." A follower of the religion of Islam.

nabi   A prophet from God.

nafs   The Islamic term for the *id*, or self. The real you; your personality and character.

Nasara   The Islamic term for Christian. It comes from the name Nazareth. It is also related to the term for *helper*, which is how Jesus' disciples are viewed in the Qur'an.

nikah   The Islamic marriage ceremony.

Orientalist   The term used to describe Western Christian and Jewish scholars who made the study of Islam their vocation in the nineteenth and twentieth centuries.

Ottoman   The name of a Muslim dynasty that ruled over the Middle East and part of Europe until 1918.

qada   "Determination." Often mistranslated as "fatalism." It refers to God's overall plan for the universe. Muslims understand this to refer to physical laws and moments of Divine intervention.

qadr   "Measurement." Often mistranslated as "predestination" or "fate." It refers to the five areas of our overall existence that are known only to God: our span of life, our overall economic state, the place of our death, whether we will believe in God or not, and whether we will be content or filled with stress in our worldly life.

qiblah   The technical term for the geographical direction of the Ka'bah in Mecca toward which all Muslims face when they pray.

Qur'an (Kuur an)   "The Reading or Recital." It is the name of the Islamic Holy Book. Muslims believe it is the direct word of God, delivered to Muhammad by an angel in small portions from the years 610 to 623 C.E. Also spelled *Koran*.

Ramadan (Rama Dan)   The ninth month of the Islamic lunar calendar. Muslims observe a dawn-to-dusk fast for the 29 or 30 days of this month.

rasul   A messenger from God who receives a scripture.

riddah   Apostacy.

ruh   The Islamic term for the soul.

sabr   Patient resolve and perseverance in the face of adversity. This quality is a sign of true faith in God.

sadaqa   Charity that is done for extra merit from God.

Sahaba   Companions of the Prophet. The people who accepted Islam and saw or heard the Prophet directly. They are our "primary sources."

salat   "Red-hot connection." The ritual Islamic prayers performed five times daily. Also spelled *Salah*.

Saum   Fasting. Also spelled *Siyam*.

Seerah   A biography of the Prophet Muhammad. Most early biographers compiled their works between one and four centuries of the Prophet's passing.

Shahadah   "To witness or testify." The Muslim statement of belief: I declare that there is no god but Allah, and I declare that Muhammad is the Messenger of Allah.

shaheed   A martyr.

Shari'ah (Shareeya)   "The path." The term for Islamic Law.

Shaykh   "Respected elder or chief." Among Sunnis, it is commonly used as the title for a religious scholar. Also spelled *sheikh* or *sheik*.

Shaytan   "To pull away from." Satan in Arabic.

Shi'a   The second-largest sect of Islam. Shi'as claim that Muhammad's son-in-law, Ali, and his descendants are the only rightful rulers of the community.

shirk   "Associating." Making others equal to God. The only unforgivable sin if a person dies while doing it.

shura   "Mutual consultation."

Sijjin   The register in which the people of Hell have their names written.

Sirat   The path or bridge over the pit of Hell that all souls must travel after they have received their verdict from God. For those who make it over, Heaven awaits. Sinners will fall into Hell.

Siratal Mustaqeem   The straight path (of Islam).

Sufi   The mystics of Islam.

Suhuf (Soo hoof)   The Islamic name for the revealed scrolls of the Prophet Abraham. Literal meaning: scrolls or sheaf of leaves.

Sunnah   The example of the Prophet Muhammad as contained in his *hadiths*, or sayings, including his actions and silent approval of actions done in his presence.

Sunni   The largest sect of Islam that claims to follow the example of Muhammad and his companions.

surah (Soo ra)   "A step-up or gate." The name for a chapter of the Qur'an.

talaq   A husband-initiated divorce.

Taliban   "Students." The name of a Muslim militant group that arose in Afghanistan in the late 1990s.

taqwa   The conscious awareness that God is watching you.

Tariqa   A Sufi lodge.

tauhid (Tauw heed)   "Oneness or monotheism." A term used to emphasize the unitary nature of God.

Taurah (Taw rah)   The Arabic name for the Torah of Moses.

tawba   "Repentance." Asking sincere forgiveness from God for a sin one has committed.

thanbi   Sin or evil deeds.

'ulema   *See* alim.

Umayyad   The name of the first Muslim dynasty. It is derived from the name of the tribal clan, the Banu Umayyah, whose foremost member, Mu'awiya, became the fifth Caliph in 661.

Ummah   The Muslim community or motherland.

wahy   Revelation or inspiration from God given to chosen men and women.

wali   The woman's representative during the courtship period. His or her job is to make sure the prospective groom is legitimate and will not take advantage of the woman.

walima   The wedding reception after a marriage ceremony.

wudu   The Islamic practice of washing the face, hands, and feet with water to achieve a ritually pure state.

Yahudi   The Arabic term for a Jew.

Yathrib   The former name of the city of Medina.

youm   A unit of time usually used for a day but with no set length.

Youmud Deen   The Day of Judgment for all ways of life.

Youmul Qiyamah   The Day of (standing for) Judgment.

Zabur (Za boor)   The Arabic name for the Psalms of David.

Zakah   "Purification." The annual required charity from all Muslim adults in the amount of 2 $\frac{1}{2}$ percent of one's yearly average savings after any debts have been discharged.

Zuhr   The afternoon prayer. Also spelled *dhuhr*.

Index

Y–Z